Anne Bancroft

Anne Bancroft

A LIFE

Douglass K. Daniel

UNIVERSITY PRESS OF KENTUCKY

Scholarly publisher for the Commonwealth,
serving Bellarmine University, Berea College, Centre College of Kentucky, Eastern
Kentucky University, The Filson Historical Society, Georgetown College, Kentucky
Historical Society, Kentucky State University, Morehead State University, Murray
State University, Northern Kentucky University, Transylvania University, University
of Kentucky, University of Louisville, and Western Kentucky University.
All rights reserved.

Editorial and Sales Offices: The University Press of Kentucky
663 South Limestone Street, Lexington, Kentucky 40508-4008
www.kentuckypress.com

Library of Congress Cataloging-in-Publication Data

Names: Daniel, Douglass K. author.
Title: Anne Bancroft : a life / Douglass K. Daniel.
Description: Lexington : University Press of Kentucky, 2017. | Includes
    bibliographical references and index.
Identifiers: LCCN 2017012533| ISBN 9780813169682 (hardcover : alk. paper) |
    ISBN 9780813169699 (pdf) | ISBN 9780813169705 (epub)
Subjects: LCSH: Bancroft, Anne, 1931-2005 | Actors—United States—Biography.
Classification: LCC PN2287.B164 D36 2017 | DDC 791.4302/8092 [B]—dc23
LC record available at https://lccn.loc.gov/2017012533

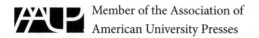

To Jason Schaff, my first editor

Contents

Photographs follow page 144

The Girl from
St. Raymond Avenue

Darkness. Heat from the sun warming her face. Wind rushing through her hair. The rollercoaster roaring with each rise and fall, every twist and turn. Others screaming with delight while she is silent with fear. Her hand tightening its grip on the arm of a friend. Hurtling through the darkness and feeling so helpless. Not knowing until now what it is like to be blind.

A simple mask over her eyes might have done the trick, even a pair of sunglasses, but Anne Bancroft wanted more. Before she left her room she closed her eyes and placed adhesive tape over each eyelid, then donned the dark glasses. In public she appeared to be a blind woman with an escort enjoying a day by the ocean and a visit to the amusement pier, not an actress developing an approach to playing a role. "I wanted to see how it felt to feel so dependent," she said, "really dependent on other people, *really*." No one on the rollercoaster that summer day in 1959 could have any reason to think that this pretty young woman, a slender five-feet-six with dark hair, could possibly have appeared in fifteen movies, scores of television dramas, and a Broadway hit and been an engaging guest now and then on Jack Paar's popular late-night television talk show. After all, she was blind.

Anne would not play a blind woman in her upcoming role. In her life Annie Sullivan had endured serious problems with her eyes, but, unlike the children she had taught, she was not without her sight. Like millions around the world, the playwright William Gibson had read about Sullivan teaching the deaf and blind child Helen Keller. His new play, *The Miracle Worker*, would dramatize the events leading to the moment Helen became aware of her surroundings. Keller had fascinated the public for decades and agreed to allow Gibson to dramatize her life for the stage. Dead for twenty-three years, Annie Sullivan had no say in the matter.

It would not be an overstatement to say that Anne Bancroft had found a miracle worker of her own. He was Arthur Penn, a director of television dramas when he had met her two years earlier as he and the producer Fred Coe were casting the female role in the play *Two for the Seesaw,* also written by Gibson. Anne had impressed the three men with her initial take on Gittel Mosca, a bohemian dancer from the Bronx who would enter a romance with a buttoned-down midwestern lawyer working in New York City. Penn wanted to test Anne's mettle before signing her for *Two for the Seesaw* and cast her in a production for the CBS television anthology *Playhouse 90.*

In the episode "Invitation to a Gunfighter," a Western drama scheduled for broadcast in March 1957, Anne would play the love interest to the actor Hugh O'Brian. At one point the script called for her to tell O'Brian, "Come to me." But in rehearsing the scene, O'Brian was already beside her. Anne was befuddled. The line made no sense and she insisted that it be cut. Penn encouraged her to reinterpret the line—to think beyond the physical sense of the words and consider instead their emotional subtext, the feelings that might lie beneath them, and connect it to her own emotional experiences: *Come to me.*

"I didn't know what he meant at first," Anne said, "but then it was like, I can't tell you, it was like getting one of those great insights you get on the couch when you're in analysis. It just came to me like that, and I said, 'Holy mackerel!' And then I could say that line meaning five hundred things." A simple line in a forgettable TV script had led to an awakening that would change her life. "Whatever it was in me that was lying dormant and waiting for someone to make me aware, Arthur did it," she said during one of the many times she revisited the moment. "In acting I had always just done it—let my instincts guide me. But Arthur Penn taught me something else. He taught me how to use my imagination and past experiences and the way I felt about everything. So it was the beginning for me. A whole world opened up." Helen Keller was not yet seven years old when her miracle happened in 1887. Anne was all of twenty-five in 1957.

At first *Two for the Seesaw* drew attention because it starred Henry Fonda, a film and theater favorite twice Anne's age. After its debut in January 1958, the play was all Anne's. She became a Broadway star overnight and won a Tony Award. Yet she knew she needed more training in this new way of looking at a role. Arthur Penn sent her to the Actors Studio and its director, Lee Strasberg. Learning about "the Method" and the ways she could plumb her own emotional life for her roles led her to tape shut her eyes and seek the feelings of fear and helplessness that came with blindness. It was a supplement to her research about Annie Sullivan and Helen Keller, the hours she spent observing how blind children were taught, and her own lessons in sign language for the deaf and blind.

The team behind *Two for the Seesaw* reassembled for *The Miracle Worker* in the fall of 1959. Coe produced Gibson's play and Penn directed Anne and her young costar, Patty Duke. The nightly battle waged onstage by Annie Sullivan and Helen Keller over a spoon turned their show into the sensation of the season. The *New York Daily News* was among those hailing Anne as "the best actress on Broadway." In the years to come, others would call her the best actress in America. "She may not be the most beautiful woman in the world," Penn said, "but more happens in her face in ten seconds than in most women's faces in ten years."

Anne's experience with *The Miracle Worker* carried many of the qualities that would mark her life and career, among them curiosity, commitment, passion, and loyalty. The emotions she learned to tap so successfully for her roles in film, television, and theater during the next forty-five years were already on display in her day-to-day life and would remain so. "She was quick to anger, the same way she was really quick to laugh," said her friend Robert Allan Ackerman. "She would giggle more easily than anybody I ever knew. She was gorgeous and she had the most beautiful smile, and it was right there and she was a totally loving, compassionate friend." There was conflict inside her and a sense of peace yet to be attained. She would struggle with competing desires at work and at home, often pursuing one goal at the cost of another of equal importance to her. She tried, not always successfully, to solve those conflicts by putting more and more of her energy into her efforts to have all that she wanted.

"Know what creates a miracle?" Anne asked the columnist Earl Wilson. "Hard work. That's what *Miracle Worker* teaches you." She first learned the value of hard work through the example set by her mother and father. Their home was also the place she first expressed a desire to perform as a way to fulfill a simple need that would turn into a craving: *Look at me.*

Family was at the center of Anne Bancroft's world for the first twenty years of her life. Until she moved to Hollywood in 1951 and took Bancroft as her professional name, she had never lived away from the modest apartment she shared with her parents and two sisters in a southeast section of the Bronx, New York. Her world then was a small one. The public schools she attended were within walking distance of her home on St. Raymond Avenue, and the Roman Catholic church her family attended was just a few steps away on the same street. Aunts, uncles, cousins, and grandparents lived within four or five blocks of her home. Little took place in the neighborhood without either the Italianos or the DiNapolis hearing about it. In those early years, what they often heard was little Anna Marie Italiano singing.

Her parents were native New Yorkers. Michael Italiano, born in 1905 and raised in Brooklyn, was the oldest of seven children. Her mother was given the name Carmela when she was born into the DiNapoli family in 1907, but she never liked her given name and went by Mildred or Millie instead. She too was one of seven children and was raised in Manhattan. Both Mike's and Millie's parents had come to the United States from the Naples region of Italy. One family story related how Grandmother Italiano was sent to America at thirteen to thwart a local crime boss's plan to marry her. Dressed as a boy by her mother, she slipped aboard a ship bound for New York and was taken in by *paisans* already living in her new homeland.

Nothing so dramatic marked the childhood of the Italianos' middle daughter. She was born Anna Marie Louise Italiano on September 17, 1931. In the family she was known as Marie; only after she began her acting career did relatives regularly call her Anne. Her older sister, named JoAnne but called Joan, had been born in 1928, and a younger sister, Phyllis, would follow in 1936. The Italian influence on their lives did not extend to the language. If their parents knew Italian, they did not speak it around their three daughters. As Grandmother DiNapoli advised, "In America you speak English." The matriarch also kept an eye on the spiritual responsibilities of her grandchildren, waiting outside Santa Maria Church after the eight o'clock Mass on Sunday to see that they attended the nine o'clock Mass set aside for neighborhood children.

Santa Maria was a modest parish for the Catholics who lived in the area, most of them Italian, Irish, and German. Unlike the towering Church of St. Raymond a half mile northwest on Oak Hill Avenue, with its twin towers and vast cemetery, Santa Maria was a two-story brick building on the corner of St. Raymond Avenue. Its basement was set aside for activities. Years later, both Joan and Anne would have weddings at Santa Maria.

"They were a typical Italian family, in the sense of the closeness of the family, attention to church and family, looking after their children," remembered Father Antimo Fiorillo, the priest for Santa Maria beginning in the late 1940s. "They were very well-liked in the area because in case of anything, they used to offer their help in some way. Very honest, respected people."

Mike Italiano had not gone beyond the eighth grade and worked as a clothing cutter in the garment industry. It was not the most reliable work because of unexpected layoffs and factory closings. In lean times—the years of the Great Depression were full of them—Mike and Millie shielded their daughters from harsh economic realities as much as they could. Money matters were not discussed in front of them. They did not have much, but, then, no one did.

The Italianos were one of five families living in apartments in the three-story building at 2402 St. Raymond Avenue. A drugstore and one apartment were on the street level. Mike and Millie and their daughters lived in a two-bedroom apartment on the second floor of the walk-up building. The sisters shared a bedroom. Not until the late 1950s would Mike and Millie leave the apartment for a house in Yonkers, New York.

The federal census taker came calling in early 1940. Mike reported earning two thousand dollars the previous year but being out of work for ten of fifty-two weeks. Millie, who had completed one year of high school, was not working outside the home while caring for eleven-year-old Joan, eight-year-old Anne, and three-year-old Phyllis. Rent was forty-five dollars a month. That Christmas, Anne broke into tears because the family could not afford a tree. Her mother placed their small gifts around the old parlor sofa.

Sometime later, during one of Mike's periods of unemployment, Millie went to work at a mail-order house. She later became an executive telephone operator for Macy's department store in Manhattan, a job she held for forty years. Mike attended night school for ten years to improve his skills in what was then called "the rag trade." He became a pattern maker, which put him on a path to management. If Anne wanted a model for hard work and perseverance, she did not need to look beyond her home.

The Italiano children attended Public School 12, six blocks from their apartment, and later Christopher Columbus High School, which required a two-mile trek north. After the girls had left for school, Millie would ride the subway for thirty or forty-five minutes to reach the huge Macy's department store on 34th Street. Most days she would return just after the children had come home. Mike would join them around six unless he had night school.

The family spent many evenings listening to music, drama, and comedy programs on the radio. On a Saturday afternoon, the Italiano girls and some of their cousins might walk to the Westchester Square Theatre off Tremont Avenue to see a movie. On a Saturday night, Mike and Millie might go to a neighborhood club for a dance. When they could afford it, the family took a trip once a year to the Catskills.

A special treat closer to home began with a drive up the Bronx River Parkway to Blue Mountain, a 1,500-acre park near Peekskill in northwest Westchester County. The extended Italiano-DiNapoli family, which could number in the dozens, made the forty-mile trip on weekends or holidays to enjoy swimming in the park's lake, walking its trails, and eating and talking at the picnic grounds. One of Anne's uncles would go up early to begin cooking and be ready with bacon and eggs on a charcoal fire when the others arrived. Spaghetti was the main meal for the large group.

At these gatherings a relative or a family friend would bring out a guitar or an accordion or some other instrument and begin to play. Anne, just six or seven, would stand atop the table and sing. Other park visitors would walk over to listen and watch as the dark-haired child sang tunes like "College Rhythm" or "Snap Your Fingers, Turn Around a Bit." Even then she was hungry for such attention.

"No one had to coax me, not for too long, anyway," Anne said. "When I was a kid all I needed was a crowd of two people and I'd be on my feet snapping my fingers and going into my song. . . . It was my way of saying, 'Look at me, everybody. Look at me.'"

The picnic table was not her first stage. When she was even younger, perhaps just two years old, she could sing "Under a Blanket of Blue." At three or four she was asking passersby in the neighborhood if they would like to hear her sing. For a while she found a regular audience a few blocks from home at the corner of Seddon Street and Maclay Avenue. Two construction workers digging up the street would stop to listen.

"The neighbors used to take me from house to house," Anne said. "Sometimes my mother didn't know, and I think I scared hell out of her more times. Boy, did I get a beating every time for disappearing."

Millie was a woman of action, a ball of fire who ruled over all aspects of her home and handled the discipline of the children. The girls were expected home at certain times and were required to tell their parents where they were going and what they were doing and with whom. In contrast, Mike was a soft-spoken man whose quiet personality balanced his wife's emotionally explosive nature. He would tell his children, "When life bothers you, put on the radio and start to sing."

"My mother is the fire, my father the cold water that calmed everything," Anne said in describing her family to a journalist. Turning to movie terms, she called her mother an Anna Magnani type—the hot-tempered and emotionally raw Italian actress had become an international film star in Italian and American movies after World War II. In an effort to present Anne to fans in her early years in Hollywood, journalists would suggest that she too was like Magnani. For mother and daughter alike, the comparison was a compliment as well as a warning.

As angry as she was over Anne's disappearances, Millie recognized that her daughter had a natural inclination for performing. "Whenever I couldn't find her, I knew that kid was out singing again," Millie said. "She'd show off for street workers, the delicatessen man, anyone."

Among her talents was an ability to watch someone do a trick or a dance step and then devote herself to copying those moves. After watching a juggler in a vaudeville show, Anne told her mother, "Momma, I could do that." Over the next few days the youngster taught herself, with some success, to keep in the air some fruit, spoons, and other things she had found in the kitchen. Her sister Joan would show her steps she had learned at dance class, and Anne would soon be able to repeat them with more style and grace.

Anne would later say that Joan and Phyllis were just as talented as children but that she was the sister who had a desire to perform. It was a sweet gesture, but no one in the family believed it. Joan, for one, was far too shy to burst into song in front of other people. By the time Anne was in grade school, she had expanded her audience from appreciative ditchdiggers to people at block parties and church picnics as she sang "Sleepytime Gal" or "It Had to Be You."

Friends and relatives applied an Italian saying to Anne: "born with the veil." It meant that she had God-given talent. Millie did her part by getting Anne singing lessons and dance classes at a young age. The question as she grew older was whether she could do more with her talent and desire than entertain the neighbors. Anne wanted—needed—to do more.

She had scribbled on the back wall of her apartment house, "I want to be an actress."

Christopher Columbus High School was widely considered the second-best school in all the Bronx. Unlike those at the prestigious Bronx High School of Science, Columbus students were not required to pass a special exam to attend. Reflecting the area, its students and teachers were mostly Italian and Jewish, and some were Irish. For many parents, the expense of Catholic school was not an option. Yet middle-class to poor families who sent their children through Columbus's trio of double doors facing Astor Avenue—the boys in shirts and slacks, the girls in skirts and blouses— could be confident of an education that was better than average.

In the latter half of the 1940s, during the school's second decade and at the beginning of the economic upswing that followed World War II, Columbus boasted a strong faculty, a respected music program, and popular intramural sports for boys and girls. Anne played basketball and swam, one reason she enjoyed a slim figure as a teenager. The long walk to school and back to the apartment on St. Raymond Avenue was another. She was almost a year younger than most of her classmates, having been advanced a grade in elementary school.

Among the faculty at Columbus when Anne was a freshman in 1944–45 was John McGiver, a thirty-two-year-old army veteran who had returned to teaching after the war. He was an actor, too, and taught the school's drama class and directed school plays. McGiver moved between the classroom and the stage for years before he became a busy character actor in the 1950s. His round face, bald head, and stern to sweet countenance would be seen in *Breakfast at Tiffany's* (1961), *The Manchurian Candidate* (1962), and other films and on *The Patty Duke Show, Gilligan's Island,* and many other television series from the 1950s into the 1970s.

McGiver greeted Anne and other students who answered a call for auditions in the music room for the next school play. Its small stage and theater seats were not as imposing as the school auditorium, which could swallow up such a small group and make anyone already nervous feel overwhelmed. For Anne, a high school play would not be her first stage work—she had been in a kindergarten production of *The Three Little Bears,* her face hidden behind a Momma Bear mask made from a paper bag.

"Mr. McGiver gave us a brief description of the plot of the show,"

8

remembered Richard Monaco, then a Columbus freshman. "We were asked to read the script for several minutes and then recite the lines. Most of the students didn't do a good job, but they gave it their best shot. Finally, McGiver called Anne Marie Italiano to come to the stage and recite. She was beautiful, poised, confident, and possessed of an amazing composure. As she read, we all sat in our seats with our mouths open." More important, she impressed her director.

McGiver asked Anne and a few of the other students at the audition to serve as the cast for a melodrama, *Curse You, Jack Dalton*, written in the 1930s. The old-fashioned tone of the play, complete with a hero and a villain and a damsel in distress, had made it popular in schools. Anne would play the innocent chambermaid who is an object of affection of her wealthy employer's son, Jack Dalton, but is pursued by a greedy and malevolent suitor. Goodness and love triumph, and the villain utters the line, "Curse you, Jack Dalton!" as he is hauled away.

Rehearsals were fun for the students and brought them closer together. McGiver sat in the back of the room and said very little, which the cast found disconcerting. "We would stop and ask him if he had any comments or suggestions, and he would say, 'You're doing great, continue,'" Monaco said.

Playing grown-ups meant acting like grown-ups. "Anne and I had our first boy-girl kiss onstage," said David Lunney, who played Jack Dalton in the show. "She was not totally into that we had to kiss in the play. She was as reticent about it as I was. You know, 'How do we do this?' Her demeanor was a little bit more shy. We were freshmen entering into a whole new arena."

A different kiss during the performance presented a practical problem. Playing a long-lost brother, Monaco embraced Anne and pecked her cheek. Later, Anne told him: "Dick, next time, make believe you kiss my cheek." His makeup had left a large red lipstick mark on her face for the rest of the show.

Curse You, Jack Dalton was a hit with the student body and gave its cast a sense of theatrical accomplishment and a taste of celebrity. "We couldn't walk down the halls without someone calling us by our stage names," Monaco said. A decade later, when she was well into her professional career, Anne remembered the experience with a dash of the self-criticism that was typical of her: "I wasn't any good," she said of that role, "but I was determined."

Anne and her castmates joined the school's drama club, a clique that gave its members an identity outside the sea of other Columbus students. Its members saw themselves as more mature and more sophisticated. They hung out in the auditorium's dressing room, ostensibly to clean it up, then had lunch there and sneaked cigarettes. "That was a drama club thing—to be just a little bit older," said Dale Brown, a classmate who spent his free time at the school newspaper. "They were giddy—and taking just a little bit more dangerous leaps, like smoking backstage. I think they liked that edge that separated them from the others. But they were just kids."

The school auditorium turned out to be a foundation for Anne in many ways. "Until my teens I wanted to be famous and known and loved by everybody," she said years later. "Then in the teens it became a question of identity. High school plays were a way of getting appreciation and recognition."

Anne was far shier—and much more ambitious—than she let on to people outside the drama club. When she presented a more aggressive demeanor and appeared confident in herself, it was another kind of performance. An interviewer asked if she had acted as a teenager all those years ago, and Anne responded: "Did I act? Of course I did. Did you ever know an Italian family in which there wasn't acting going on every minute? I acted at home and at school."

Her home was not the best venue for a performance—teenage drama did not go over well with Millie—but the stage at school was a place where Anne could let go. In addition to plays, the school put on variety shows, which gave her a chance to perform a slyly suggestive song like "Ain't Misbehavin."

"She brought down the house because she could turn it on in terms of personality on the stage," Lunney said. "To get up and do that variety show performance and to sing that song to hoots and hollers. . . . This was in a remote area of New York City, the northeast Bronx, with many blocks of open space. There was a little sexual play in it, in the performance. It takes guts to do that. It really takes guts."

The hallways of Columbus were another venue in which Anne could show off. She did some modeling one summer and returned to school fashionably dressed. "It was the introduction of the Dior New Look, which had suddenly come down to young women's wear and things—a cinched waist, the large, billowed skirt with the crinoline petticoat underneath, the low-heeled shoes," Lunney said. "She came back to school and suddenly was this kind of fashion plate. And you could identify Anne walking through the halls of the school because she was in vogue."

By her senior year Anne had developed a special allure. "She had become rather elegant," Brown said. "She had a certain dramatic way of speaking." Even if it was a bit of an act, Anne carried herself with confidence. She also had a sense of humor and an ability to be playful and enjoy someone else's jokes. There was a sexual energy to her as well, Lunney said, a natural part of her being that she did not need to flaunt. It was all part of a blossoming.

"Anne was so beautiful, I cannot tell you," said Grace Milo, a classmate. "She used to come to school all dressed up, with heels. She dressed beautifully and she was always dramatic. You couldn't miss Anne if you saw her in the halls." Milo often ran into Anne in the office of a teacher who was a favorite of theirs. "On this one particular day she flung open the door and walked into the office," Milo remembered. "She had on a black suit with an orange scarf. She was gorgeous. She asked for this teacher like she was onstage. When she left I ran outside and performed the same thing. She was good, she was good."

There were dates—Anne later admitted to being boy crazy then—but she may have spent more of her social life with her fellow actors. "Our drama club clique became a veritable rat pack," Monaco said. "We'd party in restaurants on City Island, Williamsburg Road, and any number of other Bronx places." In a nod to their efforts to be mature, Dale Brown's mother served her son's friends a pitcher of Manhattans during a party at their home.

A new drama teacher, twenty-two-year-old Elisa Coletti, took over from John McGiver in Anne's senior year. Coletti found a few of the drama club students rehearsing a play on their own, such was their dedication. The new director of school plays chose it as one of three short plays to be performed that year.

Anne impressed Coletti with her ability to interpret a character. "If I were doing a play and she was in it, I would say to Anne, 'Don't you think this character would feel such and such?' And she would give me exactly what I was intending and do it perfectly," Coletti said. "She was a magnificent actress as a kid."

For the big play of the year Coletti picked the comedy *What a Life,* a Broadway hit in the late 1930s that introduced the character Henry Aldrich, later the focus of a popular radio show and film series. It provided several unusual characters that the students enjoyed playing, and Anne appeared as a secretary in the ensemble production. There was a Christmas show, too. One snowy day during a break in rehearsals, as someone went out for food, Anne took the stage by herself.

"She gave us a show. She sang, she danced—she was fantastic," Coletti remembered. "I don't think she was a showoff. I think she just loved to perform. She really loved to perform. It came so naturally to her. She felt so good doing it. I really think that was it. I don't think it was a case of wanting to be somebody else. She just felt so good doing it."

Looking back over the nearly forty years she spent as a teacher at Columbus, Coletti regretted not choosing a play that showcased Anne in her final year of school. "I was young and I made a lot of mistakes," Coletti said. "Later on I got a little better. I didn't know I had gold in those kids." Another regret: Anne was not Coletti's first choice for the school's drama medal. The boy she chose to receive the medal for being an all-around contributor to the effort needed the symbolic encouragement more than Anne. Then he ended up falling short academically for the honor. The award went to Anne, but being second choice still rankled.

"She was pissed. She really deserved the medal," Lunney said. "Anne could get pissed. That was part of her character, too. There would be a tempestuous flare-up."

Anne had her pride—and her goals. Yet she tried to tamp down the intensity of her desire to succeed. "I squelched ambition. I never realized that ambition was a healthy thing to have. I thought nice girls didn't have it. I was resisting my own potential," she said. "I have never doubted I could do anything. My trouble was letting other people know I knew I could do anything."

To close friends she expressed the disappointment and anger she felt over the medal. Lunney remembered sitting in the sand with Anne at the Bronx's Orchard Beach after they had graduated from high school. When the subject of the tainted honor came up, she dug her heels in the sand and slowly pushed her feet back and forth as she recalled the slight. She told her friend, "I'll show them."

Anne had applied the same determination to her studies as she had to her acting. "Everything that she did in school was always done to perfection," her classmate Dick Monaco said. "Her French teacher was greatly impressed with how quickly she mastered the language, and how beautifully she pronounced the words." Being an actress—living the life of glamour depicted in the fan magazines and the newsreels about Hollywood stars—was her fantasy. One of her aunts laughed at the notion that Mike and Millie Italiano's daughter could be on the stage or in the movies. "Some dreams, some pipe dreams," she said, and her dismissive tone made Anne want to prove her wrong.

Her practical side understood that she would need a job to support herself and to help support a family in the future. Her sister Joan had taken that path, spending half days in high school in a program that allowed her to work as a messenger or a file clerk. While Mike and Millie were putting money aside for her education after high school, Anne considered the possibilities. Science interested her, and for a time she talked about going to college to become a lab assistant. After all, she thought, who from the Bronx becomes an actress?

Her drama teacher, Elisa Coletti, went to Anne's parents and told them she thought Anne had a true talent for the stage and urged them to help her go to drama school. Mike was not convinced and opposed Millie's using their money for that purpose. "The dream, the theater, is what she wanted for me, and she begged my father for money for acting school," Anne said. "I remember his response very clearly. He would say, 'Who are we to dream these dreams?' And my mother would say, 'Well, we're gonna dream 'em.' And we did."

Her mind made up, Millie Italiano was not sure where to send Anne for professional theater training. At the same time she felt that her sixteen-year-old daughter was too young to leave home. The family had a set of the *Encyclopaedia Britannica*, and she called the local sales representative for advice. He told her that the best school was the American Academy of Dramatic Arts, the nation's oldest drama school. Scores of major stars of Broadway and Hollywood had studied there—the veterans Spencer Tracy, Edward G. Robinson, and Rosalind Russell and newcomers Kirk Douglas and Lauren Bacall among them. At that time the academy was on an upper floor of Carnegie Hall, at 57th Street and Seventh Avenue in Midtown Manhattan. That meant Anne could attend classes each day and still ride the subway home each night.

The academy offered a two-year program divided into two six-month terms called a junior year and a senior year. Prospective students were required to audition and, if accepted, were admitted to a class in October, January, or April. They could stay on for the second year by invitation only.

13

Tuition was five hundred dollars each year, which was almost two months' income for the average American at the time.

Anne auditioned in June 1948 for a spot in the next fall class. She stood five-feet-six, according to her registration card. No weight was listed, but she was described as brunette and having good proportions and physical condition and an interesting personality. "Very pretty," the card noted. Her reading was deemed intelligent with good spontaneity. Notes from her audition were positive: "Anne has a good combination of qualities, pretty and if sincere and a good student can develop very well." She was admitted to the junior class starting in October. By then she would be seventeen.

Students were encouraged not to try to hold down a job, which would take time away from their studies, rehearsals, and the theatergoing they needed for professional perspective. Most worked anyway to meet personal expenses. Anne had a part-time job during her academy years as a telephone operator a few hours a night for a Girl Scout council, a gig her sister Joan helped her secure.

Anne had another on-the-sly activity during her time at the academy. Her friend David Lunney organized a troupe to perform at a small radio station in Peekskill, New York, where a friend had a show. Lunney persuaded the manager to give them a slot on Saturday afternoons. Taking their name from the street where Dick Monaco lived, the Radcliff Radio Players performed fifteen-minute versions of stories by William Shakespeare, Edgar Allan Poe, and other authors that were based on scripts Lunney obtained from a mail-order service. Friends joined them when the Radcliff Radio Players needed more voices.

"Since the studio was basically for news and music, they had no sound effect equipment," Monaco said. "We would bring our own sound effects—cellophane for the sound of fire, buckets for the scary echo effect. . . . The studio personnel got the biggest kick out of seeing teenagers come every Saturday to perform these short horror stories." Anne was not supposed to do any acting outside her studies, as Lunney recalled, and on the air the girl from St. Raymond Avenue went by a stage name: Anne St. Raymond.

The junior year at the American Academy of Dramatic Arts focused on such basics as vocal training (voice, speech, English diction), stage training (makeup, costuming, stagecraft), pantomimic training (dancing, fencing, carriage), and radio technique (voice projection, sight reading). Dramatic analysis and dramatic literature were other subjects. The medium in mind was the theater, and radio got a slight nod. Teaching the finer points of performance for film or for television—the latter was just making its debut nationally—was not considered necessary.

A few hundred students joined Anne in the junior class of October 1948. One was John Cassavetes, an intense actor who would use roles in movies such as *The Dirty Dozen* (1967) and *Rosemary's Baby* (1968) to get by while writing and directing his own films. "We hated Hollywood," Cassavetes told an interviewer when reminiscing about his days at the academy. "Hated everything it stood for. Mainly because there was no chance for us to ever get there."

The academy's dean for more than fifty years was Charles Jehlinger, then eighty-two. He had been in the academy's first class, in 1884, and joined its faculty after a dozen years as a stage actor and director of Broadway productions. Thousands of students had passed under his gaze, and he could be unsparingly critical even as he was encouraging. A typical remark after an audition: "Crude, but there are possibilities."

In the eyes of many of the new students, Jehlinger was a tyrant. "The only compliment I ever heard him give was to Anne," said Harry Mastrogeorge, a classmate who later joined the academy faculty. "And it was 'You're on track.' That was it. And that, coming from Jehlinger in those days—you're young, teenage—it was like Beethoven's Seventh, Beethoven's Ninth. I never forgot that."

Unlike the Method approach that connected an actor's interpretation of a character to the actor's own experience, no technique guided Jehlinger. "Absolutely none," Mastrogeorge said. "What he wanted us to be was real. . . . It was all based on simple imagination—on the commonsense logic of human behavior." Jehlinger's more practical approach may have appeared out of step with the internalized acting style that Marlon Brando was making popular. Cassavetes came to consider Jehlinger "the greatest teacher who ever lived" and the leader of a very good faculty. "He was a terrific man. He was a man who said only two things: he said, 'You're not talking' or 'You're not listening,'" Cassavetes said. "Finally, five years later, I understood what he meant. Most actors today still don't know how to talk and how to listen."

Working-class students of modest means gravitated toward each other, Mastrogeorge remembered. They had not been to college, as had some of the older students, who tended to intellectualize and theorize about acting. "Our little cadre wasn't like that," he said. "It was all about the work."

Anne was determined and committed from the beginning. "She had such a healthy, instinctive, and intuitive work ethic," Mastrogeorge said. "She worked harder than anybody I knew there at the time." She was also good company, "a delight to be around—just a normal teenager," he said. "She was a fun person. There was nothing pseudo, nothing phony about her—down to earth, the Bronx."

Students were allowed to pick their own scenes for their scene-study class. When she worked with Mastrogeorge on a scene, she insisted they get together at her home on Sunday to go through it. "She forced me to come on Sunday, which was my laundry day and my letter-writing day, to come to the Bronx and work with her. That was her mentality," he said. She also insisted that he stay for dinner. "Her mother made the best lasagna I've ever had in my life."

At the end of the junior year, academy students underwent an examination play. Faculty would attend their performances and decide who would be invited to return for the senior year. It was highly selective—a senior class might be half or a third the size of the junior class. Anne, Mastrogeorge, and Cassavetes were part of a senior class of whom sixty-seven eventually graduated.

Production was the focus of the second year. Several plays would be produced, and each student had to be in four of them. "We would always be in rehearsal," Mastrogeorge said. The senior productions took place in the afternoon in the four-hundred-seat Carnegie Hall Playhouse or in one of the Broadway theaters. When using a Broadway house, the student actors adapted their productions to the scenery for the production that was being staged at night.

One of the senior productions in which Anne appeared was *The Royal Family*, a romantic comedy. Mastrogeorge watched as she performed a series of uninterrupted spoken thoughts. "I sat there and thought, she is so real," he said. "And I thought, wow." She played the female lead in *The Philadelphia Story* and made the most of her small part as the maid in *The Male Animal*, which featured Mastrogeorge. Standing in the wings, she kept pointing to him as he was onstage. It took a while for him to understand her gestures: his fly was open.

Even graduates of the American Academy of Dramatic Arts faced bleak prospects in the quest to make a living as an actor. Finding a job usually meant months or even years of making the rounds, visiting the offices of agents, producers, directors, writers, and anyone else who might have a lead on a job. An exception had been Grace Kelly, an academy graduate in a class the year before Anne finished. Kelly had roles in two summer productions and then made her Broadway debut that fall.

Anne was set to graduate in March 1950. "It was the greatest school one could go to," she said later. "You learned to be concentrated and focused." One day a few weeks before graduation she spent the lunch hour alone in the academy's theater working on a scene from the play *Fly Away Home*. Dedication and determination were not all that drove her. "I had no money for malteds and no dates," Anne said. "What the hell was there for me to do but stay onstage when the other kids were out?" Admitting to having had a driving ambition at such a young age still did not come easily to her.

As it turned out, Anne was not by herself in the theater. A member of the faculty, Frances Fuller, had noticed her and stopped to watch. Fuller had enjoyed a successful Broadway career before turning to the classroom, appearing in eight shows, including *The Front Page* (1928), *The Animal Kingdom* (1932), and the behind-the-curtain drama *Stage Door* (1936). She already knew Anne—who on the faculty did not?—yet the solitary lunchtime session was another reminder that Anne was dedicated to her craft.

Not only did Fuller know talent and dedication when she saw it; she also knew Worthington Miner. He had been a Broadway director in the 1920s and 1930s, then joined the Columbia Broadcasting System in 1942 to manage its fledgling television department. Miner later guided the expansion of prime-time programming at CBS, filling its evening hours with live shows. Fuller was Miner's wife as well as his unofficial talent scout, and she was always on the lookout for a promising student to send his way. She thought she had found one in the young Italiano girl.

2

Television Nights and Hollywood Days

Television was blossoming as a national medium about the time that Anne Italiano was turning the heads of high school boys. Its roots went back to the 1920s, but the Depression had hobbled television's development outside New York City, and World War II had put the medium in limbo as resources went to the war effort. Once victory was achieved, television stations began to sprout in major cities around the country. Most stations joined a network—ABC, CBS, NBC, or DuMont—and the rapid growth in the sales of TV sets created a demand for programming.

When Anne began her studies at the American Academy of Dramatic Arts, national network television was set to flourish. Two years later, as she finished her theatrical training, television had entered what would become known as its golden age. TV shows were so new and production budgets so small that creative people were allowed to try almost anything that might draw an audience or impress the newspaper critics. People who tuned in might witness a great accomplishment or a dismal failure—and it was all live.

"Television in the early fifties had the excitement of a reckless, pioneering adventure," recalled the producer Worthington Miner, whose wife Anne had impressed. "In a nutshell, the Golden Age was crude, inept, and desperately poor. . . . At the same time the era was young, undaunted and, in its aspirations, rich."

Finding talent was part of the excitement and the challenge. Major movie stars wanted nothing to do with television, and studios could forbid performers under contract from appearing on TV shows. For many young actors in New York, Broadway may have been the destination of choice, but television could provide a meal along the way. It was experience, too, and a way to get a credit. The medium offered a wide variety of roles, from Shakespeare and other classics to original contemporary dramas and comedies. "Live television was the closest thing to repertory that an American actor could be in," said Rod Steiger, himself a veteran actor of the period.

Staying in New York City for drama school had saved Anne money and freed her parents from worry. Now that decision worked in her favor professionally. Just as Hollywood was the capital of the film industry and Broadway the home of American theater, Manhattan was then the center of television production. Anne had two venues for finding an acting job, and both were a subway ride from home. Economics would become a primary concern for her once she left the academy. If she could not make a living as an actor, and relatively soon, she would have to go into another line of work.

With the encouragement of Frances Fuller—Mrs. Worthington Miner—Anne went to CBS for an audition. Open calls could attract hundreds of people carrying photographs and résumés. The network's casting director, Robert Fryer, considered Anne along with a half dozen other young women for a role in an upcoming production for its anthology series *Studio One.* Each week offered a new cast in a new setting for a new story.

Miner had brought the program to CBS from radio in November 1948 as the network's answer to NBC's *Philco Television Playhouse.* He wrote eight of every ten of its scripts, mostly adaptations, and concentrated on the visual aspects of the production. He wanted television to be more than an electronic presentation of stage dramas and comedies. In the realm of the visual he was an innovator, and his use of the close-up and the long shot, for example, helped create the visual language that defined the small screen in its early years. After *Studio One* broadcast a modern-dress adaptation of Shakespeare's *Julius Caesar* in the spring of 1949, the *New York Times* critic Jack Gould called it "the most exciting television yet seen on the home screen—a magnificently bold, imaginative and independent achievement that stands as an event of the season." Miner admitted later that the program's budget had not allowed for Roman costumes and sets. Still, how the adaptation was presented visually had been his main interest.

Fryer and Miner decided to cast Anne as a peasant girl in "Torrents of Spring," a drama adapted from a nineteenth-century novel by the Russian writer Ivan Turgenev and set for airing in April 1950. The pay was good— $125 for two weeks' work—and would have sounded even better if the work were steady, but, then, little was steady about acting. Asked how she would want to be billed, she decided to take on another stage name, Anne Marno, instead of using Italiano. The practice of avoiding a name with obvious ethnic ties was still common. Her choice quietly acknowledged her heritage, combining the first three letters of Marie with the last two of Italiano.

In spite of her outward confidence, Anne was scared to death as she prepared for her professional debut. So much could go wrong for all to see. Typically, a one-hour live program for *Studio One* required several days of rehearsals and blocking—determining where the actors would move on the set. From noon to seven on Sunday, the day before the broadcast, the production focused on camera movement during the run-through. "They move four cameras at you at once," Anne said, "and they ogle you like monsters." The cast came in several hours before the ten o'clock airtime on Monday night.

A live television show was like a theater performance in at least one respect. "For me," Miner said at the time, "it's opening night, with all the thrills and worries." Their stage was a studio sixty-five feet long and forty feet wide. Their audience could fill every Broadway house and then some. There was no videotape to record a performance until 1956. Instead, the producers pointed a film camera at a video monitor, creating a film of the show called a kinescope.

"Torrents of Spring" aired on April 17, 1950. When Anne returned to the Bronx that night, she found a sign on the door of the Italianos' apartment: "Welcome Home—The Star." Her parents, sisters, and other relatives as well as many of their friends and neighbors greeted her with clapping and cheers. Millie Italiano had made Italian cakes, and she served them with wine and coffee. Her daughter would have other opening-night parties, but never one any better than her first.

Anne's performance in "Torrents of Spring" earned the praise of Worthington Miner and the prospect of more work from the casting director Robert Fryer. "Anne had fantastic vitality," Miner said years later. "And she was so serious and so eager to learn." With hundreds of actors routinely turned away during auditions, having an "in" with the decision makers was a huge advantage for her. They gave Anne a smaller part for "The Man Who Had Influence," a *Studio One* presentation broadcast on May 29, 1950. The director of her first show, Franklin J. Schaffner, guided her again over the two weeks needed to prepare for air time.

The extent of Anne's live television work is difficult to determine with precision. Most sources list at least two dozen credits for Anne Marno in 1950 and 1951. A handful of other credits show up in searches of reviews and television listings in major newspapers. Profiles of Anne and studio publicity would later set the number of shows in which she appeared at close to forty; there may have been dozens more. If she was in that many shows, she almost certainly did not have major roles. When she reminisced about her TV work, Anne noted that if she did not have a featured part, she had to wear her own clothes. Another sign that she was not working regularly in the five months that followed her *Studio One* appearances was her need for a job other than performing. To meet that end, she worked at a drugstore.

Miner and Fryer had better roles for Anne that fall. In October she was cast as a young newlywed for an episode of the popular situation comedy *The Goldbergs*. Miner had adapted the long-running radio show for television in 1949, and its creator and writer, Gertrude Berg, continued to star as the housewife Molly Goldberg. The thirty-minute show's setting was familiar enough to Anne: a third-floor apartment on East Tremont Avenue in the Bronx. The Goldbergs are a middle-class Jewish family with a son and daughter, both teenagers, and a father in the clothing business. Molly Goldberg tackles problems of the home and the heart as she shares recipes and gossip with neighbors—and urges viewers to try Sanka, the instant coffee that sponsored the series.

In the episode that aired October 15, 1950, a friend of Molly's is upset because her new daughter-in-law, Joyce, will not call her "Mama." The newlyweds are living in the building, and Molly sets out to investigate. Joyce eventually confides that she does not think her mother-in-law likes her because she always calls her "my son's wife." Molly's well-meaning machinations produce a heartwarming reconciliation. Anne appeared prominently as Joyce in at least one other episode; whether she was in more, perhaps in stories in which Joyce was on hand but not the center of attention, is difficult to tell because not all the live shows exist in kinescope form.

Nonetheless, Anne had enough experience with the creator-writer-star of the series to complain to her friend David Lunney. "There was a little bit of tension between her and Gertrude Berg because Gertrude Berg wanted things done in a certain way," Lunney remembered. "She was very dogmatic about telling Anne or any performer that they must do it in this way—certain line readings, the way she wanted her to react, to what she should do when she'd come in—all of those kinds of things. Anne was having a little bit of a struggle with that because she wanted to do it—she was an actress. That's what they hired her for."

Anne became friendly with fourteen-year-old Arlene McQuade, who played the Goldbergs' daughter, Rosalie. "She had a warm voice and a lovely quality about her, and everybody loved Anna Italiano, especially me," McQuade told Aviva Kempner for a documentary on Berg. "We became very good girlfriends. She was a couple of years older than I was, but it didn't make any difference. We used to put each other's hair up in curlers and shop together. And she was very Italian in her manners, and of course I loved that because my mother was Italian."

Another assignment at CBS that fall gave Anne her best role yet, the female lead in "Letter from Cairo" for *Studio One.* The star was Charlton Heston, a future Oscar winner who had found work in television while seeking Broadway roles. One of Miner's discoveries, Heston was appearing in his tenth production for *Studio One* and had just made his film debut in *Dark City.* Her only other television role of any prominence in 1950 was a Christmas presentation of "A Child Is Born" for the anthology *Lux Video Theatre.* The story had been adapted from a one-act Nativity play by Stephen Vincent Benét that was a popular source for radio and television broadcasts.

Anne made a strong, positive impression at CBS. In the first five months of the new year, she was cast in prominent roles in six television programs. After a part in a February 6, 1951, episode of the half-hour anthology thriller *Suspense,* she was directed again by Franklin J. Schaffner, this time for an hour-long *Ford Theatre Hour* presentation on February 23 titled "The Golden Mouth." The future director of the films *Planet of the Apes* (1968) and *Patton* (1970) added to his files a card with the name Anne Marno and the code CDXX: she could play comedy or drama and was an excellent actress.

"Wintertime," aired by *Studio One* on April 2, presented Anne as a displaced person trying to survive in postwar Europe. In the story, a German veteran (Patric Knowles) returns home to resume his work as a tugboat captain. He tries to help Lisa, a young Latvian woman (Anne Marno), hide from local authorities, who are seeking her brother, the leader of an antifascist insurgency. The role allowed Anne a long monologue in which her character recounts how she escaped Latvia after the Russians had killed nearly all her family. Another strong scene for her came when Lisa is brutally interrogated by police.

As Anne's career took an upswing, so did her personal life. She began dating a fellow American Academy alumnus, John Ericson. Born in Germany, Ericson came to the United States at the age of three. His parents, a business executive and a former actress and singer, moved the family from New York to Chicago to Elmhurst, New Jersey. Like Anne, Ericson had considered a career outside acting—dentistry—but with his mother's blessing he sought the stage instead. The handsome, six-foot blond actor graduated from the academy in 1948 and spent a few seasons in regional theater. He was a step ahead of Anne in the name game, having changed his from Joe Meibes.

Ericson was five years older than Anne and probably did not meet her until after her graduation from the academy; her classmate Harry Mastrogeorge remembered theirs as a romance begun away from the drama school. They may have been brought together by that connection, by mutual friends, or by work for CBS. They were certainly in the same orbit at times. Ericson landed a spot in a crowd scene in a *Studio One* program in April 1950, about the time Anne was working on "Torrents of Spring." Any kind of meeting or romance may have had to wait. Just a week after her show aired, Ericson won a starring role in the MGM film *Teresa*. Directed by Fred Zinnemann, the production filmed in Italy and the United States over the spring and summer. Once he had completed his work on the film, released in 1951, Ericson appeared in a regional production of *The Glass Menagerie*. Then he was back in New York for the CBS series *Lux Video Theatre* in early October, two weeks before Anne appeared on *The Goldbergs* for the first time.

Regardless of exactly when and how they met, theirs became an involved relationship, her friend David Lunney said. "They'd been around with each other for a while," he said. "I think they were seeing a lot of each other and it was an intimate relationship. They were a romantic couple."

Ericson went through a dry spell at the beginning of 1951 while waiting for the release of *Teresa*. His luck returned when the actor and director José Ferrer cast him in a new Broadway play, the wartime comedy-drama *Stalag 17*. (Ericson played Sefton, the role that would later win an Oscar for William Holden.) In April critics gave *Teresa* strong reviews, and Ericson received even more plaudits when *Stalag 17* opened in May.

Anne's career was moving along well; she had three roles that month.

In addition to appearing on the DuMont mystery series *The Adventures of Ellery Queen,* she was back on *The Goldbergs* as the newlywed Joyce. In that episode she collapses on the Goldbergs' couch, a prelude to her discovery that she is pregnant and Molly's advice that her husband attend a class for expectant dads. The *Boston Globe* considered it "an engaging chapter in this good series" and took note of Anne and Michael Morris, her TV husband.

Her other appearance in May came on the half-hour CBS anthology *Danger* in an episode called "The Killer Scarf." It used as its background the Ringling Bros. and Barnum & Bailey Circus while at Madison Square Garden. In a lower floor of the complex where animals and performers stayed when not in the ring, television cameras followed Anne, dressed as an acrobat, and other members of the cast as they played out the story of a deadly love triangle. In a review the next day, *Billboard* considered the plot hackneyed but called Anne "refreshing." She was gaining experience and good notices.

Over the summer, Anne starred in the episode "Stranglehold" on NBC's *Kraft Television Theatre,* her first major role away from CBS. She played the silly wife of a promising young writer who takes on hack work to support her and other relatives. "Well-rehearsed and well-acted," the *Boston Globe* declared, and Anne and other members of the cast were lauded for outstanding performances. She returned to CBS and to *Suspense* for "A Vision of Death" and, in August, appeared again on *Danger* in "Murderer's Face."

Anne found time to help out a friend who was asked to direct a screen test for a twenty-four-year-old dancer, Doug Rogers, who had caught the interest of Twentieth Century-Fox. Rogers had already done tests showcasing his singing and dancing, and Fox now wanted to see if he could act. Rogers was asked to prepare for a scene taken from the novel *The Girl on the Via Flaminia* by Alfred Hayes, a love story published in 1949 about an American soldier in Rome and his affair with an Italian girl. The test was shot at a Midtown studio.

"She came in and we, meaning me and my agent at the time, looked at her and said, 'She looks great.' She'd certainly had more acting experience than I'd had," Rogers remembered. They spent the afternoon going through the scene, the camera shooting over Anne's shoulder to focus on Rogers and then over his shoulder to focus on her. "She was great to work with," he said. "She was a wonderful actress and very giving."

Anne may have looked the part of an Italian girl, but nothing about the story resonated with her. She had never been to Rome, did not know any soldiers, and had not had an affair. She also had little idea how to perform for a movie camera. "I didn't even know it was there," Anne said. "I just wanted to act. Imagination took over." Rogers had one advantage in that sense. He had been in the Army Air Corps during the war and did not have to imagine what it was like to be a soldier. Still, he did not get a contract offer from Fox.

Anne had more roles—two came in September on NBC's half-hour *Armstrong Circle Theatre* and CBS's half-hour *The Web*—and a larger audience for her performances than her boyfriend John Ericson, thanks to television's demands for programming and its long reach into viewers' homes. He was working in the more respected venues of film and the New York stage, however. When the Broadway columnist Earl Wilson reported that they planned to wed in October 1951, the news was that the Broadway star John Ericson was marrying the TV star Anne Marno. It may have been her first appearance in a New York gossip column.

A call from Anne's agent, Mort Millman, rocked any idea of an October wedding date. People at Twentieth Century-Fox had been impressed by her performance in the screen test she had done for her friend over the summer. The studio was offering a standard contract at $20,000 a year, an average salary for a newcomer to films but a huge amount to the typical working-class American family at the time (about $185,000 in today's dollars).

How had Doug Rogers's screen test led to Anne's getting a studio contract? He saw the test a few months later. "In the editing of it, in all of my important parts of the scene, they were shooting over my shoulder into her face. My close-ups were not in the final edit. It was clearly geared toward making her look good." He believed that the director, being a friend of Anne's, had cut the test to favor her. "There were no really great shots of me acting. It was all the back of my head and her face. It's no wonder that she got to Hollywood. It sounds like sour grapes, but it isn't. It's the truth." Rogers continued his dance career, became a choreographer and stage director, and directed dozens of episodes of popular television sitcoms in the 1970s and 1980s.

Sabotage could have been on the mind of Anne's friend when he directed the test and supervised its editing. On the other hand, he probably would not have been so bold as to turn in footage that showcased only her. It is more likely that he used the occasion of Rogers's test to stage one for Anne as well. The director and film editor could have made two tests from the film negative, one for Rogers and one for Anne. That was close to the way Anne explained her big break. "Twentieth Century-Fox on this side, the East Coast, thought it was so good that they should make the test really for both of us," she said. "So they gave us equal footage, you know, and equal close-ups, and things like that. And it went to the West Coast and the West Coast said, 'Well, we'd like to sign up that girl.'"

How she felt the moment her agent told her Hollywood wanted her stayed with Anne. "It was the most thrilling thing that had ever happened—the end of the road, a dream come true," she said decades later. "There was no greater dream in the world." The opportunity had come out of good luck, but it was also the payoff for the experience she had received from appearing so frequently on television. On Columbus Day, October 12, 1951, while on a Fifth Avenue sidewalk watching the parade celebrating America's Italian heritage, Anne signed the contract that Millman had brought to her. Within four days she was listed among the cast of a movie scheduled to begin production in late November.

Getting to Hollywood had probably been on the minds of Anne and John Ericson. The optimistic view would have been for Ericson to join her and pursue his own film career after *Stalag 17* ended its Broadway run. With a well-received movie and a hit play to his credit, it was a reasonable plan. Later that month, Earl Wilson's gossip column reported that their wedding was being delayed until November. It was wishful thinking on someone's part, given that Anne was preparing to move across the country and Fox expected her on a soundstage after Thanksgiving.

For an energetic woman brimming with confidence and a career burnished with success, all those problems would have seemed surmountable. Twenty-year-old Anna Marie Italiano, known as Anne St. Raymond on radio and Anne Marno on television, had dreamed of being a movie star for most of her young life. She was about to get her wish—and yet another name.

After one more television appearance, an episode of the CBS mystery and suspense series *Lights Out* on October 22, 1951, Anne left New York City for Los Angeles accompanied by her parents. To help her get settled and make the transition from Mike and Millie Italiano's care and support, she moved in with the family of her agent, Mort Millman. ("Where are the subways?" she asked.) She would eventually rent an apartment of her own just a few blocks from the Millmans.

The most important person she met in those first few days in Hollywood was Darryl F. Zanuck, the head of Twentieth Century-Fox. Her new employer was not keen to see the name Anne Marno on his roster of stars. Worried that an ethnic-sounding surname and her dark features could typecast her, Zanuck handed Anne a list from which she could pick a new name. The choices struck her as better suited to a stripper than an actress. She managed to find one that she liked and later remarked, "Bancroft was the only name that didn't make me sound like a bubble dancer."

Zanuck had more on his mind than the name of yet another starlet. His studio, like the rest of Hollywood, was facing a financial and artistic crisis. The days when the movies served as a national retreat from the troubles of economic depression and war were over. Theater attendance was dropping by 10 percent in 1951 and would drop nearly twice that the next year as television extended its reach into American homes. The whole country was changing in ways that hurt movie attendance. People were moving to the suburbs, spending their money on other kinds of entertainment and leisure activities, and putting more toward having babies and raising families.

The studios also were losing their monopoly on production, distribution, and exhibition after the Supreme Court ordered them to sell off their theaters. On top of that, the federal government had renewed its investigation into communist influence in the film industry. Fox talent in front of the camera and behind it was being scrutinized for "reds." How to respond to what would become a blacklist and grappling with all those other issues while still producing movies that sold tickets was Zanuck's immediate challenge. The decisions he made would affect Anne and her career as well as the thousands of others who relied on Fox for a paycheck. The situation was almost the opposite of what Anne had found in early television in New York. Instead of enjoying the energy and optimism brought on by a new medium, Hollywood was operating in a climate of fear and uncertainty.

The immediate problems Anne faced were personal and professional. She was underage in the eyes of California law when it came to entering into a contract. On November 20, 1951, she appeared in Santa Monica Superior Court with her parents as Judge Orlando H. Rhodes reviewed the terms of the agreement with Twentieth Century-Fox. When the judge asked Anne if she was satisfied with the contract, she just nodded her head, perhaps too excited to speak. Mike and Millie Italiano gave their approval as well, and Rhodes suggested that Anne invest seventy-five dollars a week in government bonds. A statement of expenses submitted by Millie took into account what Anne would need for her forthcoming marriage to John Ericson. The *Los Angeles Times* reported on the contract approval using her new name, thus confirming that Anne Marno ceased to exist.

November was shaping up as an eventful month in her life—perhaps too eventful. As far as the public knew, Anne was still planning to marry Ericson that month. No wedding took place. In early December, citing the demands of Anne's first movie, the Broadway columnist Dorothy Kilgallen told her readers that the wedding had been moved to February. By then Anne was expected to have completed her first film.

Don't Bother to Knock was a minor thriller by design. The script was based on a well-received novel published the previous year, *Mischief,* and for a time the movie was going to be called *Night without Sleep* before Zanuck stepped in and changed the title. The film's budget was set at $600,000, a ceiling met in part by using only interior sets on the large stage at the old Fox facility on Western Avenue.

The story was economical, too, taking place on a single night. An airline pilot, Jed Towers, and a hotel lounge singer, Lyn Lesley, are at odds over the end of their six-month relationship. In the same hotel, Mr. and Mrs. Jones hire a babysitter, Nell Forbes, to stay with their daughter, Bunny, while they go out for the evening. Nell catches Jed's eye from his window across the hotel courtyard and he calls her. His visit to the Joneses' room reveals extremes in Nell's behavior—she is innocent one moment and flirtatious the next, shows a warm and caring attitude toward Bunny followed by a threatening tone. It becomes more and more apparent that Nell is mentally unbalanced and a danger to the child as well as herself.

Anne played the lounge singer, but the studio ordered her songs to be dubbed by the singer Eve Marley. "I couldn't have reached the high notes she reached," Anne admitted. Her leading man was Richard Widmark, a Fox star who had already made a dozen movies and seemed most at home in crime pictures and other urban dramas, notably the stylish films noirs *Panic in the Streets* (1950) and *Night and the City* (1950). The supporting cast of veteran character actors such as Jim Backus and Elisha Cook Jr. gave the slight production a sturdy foundation. Its director, Roy Ward Baker, was a native of London who had worked in the British film industry since the 1930s and had been brought to Fox by Zanuck. *Don't Bother to Knock* was his first Hollywood film.

All the attention, for better and for worse, was on the actress playing Nell, in her first starring role in a drama: Marilyn Monroe. She had made an impression in a handful of movies in the late 1940s and garnered more attention in 1950 in the Oscar-winning backstage drama *All About Eve* at Fox and the crime drama *The Asphalt Jungle* at MGM. In both movies Monroe played a supporting role as the sexy if innocent plaything of older men. She had signed a contract with Fox that year, too, and the initial budget for *Don't Bother to Knock* showed her earning $500 a week, the same money as Anne. (Widmark was being paid $1,750 a week.) Zanuck still required Monroe to do a screen test for the role of Nell, unsure that she was ready to carry a film. His lack of confidence in the endeavor was another reason for the low budget. With a new director and two actresses of limited experience, the studio chief was willing to gamble only so much money.

Unlike Anne, who was five years younger, Monroe was beset with doubts about her abilities and made those doubts known to everyone around her. The problems that would mark her entire career—an overreliance on an acting coach on the set, turning up late for work or not at all, and a tendency to blow her lines—showed themselves to some degree during production of the film she made with Anne. Still, Monroe had an undeniable appeal that went beyond good looks. Her sweet nature made most people protective of her.

"We had a hell of a time getting her out of the dressing room and onto the set," Widmark remembered years later. "At first we thought she'd never get anything right, and we'd mutter, 'Oh, this is impossible—you can't print this!' But something happened between the lens and the film, and when we looked at the rushes she had the rest of us knocked off the screen."

Monroe had little opportunity to knock Anne off the screen—they shared only one scene in the entire seventy-six minutes of the film. It came at the end, when Lyn and Jed quietly talk Nell out of killing herself. Anne's scenes with Widmark were about their characters' breakup and did not include any intimate moments. She later said that her sisters were disappointed that she could not tell them what it was like to kiss one of their favorite stars. "I found that Richard Widmark holds hands very nicely," she said.

Monroe biographers tend to brand the director Roy Ward Baker as unsupportive of her and at times nasty. There is no doubt that she gave Baker reasons to be exasperated, one being her desire to perform not according to his direction but to the approval of her acting coach. In contrast to Monroe, Anne was professional in her attitude as well as impressive in her acting. Baker had seen her *Girl on the Via Flaminia* screen test and thought at the time that Anne was inexperienced but promising. She exceeded his expectations once *Don't Bother to Knock* began filming. "She was a revelation," Baker told the film scholar Wheeler W. Dixon. "I mean, it's unbelievable, she was so good."

Anne had two other advantages while making the film besides a supportive director. Widmark was easy to work with and helpful to Anne, Baker recalled in a memoir. "Another bonus for her was that she had no scenes with Marilyn, except at the end of the film," he said, "and that was a reaction, which she did superbly, making a great contribution to Marilyn's performance." Whether Monroe's problems would have affected Anne's performance had they shared more screen time is impossible to judge, but the blonde star's anxieties drove Widmark to grumble, "Come on, will ya, for crissakes!" Baker felt that Zanuck had little interest in *Don't Bother to Knock* once it was completed, "except to give it its stupid title." He would always be asked about his experience with Monroe, but he seemed more pleased to have helped Anne on her way to a long career. "She was good news," Baker said. "And she never looked back. So the picture made two stars; it did Richard Widmark no harm, either."

When *Don't Bother to Knock* reached theaters that summer, critics focused on Marilyn Monroe, naturally, and they were divided over her performance and the movie. Only a sentence here and there in reviews of the movie noted Anne's portrayal of the lounge singer. The *Los Angeles Daily News* said she registered common sense in a difficult role, whereas the *Los Angeles Times* said the newcomer "lands a Sunday punch as Widmark's singer sweetheart." *Variety* allowed that she "scores brightly" and lauded her delivery of five songs in the film, apparently unaware that she had been dubbed. Judging from those kinds of reactions, Anne had made a positive impression in a so-so film. Moviegoers thought so—she began getting fan mail.

A different kind of reception greeted *Don't Bother to Knock* when it played near her neighborhood in the Bronx. "We all went to see it at the RKO Pelham," remembered her high school classmate Grace Milo. "When she got on the screen, we all screamed, 'Annnnnne!'"

With barely a break she went to her next assignment, *Treasure of the Golden Condor*. The movie was as different as it could be from her first film. Its director, Delmer Daves, had written an exotic adventure film set in eighteenth-century France with a side trip to Guatemala. Its hero, Jean-Paul, seeks to escape his life as a bondsman to his uncle, the evil Marquis of St. Malo, and make a claim to the title and holdings in spite of his illegitimate birth. He joins a visiting Scotsman, MacDougal, on a quest to find a Guatemalan treasure with hopes of returning wealthy and claiming the marquis's beautiful if selfish daughter, Marie. Jean-Paul and MacDougal sail across the ocean and, joined by the Scotsman's daughter, set out to find the treasure hidden deep in the jungle.

In the role of the duplicitous Marie, Anne wore several gowns and other costumes befitting her character's standing as the belle of the château and the production's use of Technicolor film. Her character had more shadings than the one in her first movie, and she spoke such lines as "I've been a countess all my life—I don't want to be a nobody!" and, while deciding whether to help her father or her lover, "I've been weighing one thing against the other. You've taught me well, Father." Daves's script avoided overly flamboyant dialogue and action, as Zanuck had demanded, but it was still a period piece with clinches and fisticuffs. Anne made up for lost time in the onscreen kissing department, embracing the film's star, Cornel Wilde, and kissing him in nearly every scene they shared.

A breathless publicist for Fox apparently did not read Zanuck's memo about avoiding flamboyance. "Although she looks to be a demure young miss, she has plenty of fire," read a paragraph about Anne in publicity material handed out to the press. "In one passionate scene with Cornel she pulled his hair, slapped his face and threatened him with a hammer before submitting to his embrace. It left the crewmen gasping."

Wilde had appeared on Broadway before beginning his movie career and reached star status by the mid-1940s. He had just completed his role in Cecil B. DeMille's circus epic *The Greatest Show on Earth* (1952) when Daves was considering a leading man for his adventure movie. Zanuck himself wanted Wilde cast as Jean-Paul to take advantage of his role in what was expected to be another DeMille blockbuster. (It later won the Oscar for best picture.) *Treasure of the Golden Condor* became Wilde's twenty-eighth movie. Anne described him at the time as a generous actor. "He was always urging me to keep my face toward the camera so I could have the photographic advantages," she said. "I'd always heard you had to fight for your close-ups, but he insisted that I get the good ones." Wilde could afford to be generous; he was earning $6,250 a week compared to Anne's $500.

When Fox released *Treasure of the Golden Condor* in the spring of 1953, nearly a year after filming had ended, Anne again picked up one or two positive notices for her supporting role. "Miss Bancroft comes over effectively as Wilde's calculating love," the *Hollywood Reporter* wrote. Critics tended to see the movie as above-average if not particularly memorable entertainment. The *New York Times* commended the entire cast and gave the film the backhanded compliment as "the tastiest corn in a blue moon."

In between *Treasure of the Golden Condor* and her next movie, *Tonight We Sing,* Anne visited her family in New York. She also took the opportunity to end her engagement to John Ericson. He had not been able to land a Hollywood assignment and instead stayed with *Stalag 17.* The distance probably proved to be deadly for their relationship—Anne suggested as much in an interview—and it kept them apart during an exciting time in their young and all-too-separate lives. The Hollywood gossip queen Hedda Hopper told her readers on March 28, 1952, that Anne had returned her engagement ring to Ericson and that he gave back a set of diamond-studded cuff links.

So far, Anne had appeared in one suspense film and one swashbuckler. *Tonight We Sing* fell into another category, musical biography, a film genre that celebrated a well-known figure with a largely fictionalized version of his or her life punctuated by musical numbers. Fox held the film rights to the impresario Sol Hurok's life and decided to put a movie into production after MGM had a hit with *The Great Caruso* (1951). Fox was filming another entry in the genre, the John Philip Sousa story *Stars and Stripes Forever,* while Anne worked on the Hurok project that spring.

Hurok was a different kind of subject for a musical biography because he was not a performer or a composer but a manager of musical talent—arguably the most important impresario of his time. In the film, Hurok (David Wayne) devotes himself to bringing music to the world no matter the cost to him financially and personally. His wife, Emma, played by Anne, is understanding and supportive until his neglect of their marriage drives her away. She returns to help him recover from bankruptcy and reach even greater heights.

The role of Emma can be summed up in one of her lines of dialogue: "Don't worry, Sol, everything will turn out all right." For Anne, the picture's dramatic shortcomings were balanced by lavish outfits evoking the 1920s—the studio claimed she had twenty-eight different costume changes for the movie. Far less colorful in the movie was her costar, David Wayne, typically a supporting player on Broadway and in movies who was saddled with a character as bland as the script for a rare leading role. Its director, Mitchell Leisen, had guided forty films by then—most of them in the 1930s and 1940s with top stars of the day—and he was nearing the end of his film career.

Hurok served as a technical adviser, but the story was almost totally fiction. There were two Mrs. Huroks, for example, and the impresario could be as vain as any of his star clients when not displaying the bullying and cunning that had helped make him a towering figure in a cutthroat business. The real purpose of the narrative, as in most musical biographies, was to connect the musical numbers. *Tonight We Sing* offered a dozen from operas, ballets, and other classical compositions. The producer George Jessel, a top comedian and for nearly a decade a producer at Fox, wanted the numbers in *Tonight We Sing* to stand out. He hired such artists as the choreographer David Lichine, who had worked on the ballet drama *The Red Shoes,* to give the movie prestige.

Jessel spent the money he saved by casting David Wayne at $2,100 a week and Anne at $500 a week on those who performed in the musical interludes: the opera singers Ezio Pinza, Roberta Peters, and Jan Peerce (who dubbed the actor Byron Palmer), and prima ballerina Tamara Toumanova and violinist Isaac Stern. All appeared as performers from Hurok's early career. A partial budget for the film showed the real stars: Pinza was paid $10,000 a week for twelve weeks, and Stern drew $8,500 for a single week. Pinza had not only the most numbers in the film, but also the heartiest role as the opera singer Feodor Chaliapin, and he played the Russian as comically vain and grandiose.

Musicals had never been Fox's strongest product—that was the province of MGM in the 1950s—but the musical sequences if not the narrative in *Tonight We Sing* impressed critics. *Time* magazine called it an "opulent, star-spangled, two-hour film concert" with a fairly lowbrow offstage story. "A magnificent piece of entertainment that is sheer delight," wrote the *Hollywood Reporter,* which described Anne as giving an appealingly persuasive performance as Mrs. Hurok. *Variety* said she "impresses favorably." The critic at *Newsweek* was among those who understood what the film was all about: "a Technicolored musical extravaganza."

In that first year in Hollywood, Anne worked hard to learn how to perform before a film camera. As opposed to the multiple cameras used in television production, a single camera recorded her efforts. "They make you look so wonderful," she said at the time, "you feel like you're Cinderella and the camera is the good fairy and your glass slipper rolled into one." The wardrobe for movies was far more extravagant than it had been for television, with silks, satins, and imported fabrics she had never before seen. Broadcast in black and white on a tiny screen, no actress looked her best on television. Film could produce a sharp image with arresting shadows, particularly in black and white. Technicolor created another world entirely.

The depth of her acting was not on her mind. "The script said 'Laugh' and I laughed; 'Cry' and I cried," she said later. "I was just doing me." Nor did she pay much attention to the quality of her roles. The clothes, the premiers, the parties, and all the other trappings of the movie star were enough. As ambitious as she was, Anne tended to do as she was told and not raise a fuss about things that bothered her. "It never occurred to me that there was anything else worth happening to me," she said.

Like Jean-Paul in his quest for the Golden Condor, she had found her treasure. "I had no desire to be anything more than I was," she said in looking back at that time in her life. "To be a movie star, oh, that was it! It was a single-minded dream." Fox rewarded her in October 1952 with an extension of her contract and a 20 percent increase in her salary, to $600 a week. The dream would continue—at least for another year.

3

Stuck in a Low-Budget Rut

Several months passed before Twentieth Century-Fox cast Anne in another movie. Her contract may have specified a certain number of films each year or a certain number of weeks to be worked per year. For that matter, the studio may have had little for her to do in front of a camera.

Not that acting was her only chore as a contract player. Away from the soundstages at Fox, Anne had premieres to attend, interviews with newspapers and fan magazines, and photographs to pose for. A picture of her frolicking on the beach in a striped swimsuit had appeared the previous summer in the *Chicago Tribune,* and the newspaper published a glamour shot of Anne in a gown that December. She also endorsed products like Lustre-Cream Shampoo, appearing in an ad in *Variety* as "one of television's loveliest contributions to motion pictures." Such off-screen activities generated publicity to build up her image as a young actress worth watching.

The long period Anne spent in between pictures coincided with her twenty-first birthday. She became a full-fledged adult in September 1952, at least in the eyes of the law and American society. Even then she remained emotionally immature, or so she thought years later, and she no longer had the personal discipline that came with the watchful presence of her mother. "Hollywood was the ideal place for being young and irresponsible and having fun," Anne said as she looked back on that time. "It was one big party with palm trees and swimming pools." Only from the perspective of time did she realize that she was undergoing a kind of delayed adolescence.

Parties were one way Anne dealt with the boredom that came amid the constant sunshine and unchanging palm trees. Such gatherings were also a patch for the loneliness she was feeling. It was difficult for her to meet people when making a movie that demanded she rise at five or six in the morning and work all day. Night came with exhaustion. When she was not working, she had time to consider how empty her life had become without her family and friends.

Anne now lived alone in a West Hollywood apartment on Miller Drive, just off Sunset Boulevard. Temptations were close at hand. A few blocks east on Sunset was the nightclub Ciro's. Its competition, the Mocambo, was a few blocks west. Anne went to enough parties and showed up on the arms of enough different men that her name landed frequently in the gossip columns. But parties were not always the answer. When she found herself in a circle of intellectuals discussing all manners of things, she felt inferior. Besides having a high school education, what did she know about life?

In the movies back then, an immature girl who enjoyed a good time usually ended up in all kinds of trouble. Such a cautionary tale loomed as a reality for Anne. "There was a lot of drinking in Hollywood," she said. "When I would be driving and get home and wake up in the morning and not know how I got there, I was scared to death—absolutely." She did not offer details when she reflected on those days—and she expressed no personal regrets about them—but she made it clear that she remembered being a lonely, frightened young woman at times in spite of all the glamour.

Work provided a measure of relief. In March 1953 Anne began shooting *The Kid from Left Field,* a lighthearted baseball tale with a little bit of romance wedged in between innings. There were two stories off the field, the one between a boozing former player and his nine-year-old son, groomed for the game, and the one between a member of the team and his fiancée. Fox's studio chief, Darryl F. Zanuck, was wary of baseball movies because they performed poorly abroad. He urged the producer Leonard Goldstein to make *The Kid from Left Field* as cheaply as possible. A master of the low-budget film, Goldstein cast one star, Dan Dailey, and filled the other roles with low-cost talent and then shot in black and white. The love interest—between Anne and her costar, Lloyd Bridges—was a way of coaxing women to watch a male-oriented story.

Anne received her first above-the-title billing with *The Kid from Left Field.* It was a bit of a sham, however, as were the posters that showed her with Dan Dailey and young Billy Chapin as if they were a happy threesome. Chapin had more screen time than anyone, and there was no love interest between Dailey's and Anne's characters. Their nearly equal billing did not mean parity in pay. Dailey earned $3,250 a week to her $600. Shot in a matter of weeks and released that summer, *The Kid from Left Field* required only that Anne look pretty and play the supportive female. At least the benign entertainment did her career no harm. The *Hollywood Reporter* said she made "a warmly appealing femme lead." The movie played on a double bill, further evidence that it was considered a low-end product.

Nothing was low end about *Demetrius and the Gladiators,* a lavish sequel to *The Robe* that followed characters introduced in the Lloyd C. Douglas novel about the crucifixion of Jesus. The book, published in 1942, had topped the annual list of best sellers for several years. To make the most of the massive sets built for *The Robe,* Fox put the sequel into production almost immediately after filming on *The Robe* ended in April 1953. It was a gamble to undertake a sequel before the release of *The Robe,* even though the popularity of the novel seemed to ensure an audience for both movies.

The Robe had been the first major film production to use the widescreen process CinemaScope, which Fox developed itself. Making the projected image more than twice the size of those shot in the conventional format and joining it with stereophonic sound were Hollywood's most significant responses to the incursion of television. Although *Demetrius and the Gladiators* would naturally be filmed in color and in CinemaScope because of its ties to the first film, Zanuck decided that all new Fox features would be in its new widescreen format. In time all major studios either licensed CinemaScope for their own use or turned to other formats designed to dwarf home screens and entice people back to theaters.

Victor Mature appeared again as Demetrius, and Michael Rennie reprised his role as the disciple Peter. In her part as the unfaithful wife of Claudius, the emperor's uncle, Susan Hayward provided the film's main sex appeal. Demetrius needed someone to love, too, and for that purpose Debra Paget appeared as Lucia, the daughter of a pottery maker. The only other female character of note was Paula, one of the many women brought in to provide companionship for the gladiators during their celebrations. In studio memos they were referred to as prostitutes, though not in the film itself.

The film's director, Delmer Daves, may have chosen Anne from other Fox contract players to play Paula because of their association on *Treasure of the Golden Condor.* Paula was not a memorable role. Billed fifth in the biblical epic, Anne appeared in just three scenes. With dark, curly hair, dangling gold earrings, and a knowing smile, Paula commiserates with Demetrius over a plate of food when he arrives at the gladiator school. She later sneaks Lucia into the gladiators' banquet hall so that Lucia can see the man she loves. When Lucia succumbs to shock in the arms of a gladiator rather than be ravished by him, it is left to Anne's character to scream, "She's dead!" With that, Anne disappeared from the movie.

Being part of a major film, even in a small role, was a plus for a young actress. *Demetrius and the Gladiators* ended up being one of the most popular films released in 1954. Unlike *The Robe,* the sequel was an action movie with a religious theme for those who looked hard enough. Audiences and critics responded positively to the spectacle. In terms of box office, it was the biggest hit Anne appeared in until *The Graduate,* more than thirteen years later.

As she completed work on her fifth film, Anne found what she hoped would be the cure for her loneliness and longing: a husband. She had been almost desperate to marry—she later joked that she had even thought about marrying the comedian and producer George Jessel. The notorious womanizer was older than her father. (Part of the joke lay in the fact that a decade earlier Jessel, then forty-four, had married a sixteen-year-old.) When it came to her desire for a husband and a family, Anne was serious.

The man she did marry, Martin May, was older by nine years and far removed from show business and city life. Raised in Lubbock, Texas, May had come to Los Angeles to study law and was preparing for the bar exam when they met. Newspaper articles described him as tall and handsome and the son of a family made wealthy either by oil or by ranching. In interviews then and later, Anne said little about her husband.

Even by Hollywood standards, the circumstances of their marriage were odd. Public records show that Martin May and Anne Italiano married on July 1, 1953, in Riverside, California. Yet, for the next ten months, she pretended publicly that she was still a single actress looking for the right man. When the *Los Angeles Times* film critic Philip K. Scheuer interviewed her a few weeks after the marriage, he reported that while Anne expressed her desire to act in any medium, "in the next breath, though, she said she'd like to get married and have kids." Unbeknown to Scheuer, she was already halfway there.

For most of the early months of their marriage, Anne and May lived in separate apartments. There appeared to be some accommodations to reality. On her next movie, begun two months later, the contact sheet listing her address—by then she had moved to South Burnside Avenue—noted two phone numbers. When *Time* magazine wrote a cover story about Anne in 1959, the first year of *The Miracle Worker's* run on Broadway, Marty May explained away the secrecy by saying that he had wanted to tell his mother about the marriage in person. Why so many months had to pass was not explored. In interviews Anne never offered an explanation for keeping the marriage secret. When looking back, she often said that she had realized quickly, even within days of taking her vows, that marrying May was a mistake.

While Anne and Marty May were living apart in their effort to keep their summer marriage out of the newspapers, financial worries at Twentieth Century-Fox were all too public. Zanuck had rolled back production by one-third as the studio retooled for CinemaScope. In spite of the realignment, Fox still needed low-budget movies to send to theaters if it wanted to remain competitive with other distributors.

In late July, Fox announced a deal with the producer Leonard Goldstein, the man behind *The Kid from Left Field,* to distribute movies he would make elsewhere while using non-Fox financing. Since the studio had talent under contract with nothing to do because of the scaled-back production schedule, Goldstein tapped those idle Fox employees for his new independent venture, Panoramic Productions. Anne was among those whom Fox sent to Goldstein's offices at the RKO-Pathé lot in Culver City. It was work but not necessarily a step up for her.

Goldstein had produced scores of films for Universal-International and then Fox in the six years before he formed Panoramic Productions. Though Fox occasionally backed issue-oriented movies like *Gentlemen's Agreement* (1947) and *Deadline U.S.A.* (1952), Goldstein was interested in popular entertainment. He made no pretense to presenting artistic-minded or socially significant films. "There are more people going to the movies with my mentality than any other," he told the press. "Let's face it: I don't dig this highbrow stuff. I always say that for messages I will go to Western Union." Proving his point were the Francis the Talking Mule series and the Ma and Pa Kettle films, all made on tight budgets under tight schedules at Universal and earning good money.

Following his tried-and-true strategy, Goldstein developed *Gorilla at Large,* a melodrama of greed, jealousy, and murder set at a carnival featuring a ferocious ape. He put slightly more than $400,000 into *Gorilla at Large* and may have sensed that it needed more than a man in a gorilla suit and Anne in a crimson leotard to sell tickets. He turned to 3-D, which was then a craze. Though it was short-lived and often gimmicky, 3-D was another response to the threat posed by television. The process spanned all genres—even the Western (*Hondo* with John Wayne) and the musical (*Kiss Me Kate*)—but 3-D may have been most effective for horror films such as *House of Wax* and *Creature from the Black Lagoon.* Fox released its first 3-D movie well into the craze, the suspenseful desert drama *Inferno,* in the summer of 1953. Zanuck all but banned 3-D for other Fox projects as a sign of its commitment to CinemaScope. Except for *Gorilla at Large,* Fox did not distribute any other 3-D movies during that era.

No other movie showed off Anne's lean and well-proportioned figure as well as *Gorilla at Large.* It was also the first movie in which she was a decidedly bad girl. If her talent was being squandered, she was in good company. The carnival owner was played by Raymond Burr, still a few years from television's *Perry Mason.* Lee J. Cobb and Cameron Mitchell, both stars of the original Broadway production of *Death of a Salesman,* were in the cast. Cobb would appear as the union boss in *On the Waterfront* five months later. Also onscreen was the future Oscar winner Lee Marvin as a bumbling policeman. Everyone needed a paycheck.

Television's golden age had served Anne well, but the golden age of 3-D did not. She would point to *Gorilla at Large* as the kind of movie that made her early film career seem like a waste of time. Actually, the movie delivered its promise of cheap thrills and chills, and critics either accepted it on those terms ("diverting and persuasively acted," contended the *Hollywood Reporter*) or dismissed it ("melodramatic muck," chided the *New York Times*). Then again, the bar was quite low for a B movie in 3-D featuring a man in a gorilla suit. After showing off so much of her body, Anne could not be ignored. The *Hollywood Reporter* gushed, "Anne Bancroft makes a gorgeous one-woman crime wave." To her chagrin, the film resurfaced in the early 1980s when television stations in Boston, Los Angeles, and other cities began showing 3-D movies from the 1950s as a novelty. If an ad appeared, it was likely to note *Gorilla at Large* "starring Anne Bancroft."

The worst movie Anne would make in those early years also signaled the end of her two years under contract with Twentieth Century-Fox. The studio was dropping the contracts of stars big and small as part of its cost-cutting efforts. Unless she signed a long-term deal with another studio,

Anne would be a freelancer. All the major studios, however, were moving toward shedding their contract talent in the face of financial uncertainty. The independence that came with picking and choosing roles could not be separated from the loss of security represented by regular employment.

"They did not know what to do with her," recalled the actor Robert Wagner, whose long film career began at Fox at nearly the same time as Anne's. "It's very frustrating when you're at a place like that and they don't get who you are. Her talent hadn't really been exposed yet. People didn't really know what she had."

Though they were not close friends, Wagner remembered Anne fondly. "I used to see her around on the lot as young actors. We were both young, very enthusiastic young actors. And she was great. I really liked her so much—such a lovely person." Her departure came amid some talk about her wanting a raise and not getting one. "I don't know what happened," Wagner said. "Who knows what happens with careers. It's like a marriage—who knows? I don't think that they recognized this talent that she had, and I think it took a while for that to surface."

Anne did not work on any other films in 1953. If the movie studios had nothing she wanted or if they had not wanted her, there was still television. It offered Anne money and interesting roles as well as a trip to New York, where she could visit her family. She appeared with Sal Mineo and Leslie Nielsen in an adaptation of an Ernest Hemingway short story about matadors in Madrid, "The Capital of the World," for the CBS series *Omnibus* on December 6. The director was Yul Brynner, who had managed to keep his job as a director of television programs for CBS even as he starred on Broadway in *The King and I.* Anne then appeared in "To Live in Peace," a story set in Italy during the Napoleonic wars that aired on *Kraft Television Theatre* on December 16.

Marriage was proving to be another adjustment for her. She later described Marty May as a rich, spoiled kid and hinted at a darker side when she remarked that her husband always slept with a loaded handgun under his pillow. When he discussed their marriage with *Time* magazine, the law school graduate working in real estate sounded like a fish out of water. In his telling, their apartment was often filled with actors sitting up for hours reading plays. "Annie was intense about everything," May said. "She'd lie on the floor and watch television by the hour, or she'd fry an egg, standing there leaning over the skillet staring as if the fate of the city depended on that egg. She was either a hungry tiger or a lovable lapdog."

Her high school friend David Lunney visited the couple after they had moved into an apartment on Doheny Drive in Beverly Hills. He sensed the tension between them. "It seemed that relationship was not going that great," he remembered. "That was a problematic relationship, it seemed to me." She mentioned the gun under the pillow to Lunney, and he thought it disturbed her greatly. Even at that, he recalled, she was not saying the marriage was over.

As a freelance actress, Anne offered good value for the money, on the basis of her talent, experience, and good looks. The competition for parts in high-quality films was fierce, however. Her age, twenty-two, worked against her for mature roles that went to Susan Hayward, Donna Reed, Ruth Roman, Gloria Grahame, Virginia Mayo, and other actresses in their thirties. As pretty as she was, Anne could not match the dark beauty of Ava Gardner, Elizabeth Taylor, and Jean Simmons or the blonde sirens Marilyn Monroe, Lana Turner, and Grace Kelly. Those within a few years of her age—among them Debra Paget, Pier Angeli, Janet Leigh, and Eva Marie Saint—were busy seeking roles at the same time Anne was looking for work.

Leonard Goldstein knew Anne could deliver onscreen and on time. As 1954 began, he cast her in two more movies, paying her $2,500 a week for the four weeks he needed her for each of his low-budget films. Although the money represented a huge boost compared to her weekly Fox salary, it was still work for hire.

Fortunately for Anne, Panoramic Productions had better movies for her than *Gorilla at Large*. In January 1954 she began shooting *The Raid*. The screenplay was based on historical events surrounding a Confederate raid in 1864 that was the northernmost action of the Civil War. About two dozen Confederate cavalrymen invaded St. Albans, Vermont, and robbed its three banks before heading to Canada with their loot. In the Hollywood version of history, the undercover Confederate major in charge of the raid (Van Heflin) develops tender feelings for a widowed boardinghouse owner, played by Anne. Though set in New England, the movie had all the trappings of a Western—horses, wagons, six-shooters, and rifles—plus a fiery climax as the raiders set the town ablaze.

The Raid was a step-up for Anne as well as for Panoramic Productions. Heflin, a Broadway-turned-film actor, had won an Oscar as a supporting player in the crime film *Johnny Eager* (1942). He had appeared in more than thirty films, including the classic Western *Shane* the previous year.

Filmed in Technicolor at the RKO-Pathé studios using old sets from *Gone with the Wind*, *The Raid* was a low-budget movie, costing under $600,000, with a better-than-average look. Critics tended to like the film for its action and unusual story. The *Los Angeles Examiner* considered it dramatic and suspenseful—and noted that Anne had provided excellent support as the comely widow.

With barely a break from the camera, Anne traveled to Mexico City in February to shoot her third Panoramic film, *A Life in the Balance*. Joining her were the Mexico City–born star Ricardo Montalbán and the supporting player Lee Marvin, who had appeared as a miscreant Confederate in *The Raid*. Marvin's career was rising in the mid-1950s, though he had become typecast as a brooding and often deranged criminal. That was his role in *A Life in the Balance*, based on a novella by Georges Simenon. Goldstein had purchased the rights to the story from Fox, which at one time planned to film it with Richard Widmark in Paris, the story's setting. Instead, Goldstein took the production south of the border and used a Mexican crew and studio, perhaps with an eye on feeding the Latin American market after its run in the United States.

Black-and-white photography suited the film's story about an unemployed and quick-tempered composer suspected of a murder actually committed by a serial killer. Anne played the woman he meets at a pawn shop and spends the evening with at a street festival. Lee Marvin and Anne were the only Anglos in the cast, and she was made up to be slightly darker for her role. While she fell into the stereotype of the supportive female, she appeared more natural and charming than in her previous films and seemed at ease in the contemporary urban setting. Ricardo Montalbán was ten years older than Anne but still closer to her age than most of her male costars so far. Such dramatic roles were helping him move away from his early portrayals of lighthearted Latin lovers.

Marvin dominated the screen as a psychopath driven by a desire to bring God's wrath on his hapless victims. The film's climax brought the cast to the campus of the newly completed University of Mexico. Harry Horner, an art director who guided only a handful of films from the director's chair, took full advantage of the striking murals and modern architecture as he staged the confrontation between the composer and the killer. (A half century later the United Nations designated the campus a World Heritage Site.) Once more, Leonard Goldstein got his money's worth from cast and crew.

A *Life in the Balance* ended filming in mid-March and reached theaters more than a year later, in the summer of 1955. Critics disagreed over whether the movie was "artful suspense" (*Los Angeles Examiner*) or "generally slack and uninspired" (*New York Times*). Anne received good reviews for her last Panoramic film. It turned out to be the last for Goldstein as well. A few months later, while in a meeting with Darryl F. Zanuck, he suffered a stroke and died at fifty-one.

After completing work on *A Life in the Balance,* Anne announced to the press in April that she and Marty May had married. Up to that point they were still only engaged as far as the public was concerned. The *Los Angeles Times* reported on April 28, 1954, that a justice of the peace had married them the previous weekend in a town near Las Vegas—not ten months earlier in Riverside, California. The couple kept the full story to themselves as best they could. When the Hollywood columnist Louella Parsons asked where the wedding had taken place, Anne became flustered and replied, "I don't remember." Parsons kept the strange response to herself for the time being. The columnist Hedda Hopper told her readers that the two were driving to Texas to visit May's family and continuing on to New York to meet the Italianos and then marry in Santa Maria Church in the Bronx. A Catholic wedding was important to Millie Italiano, and the couple planned the ceremony to coincide with their first anniversary—the real one.

When Anne returned to Los Angeles in mid-July, she began filming the first of two hard-boiled crime movies for the independent producer Edward Small. A congressional investigation led by Senator Estes Kefauver in 1950 and 1951 had made organized crime a hot topic. Small had the film rights to the book *New York: Confidential,* a collection of true tales of crime and corruption written by Jack Lait and Lee Mortimer, both newspaper veterans. (Mortimer may have been most famous for taking a punch from Frank Sinatra outside Ciro's nightclub in 1947.) In keeping with a tight budget, filming took place at the Goldwyn studios in Los Angeles.

New York Confidential allowed Anne to play a contemporary New Yorker for a change. The main characters were a volcanic syndicate boss, his daughter, and a newly hired gunman struggling with domestic problems amid a gang war. The daughter is ashamed to have a gangster for a father and leaves home, only to develop feelings for her father's newest employee. When he rejects her, she dies in a suicidal car accident. The cast for the grim story was strong, led by Broderick Crawford as the crime boss and Richard Conte as his protégé. Crawford had broken out of B movies to win an Oscar for playing the political boss Willie Stark in the film version of the novel *All the King's Men* (1949), then settled into a series of tough-guy roles in movies of varying quality.

It took an unheralded potboiler to show Anne the limits of her acting technique. Though the script called for her character to kill herself off-screen, Anne tried to keep that in mind and shade her performance accordingly when she played her breakup scene with Richard Conte. She struggled, having no idea how to empathize with a young woman in such distress that she would commit suicide. Russell Rouse, a screenwriter who was directing his fourth film, was of no help to her. "All he did was just take the scene, thirty-three takes," Anne said, "and each time he was like expecting God somehow to come down and strike me with the right meaning to the scene." Ultimately, Anne delivered what she considered one of the few moments in her early films of which she could be proud. Yet, she determined later, the experience also showed that she had more to learn.

Moviegoers who liked their crime stories with grit and gunplay would have been entertained by *New York Confidential.* Some critics were not. Richard L. Coe of the *Washington Post* considered it cheap and sleazy, as befitting the source material. The *Chicago Tribune* faulted the script as being thin and tossed together. Though the *Los Angeles Times* thought the movie was competent if familiar, it joined the *Los Angeles Examiner* in commending Anne and her costars for effective performances. *Variety* echoed that praise and said that Anne, "showing continuing progress and talent, scores with a standout performance."

Anne seemed to move easily between movies and television after leaving Fox. She starred in an adaptation of John Steinbeck's story "A Medal for Benny" on *Lux Video Theatre* in November before returning to Edward Small's independent film operation for *The Naked Street* in February 1955. The broad outline of the role must have seemed laughably familiar to her: the sister of a New York mob boss whose family problems cross over into his business. This time, instead of playing a daughter who could go toe to toe with her father, Anne appeared as a timid if loving sister who could not believe her brother was a bad man. At least *The Naked Street* put her in good company: Anthony Quinn, already an Oscar winner for *Viva Zapata!* (1952) and a year from another for *Lust for Life* (1956), played her brother and Farley Granger her homicidal boyfriend.

Top billing went to Granger, a veteran of two Alfred Hitchcock films,

Rope (1948) and *Strangers on a Train* (1951), and several other movies. He was disappointed with the quality of his latest vehicle. "We all struggled to inject some kind of drama into a script that was preachy, trite, and pedestrian," Granger recalled in a memoir. The *New York Times* and *Variety* agreed for the most part, though *Variety* deemed Quinn and Anne excellent in their roles. Granger longed for New York and the theater, where he hoped he could break out of the mediocrity he found all too often in the movies. "Anne and I would spend our lunches talking about the theater and life in New York," he remembered. "This was her tenth film, and she was not happy about any of them. I felt that she was too special and too good for Hollywood to ever figure out how to use her well and suggested she go back to the theater." At that point, though, she had never been in the theater. Movies and television were all she knew.

There could be no question that Anne was in a low-budget rut. The money was good—she said as much—and her costars were respected actors. The directors, however, tended to be industry journeymen with little standing among critics or the more artistic filmmakers at work. The production values were obviously low. None of her films, not even the big-budget *Demetrius and the Gladiators,* had drawn a single Oscar nomination. Another blow was missing out on a role in *The Ten Commandments,* a star-studded spectacular from the director Cecil B. DeMille that would become second only to *Gone with the Wind* in ticket sales. DeMille had auditioned Anne for the role of Sephora, the wife of Moses, but she failed to impress him. "Her voice isn't very pleasant," he wrote in his casting journal. "Looks the part; not a very good actress." The role went to Yvonne De Carlo instead. Such a rejection, had Anne known of it, could have pushed her to abandon Hollywood as Farley Granger had suggested.

Good news from her agent must have quieted any thoughts Anne may have had about going onto the stage in search of better roles. Columbia Pictures was offering a two-picture contract, while MGM was interested in having her appear in an upcoming Western. Offers from not one but two major studios suggested that her career was primed for a rebound. The production values at Columbia and MGM promised to be of higher quality; her costars would be on a different tier and her directors possess a more solid body of work as well as a sharper sense of visual and dramatic style.

The Last Frontier was no back-lot Western made for children on a Saturday afternoon. The story of conflict between the U.S. Army and Sioux

Indians demanded a huge cast and a vast outdoor setting. Its subplot, a love triangle involving a cavalry officer and his wife and the mountain man who comes between them, added a sexual flavor that was unusual for most Westerns at the time. The director, Anthony Mann, specialized in providing the genre a psychological undertow. He had directed two dozen movies in his twenty years in Hollywood, but the Westerns he made in the 1950s with James Stewart—*Winchester '73* (1950), *The Naked Spur* (1953), and three others—along with the popular biopic *The Glenn Miller Story* (1954) had put him in the ranks of major directors.

Location shooting in early spring 1955 took place forty miles southwest of Mexico City in the shadow of the icy volcanic peak Popocatépetl. The story, however, is set in Wyoming during the army's 1860s war with the Sioux chief Red Cloud. Anne was billed below Victor Mature as the trapper, Robert Preston as the cavalry commander, Guy Madison, and James Whitmore. The only woman with a significant role, her hair was turned a flat blonde for a character at least ten years older than her true age, and her face was given a pallid tone. Mann probably saw the makeover as important to highlighting the differences between civilization, represented by the fair-skinned eastern woman, and nature, represented by the dark-haired and darker-skinned mountain man. As the film scholar Jeanine Basinger suggests in her study of Mann's films, such symbolism gave depth to his Westerns—man versus society was a favorite theme— and set them apart from other entries in a tired genre.

A low-key performance marked Anne's scenes with Robert Preston and even those with Victor Mature. Her *Demetrius and the Gladiators* costar was one of Hollywood's popular if colorless performers, but the mountain man gave Mature a dynamic character who brawls and laughs and lusts with equal fervor. As the two men vying for her character's attentions fought savages and challenged each other, Anne had little to do. A scene in which she repeatedly stabs an Indian warrior was eliminated from the film after the industry's censorship office decided it was too brutal.

The Last Frontier fell far short of Anthony Mann's other Westerns. The weaknesses of the screenplay—without a star of James Stewart's caliber and lacking a brisk pace—were all too obvious. "The story is so disordered and the color photography is so deliberately dim that the whole thing is thoroughly obscurist," complained Bosley Crowther of the *New York Times*. The *Chicago Tribune* called the plot trite, and *Variety* thought no one was outstanding in what came off as a routine Western. The *Hollywood Reporter* compared the film to a frontier rifle, calling it "a long, smooth bore."

As production continued on her first Columbia feature, Anne made herself available to MGM in mid-April for costume tests for another Western, *The Last Hunt.* The wardrobe department anticipated she would need four leather jackets, one of them bloodstained, for her role as a young Indian woman. One budget for the production showed MGM was investing $1.7 million, more than three times the money that went into one of her Panoramic Productions features. Set aside for the role Anne would play was $19,500.

Her previous Western had sacrificed an authentic location for a picturesque one in Mexico that probably offered some cost advantages. The writer and director of *The Last Hunt,* Richard Brooks, would put authenticity first. The former newspaper man and radio reporter researched his films like the journalist he had been and demanded a high degree of accuracy. *The Last Hunt* was his eighth film directed for MGM, which gave him leeway to make a big-budget Western after his previous effort, *Blackboard Jungle,* proved to be a surprise hit. Brooks preferred to write as well as direct and had adapted Milton Lott's award-winning novel about buffalo hunters in the Black Hills.

Everything about *The Last Hunt* was first-rate and promised Anne the best venue yet for her talents. Its producer was the studio chief of MGM, Dore Schary, who personally oversaw only one or two movies a year. Set to star as the buffalo hunters were Robert Taylor, still one of Hollywood's most popular leading men, and Stewart Granger, a British transplant who had become a major star of adventure films and period romances. The production would have the typical MGM gloss and the stature of being released by what many still considered best of the Hollywood studios.

That summer Richard Brooks took the cast and crew to South Dakota to film the 1,500 buffalo at Custer State Park, the largest buffalo herd in the country, and make use of arresting locations in the Badlands. For a movie about the slaughter of the great herds of the High Plains, the writer-director wanted to film the actual killings of buffalo during the annual thinning of the herd. The forty-seven days set aside for filming would be almost evenly divided between locations in South Dakota and soundstages at MGM.

Good weather led the crew to cut its location shooting in the Black

Hills by nearly ten days. For one scene, Anne bathed in French Creek, prompting a technician to tell a visiting journalist, "I hope it gets by the censors." In case her bare back somehow caused a stir, Brooks also filmed her in the water's reflection.

On July 28, one of the final days of filming, the script called for Stewart Granger to lift Anne onto the back of his horse and ride off with her. "Not an easy thing to do," Granger recalled in a memoir. Brooks rejected using a double, according to Granger's account, and they prepared the scene. "The horse was one of the Hollywood types who, on the words 'get ready' starts to play up and when 'action' comes, takes off like a bullet," the actor said. "Trying to control him with one hand, I lifted Anne with the other, but the horse put in a buck at that moment and she landed hard, hitting her coccyx painfully on the pommel. I did my best to hold her off and stop the galloping horse but I'm afraid the damage was done and by the time I finally pulled up she was in agony." She was taken to St. John's Hospital in Rapid City for treatment of the injury. The cast and crew left for Hollywood within a day or two, Anne among them.

Various reports then and later had it that Anne had broken her back, that a vertebra had been fractured or punctured, or that she had suffered a severely pinched nerve between vertebrae. It was probably a less serious injury, if still painful, that did not involve a broken back. Consigned to bed rest for the next three months—some reports had it that she was in a cast for most of that time—she withdrew from *The Last Hunt*. MGM turned to Debra Paget, her *Demetrius and the Gladiators* costar and a veteran of Native American roles. The studio was not willing to discard the footage shot with Anne and inflate the budget restaging them with Paget. (Location shooting on the film cost nearly $50,000 a day.) The final cut of the film included outdoor scenes in which Anne appeared, at a distance, as the Indian woman.

When *The Last Hunt* reached theaters in 1956, it barely covered its costs. Many critics felt that Richard Brooks had put a message about destroying the buffalo and Indian culture ahead of a compelling drama. The use of real footage of buffalo being shot down reportedly nauseated some moviegoers and prompted cuts by censors in other countries.

Regardless of such shortcomings, a role in an MGM film would have been better than the parts Anne had been playing. Even though ticket sales were disappointing, more people paid to see *The Last Hunt* than any of the other movies she had made as a freelancer. Thanks to a quirk of fate, a major opportunity for Anne to move her career to a higher level had become a professional and personal disaster. She returned home to endure months of painful recuperation amid a marriage showing signs of strain. Her future as an actress was uncertain as well.

4

A No-Name Actress
Starts Over

Three months of limited activity gave Anne the time she needed to think about her work and her marriage. By mid-November 1955 she had decided to take action on both fronts. She signed for a new Western being produced by Universal-International, a major studio for which she had yet to work. *Walk the Proud Land* would film its outdoor scenes near Tucson, Arizona, giving her a break from Los Angeles and her husband.

As she prepared for the role, Anne announced that she and Marty May were separating after two years of marriage. (No reporters seemed to notice that that meant their marriage dated back to 1953 and not 1954, as had been previously published.) She gave the press no reason for the split but said she did not want a divorce. Instead of May's leaving their home, Anne moved in with her manager and his wife. Curtailing her career did not appear to be part of any plan designed to make the marriage work. Why would it be if she already believed it was doomed? A few years later she suggested that she and May had little in common and spent too much time apart. "We just came from two entirely different backgrounds," she said. "All our lives we lived two different kinds of lives, and we could never get them together to make anything constructive. And I don't care who you are, love has to be fired to live. When lovers part, it just fades away."

Walk the Proud Land was a vehicle for the biggest star at Universal-International, Audie Murphy. His exemplary service in the U.S. Army during World War II—he was hailed as the nation's most-decorated soldier—was the root of his celebrity. Once he was out of the service, Murphy was enticed to Hollywood to try acting. On the screen since 1948, he built a solid if artistically undistinguished career in Westerns for Universal-International. He made eleven for the studio before appearing as himself in the movie version of his wartime memoir, *To Hell and Back,* in 1955. Directed by Jesse Hibbs, it became the biggest-grossing movie in the studio's history. Murphy and Hibbs made three more films together in rapid succession, the second being *Walk the Proud Land.*

Based on the memoir of a historical figure, the movie follows an Indian agent, John Clum, as he takes over the San Carlos reservation in Arizona. He holds an atypical view of Apaches, seeing them not as savage prisoners but as wards of the government deserving dignity and as much autonomy as possible. The Apache chief assigns Clum a housekeeper of sorts, Tianay, a widow raising a young son. Clum's feelings for her, and hers for him, complicate his forthcoming marriage just as the conflicts between whites and Native Americans complicate his assignment.

Amid the hundreds of Hollywood films in which American Indians were vilified, simplified, stereotyped, and misrepresented, *Walk the Proud Land* was a rarity. The enlightened attitude did not extend toward casting. Anne was just one of several non–Native Americans playing Apaches. Her olive complexion was further darkened for her role as Tianay, as was the skin of the seven-year-old actor who played her son in the film, Eugene Mazzola. "I played all kinds of ethnicities in my career," Mazzola remembered. "Being Italian meant that we had Mediterranean features. These features were consistent with other ethnic features." Anne's costume covered most of her body, but Mazzola was shirtless and obliged to endure a chilly morning ritual of body makeup applied with a large, wet sponge.

The top cast members stayed in one of Tucson's better downtown hotels. Many extras in the film came from a reservation nearby. "Not all the extras were good horsemen," Mazzola noted. "There is one scene in the film when a band of Indians leave the compound at a gallop. When the dust settled you could see the wigs of the Indian extras hanging from a couple of trees the horses ran them under. The entire company had a great laugh over this."

A Western movie set could be fun for a young boy. City born and bred and a twenty-four-year-old woman to boot, Anne tended to spend little time there when she was not working. "As you can imagine, there was not a lot that Ms. Bancroft would have in common with a youngster like myself," Mazzola said. "When I was on set, Ms. Bancroft was attentive and supportive, but we did not socialize." By contrast, Audie Murphy, a native of rural Texas, was in his element. "Mr. Murphy was great," Mazzola said.

"Mr. Murphy was always encouraging and supportive of my effort on set." In their free time the movie's wranglers taught Mazzola how to ride.

If the boys' club atmosphere did not interest Anne, she may have been even less drawn to horseback riding, given her recent accident. She kept to herself to a degree, perhaps careful not to overwork herself and fearful of a dust-borne illness common to the area, San Joaquin Valley fever. A large number in the movie company came down with the illness, Mazzola recalled, to the point that production had to move to soundstages in Los Angeles.

Universal-International was pleased with Anne and her work on *Walk the Proud Land*. In February 1956, several months before its release, the studio signed her to a five-year contract calling for two pictures a year. It was a nonexclusive agreement, allowing her to appear in other films and on television. The columnist Louella Parsons reported that Anne looked happy and well as Universal-International announced their deal. It was a welcome turnaround for her professionally. On the personal side, she had reconciled with her husband at year's end. "Things are shaping up very nicely in 1956 for this girl, who was so depressed a short time ago," Parsons wrote.

If spending too much time apart from Marty May was an issue, Anne did not appear to let it hinder the upswing in her career. Two weeks after signing the contract, she was back on NBC's *Lux Video Theatre* in a program titled "Hired Wife." More television production was moving from New York to Los Angeles, especially after the introduction of videotape, which made it easier for Anne and others to shift between the big and small screens. The next month she began *Nightfall*, the second movie in her two-picture deal with Columbia. Another crime drama—an innocent man is caught up in a bank heist gone wrong—the story assigned Anne the familiar position of romantic helpmate. At least her character was not part of a mobster's family again.

The pedigree of *Nightfall* could not be faulted. The director was Jacques Tourneur, who had made the essential film noir *Out of the Past* (1947). The screenplay was an early effort by Stirling Silliphant, soon to be ubiquitous on the credits of the television series *Naked City* and *Route 66* and later an Oscar winner for *In the Heat of the Night* (1967). In charge of photography was the veteran Burnett Guffey, who had won an Academy Award for Columbia's *From Here to Eternity* (1953). Leading the cast were Aldo Ray and Anne, backed up by two familiar supporting players, Brian Keith and James Gregory.

No matter how good they were, black-and-white films running eighty minutes and featuring mid-level stars did not generate much interest. Besides, television series like *Perry Mason* and *Alfred Hitchcock Presents* were offering a free dose of suspense at home on a nightly basis. The *Los Angeles Express* and the *Hollywood Reporter* recommended *Nightfall* as a good thriller upon its release late that year. The *Boston Globe* critic Marjory Adams even thought it "a wild and terrifying experience." The *New York Times* was underwhelmed, saying *Nightfall* "is not sleep-inducing, but it isn't overly exciting, either." Anne received solid notices again for another movie in which her character was tangential to the events at hand.

Television provided Anne with more work. In June she was in "The Corrigan Case" on *Lux Video Theatre,* and in July she appeared on *Climax!* in "Fear Is the Hunter." Her name was showing up in movie columns as producers and directors considered whom to cast in projects under development. The producer Edward Small said he wanted her back for the female lead in a biopic on the boxing champion Barney Ross. Another producer was interested in casting Anne as the American opera soprano Geraldine Farrar.

In September 1956 Universal-International released *Walk the Proud Land.* The Western was a well-produced film, shot in Technicolor and CinemaScope, but it had little effect on ticket buyers or critics. Although the *Los Angeles Times*'s critic Philip K. Scheuer was lukewarm about the film, he used its release to praise Anne and chide the industry. "As the Indian widow, Tianay, devoted to Clum, Anne Bancroft reinforces the conviction that she would really distinguish herself if Hollywood ever gave her the self-respecting opportunity to do so," Scheuer wrote. "Even in such a stereotype as this Tianay proves winning." Her next two movies, made before the release of *Walk the Proud Land,* would not provide the kinds of opportunities he had in mind.

The Girl in Black Stockings was as lurid as the title implied. Filmed over the summer at a resort in Kanab, Utah, the black-and-white film placed Anne's character among several suspects in a young woman's brutal murder. In *The Restless Breed,* a Western shot that fall, Anne played a lusty half-breed dancer who falls in love with a man on a mission of revenge. Both were insignificant entries in their genres—so much so that the *New York Times,* the *Los Angeles Times,* and the *Chicago Tribune* did not bother to review them.

Though critics usually complimented Anne for her screen performances, there also had been echoes of a comment by the *Los Angeles Mirror* in its review of *The Restless Breed*: "Miss Bancroft doesn't have much to do except bandage her beloved's wounds and plead: 'Don't go out there! You'll get yourself killed.'" The *New York Times* had put the issue succinctly in a remark about Anne's role in *Nightfall*: "Decorative and understanding." Terse and all too true.

Anne had begun to ask herself what she was doing with her talent besides making money. She was not widely known, even though she had worked steadily and collected good notices. "She seemed just another pretty girl with high movie hopes," according to Louella Parsons, "not too distinguishable from hundreds of similar young actresses playing routine leading lady roles." There was another sign that she was spinning her wheels professionally: when the film industry had concocted a contest to have moviegoers pick their favorite female newcomers from a list of twenty actresses, Anne was among them even though she had made a dozen films by then. The winner was the singer Peggy Lee, who actually was a new-comer to films.

Anne had her own take on why she did not stand out. "She always said her tits were not big enough and that's why she didn't have a big Hollywood success," observed a friend, the playwright William Gibson. If that were the case, few women could measure up to the more buxom beauties of the 1950s—Marilyn Monroe, Jayne Mansfield, Sophia Loren, Mamie Van Doren, and Yvonne De Carlo among them. It was too simple a criticism, however, because it overlooked sexy stars like Lauren Bacall, Leslie Caron, Piper Laurie, and Audrey Hepburn, whose builds were closer to Anne's. The question that began to bother her was not about her looks but about her professional choices. What had she accomplished over the last four years?

One of the most sought-after leading-lady roles that fall was the lead in a Warner Bros. biopic about the singer Helen Morgan. Deciding who would play the tragic nightclub and movie star—Morgan drank herself to death at an early age—drew intense interest around Hollywood. By November, the director Michael Curtiz had considered Jennifer Jones, Susan Hayward, and Doris Day among a dozen actresses. After he tested Anne, the director of *Casablanca* and many other Warner Bros. films was impressed enough to take the footage to the studio's chief, Jack L. Warner. She did not get the part—it went to Ann Blyth—in spite of Curtiz's support.

"He wanted me," Anne said. "And I remember his exact words. 'This test is the best by far, but you have no name.'" Warner was a businessman and not a filmmaker. He would have wanted a star to carry the film, not the risk that came with trying to make a star over whom he would have had no control.

Somewhat belatedly, Anne realized that being cast in a film might not have had as much to do with her talent as with her box-office potential. It was naive of her to have thought otherwise. She must have known too that none of her films yet to be released held any possibility of highlighting her talents. Indeed, *The Restless Breed* and *The Girl in Black Stockings* would be distributed as B movies destined for small audiences. Curtiz's words—"You have no name"—stung because they were true.

At the same time Anne was coming to grips with her disappointing career prospects, problems in her marriage resurfaced. In October 1956 she and Marty May separated again; he filed for divorce in December. May's failings as a husband managed to escape public scrutiny. No Galahad, he let her shoulder the blame in the press. If their marriage suffered to a great extent because of her career, Anne was also facing the unwelcome reality that her career might not have been worth it.

Also in October she appeared on NBC's *The Alcoa Hour* for an adaptation of the play *Key Largo*. Work had been a solace for her in her unsettled personal life, the arena in which she could feel good about herself. Now, though, she was even unsure about that.

Everything began to change—and at a surprisingly fast pace—in the early months of 1957. Psychoanalysis provided the spark that set events in motion. Anne had decided months before that it was time to try to understand what was wrong with her life—the failing marriage, the unsatisfying films, the feeling of wanting two different things (husband and career, acting and stardom) when holding on to one might mean having to let go of the other. She put herself in the care of an analyst as she sought to understand and control the forces that were threatening her with self-destruction.

"Through analysis—you really have to stop and look at yourself. And in looking at myself I realized that I was lost," she told the writers Lewis Funke and John E. Booth. "I knew something was wrong, that the picture I had of myself and the picture of what I saw of myself on the outside—the reality of it on the outside—well, they were different."

Her analyst concluded that she was a victim of a prolonged adolescence. "He helped me to find the answer to many questions which added up to knowing who I was and what I wanted out of life," she said in a different interview. "He had me examine with honesty what I really enjoyed and to separate this from what I thought I enjoyed or should enjoy. When you are not aware of what gives you pleasure, many hidden conflicts arise. Enjoyment is the secret of happiness. And when you get to know yourself, to evaluate your taste in people, clothes, creative expression and philosophy, you become a well-adjusted individual."

Anne began to see her career in a harsh light. Before then she had considered herself on the same plane as Greta Garbo—an exaggeration, certainly, but an indication of how deeply she had believed that she was doing fine work in the movies. Now she viewed her films with disdain and embarrassment. She was unsparing about her love life, too, seeing her involvement with men as just one disaster after another.

So much had come so early. Out of high school at sixteen, on television at eighteen, in a profession that sought to offer an interpretation of life when she had hardly lived at all. Her training as an actress had not continued in Hollywood. Directors had told her where to stand for the camera, not how to think about the role. Her trouble with the suicide scene in *New York Confidential* was the most glaring example of how her ability to use her talent had come up short. Pretending was not enough.

"All my life, you see, I'd told myself that I was the greatest thing that had ever lived, and all my life I believed it," Anne said, "and it was obvious that the outside world was telling me at this point that it wasn't so." She determined that she had to challenge herself—to face herself—to see if she actually had any talent.

Marty May was not going to accompany her on this journey of self-discovery—not that she would have welcomed him. In February 1957, the day before Valentine's Day, he appeared in Superior Court to present his case for divorcing her. Anne did not attend the hearing before Judge Fletcher Bowron, but newspaper reporters did. "She worked from 4 A.M. to 6 P.M. She came home and couldn't talk. Once she wouldn't talk to me for three weeks," May testified. "There was a lack of companionship with millions of people tracking into the house. She tried to combine two loves—one a marriage and the other a career. The career turned out to be the greater of the two." Bowron granted May a divorce and approved a settlement that was not disclosed.

Then and in later years, Anne would neither publicly criticize her ex-husband nor reveal the details of their estrangement. "That marriage lasted three years," she said in 1983, "but to tell you the truth, I knew at the end of three days. It was all wrong and it took me those three years to gather up the courage to stop trying and say no." Extending that courage to her career would call on her to do more than skip divorce proceedings.

While Anne was deciding how to deal with her crisis of artistic confidence, an unusual threesome in New York grappled with a creative predicament of their own. They were wrestling, unsuccessfully, with the problem of casting a new two-character play, *Two for the Seesaw*, that explored the loneliness of a decidedly mismatched man and woman and their eight-month affair. The play was in danger of being shelved in spite of their enthusiasm for it. The playwright, William Gibson, had never had a play staged professionally. The director, Arthur Penn, was a veteran of hours and hours of live television but had no Broadway stage production to his credit. The producer was Fred Coe, a top television producer who was just then turning his attention to the stage. Unless they could land a major actor or actress, financial backing for *Two for the Seesaw* would be nearly impossible to secure.

Finding a bankable actor or actress willing to be onstage nearly alone for two hours was one reason for their trouble. Another was the role of Jerry Ryan, a lonely Omaha lawyer who has all but run away to New York to escape a troubled marriage. Even Gibson thought the role was underwritten and essentially unsympathetic. Jack Lemmon and Paul Newman were among those who turned it down.

One actor interested in the play was Richard Basehart. He had appeared in two dozen movies since 1947 and a half dozen Broadway productions. To the delight of Gibson, he called *Two for the Seesaw* one of the best plays he had read in years. Basehart and his agent met Gibson and Coe for dinner in late January 1957. The actor mentioned in passing that they should consider Anne for the female role. He had just appeared with her in a *Playhouse 90* program, "So Soon to Die." Her name meant nothing to Gibson, but Coe promised to see her for the role of Gittel Mosca.

Gittel, a feisty if fragile Bronx-born Jewish dancer, was clearly the play's leading role. Yet finding an actress to play her had been no easier than finding an actor to play Jerry Ryan. Gwen Verdon had declined, as had Julie Harris, and Kim Stanley never responded to their entreaties. Lee Grant was a strong possibility, and the creative team was all but set on her.

She was no guarantee at the box office, which meant that the male role would require a star to attract investors and ticket buyers.

Gibson traveled west to Los Angeles to work with Penn on a live television production of a script Gibson had written about the teacher of the blind and deaf child Helen Keller. "The Miracle Worker," starring Teresa Wright as Annie Sullivan and Patty McCormack as Helen, was set to air on CBS's *Playhouse 90* the night of February 7, 1957. That morning, Fred Coe waited in his office in New York's Radio City to hear Anne read for the part of Gittel Mosca. The interest in her for *Two for the Seesaw* happened to coincide with a trip to New York for her sister Phyllis's wedding.

If Anne had read for a part in a Broadway play before then, she seldom if ever mentioned it. She had heard that producers had no imagination and decided she needed to look and act the part before Coe ever laid eyes on her. She left Mike and Millie Italiano's home as their daughter and became a different person on the way to Manhattan. "I was Gittel from the moment I got on that subway," she said. "And when I entered that office I did everything that was that character."

In Gibson's play Gittel comes off as a bohemian girl, unaffected and unsophisticated and slightly crude. To that end, Anne took off her shoe as she engaged Coe's secretary in an animated conversation. She made a point to start scratching her foot as he opened the door to greet her, and then naively picked up her shoe to follow him inside. "I knew that's what the character would do," she said. The first thing she said to Coe was similarly Gittel-like: "Where's the john? I gotta go so bad . . ." She went to the bathroom even though she did not need to use the facilities. The session ended with Coe's asking Anne to return the next morning to meet the playwright. He called Gibson on the phone to declare her "the best Gittel yet."

For her meeting with Gibson, Anne stayed with what worked. He was just off an overnight flight from Los Angeles when he came to Coe's office. The TV presentation of "The Miracle Worker" had been an enormous hit, moving viewers to the point that they jammed the network switchboard with phone calls. Sitting in Coe's office, Anne—or, more accurately, Gittel—asked the playwright: "How was the coast? Lousy, huh?"

"My mind blinked," Gibson wrote in his memoir about the production. "She could have walked off my pages. Fred called in an actor for her to read with, and she read excitingly, with the exact turns of voice—this was eerie—I had heard when writing the lines and had not heard since; I felt we had fallen into a diamond-in-the-rough mine." Coe and Gibson were even more impressed once Anne lifted the mask and showed them who she really was—a talented actress who understood the material. Gibson came to believe that Anne shared his own connection with the character. He had been born in the Bronx a mile from Anne's neighborhood, though seventeen years earlier, and believed that they both had a feel for his creation. "She dug the lingo that I had written for Gittel," he said later. "It was part of her blood, as it was with mine."

They were sold on Anne for the part even though they knew that she would not bring in a dime of financial backing. At the moment that did not matter. Half of their casting problem had been solved even if all the financial problems remained. Arthur Penn had yet to weigh in, however, and they arranged a meeting between him and Anne in Los Angeles. Penn soon cabled his approval: "Gittel on the hoof." He did not change his opinion that Anne was right for the role after directing her in a March 7 *Playhouse 90* production, "Invitation to a Gunfighter." For her part, she was eager to work with a director who could open a new world for her as an actress.

Why had that world seemed closed to her for so long? Anne did not fault her education at the American Academy of Dramatic Arts. Part of her new understanding of herself was realizing that at seventeen she would not have known what to make of motivation and justification as acting techniques even if Charles Jehlinger had taught them. In Hollywood no one had taught her anything, good or bad, and her raw talent merely went undirected instead of misdirected.

After working with Penn on *Playhouse 90*, acting excited and interested Anne as never before. With a new horizon before her, she asked herself whether the path she was on would take her there. For so long she had put herself in the hands of others and allowed them to mold her. No one but Penn had tried, at least in her estimation, and there was no reason for her to think anyone she would work with in Hollywood would try.

Anne decided to do something unheard of for an actor with her experience: she would start over.

"That was the first time in my life I made a decision entirely on my own," she said. "And that was when I was ready to be an actress. Of course, it wasn't that simple. Life doesn't change overnight."

After two more television appearances, in "The Black Angel" for *Lux Video Theatre* on March 28 and "The Mad Bomber" on *Climax!* on April

18, she announced she was leaving Hollywood and returning home to New York. If she was to further her acting studies, she believed she would learn more there. "I've had some roles lately that haven't done my career any good," she told the *Los Angeles Times*. "Fortunately most of them have been in movies. TV has been very kind to me. But I believe everyone can still learn something new. That's why I have to get back to my schooling in New York."

Unspoken was the possibility of starring in a Broadway play. It was only a possibility, which made her decision to leave Hollywood with a slap in the face all the more daring. Starting over was a financial gamble, too. She later said she was broke when she returned to her parents' home in New York, having spent all her money on clothes, cars, and good times. Whether that was the exact truth or not, she apparently put aside her deal with Universal-International and was not taking other film work for the time being.

At that point *Two for the Seesaw* was still a play in search of a star. Anne could not be signed before the male lead—on whom so much would depend—was engaged. Negotiations with Richard Basehart had proved difficult and he had bowed out. Among the other actors contacted were two Anne had worked with before, Robert Preston of *The Last Frontier* and Van Heflin of *The Raid*. Both said no, as did Barry Nelson, Eli Wallach, and Don Murray.

Henry Fonda said maybe and accepted a script to read while in New York working on the movie *Stage Struck*. He had been on the early list of possible Jerrys—almost every star imaginable had been—when they began the casting process eight months earlier. As Fonda read, a few more actors declined. One of them, Fritz Weaver, thought the play incredibly good, but he had committed to another project. Gibson and Coe had just about given up when Fonda called and asked to meet them.

Fonda was one of America's most popular movie stars; he had twenty years of filmmaking behind him. He was also a huge draw on Broadway after long runs in the 1948 comedy *Mister Roberts* and the 1954 drama *The Caine Mutiny Court-Martial*. The flaws in *Two for the Seesaw* did not escape him, and he agreed with those who thought the male role was underwritten. Fonda was an Omaha native like Jerry, but Jerry's words did not sing to him as Gittel's had to Anne. Getting Fonda meant Gibson needed to rewrite and deal with a problem he had been avoiding.

Before Gibson undertook that chore, Fred Coe suggested that he take

Anne to Fonda's home in Manhattan for a reading. Fonda objected, fearing that if Anne did not get the part she would blame him. Coe insisted and Fonda agreed to host Anne, Coe, and Gibson at his home on Seventy-fourth Street. They would read just the first act and send Anne home so they could talk business. "After the first act, I didn't want to stop," Fonda said in his autobiography. "She was just great." They ended up reading the entire play. "I thought the woman's part was very impressive," he said, "but I was more convinced than ever that the man's role had problems." Fonda made it clear that he would withhold a decision about appearing in the play until he saw the revisions.

That summer Gibson rewrote, Fonda vacationed in Europe with his family, and Penn and Coe worked on their first movie, a psychological treatment of Billy the Kid with Paul Newman called *The Left Handed Gun.* Anne, meanwhile, settled down in New York to take a fresh look at her craft. For an appraisal of her talents she went to Herbert Berghof, one of the theater's most respected acting teachers. "If he said I didn't have it," she decided, "then I'd quit." The Vienna-born Berghof was an actor and director as well as a teacher. His approach drew from the theories of the Russian actor Constantin Stanislavsky, who believed that an actor should connect his own feelings to a character and develop an understanding of the character's motivations. Following this method, Stanislavsky hoped, would result in a more naturalistic performance. In 1947 Berghof became a charter member of the Actors Studio, the American institution best known for applying the principles of Stanislavsky's Method. Future Berghof students would include Al Pacino, Robert De Niro, and Matthew Broderick.

When Anne went to the Herbert Berghof Studio in its loft in Manhattan's Chelsea district, she got a bonus of sorts. She had not known what a loft was and she needed to—in the play Gittel Mosca wants to rent one. Anne was there for an appraisal, not to study the architecture. Whatever it was that she did for Berghof—give a line reading, perform a scene, or reveal her doubts about herself—his conclusion renewed her self-confidence. "You must stay in the theater," he declared. He also gave her a scholarship, a sign that her financial standing was indeed precarious.

An intellectual approach to acting was just what Anne craved at the moment. That had not been the case when the actor Rod Steiger had tried to introduce her to the Method technique years earlier. "On the third TV show I ever did, Rod Steiger told me about Stanislavsky," she recalled. "I said, 'Who's he?' Rod gave me Stanislavsky's book about acting." She still had not read it when she studied with Berghof as she waited for the production of Gibson's play either to flourish or to fold. To earn some money, she worked in another television appearance, on July 7, 1957, in "Hostages to Fortune" for NBC's *The Alcoa Hour.*

With September came William Gibson's revisions to *Two for the Seesaw.* He had tried to put out of his mind that he was writing for Fonda specifically. "I defined the task as one of so writing the character that any actor would take pleasure in playing him," Gibson said. He added the equivalent of a half hour of stage time to the role of Jerry in the first two acts. The pages went by airmail to Fonda, and Gibson and Coe waited for a response. The play still did not feel right to him, but not working may have felt worse. He sent a cable to Coe: "Start it rolling. I am yours. Fonda."

As if by magic, Henry Fonda's name opened doors and pocketbooks. Within a short time they set a budget of $80,000, the amount needed to mount the production, and scheduled rehearsals for November, out-of-town openings for December, and New York previews and the official opening for January 1958. Fonda put in $20,000 as part of his deal calling for one-fourth ownership of the show. He was guaranteed $2,500 a week against 15 percent of the gross at the box office and could leave the show after six months. His value was acknowledged further when investors eager to back a Fonda vehicle readily put up the remaining $60,000 needed to get started. The advance box office reached $350,000.

Anne's contract affirmed her lack of status on Broadway. She would be paid $550 a week, less than she had made for some of her early movies. If *Two for the Seesaw* was a hit, she would be obligated to remain with the show for two years. On the other hand, Anne could be replaced before the show reached New York. For most of the weeks in rehearsal she would receive the standard rehearsal pay of $65 a week. A CBS television gig that November, a *Zane Grey Theatre* entry called "Episode in Darkness," in which she played a blind woman, brought in a little extra money. To make ends meet she remained with her parents. Without question, leaving the movies came at a price for her.

A play featuring just two characters was not common for Broadway but not unheard of, either. Some viewed such an offering more as a stunt than as a basis for a viable evening of theater. When he first wrote about Gittel and Jerry, William Gibson had toyed with introducing a third character and even produced a draft with that extra voice before returning to his original idea. More than one observer would note that there is indeed a third character in the play—the telephone that connects Gittel and Jerry to each other and to the outside world.

Two for the Seesaw opens the first of its three acts with Gittel and Jerry occupying separate apartments in different buildings in New York. (Gibson's script called for two distinct sets on the stage.) Having met Gittel through a friend the previous evening, Jerry calls to ask her out. Over the course of the next eight months, from September to May, they share their anxieties in a bittersweet if humorous relationship that seems to mirror the seasons. They come together in a lovely fall, face uncertainties in a cold winter, and grow apart in a fresh spring.

Uncertain about the unfaithful if loving wife who is divorcing him in Omaha, Jerry desperately wants someone to need him. Gittel is so used to being the doormat in a relationship—her personal misfortunes have given her a bleeding ulcer—that she worries that Jerry just feels sorry for her. For her part, she encourages him to take the bar exam in New York. "Jerry," she says, "you know what I think you got too much of? Lack of confidence!" She also subtly pushes him to cut his ties to the wife, who has an unhealthy hold on him but will not follow through with a breakup.

Act 2 begins with Gittel returning slightly drunk to her apartment, which they now share. Jerry accuses her of sleeping with the old boyfriend she had visited, and Gittel accuses him of being only half hers, the other half belonging to his wife in Omaha. He assures her that other men do not matter but admits that he has failed to reach the deepest part of her. As Jerry turns to leave, Gittel breaks down and confesses that her main activity that night had been fainting in her friend's bathroom. She reveals that her ulcer has hemorrhaged and she is bleeding. She cries, "Don't leave me, don't leave me—" and Jerry assures her as he calls a doctor: "I'm here, infant. Take it easy, can't you see I'm here?"

Jerry is there, but he is not completely there for her. In the final act, set weeks later, the two are still living together and even planning a future. Then Gittel discovers Jerry has kept from her the fact that his divorce is final. He admits he cannot put his ex-wife out of his mind and that while he cares for Gittel, he cannot love her completely, let alone ever marry her. Both realize they will be settling for less and decide to part ways, Jerry for Nebraska to reunite with his wife and Gittel to keep looking for the right man. They have helped each other understand what they need in their lives.

Neither growing up in the Bronx nor being in her mid-twenties led

Anne to feel a connection with Gibson's character. "It was the emotional life of the girl that I felt similar to," she said. "It was the emotional life of Gittel and myself that was so close." In true Stanislavsky fashion, she began developing her own understanding of the fictional person she would portray and linking her emotions to it even before rehearsals. Anne took two main tacks. She studied her sister Joan, believing that she was just like Gittel emotionally—Anne described her to the writers Lewis Funke and John E. Booth as a sweet and lovely soul surrounded by a hard, funny, flippant, and coarse exterior. While she also studied Joan for her speech and mannerisms, Anne drew from her own experiences in empathizing with the character's failed emotional relationships. (Gittel exclaims at one point, "When it comes to men I expect the worst!") Happily married siblings were of no help there.

Since Gittel is a dancer, Anne took classes for a few weeks with the modern dance instructor José Limón. She paid particular attention to those in the classes who lacked talent because she believed that was part of Gittel's persona. When in Greenwich Village for Herbert Berghof's classes, she studied the people there because they were Gittel's neighbors and not unlike Gittel herself, as Anne was coming to know her.

For the first week of rehearsals that November, sitting at a table in a room on Fifty-seventh Street, Arthur Penn listened to Anne and Henry Fonda read their lines in a scene and then went back over them to discuss the meanings and tones they sought to convey. The afternoon was reserved for a complete reading, then Penn and Gibson worked on trimming the play. Meant for a two-hour performance, it was running long by at least twenty minutes.

Anne's education continued with Penn, another artist influenced by Stanislavsky. For example, she did not know what to make of the play's third act. "He gave her no answers," Gibson said, "but by patient Socratic questioning let her make discovery after exciting discovery on her own." This aspect of acting—discovering the character during rehearsals and other preparations—would become her great joy as an actress. Whereas Fonda was more concerned about the physical aspects of the play—where he would be standing or sitting at a particular moment and how he would move about the stage—Anne asked about Gittel's inner life. Clearly, she was eager to apply the Stanislavsky-inspired techniques she had learned from Berghof and which Penn was reinforcing in his direction.

Fonda came from a different tradition, one closer to what Anne had learned from Charles Jehlinger. He was from another generation, twice Anne's age, and had far greater experience on the stage than either she or Penn. Fonda was finding himself at a dual disadvantage, left out of the intensity that Anne and Penn brought to their discussions of the play and dealing with a role he still thought was secondary to hers. He did not understand Jerry and did not particularly like him. It was also the kind of role that audiences did not associate with the movie and stage star.

"Henry Fonda was not a risk taker," said Gene Lasko, a longtime associate of Arthur Penn. "That's a terrific role, and my opinion is that he didn't take sufficient opportunities for it. He was very cautious. Arthur once said to me that Fonda couldn't talk and take off his jacket at the same time. But it really had to do with—it was one thing at a time with him. He couldn't layer it the way Annie could." In fact, trying to get under the skin of Jerry Ryan only seemed to perplex Fonda and increase his unhappiness with the enterprise. Gibson felt Fonda did not appreciate the irony at the heart of many of Jerry's lines. When the director and the playwright reminisced about the problem many years later with Penn's biographer Nat Segaloff, they put a great deal of it on Fonda's misreading of the play.

"I asked Fred," Gibson said, "while we were on the road, 'What did he see in this play?' and Fred said, 'He fell in love with the girl.'"

"He clearly made it known that he didn't like the play," according to Penn. "He said, 'I thought this was a play about two charming people.' That was his statement when he had read it in the south of France. I said, 'Yes, but, Hank, this woman has a hemorrhage in the middle of the second act. You may find that charming, but . . .' No, we never satisfied Hank. But what we did was, we mined the gold mine that was Annie. She was extraordinary."

Not from the beginning. Reading at a table was incomparable to moving about on a stage. Besides, the stage design for *Two for the Seesaw* featured different environments, Jerry's living room in his East Side flat and Gittel's in a rundown Midtown brownstone. Each was decorated to fit the character's personality. George Jenkins, the designer, placed the sets on twin turntables to allow various views of them as the scenes changed, which would give a little more life to a play with only two characters.

Henry Fonda was at home on a stage, but Anne was unsure of herself, and it showed. More nervous observers wondered whether she should be replaced while there was still time. Penn and Coe remained calm. "She didn't know very much," Penn said. "But she was absolutely open and defenseless." She took his direction and did not have to be told twice to move or deliver a line a certain way. One example was when she developed a tendency to mug or otherwise overplay. Once Penn and Gibson brought it to her attention, it stopped. She handled other criticism the same way. "Anne took a hell of a beating," the director said, "but she had the courage to stick it out." As rehearsals progressed, so did her ability to negotiate the stage.

Also progressing, unfortunately, were the anxieties surrounding Fonda and his unhappiness with Jerry's different complexes. "I can't follow this guy!" he exclaimed. Gibson continued to revise, even though it meant changing his concept of the male character to satisfy Penn and Coe as well as Fonda. The playwright came to believe that Fonda was less concerned with the character than the size of the role itself. "Hank was wanting the play should somehow change so that he could be the star again, and he wasn't. Annie was," Gibson said. Coe and Penn generally sided with their star and kept Gibson at the typewriter.

In his autobiography, Fonda said little about working with Anne except to compliment her. In Penn's and Gibson's accounts, Anne's emotional performance as Gittel bothered Fonda, especially when the script called for Gittel to break down in Jerry's arms. Anne was learning to draw from within to give the moment the power it needed, a Method approach that was outside Fonda's expertise. "I can't kiss her," he complained to Penn. "There's snot running out of her nose."

Gibson's admiration for, if not infatuation with, Anne grew as they worked on the play. While the company performed *Two for the Seesaw* in Washington, D.C., the first time for a paying audience, he approached her with an offer. To stay sane, he was already moving on, at least in his mind, from the project bedeviling him on a daily basis. He had decided to adapt his *Playhouse 90* television script about Annie Sullivan and Helen Keller for the theater. (Arthur Penn told him such a notion was crazy.) Would Anne want to play Helen's teacher? "You think I'm right for it?" she asked. Gibson was so certain that she was perfect for the part that he made the offer without consulting Penn or Coe, both of whom were likely to be his partners in the production.

From rehearsals in New York and performances in Washington and Philadelphia to a return to New York for opening night, the company labored for ten weeks. It was a round trip paved with revisions, clashes of temperament, and hurt feelings. Anne remained largely out of the line of fire, the combatants being the star, the director, the playwright, and the producer. Having no name and no standing carried an advantage after all.

For Anne the biggest concern as Broadway beckoned became her health. Exhaustion was setting in for all involved, and in Anne's case her voice suffered the most. At one point she developed a boil in her throat; a doctor came in to lance it. Laryngitis was a constant worry, and she was ordered to rest her voice whenever possible. Her frequent cross-legged sitting on the stage led to a hernia in the pit of a knee. As opening night neared, she took a room at the Hotel Manhattan to be close to the Booth Theatre. At least the early reviews in the Washington and Philadelphia newspapers were promising—mixed, certainly, but still promising.

The revisions continued, even hours before the play's first performance at the Booth. Not having the script set annoyed Henry Fonda. The last person he wanted to see was William Gibson. When the playwright stuck his head inside Fonda's dressing room to wish him well, the star of the evening would not hear of it. "I lost my temper like I never had before in the theater," Fonda recalled. "'You get your ass out of here,' I told Gibson. 'I don't ever want to see you again. Don't come into my dressing room to wish me good luck. You've been of no help to me!'"

For many reasons Gibson would have agreed. Looking back at Fonda's displeasure, Gibson noted with a touch of irony that would have fit Jerry Ryan, "He made a lot of money out of his misery."

A hit can soothe many wounds and turn enemies into friends. *Two for the Seesaw* opened at the Booth Theatre on January 16, 1958, and generated critical reaction so positive that Fonda was left almost speechless. "Jesus!" he said as he read the early editions of the papers. "I never expected reviews like this!" Not that his costar and other colleagues could enjoy his astonishment. Fonda had decided to gather with friends at Sardi's restaurant rather than attend the company's party and await the first reviews with them.

Among those working for the several newspapers publishing in New York, the theater critics for the *Times* and the *Herald-Tribune* mattered most to a play's good health. Fonda broke even with them, perhaps better than even. Brooks Atkinson of the *Times* declared Fonda "a wonderfully straightforward actor who plays at low pressure. As Jerry in Mr. Gibson's play he gives his most limpid and moving performance. What he does not say in the dialogue, he says with the silent eloquence of a fine actor." The *Herald-Tribune's* Walter Kerr was lukewarm about the play but seemed to lay the fault for a lack of power in the production on Gibson's writing. Other critics, however, lauded Fonda much as John McClain did in the *Journal American:* "Henry Fonda has never given a poor performance within my memory, but this may be one of his best." After believing he was heading for a downfall, Fonda had come up with another winner after all.

Two for the Seesaw drew overwhelmingly positive reviews, many of them effusive. "It has style, beauty, and a delightful point of view," Atkinson wrote. "An absorbing, affectionate, and funny delight," said John Chapman of the *Daily News.* The *Mirror's* critic, Robert Coleman, said the play was "a whale of a hit" and advised theatergoers not to waste time getting in line for tickets. "A runaway hit," declared McClain. On the negative side, Frank Aston of the *World-Telegram* thought the play could have been better and found neither Gittel nor Jerry to be at all believable.

And then there was the matter of Anne Bancroft. If Fonda was the old hand at work, she was the discovery of the season in the eyes of the critics. Atkinson called Anne "an attractive young actress unknown to this department until last evening, but sure to be known to thousands of theatergoers before the season is over." Kerr clearly considered her the play's main attraction. "The young actress, who seems to have just come to us from television, has the kind of natural, offhand, nobody-asked-me warmth that turns red-hot gas grates chilly by comparison." He added: "But Miss Bancroft has something more than the tart, shoulder-shrugging, know-it-all innocence of the patsy she is playing at the Booth. She has, in addition, the range of one of the newer guided missiles."

Other critics piled on the praise. In their opinions, Anne displayed flawless timing and was a perfect treasure, the most engaging gamine in years, deliriously captivating, a rich discovery, an exceptional young actress. Just in case anyone failed to make the connection to a timeworn sobriquet, Coleman of the *Mirror* proclaimed that the opening night audience had witnessed "the birth of a new star."

A year after she had decided to begin anew, Anne won her gamble. She took a path without certainty of success and allowed her usual standards of focus and resolve to guide her. In challenging her view of herself, she discovered new qualities she could apply to her craft and to her life. Her indefatigable work ethic also played in her favor as people impressed by her talent and her determination came to her side once more.

That the critics made little reference to Anne's scores of television roles or her fifteen film appearances was testament to the minimal significance of her earlier work and to Broadway's unique provincialism. Michael Curtiz had been correct if cold when he told her: "You have no name." With the success of *Two for the Seesaw,* Anne finally had a name—at least in New York, at least for that moment.

5

One Miracle Happens, and Then Another

The morning after *Two for the Seesaw* opened, the understudy for the role of Gittel Mosca, Gabby Rodgers, ran into Anne Bancroft at the Booth Theatre as she prepared for her second performance. "How does it feel to be in a hit?" Rodgers asked. "I don't know," Anne replied. "I've never been in a flop."

For performers in a play about to open on Broadway, life takes on the quality of a small plane in a heavy fog; they are unsure where to land or what to do next. Nothing could be determined until the critics and the public weighed in on their efforts. The acclaim Anne received for *Two for the Seesaw*, however, left little to the imagination as far as how she would be spending the first half of 1958. "She was so wonderful in that role. She got great reviews and she was the toast of Broadway," remembered the actor Robert Wagner, who had been in the opening-night audience with his wife, Natalie Wood, and visited Anne backstage. "It's like that story you'd see in the movies. 'Look down there, darling, that's Broadway. And tomorrow it's yours.' I'm telling you, it was just incredible."

The celebration left Anne exhilarated if tired. She had stayed up well after midnight going over the reviews. "I don't want to read them again," she said later. "It might be dangerous. It might make me stop wishing to grow. I might feel too self-satisfied." She talked into the morning with her friend Ruby Rick, a visitor from Los Angeles, before falling asleep at eight-thirty.

More than another performance awaited Anne when she woke. She gathered up her things and moved out of her room at the Hotel Manhattan, bound for a sublet apartment in the East Fifties. Although she was no longer living at her parents' home in Yonkers, she could still see them regularly since both worked in the city. Her father would visit the theater during his lunch break on Wednesdays, one of her two matinee days, and bring Anne a bag of figs from the tree in their backyard.

Before long Anne moved again, this time into a three-room apartment on the first floor of a Greenwich Village brownstone on West Twelfth Street. It was inexpensive and simply furnished: a sofa bed, a few chairs, a small table, and some framed prints and oil paintings for the walls. It was all she felt she wanted and needed at the time. She liked the idea of living in a small, self-contained community where she could get to know the grocers, vendors, and local characters. She hoped it would remind her of the kind of warm and friendly neighborhood where she had grown up.

Whether it was returning to her roots as a child of the city or the spirit of Gittel Mosca mixing with her own, Anne was no longer the young movie star swept up by the glamour of Hollywood. She began wearing sandals more often and dressing in sweaters and slacks in the casual style many people associated with the era's beatniks—and with Gittel herself. A bohemian lifestyle in the Village suited Anne's new outlook, and it may have suited her modest weekly paycheck even more. She had debts to pay from her quick exit from the West Coast and still saw an analyst regularly. A posh home, fancy clothes, even nylons, would have to wait.

As Anne settled in at the Booth Theatre, Henry Fonda remained unhappy in spite of praise from peers and applause from appreciative audiences. "He was really upset," his wife at the time, Afdera Franchetti, told Fonda's biographer Howard Teichmann. "He had worked so hard, but his part was not the charming one. . . . He was the hard one." Success ended any possibility that the play would close and Fonda could escape sooner than called for in his six-month agreement. Owning a sizable piece of a hit did little to ease his disappointment with the experience. He would later consider Broadway first-timers William Gibson and Arthur Penn "bushleague" for the way they had treated him in rehearsals and the deference they had paid to Anne.

"I'm not putting her down and I wouldn't for a moment because I loved her in the part and I loved her as a person," Fonda told Teichmann for their 1981 book. "She's one of our better actresses. But there was no reason for her to be upset. She had a beautiful part with four dimensions, and I was fighting a guy with one dimension and trying to make it balance and getting no help from the author." Praise for Anne aside, Fonda seemed to take a touch of pleasure in looking back at Anne's own difficulties on

Broadway in plays in the 1960s and 1970s that did not work as their star had hoped. "Now she knows what it's like," he told Teichmann.

At the time and over the years that followed, Anne avoided saying anything negative about Fonda in the press. The year after his play's debut, William Gibson wrote a revealing memoir about the genesis of *Two for the Seesaw* that highlighted Fonda's complaints. Hedda Hopper asked Anne about those difficulties during a 1965 interview. "I didn't steal the play from Hank—he gave it to me," Anne told her. "Somewhere along the line he didn't seem to be trying. There were some early rehearsals in which he was breathtaking, but later he gave up. Every new line the author wrote Hank didn't like, and he didn't like taking direction." Her defense of Gibson and Penn was as much about loyalty as criticism of her costar.

To those close to her she confided how Fonda could make her performance unnecessarily difficult. "Anne was really pissed about the problems with Henry Fonda," recalled her high school friend David Lunney, who saw her during the run of the play. "And Henry Fonda was not being cooperative, and, of course, he was the star and he wanted it his way. I guess he felt that he was being a straight man for her." While Anne obviously enjoyed her stage triumph, "it was still an incredibly difficult circumstance that she endured," Lunney said. "It never stopped." Years later, when the documentarians Joan Kramer and David Heeley asked Anne to participate in their film about Fonda and his career, she politely declined. She told them that she would give her reasons only to his daughter Jane, if she wanted to hear them.

Henry Fonda was not interested in extending his appearance in *Two for the Seesaw*, even in the wake of its success, and Penn and Fred Coe had to contend with finding another leading man. No replacement would have been needed if their production had received a lukewarm response or cooled off at the box office, yet through that spring the Booth was still selling out its performances. Nor would a replacement have been called for had the play's popularity relied solely on Fonda's participation, as it had in getting the initial financial backing. Ticket sales were so strong and Anne's star burned so bright that a different leading man did not necessarily spell doom for the show.

"That turned out to be a bigger hit than we expected," Penn said in reflection, "because we knew of Hank's displeasure and we knew he was going to leave after six months, but what we hadn't counted on was that Annie would get such good reviews that she was carrying the play by that point."

Another reason people were still buying tickets: the play featured a Tony Award–winning performance. Not from Fonda, who had not been nominated. Anne was among the nominees for best supporting or featured player in a drama—and won the play's only award during ceremonies on April 13, 1958, at the Waldorf Astoria. (The best drama award went to *Sunrise at Campobello* and the best musical award to *The Music Man*.) Though her champions, Arthur Penn and William Gibson, lost their bids for a Tony, they gained a shot at Hollywood when Gibson sold the screen rights to the play with the caveat that Penn be its director. Anne was not part of the deal, which was understandable given that the role of Gittel Mosca would require a box-office star to gain studio backing. Whether she would rise to that level by the time production began was an open question. William Holden was already being discussed for the role Fonda disliked.

On the stage Anne found a more agreeable Jerry Ryan in Fonda's replacement, Dana Andrews, a star of popular 1940s films such as *Laura* and *The Best Years of Our Lives*. (He also had played one of the cowboys Fonda could not save from a lynch mob in 1943's *The Ox-Bow Incident*.) By the late 1950s Andrews's career was on a downswing—alcoholism had damaged his standing in Hollywood—and he was easing into television appearances. A *Playhouse 90* role had brought Andrews to Fred Coe's attention. Whether Jerry's character was underwritten was probably not an issue for Andrews, who had stage experience but had yet to appear on Broadway. *Two for the Seesaw* was an excellent vehicle at that point in his career, especially with Anne still filling seats as Gittel Mosca. Andrews's Alcoholics Anonymous sponsor was on hand as needed at the Booth Theatre, testament to his efforts to remain sober. He joined the show in June 1958 and stayed with Anne for the next twelve months, garnering favorable reviews himself.

Becoming a Broadway star brought Anne offers of all kinds—someone proposed that she put together a Las Vegas nightclub act—as well as promises of a big payday. Having already known the emptiness that came from money without professional satisfaction and personal happiness, she turned down almost everything and stayed focused on the stage and her talents. An exception was a print advertisement for Rheingold Extra Dry Lager Beer. "I can't keep a good thing to myself," read the ad copy that accompanied a color photo of Anne dressed in black with a white phone to her ear and a glass of beer on a table. Gittel herself might have excused the ad and the extra money it brought by saying, "Look, a girl's gotta eat."

At least one of the rejected offers was tantalizing. The composer Richard Rodgers heard that she was taking singing lessons and hoped one day to appear in a stage musical. When the composer of *Oklahoma!* and *South Pacific* asked if she would sing for him, Anne doubted that she was quite ready for such an audition. "I never dreamed I'd be saying this to Richard Rodgers," she admitted, "but . . . don't call me, I'll call you." Besides, her friend William Gibson was writing his play about Annie Sullivan and Helen Keller. She could afford to wait.

Singing lessons were not just to serve her ego or to lay the groundwork for appearing in a musical. Her voice was taking a beating in the two-character play and nodes had appeared on her larynx, the voice box. Told by her doctor that she was improperly projecting her voice—as she described it, "I'd bang my vocal cords together"—she faced the choice of surgery or hiring a voice coach. Singing lessons were her main therapy, and she used the opportunity to begin developing a contralto. When Anne could get away from the city for a day or two, she would try out her husky singing voice at a resort in the Catskills. Photos in the magazine *Cue* showed her giving a rendition of the song "Some Sunny Day" and trying her hand at oil painting as part of her relaxation.

Another professional challenge arose during Anne's eighteen months in *Two for the Seesaw*. She was having problems retaining her take on the character, and Arthur Penn was not on hand to help her. Much as she relied on regular sessions with her therapist to explore her understanding of herself, she needed to explore her craft to understand her abilities and how to use them. Penn suggested that she enroll in the Actors Studio, thereby entrusting his discovery to the acting teacher Lee Strasberg.

The Actors Studio was in its second decade when Anne prepared to audition for a spot in its classes. Founded in 1947 by Robert Lewis, Elia Kazan, and Cheryl Crawford as a laboratory or training ground for working actors and others, it promoted Stanislavsky-style approaches to performing. Strasberg became its artistic director in 1951 and would spend three decades guiding actors in his own version of Stanislavsky's teachings, becoming the prime proponent of Method acting.

"This is oversimplifying," the actor Martin Balsam once said in describing what he gained from the sessions he attended, "but what the Studio techniques ask, basically, is that the individual get in touch with himself.

The actor really has to understand what his own machinery is and what his own feelings are—not what he thinks they should be. It's the use of one's own truth. Once you get acquainted with that truth, then you can add on the rest of the things that are necessary for the rest of the character you're portraying." It was just the sort of intellectual exploration of her craft that Anne was learning to cherish.

Many of her past and future costars and friends would take part in sessions with Strasberg, among them Marilyn Monroe, Jane Fonda, Dustin Hoffman, Patricia Neal, Rod Steiger, Inga Swenson, and Sidney Poitier. Typically, an actor would prepare a scene and perform it for Strasberg and those in the class or observing it, then Strasberg would offer a critique before others gave their opinions. Not everyone warmed to Strasberg and his penetrating remarks. John Cassavetes, Anne's classmate at the American Academy of Dramatic Arts, walked out after a few weeks. Even Penn had some misgivings, particularly with what he considered an excessive reverence paid to Strasberg, and felt that Strasberg ignored the practical matters facing a director trying to put on a play in three or four weeks.

Anne auditioned for admission to the Actors Studio in fall 1958. It had been just three years since the Studio established its new headquarters in a renovated Presbyterian church at West Forty-fourth Street between Ninth and Tenth avenues. For her audition she performed a scene from *Two for the Seesaw* with Kevin McCarthy, a Studio member who had been Henry Fonda's understudy in the play. If Anne had any hesitations about Strasberg and the Studio, he quickly eased them. "You are not a personality," Strasberg told her. "You are an actress."

"These were the sweetest words I had ever heard," she said when remembering the moment. "I had an identity at last. I knew I was an actress."

Another Studio alumna, Kim Stanley, once compared Strasberg's approach to undergoing analysis: "Lee tries to make you find things in yourself that you can use." In that sense, the sessions with Strasberg were another kind of therapy for Anne. "At the Studio I learn a lot about my real-life problems," she said after having spent several years under Strasberg's tutelage. "I also get a chance to work out many emotions that would make trouble for me if they were bottled up. For instance, I can act out my destructive tendencies where they can't hurt anyone." Anne did not go into detail about destructive tendencies, at least not with reporters. Yet she acknowledged now and then what she considered to be her self-centered nature and highly emotional disposition.

Anne was not afraid to stand up for herself, either, and was no one's fool. Not long after she began attending the Actors Studio she clashed with the author Norman Mailer during a series of readings of his stage adaptation of his Hollywood novel *The Deer Park*. Mailer had brought the play to the Studio at the suggestion of a friend, the actor Mickey Knox, whose friend Frank Corsaro was a director and a Studio member. Corsaro enlisted Anne, Rip Torn, Kevin McCarthy, Patrick O'Neal, and others in the effort to help Mailer shape his work and give it cohesion.

The role of the beautiful, volatile dancer Elena fascinated Anne, whom Knox remembered as "bright and funny and very good in the part." Mailer, meanwhile, was growing fascinated with the actress playing the character he had created on paper. Corsaro accompanied Mailer on a visit to Anne's apartment one night and quickly realized that the married writer was not there to talk about the play. "It was obvious he was trying to make her, and she said, 'No way. Sorry, buster,'" Corsaro told Mailer's biographer Peter Manso. "Anne Bancroft was very peasant—smart, with a good shit detector." It probably was not a coincidence that Mailer and Anne began having major differences over how Elena should be played.

"Finally he and Annie had a big blowup," recalled Mailer's wife, Adele. According to her version of events, Mailer kept interrupting the actors at rehearsal and then criticized Anne's interpretation of the character. She threw the script at him.

"You know what you can do with this part?" Anne told the famous writer before walking out. "Get Adele to play it. That's what you've wanted all along."

"Fine," Mailer replied, "because you'll never amount to anything anyway."

Adele Mailer later remarked: "It was a strange thing for him to say considering she had been a big hit in *Two for the Seesaw*. We had both seen the play and thought she was wonderful." Even though Adele Mailer was a painter and not an actress, she took over the part, at least in the Studio readings. Two years later, a drunken Mailer stabbed his wife with a penknife, nearly killing her, and their marriage ended in 1962. His play eventually reached off-Broadway in 1967.

Most significant for Anne, the *Deer Park* episode did not sour her on the Actors Studio. She continued to believe in its goal of providing actors and other artists an opportunity to flex their creative muscles in a professional but private setting and to try new things without fear of failure. As the actress Inga Swenson put it, "The Actors Studio was like a gymnasium. You went there to exercise."

While Anne worked out, she inspired others. "It was very brave of her to go there," recalled Lane Bradbury, an actress who attended sessions with Anne. "The fact that she had success—and still had the courage to go. There was something that she wanted, something more than what she had. ... She was somebody that was passionate about being an actress and passionate about discovering the truth about herself—and willing to bare her soul and be bad to discover herself."

There were lighter moments in Anne's professional life, too. In February 1959 she made her first appearance on Jack Paar's *Tonight* show, then broadcast live on weeknights from New York by NBC. She became a favorite of Paar because of her warmth and sense of humor and her ability to engage him in playful banter. "She was very funny," remembered her friend David Lunney, who was working at NBC at the time. "She could be politely outrageous—she was fast in terms of thinking." Lunney was not alone in thinking that Anne was channeling Gittel Mosca at times during those appearances, so much so that people who did not know her well wondered if she was becoming Gittel or even had been like the slightly kooky character all along. It was a put-on, to some extent, and Anne took home a couple hundred dollars for a few minutes of fun. She joined Paar five more times that year alone.

Performances at the Booth Theatre, voice lessons three times a week, regular sessions with her therapist, twice-a-week sessions at the Actors Studio, an occasional talk show—Anne liked to stay busy even as she valued time to herself. Knowing what was in store with *The Miracle Worker,* she added to her offstage activities by studying sign language for the deaf and blind. She even experimented with some approaches to the role of Annie Sullivan at the Actors Studio before William Gibson had finished his play. "I didn't want to use up rehearsal time," Anne said. She felt secure and artistically free in the company of her peers. "If you fall on your face," she said, "you don't do it in front of the world." She told reporters that she hardly had time for a boyfriend, and what dates she had made no particular impression on her family in terms of a serious relationship.

Whether she lived as monastically as her press interviews suggested, Anne was not in the gossip columns as she had been during her Hollywood years. One reason may have been that she had not yet become—and was not interested in becoming—the kind of celebrity whose daily life was fodder for the press and an eager public. To her professional benefit and personal chagrin, that would soon change.

When William Gibson first turned his attention to adapting his teleplay *The Miracle Worker* into a work for the stage, he had the Broadway star Julie Harris in mind to play Annie Sullivan. As rehearsals for *Two for the Seesaw* progressed, however, Gibson grew even more enamored of Anne and soon saw her as the only actor he would consider for the role. His television drama had been just the latest rendering of the unique relationship between Annie Sullivan and Helen Keller. For generations people around the world had been fascinated with the life of the woman who had lost her hearing, sight, and ability to speak at eighteen months, yet overcame those handicaps to graduate from college, write an autobiography, and crusade for humanitarian causes. Though Keller was the greater celebrity of the two, Sullivan was her teacher and companion until Sullivan's death in 1936. There had been more books, lecture tours, a vaudeville act—even motion pictures, mainly documentaries, as far back as 1919, when Keller appeared onscreen in *Deliverance,* itself a silent film.

Writing the play from Sullivan's letters and other material was easy for Gibson when compared to the difficulties he had had with *Two for the Seesaw.* "Like falling off a log," he said. There would be no struggle over major revisions this time, only small cuts here and there and some polishing. Compressing time, combining incidents, and inventing dialogue were compromises of fact for the sake of drama. Sullivan's biographer and Keller's legal representative, Nella Henney, had been given script approval. Both Keller and Henney would receive 10 percent of Gibson's share of the profits since they had provided source material, which gave them a reason to support the playwright's efforts to make the drama entertaining.

Gibson opened the three-act stage play at the Alabama home of the Kellers, whose deaf and blind daughter lives a nearly feral life in their household because of her lack of understanding of the world around her. Mrs. Keller persuades her husband to try once more to help Helen by hiring a young governess from a school for the blind in Boston. The teacher, Annie Sullivan, is trying to overcome a childhood marred by the loss of her parents, the separation from her younger brother at an orphanage and his subsequent death, and her own poor eyesight. Captain Keller takes an immediate disliking to Sullivan, as does Helen when Sullivan begins to discipline the child for her tantrums. The second act is full of conflict—

between members of the Keller family, Captain Keller and Sullivan, and Sullivan and Helen. The teacher and pupil engage in an exhausting battle over using a spoon at breakfast. Sullivan persuades the Kellers to allow her to take Helen to a garden house for a period of separation as she tries to teach her manners and the language of the deaf and blind.

The final act begins with the Kellers insisting on Helen's return in spite of some progress by the child. At dinner Helen tests everyone by reverting to her old habits and throws a pitcher of water in Sullivan's face. She drags the child outside to the water pump and spells out "water" as they refill the pitcher. At that moment the "miracle" happens: Helen connects the word Sullivan spells on her hand with the cool liquid flowing from the pump. She eagerly asks to know the names for everything and Sullivan calls for the family to share in the miracle. As the play ends, Helen learns new words: mother, father, and teacher.

The Miracle Worker is the story of the title character, not Helen Keller. Gibson saw the theme of the play in terms of Annie Sullivan's struggle with the ghost of her younger brother and her own failures. The playwright described Sullivan's motivation to Arthur Penn succinctly: "Her business in life was to redeem a life lost." At the end of the play Helen has changed, as she is now able to begin to discern the world. Her teacher has changed, too, as Gibson presents Sullivan achieving her goal of redemption. Anne herself identified with Sullivan's internal battle to find peace with the past through determination to succeed in the present.

Even while she performed in *Two for the Seesaw,* Anne was delving into the world of the blind. "Before I could understand Annie Sullivan—or Helen Keller—I had to know the blind and know myself what it was like to be blind," she said. In her free time she observed blind children at the Institute for Physical Medicine and Rehabilitation in New York City. Later she attended a conference for teachers of the blind and deaf at Northwestern University. A weeklong stay at a camp for the blind in Spring Valley, New York, helped her perfect her use of the manual alphabet that was central to Helen's education.

At times Anne actually worked with handicapped children. On a visit to the home of an eleven-year-old girl who was blind and deaf, she spent a few hours playing with the child and observing her. Unlike Helen at the end of the play, the child had not yet developed a way to communicate with others. Anne went home greatly disturbed at the prospect of a child living in such isolation. At the institute in New York, a blind seven-year-old boy had trouble filling his spoon as he ate, and Anne spent days trying to teach him. "The most important thing you can do with these children is to form a relationship with them," she said. "After that, anything is possible." When he finally achieved this seemingly small task, Anne wept with joy and understanding of how great a step it had been for him.

Those experiences enhanced her understanding of Sullivan's goals and what Gibson was trying to show in his play. Still, it was not enough. She wanted to have a feeling for what it meant to be blind, and she undertook an experiment. She checked into a hotel in a strange town. Taping her eyes shut, she put on dark glasses, then tried to live as if blind. In the two days that followed, she felt fear, loneliness, and frustration with the unseen world around her. She discovered for herself that learning to use a spoon without the benefit of sight required considerable effort.

Anne completed her contractual obligation to *Two for the Seesaw* in late June 1959 and took a brief vacation before plunging into rehearsals for *The Miracle Worker*. Replacing her as Gittel Mosca was Lee Grant, her standby and one of the actresses the production team had considered for the role in the beginning. Anne's first Broadway play had been good to her, but it had been even better to its backers. By the time *Two for the Seesaw* closed on October 31, 1959, after ninety-four weeks at the Booth Theatre, the original $80,000 investment had returned a profit of about $570,000. Anne had been little more than a hired hand, but she was looking forward to a better salary and a share of the profits when she returned to Broadway.

Her connection to *Two for the Seesaw* ended on a sour note. As the rights to the play bounced between studios and producers, the original team—William Gibson, Arthur Penn, and Fred Coe—were eased out of the project. A movie version ended up being produced for United Artists by the Mirisch Company, an independent operation that was becoming a major player in the industry. The producer Walter Mirisch had seen Anne on Broadway but could not offer her the part in the film because the studio did not believe she would have the box-office draw of other actresses. Anne was heartbroken—the film could have made for a triumphant return to Hollywood and preserved her unique performance. Instead, Shirley MacLaine and Robert Mitchum were cast, the screenwriter Isobel Lennart adapted Gibson's play, and Robert Wise directed. When the movie reached theaters in 1962, the critical and audience response did not begin to rival that of the Broadway production.

Rehearsals for *The Miracle Worker* began in August 1959 at the

Playhouse Theatre with an eye on an October opening. Almost immediately a problem with Anne's approach to the role became obvious—at least to Gibson. "She played Annie Sullivan as though she were Gittel," he recalled. "I said to Arthur, 'I've made a terrible mistake.' And he said, 'I'll fix it.'"

Penn knew that Anne was not a one-trick pony. She had been wrapped up in Gittel Mosca nearly every day for a year and a half, so some spillover might have been expected. Penn "fixed it" in part by making Annie Sullivan's voice sound quite different from Gittel's Bronx accent. "He gave her an Irish accent, a brogue, which Annie Sullivan did not have," Gibson said. The playwright could live with that bit of fiction. Sullivan's letters and information from Nella Henney indicated that Sullivan knew how to speak in a brogue because of her Irish Catholic roots. "All over the world Annie Sullivan has had a brogue ever since," the playwright said, "because Arthur was trying to get rid of Gittel in Anne Bancroft."

Others in the cast included the stage and film performers Patricia Neal as Helen's mother and Torin Thatcher as Captain Keller. The actress chosen for the role of Helen Keller, twelve-year-old Patty Duke, was a bit small for her age at four feet and not quite five inches. That worked well since Helen was not yet seven when she first met Annie Sullivan. Duke had been appearing in films, television anthologies, and other television series for a few years but had not been on a Broadway stage. Under Penn's soft-spoken guidance, she developed an incredible concentration that allowed her to be completely convincing as a child who could not see or hear.

Duke coped with a myriad of personal problems away from the theater, later detailed with startling frankness in an autobiography. She found sources of comfort in her female costars and her director. Anne, in particular, was a friend to her even though Duke could be very demanding emotionally. "What I felt from Annie, the sense that it was truly possible for someone to care about and accept me, to want me to be intelligent and mature, has stood me in good stead ever sense," she wrote. They would share a special camaraderie for the years they worked together. Anne would listen to Duke talk about her problems, kid around with her, and treat her like a young person entering adolescence rather than a perpetual child.

The most memorable scenes in *The Miracle Worker* were the breakfast battle to get Helen to use her spoon instead of grabbing food from the plates of others and the confrontation over the folded napkin that leads to the revelation at the water pump. The first scene would bring audiences out of their seats; the second would leave them in tears. Sullivan's letters had referred to "a battle royal" with her pupil over table manners, and Gibson imagined how it might have played out. Relying on the carefully written scene—in the published play it takes four pages and has no dialogue—Penn choreographed the dining room confrontation into a brawl. He began with Annie Sullivan facing the audience, but the scene just seemed limp to him. Penn realized that he should be thinking in terms of the characters, not the audience. He placed Annie Sullivan with her back to the audience as she tried to teach Helen to use a spoon.

"Helen would refuse to do it," Penn said. "Then Helen would crawl away, and then crawl under the table, and Annie would run around, pick her up, bring her back, and that gave us a kind of springlike energy that kept that scene going, where, if we were able to see all the expressions and all that stuff from the outset, it would reveal too much."

Some elements of the scene were unpredictable. A spoon might fly this way one performance and that way another. Patty Duke might turn one way one time and another way another time. Sometimes the confrontation would take eight minutes; other times it would go on for ten, even twelve minutes. "They were building it themselves. It was some kind of scene," Penn remembered. "We had the blessing of these two really great actresses, and they would spare nothing. They were black and blue a good part of the time." A degree of improvisation would keep the scene fresh for the performers and their audience.

Both Anne and Patty Duke wore padding under their costumes to try to limit the physical damage to feet, shins, and knees that resulted from throwing themselves into the scene every performance. Accidents happened when, for example, Duke smacked Anne a little too hard with her doll. During rehearsals Anne ran into an upturned chair and developed a huge lump on her instep. The slaps they exchanged were real if measured, but one time Duke clenched her teeth and Anne's slap chipped a tooth. The production used bread crumbs in place of scrambled eggs because eggs turned the stage too slippery.

"The two of us did get physically fit during the play," Duke said. "We used to make jokes about having real muscles in our arms like Popeye." For both actresses, the play was physically and emotionally exhausting.

Before opening in New York, the play had two weeks of tryouts in Philadelphia and two more in Boston. The reaction that first night in

Philadelphia bode well. "There were eighteen curtain calls," Duke said, "and since I'd never been in front of an audience before, I sort of assumed this was what being onstage was like." Another member of the cast, Kathleen Comegys, took her aside. "Well, my little dear," said Comegys, who would be appearing in her nineteenth Broadway production since 1913, "I want you to take a moment and really remember this, because it doesn't happen very often."

The Miracle Worker rode excellent reviews and word of mouth from its tryouts into opening night at the Playhouse Theatre on October 19, 1959. Nearly all the major critics praised Anne and Patty Duke even if they thought the production itself had a few stumbles. "Anne Bancroft gives a glorious performance. . . . Little Patty Duke is wonderfully truthful and touching," wrote Brooks Atkinson of the *New York Times*. He faulted the play for "the loose narrative technique of a TV script" and called it an "untidy but moving drama." At the *New York Herald-Tribune*, Walter Kerr admitted that he was wallowing in adjectives: "powerful, hair-raising, spine-tingling, touching, and just plain wonderful. . . . Need I say that Miss Bancroft is magnificent, too?" In spite of minor flaws, he declared of the play: "It's not a miracle. It's honesty, and talent."

Other critics signaled that *The Miracle Worker* was the event of the season. The *Wall Street Journal:* "Illuminating and often exciting." The *New York Daily Mirror:* "Magnificent theatre . . . the power to wrench the heart." The *New York World-Telegram:* "Anne Bancroft and little Patty Duke will shatter every crowd that gathers in the Playhouse for months to come." *Saturday Review:* "Forceful theatre. Its story is honest, its impact is direct, and its concentration on the hard realities that underlie a sentimental result reaches an extraordinary intensity." More than one review noted that Anne's teacher was completely different from her *Two for the Seesaw* character. "If there was ever the slightest question about Miss Bancroft's versatility, it can now be answered," wrote John McClain of the *New York Journal-American*. "In *Seesaw* she was Jewish, now she is Irish; she is forthright, explicit, funny, and enormously endearing."

The following April, the American Theater Wing honored *The Miracle Worker* with Tony Awards for Anne as best dramatic actress, William Gibson and Fred Coe for best play, and Arthur Penn for best director as well as an award for best stage technician and a nomination for its scenic designer. (Patty Duke was not nominated for a Tony, but she won a Theatre World award.) Voters selected Gibson's play over Lorraine Hansberry's *A*

Raisin in the Sun, Gore Vidal's *The Best Man*, Paddy Chayefsky's *The Tenth Man*, and Lillian Hellman's *Toys in the Attic*. The competition for the dramatic actress award had not been weak: Margaret Leighton, Claudia McNeil, Geraldine Page, Maureen Stapleton, and Irene Worth. John Chapman's praise of Anne in his *New York Daily News* review—"the best actress on Broadway"—rang true.

Life began to change professionally and personally for the star of *The Miracle Worker*. Anne's income reached $150,000 a year in the wake of that success, giving her a financial security she had not enjoyed since returning to New York in 1957. She continued her frugal ways by sticking to a $50-a-week budget set by a financial adviser who invested her earnings. She also remained in her modest Greenwich Village apartment and tried not to let the accolades go to her head. The night she won the Tony she traveled to her parents' home in Yonkers and, finding them asleep at that hour, left the award in their mailbox. Millie Italiano added the Tony to the award room she had set aside for her daughter, confident there would be more.

Financial security and professional acclaim cost Anne a degree of the personal privacy she had enjoyed, not that she shied away from promoting herself and her career. She knew that the profession she had chosen demanded a personal touch. The national media reintroduced her to the public and began treating her like a celebrity. *Time* magazine featured her on the cover of its December 21, 1959, issue, making her one of a handful of performers each year who drew a major personality profile. In January 1960 she made the first of four appearances that year on Jack Paar's *Tonight* show. She joined the singer Perry Como for a duet on his NBC variety series that February and would return in November to guest-star along with Bob Hope. The popular CBS series *Person to Person* visited her apartment for a live broadcast in June. Feature articles about her life and career appeared in newspapers and magazines.

The *Time* profile was particularly revealing, especially on the subject of her love life. The marriage to Martin May and their subsequent estrangement and divorce were revisited, and she was reported to have been engaged to an Italian businessman, Mario Ferrari-Ferreira, a pairing that the magazine said had ended in part because of her Catholicism but also because she had been so focused on *Two for the Seesaw*. In subsequent interviews Anne shrugged off the idea of another marriage, but during the run of *The Miracle Worker* she was linked romantically to the actor Scott Brady, her *Restless Breed* costar and a Brooklyn native seven years her senior. Their relationship was serious enough that Anne introduced Brady to her parents.

She continued to participate in activities at the Actors Studio, an oasis of creativity for her even as she appeared nightly in *The Miracle Worker*. One of the Studio's projects in 1960 was a one-act play, *The Alligators*, written by Molly Kazan. A Broadway veteran, Gerald Freedman, directed Piper Laurie and William Daniels as well as Anne. "She had a sense of play, fun—and was very intelligent," Freedman remembered. "I don't feel like I directed her. We created together. She was willing to try anything and was a real team player." There were egos, of course, but Freedman recalled a healthy and respectful environment while working on *The Alligators*. "We were applying the principles taught at the Studio—talking, listening, story, theme, spine, all that," he said. "She was an actress and she wanted to grow." When the play debuted off-Broadway with a second one-act work by Kazan that November, Jo Van Fleet took Anne's part while she continued playing Annie Sullivan.

Becoming a Broadway phenomenon made *The Miracle Worker* ripe for a film adaptation. After watching *Two for the Seesaw* slip away from all involved in its stage success, William Gibson was determined not to see that happen again. To protect his work, Gibson joined Penn and Coe in creating their own company, Playfilm Productions. United Artists agreed to finance their film and serve as its distributor but, understandably, sought to protect its investment by casting a major star. Elizabeth Taylor wanted the role, and Audrey Hepburn was interested, too. A major star meant more ticket sales, which translated into a bigger budget to make the film and more money up front for the people behind it. United Artists predicted a $10 million box office with Taylor, about $7 million with Hepburn, and less than $2 million with Anne Bancroft.

Gibson understood the dollars and cents behind putting on a show. The playwright, however, also must have realized that a film of his work would be seen by untold millions and exist long after he was gone. Still regretful for having given up any involvement in the film version of *Two for the Seesaw*, he continued to pursue making a film of *The Miracle Worker* his way. The decision to cast Anne was a personal one for Gibson. "I asked Annie, 'Is it important to you to get this movie?' and she said, 'It's very important,'" he remembered. "I was sort of in love with Annie—we never had any affair, but we had some kind of an intellectual rapport that was like an affair, but intellectual—and I digested that. It was very important."

Did Gibson and his production partners believe they would surpass the expectations of United Artists with Anne repeating her role onscreen? Perhaps, but without question Gibson, with the backing of Penn and Coe, put his friendship with Anne ahead of personal gain. It was an act of loyalty she never forgot. No wonder she would soon be calling them "the three most important men in my life."

United Artists proposed providing the fledgling filmmakers about $1.2 million to make their movie plus another $100,000 to pay their star. One version of the deal had the rights to the play budgeted at $400,000; Gibson would earn $150,000 as writer and Penn and Coe would receive $75,000 apiece for their contributions. At least half of the profits would go to Playfilm, according to the deal under discussion in April 1960. At the time United Artists' president, Arthur Krim, still agitated for a different actress, making clear that the relatively low budget would remain if they insisted that Anne lead the cast. Gibson and the others stood firmly behind their star and friend.

There was, in fact, an artistic rationale for casting Anne instead of the more popular actresses whose names came up. "If they'd gone with any of those other women," said Penn's assistant on the film, Gene Lasko, "you would have seen melodrama as opposed to drama—really, truly character-driven drama." Gibson, Penn, and Coe were not averse to making money, but they took pride in their work, too.

Anne left *The Miracle Worker* in early February 1961, and Suzanne Pleshette took her place at the Playhouse Theatre. A late June start on the film gave Anne the longest vacation she had enjoyed in years. She spent part of it looking ahead to the next job, reading script after script in her apartment. Arthur Penn warned her to resist the temptation to exercise her range with a good part in a bad play. While she wanted to work, she also wanted to make wise choices.

Another guest spot on Perry Como's weekly NBC variety show, *Kraft Music Hall*, was a respite from the emotional drama she had been acting out every night for sixteen months. The show, taped at Broadway's Ziegfeld Theatre, provided the most prominent venue for her abilities as a singer. In the show scheduled for February 22, Anne joined Como and his guest star Jimmy Durante for skits and songs on the theme of marriage. Together, Anne and Como sang "Blue Room," "Whoopee," "Bidin' My Time," and

"By Myself." On her own Anne sang "Married I Can Always Get." An exuberant observer who had joined in the applause for her solo number approached Anne and introduced himself: "I'm Mel Brooks. Hiya, A."

"Just like that," she recalled some years later. "He talks that way. I liked him." Brooks had accompanied a mutual friend to the rehearsal intent on meeting Anne, and they ended up chatting between numbers.

The name Mel Brooks probably meant little if anything to her. At the time he had made his mark as a writer rather than as a performer. He had been a writer on Sid Caesar's popular 1950s comedy series, *Your Show of Shows* and *Caesar's Hour,* and had written sketches for the Broadway musical *Leonard Sillman's New Faces of 1952* as well as the book for another Broadway show, *Shinbone Alley,* produced in 1957. Brooks was about to hit a career milestone with the comedy album *2000 Years with Carl Reiner and Mel Brooks.* It would become a million-seller, spawn several more recordings, and lead to TV appearances in which Brooks and Reiner would do the album's title bit about the observations of a 2,000-year-old man.

Born in Brooklyn in 1926 and raised in the Williamsburg neighborhood, Mel Brooks was five years older than Anne. He had earned money as a teenager playing drums, studied psychology during a stint in college, then worked as an army ordnance specialist during World War II. He later worked as a musician in resorts and clubs in the Catskill Mountains and eventually became a stand-up comic. Writing for other performers had given him a somewhat more stable perch in show business.

When Brooks met Anne he was married and had three children, but he and his wife were already on their way to a divorce that year. He made a point in the days after the Como rehearsal to know where Anne would be so he could innocently run into her as if kismet were at work. She figured out the ploy soon enough—"he started following me around"—but she was more intrigued than annoyed and began seeing Brooks socially.

That summer Arthur Penn planned a forty-day shoot for *The Miracle Worker.* Exteriors were filmed at a Victorian farmhouse in the Red Bank–Middletown area of New Jersey. Interiors were shot on soundstages at a west-side Manhattan studio, the Film Production Center. Besides Anne, Patty Duke reprised her role as Helen Keller even though she was now fourteen. Penn's assistant, Gene Lasko, did not recall any effort to replace Duke with a younger actress. "You got a brilliant diamond," he said, "you don't go looking for one that's a second quality just because it's two carats bigger." One reason Penn cast Inga Swenson as Mrs. Keller was her height—

at five feet and ten inches, she would make Duke look smaller. Another tall actor, the six-feet-plus Victor Jory, played Captain Keller.

The *Miracle Worker* cast and crew labored under a tight schedule and budget. "It was all pure business. It wasn't fun and games off the set or anything. As a rule I don't think movies are," Inga Swenson remembered. Though she did not grow close to Anne, she found her costar to be warm and giving. "She was a very good actress and very professional. She never had a hissy fit or was late to shooting." Swenson thought her role as Mrs. Keller was as bland in the film as it had been on the stage. "It's not a good part. None of the parts are good. Only Annie and Patty had great roles. The others just don't matter. I mean, they fade into the background," she said. "It's just those two incredible roles. It was an accident of fate that Arthur found those two incredible actresses."

Anne and the other New York-based actors could finish a day's work and enjoy the evening at home. Lasko remembered her as a wonderful colleague and loved the time he spent with her. "She was a barrel of fun," he said, "unless there was a scene coming up and she wanted to focus herself. We had a very merry time on that picture." Occasionally Anne would look back on her previous foray into the movies. "She would be fondly bitter about it. She'd say, 'Ah, you shoulda seen me in the ape suit' or something like that," Lasko said. "I think she was goddamn happy to be a star at last— as opposed to taking out her bitterness with her past, which happens to a lot of females, and males. They make you pay back for having mistreated them in the years before they were known. She didn't do that."

Penn was directing only his second feature film but had guided dozens of hours of television programs. The stage version of *The Miracle Worker* usually ran 130 minutes, but the film ended up about twenty-five minutes shorter because of extensive trims in dialogue not needed for a medium that relied more on images than words. The director decided not to ask Anne and Patty Duke to tone down their performances for the more discerning eye of the camera. "I didn't hold back," he said. "I figured, we'd have to be as vigorous as we were on the stage." When it came time to film the pump scene, Penn pulled back his camera to let the emotional moment play out as it had on the stage. When he saw the dailies, the scene looked terrible. "It thrust us back into a spectator's role rather than a participant's role," he said. "So I came back the next day and said, 'Fellas, back we go.'" Building emotion through multiple cuts, close-ups, and a moving camera proved to be a revelation for him. "That," he said, "was where I learned movies."

In Penn's estimation, United Artists' top executives did not appreciate *The Miracle Worker* and did not back its distribution with a strong promotional campaign. They had gathered in a screening room on Seventh Avenue in New York to watch the movie with its writer, producer, and director and then left relatively unimpressed. "It didn't register," Penn recalled. "It was a matter of taste, it was a matter of taste. It didn't register on them, the real emotion of it. We should've had some women, first of all, in the audience. Here you've got three guys with cigars." It would not be the last time Hollywood would disappoint Penn, who would remain a cinema rebel of sorts while directing *Bonnie and Clyde* (1967), *Little Big Man* (1970), and other films even as he continued to bring plays to Broadway.

The Miracle Worker opened in theaters in the spring and summer of 1962. Reviews were much like those for the play, praising Anne and Patty Duke while finding small faults with the script and the execution of some scenes. The *New Republic*'s critic, Stanley Kauffmann, called the movie "clumsy and cluttered with dramaturgic baggage, but the subject and the central facts give it irresistible power" and observed that Penn had not yet dared to use all the resources of the camera—a criticism Penn would suggest himself. Generally complimentary of the film, Bosley Crowther of the *New York Times* said it "has finally brought Arthur Penn to the point of being the director of a conspicuous and exciting film." The *Chicago Tribune* was ecstatic, calling it "an unvarnished, often painful film which is one of the great ones. Anne Bancroft as Annie Sullivan and Patty Duke as Helen Keller re-create their stage roles with a ferocious intensity that is absolutely gripping." Once again, the leads drew most of the accolades. *Time* said *The Miracle Worker* offered "what is quite possibly the most moving double performance ever recorded on film."

Largely left unsaid was the unique nature of the role of Annie Sullivan in American movies that year. Few major films were portraying a woman grappling with internal and external forces that had little to do with her gender or her relationship with a man. In so many American films of the era, a woman was either seeking a man in her life or trying to get away from one. (Anne's own films in the 1950s had placed her in that box and limited her creativity.) Most of the popular movies in 1962 were not presenting women as complex human beings: *That Touch of Mink, The Music Man, Mutiny on the Bounty,* and *Hatari!* are a few examples from the year's top ten. The two most popular films, *Lawrence of Arabia* and *The Longest*

Day, lacked prominent female characters. No wonder Hollywood's top actresses had wanted to play Annie Sullivan.

How eager moviegoers were to see such characters would be a fair question. As it turned out, United Artists had been prescient. *The Miracle Worker* brought in $1.6 million in film rentals and was expected to top out at $2 million, placing it deep in the list of the year's top fifty films. (*West Side Story*, a holdover from the previous year, led the annual *Variety* tabulation with an anticipated $19 million.) Ticket sales were enough for United Artists to recoup its investment but left little for Playfilm Productions and the men who put Anne ahead of profits. She could be hailed as the greatest actress on Broadway, be a favorite for an Academy Award, and field more and more offers for movies and plays, but Anne still had no power at the box office. That was the lone drag on the career she had reinvented against all odds—a miracle of her own making.

6

A Challenging Role's Only Reward

Filming *The Miracle Worker* took two months, but nearly ten more passed as Arthur Penn supervised its editing and United Artists arranged for its release. Anne spent most of that time taking it easy and considering roles. It was to become a familiar pattern: intense work on a major project, then a period of relaxation as she weighed her options. Another regular occurrence for her was illness. During the last few days of the *Miracle Worker* shoot, she suffered from what turned out to be walking pneumonia. In time she would grapple with all kinds of ailments interfering with her work—or arising from it. On doctor's orders she stayed in the hospital for a few weeks, then continued her recuperation for several weeks more on Fire Island.

Soon enough, in the fall of 1961, she was back home in Greenwich Village and attending the Actors Studio, reading scripts, and undertaking other routines. "I want to do something I feel is worthwhile," she told a reporter. "Something that will give back to me the same life and energy I put into it, and perhaps that will reveal a different part of me." It would be a tall order to find such a part in the movies, less so on the stage. Comfortable enough financially, she could afford to be choosy.

Her name was coming up more frequently now as film producers and directors discussed casting for female roles. When Richard Burton and the director Sidney Lumet were teaming up for a movie based on an F. Scott Fitzgerald story, they wanted Anne. The producers of a Dean Martin–Lana Turner project titled *Who's Got the Action?* wanted to add her to their cast. After Marilyn Monroe fell out of a proposed television production of the W. Somerset Maugham short story "Rain," Anne's name was connected to the lead character, Sadie Thompson, for a time. She was reported to be talking to United Artists about appearing in *The Manchurian Candidate* as Frank Sinatra's love interest; Janet Leigh got the job. There was talk of trying to hire Anne to star with Charlton Heston in the historical epic *55 Days at Peking*; Ava Gardner took that part. Alfred Hitchcock was considering Anne for a supporting part in *The Birds.*

How seriously Anne explored such possibilities—or was even considered by producers and directors beyond name-dropping in the press—belied a more significant development. When practically anyone was casting a female role for the stage or a movie, she was almost certainly part of the conversation. That was the case when the stage producer Cheryl Crawford and director and choreographer Jerome Robbins mulled over the lead for what they hoped would be the first American production of Bertolt Brecht's play *Mother Courage and Her Children.* Their list of twenty-two names placed Anne in the third spot, behind Geraldine Page and Simone Signoret and ahead of Lotte Lenya and Uta Hagen. Their rundown was light on movie stars and heavy on respected actresses of the American and British stage. It was a compliment to Anne to have her name anywhere on such a lineup—another sign of her elevated status within the acting community.

Crawford was one of the founders of the Actors Studio and by then was quite familiar with Anne's work on Broadway and at the Studio itself. She knew Anne could deliver a forceful performance in a difficult work. That year she witnessed Anne and the actress Viveca Lindfors engage in what some described as a fight to the death at the Studio while they were working on August Strindberg's brief play *The Stronger.* Crawford's account had the two screaming and crying as they scratched and tussled with each other. "That was a fight," Crawford said. "Two washerwomen couldn't have done that well." Lee Strasberg would not allow anyone to break it up, content to let his Method-fueled pupils go at it.

Mother Courage and Her Children was a long way from production. As for the Hitchcock movie, Anne did not join *The Birds* as it moved toward a January 1962 start date. According to some accounts, Hitchcock did not want to meet her price; instead, he hired Suzanne Pleshette, her *Miracle Worker* replacement, for a minor character who ended up being pecked to death. As it happened, Anne did not accept any roles for films that would be shot in the new year. One reason might have been an agreement not to appear in any movie or television series (except guest spots) released in the five months after the opening of *The Miracle Worker.* Such a prohibition would have protected the significance of her performance. If her next movie turned out to be a bust, always a possibility, it would only dim the glow of her achievement.

Stage roles were another matter. In October 1961 Anne agreed to be cast in a new comedy bound for Broadway, *Rich and Famous,* written by Jay Presson and produced by her husband, Lewis Allen. The main attraction for Anne may have been the director, Arthur Penn, who also would be coproducing. Anne decided that the contemporary comedy—a married New York writer finds unexpected success with a novel—offered something she had not done before. Revisions in the script were sought, delaying the production for months, and by February Penn had turned over directing duties to his associate Gene Lasko. Soon the production disappeared altogether from the lineup of plays in the works for Broadway.

With *The Miracle Worker* in release in spring 1962, Anne promoted the film with numerous interviews. Invariably, the theme was her triumphant return to the movies. In private she harbored negative feelings about her Hollywood years, professionally and personally, but she kept any bitterness out of the public conversation. Wisely, she did not gloat over her comeback in one of the best roles of the year. Nor did she bad-mouth either the movie industry or the Hollywood culture she had held in disdain. She faulted herself, contending that her unhappiness with the pedestrian, forgettable films she had made was the result of immaturity and confusion over what mattered to her. A story by the Associated Press was typical. "I can't blame Hollywood for anything," she said. "I blame myself for what happened to me out here." It was not the time to get into the lack of demanding roles for women, the dearth of good material for anyone, the general public's taste for melodrama and low comedy, or the erosion of a studio system dominated by men who catered to traditional male tastes. Her approach—"I blame myself"—burnished a comeback story that was very much true while not ruining it by pointing out that there was plenty of blame to go around. With positive press for *The Miracle Worker* in the balance, not to mention a likely Oscar nomination by her peers and a potential victory dependent on the industry as a whole, it was a savvy presentation.

A happier and fuller truth was that Anne had every reason to look ahead with optimism. Critics were praising her new film, and she did not lack for offers of employment. She was earning enough money to afford to buy a home of her own. (In the months ahead she would pay $95,000 for a three-story brownstone in Greenwich Village.) The Actors Studio had become such a prominent part of her life that she served on a committee seeking to establish a permanent production company within the Studio, perhaps as soon as the following year, and joined those committed to being available for future productions.

Best of all, perhaps, she was spending more and more time with Mel Brooks, who had become the main man in her life. "Mel is so wonderful," Anne said. "Most people, if you pinch them, they come out with a conventional 'ouch.' But he never says anything ordinary, he's so alive to the fun of life." Her upcoming trip to Spain for the San Sebastian Film Festival (her film would be awarded the top honor and she would win the drama award) prompted wistful feelings for Brooks's company. "When you're in love," she said, "it's no fun going away."

There was one drawback to all the professional success and personal satisfaction Anne had worked so hard to achieve: her private world was shrinking. That reality became clear not long after her appearances in early July on prime-time television game shows. She was the "mystery guest" on *What's My Line?* and the next week matched wits with her fellow Broadway star Robert Goulet on *Password.* Given the reach of television in a three-network world, more people saw her those nights than had bought tickets to either of her Broadway shows or to her new movie. "I was walking in the neighborhood recently," she said later that summer, "and as I passed two bystanders, I could see they were watching me, and I heard my name. That was one of the saddest discoveries of my life."

Of all the potential roles Anne might have undertaken as a follow-up to Annie Sullivan, the most intriguing "what if" revolved around plans by David Merrick and Ray Stark to produce a stage musical inspired by the life and career of the comedienne Fanny Brice. Jerome Robbins, still discussing *Mother Courage and Her Children* with Cheryl Crawford, had agreed in February 1962 to direct the Brice show. By then his credits were a roster of Broadway hits—among them *Call Me Madam, The King and I, Peter Pan, West Side Story,* and *Gypsy*—but he yearned to take on a "serious" show like *Mother Courage and Her Children.*

Robbins presented Stark with several possible stars for the Brice show but pushed hardest for Anne. She had been a part of the casting discussion even before Robbins joined the project, but Stark questioned her ability to play Brice as Brice and not as a character of her own creation. For Stark, it was a personal decision as well as an artistic one—the late Fanny Brice was his wife's mother. In time Stark's own list of possible stars grew longer but left out Anne in spite of Robbins' wishes. Stark simply felt that Anne lacked the humor and warmth needed to play Brice as he envisioned her.

Anne had told the press that spring that the Brice musical would be her next project if she liked the script. She did not and shared her concerns with Robbins. She was dissatisfied with the songs, too. One account has her telling the songwriters Jule Styne and Bob Merrill that no one could sing "People" and "Don't Rain on My Parade."

Could Anne's voice handle a full-blown musical? Robbins was not sure of her singing abilities and acknowledged as much to Ray Stark even as he backed her talents as an actress. Robbins began putting more support behind his second choice, Carol Burnett. Stark, meanwhile, had decided that the role should go to a relative newcomer, Barbra Streisand. That season she was stopping the show in a supporting role in the musical *I Can Get It for You Wholesale* and developing a following with her nightclub and television appearances.

Script problems and casting disagreements that summer made an October opening seem unrealistic to Robbins. When another revision of the Brice script failed to solve the issues that he thought imperiled the show, he returned to Anne as his first choice. He believed that her skills as an actress would help deal with flaws in the script. Streisand, he argued, did not have the acting experience the show needed. It was a dilemma: an actress with questionable singing skills versus a talented singer with questionable acting skills.

During the time Robbins was helping shape the Brice musical, he kept close to *Mother Courage and Her Children*. He could not do both, especially with Stark pushing for a fall opening and Cheryl Crawford wanting to open her drama in early 1963. The competing projects had turned into a tug-of-war for his time and energy. In September Robbins told Stark he was out, choosing Mother Courage over Fanny Brice, but he still wanted to work with Anne.

Whether it was the songs or her singing or the script or the ongoing arguments between producer and director, Anne too had lost interest in the Brice musical. Her concerns aside, it seemed unlikely that Stark would have accepted her after Robbins, her champion, left the production. Eventually, the Brice musical would gain a fresh director, a fresh script, and a fresh title. When *Funny Girl* opened eighteen months later, Broadway audiences celebrated a new star in Barbra Streisand.

Robbins invited Anne to lunch at the Carlyle Hotel. Once he learned that she was probably not going to do the Brice play, he turned the conversation to *Mother Courage*. Cheryl Crawford had already asked her to read the play and Robbins encouraged her to join them in bringing Bertolt Brecht's masterpiece to Broadway. Brecht had written *Mother Courage and Her Children* in 1939 in response to the fascism that led to his exile from Nazi Germany. In 1949 his East Berlin theater company, Berliner Ensemble, staged an internationally praised production of what was becoming a twentieth-century classic. Brecht was best known to American audiences through his popular musical *The Threepenny Opera*, which introduced the song "Mack the Knife." Other New York theater productions of works by the German intellectual had not been audience favorites, closing within days or a few weeks of their premieres.

Nor did the plot of *Mother Courage* promise a typical night of Broadway entertainment. Spanning a twelve-year period in the seventeenth century, the play is set amid the Thirty Years' War, and its dozen scenes move the characters through battlefields in Germany, Poland, and other countries. Mother Courage enters the stage sitting on a cart pulled by her two sons, her mute daughter beside her. The matriarch sells all kinds of goods to the Protestant army, but over the course of time she switches allegiance from Protestant to Catholic and back again as her mercenary needs demand. By the play's end the war and her own greed have led to the deaths of each child. Mother Courage is left alone to drag her cart as she follows soldiers to the next battle.

Brecht's traditional staging also would be unusual for Broadway. With verse set to music, Mother Courage and other characters occasionally sing. Title cards reveal events before they occur to remove any suspense. Props and scenery are minimalist. The play's themes—antiwar, anticapitalist, antiheroic—and its biting humor and irony are other matters altogether. Brecht considered Mother Courage "the hyena of the battlefield," as one of its characters puts it, and "a great living contradiction," an apt description of war itself. Whether she was an epic figure driven to survive or a greedy conniver living off humanity's ills would spark many a post-performance conversation.

All this in a Broadway production to compete with musical shows like *Oliver!* and *A Funny Thing Happened on the Way to the Forum* and *Little Me*, not to mention *Stop the World—I Want to Get Off*. To their credit, Cheryl Crawford and Jerome Robbins were taking a considerable artistic and financial gamble. They believed they could produce a version of what was arguably Brecht's greatest work and impress drama critics and Brecht aficionados while still filling seats at a Broadway theater night after night. And the star they wanted hitched to Mother Courage's wagon was Anne Bancroft.

Except that Anne did not share their enthusiasm. Over their lunch at the Carlyle in the fall of 1962, she admitted to Robbins that she had not been able to make any connection with Brecht or his play. "She said that she couldn't read it, that she wasn't able to read it, that she just didn't get anywhere with it," Robbins said in recalling the genesis of the production. "I asked her to read it again and see whether she felt anything more about it."

While Anne tried to get a grasp on the material, Cheryl Crawford turned her attention toward Geraldine Page, the name at the top of their original list. Robbins had reservations about Page, but after discussing the play with her and spending time in Los Angeles with Page and her husband, the actor Rip Torn, he realized that she was much closer to sharing his vision for *Mother Courage* than Anne had been. They agreed to work together, but the day after his return to New York he heard back from Anne. She was now eager to join him in interpreting Brecht's work.

Part of the reason Anne had been put off initially was her desire to do something glamorous after her turns as Gittel Mosca and Annie Sullivan, the sort of role that *Rich and Famous* seemed to promise before its script came up short. "I wanted to get a part in which I could wear high heels and hose and be really beautiful and glamorous," she said. The heels-and-hose roles in the various scripts she read may have delivered in the striking beauty department, but they did not have the depth she sought. After supplementing the *Mother Courage* script with some research about Brecht and reading his other writings, she felt that she finally understood it.

Her revelation came too late. Robbins broke the news to Anne that Geraldine Page had the role. "She was heartbroken and angry, and I was sick that I had to tell such a talented girl, and one that I still cared a lot for, that we had to make a decision elsewhere," he said. "She left on the verge of tears and very angry." It had been some time since Anne had been turned down for something she wanted.

Geraldine Page proved not to be as ready to sign a contract as Robbins had thought. She put off making a commitment to *Mother Courage* while deciding whether she wanted to appear that spring in an Actors Studio production of Eugene O'Neill's *Strange Interlude*. Her dithering threatened to delay Robbins and Crawford's production schedule and probably undercut their confidence that she shared their passion for the project. They went back to Anne to offer her the part.

Anne was ecstatic and, according to Robbins, told him, "When I thought I wasn't getting the part I was ready to screw Cheryl to get it, if necessary." He was not certain that was an exaggeration. "One thing Annie has in her favor is her tenaciousness and wish and desire and what she feels is her knowledge that she can do this role," he said. "I'll buy that because I trust her, so here we go into the wild blue yonder." In December Anne signed a contract to appear in *Mother Courage and Her Children;* the opening was set for March 1963, after as many as six weeks of rehearsal.

This time, it was Anne's name that drove the pre-sales for the production. Her contract called for her to be paid 10 percent of the weekly box-office gross, or a minimum of $2,500 (nearly $20,000 today) and 5 percent of the profits. Among other things, she would receive sole star billing; only her image would appear on the cover of *Playbill;* seventy-five dollars a week would be set aside for a personal maid; and Anne would receive eight tickets for every performance (the seats had to be in the center of the orchestra section, within rows five and ten). She also would be guaranteed one week of vacation, between July 1 and September 30. In exchange, she would agree to appear for the run of the play or until January 4, 1964, whichever came earlier. These were the kinds of expectations—or demands—of a Broadway star.

The deal in place, it was time to get to work. To develop a feeling for the people in Brecht's play, Anne enlisted the help of housing officials and spent weeks visiting tenement areas of the city to observe immigrants in America. She told a reporter, "I felt they would have quite a time, with difficulties and probably the same problems, coming to a strange country and making some kind of life for themselves." On the stage, she shared Robbins's concern over her appearance, given that she would be portraying an aging, haggard woman with grown children. A visit to the Eaves Costume Manufacturing Corporation on West Forty-sixth Street—the largest maker of theatrical and historical apparel in the country—led to plenty of padding, long and sagging breasts, a blacked-out tooth, wild gray hair covering a skullcap, and other makeup and wardrobe effects. The result was far removed from her contemporary beauty.

It did not take long for *Mother Courage* to become a troubled production. Robbins was often at odds with the translator for the English version of the play, Eric Bentley, who told Robbins's biographer Deborah Jowitt that he thought the director did not quite understand the play's emotion and humor. Cheryl Crawford sent Robbins note after note on what she thought should be the interpretation behind a scene. The opening was postponed, more rehearsals were undertaken, and three weeks of previews rather than tryouts in Boston or Philadelphia became the vehicle for changes and experimentation. Following his reputation, Robbins was an exacting if brilliant taskmaster, not above belittling his colleagues.

Underlying the production's difficulties were his own doubts about whether he was up to the task at hand. "It was a change of pace for Jerry in terms of the material," recalled Gerald Freedman, a dancer and director who had worked with Robbins on *West Side Story* and other productions. "But he was always experimenting. He was growing, growing, growing—always."

Brecht had not wanted audiences to feel sympathy for Mother Courage. His approach to theater involved placing distance between the actors and the audience—he did not want tears on the stage or other actions that would draw the audience to the characters. Anne understood Brecht's philosophy—Robbins did as well—and she knew that playing a scornful creature would be a total departure for her. "The audience for the first time is against me," she said. "I have to fight for any sympathy I get, and it takes hard, steady concentration." To achieve that, she viewed Mother Courage as an ordinary person who ends up doing something heroic and deserving of admiration. Anne and Robbins may well have decided that a female antihero would be rejected if she did not create some empathy for her, an interpretation that ardent Brechtians would surely have opposed.

Mother Courage was a physically demanding role, too, though Anne considered it not half as hard as fighting Patty Duke every night. Pulling Mother Courage's wagon by herself at the end of the play was an aspect of her performance that disturbed both her mother and father. Mike and Millie Italiano worried that their slight and slender daughter could not bear that burden eight times a week. They were in the opening-night audience at the Martin Beck Theatre on March 28, 1963, and, once backstage, Millie lost no time warning her daughter to take care of herself.

"Listen, miss," Millie said, "you take your vitamins every day and get plenty of sleep or else!"

"Or else what, Ma?" a bemused Anne asked.

"Or else . . . or else you can't work here! That's what else!"

The critical response to *Mother Courage* generally fell into three camps: those who thought the production was a standout, which was the majority view; those who considered it a noble failure; and those who decided the production had let down a classic play or that the material itself had failed the production. Anne herself tended to receive compliments if not outright praise, with two notable exceptions. The varying opinions of more than a dozen critics, while two-to-one in favor of the play, allowed the perception that *Mother Courage* had received mixed reviews.

An "austere but honorable production," wrote Walter Kerr for the *New York Herald-Tribune.* At the *New York Times,* Howard Taubman called the show "a different theater experience" and added, "In its humor, irony and truth, it is a work to welcome and cherish." The *Wall Street Journal* labeled it excellent but questioned whether there was anything on the stage to stir or inform and concluded that there was not enough at the Martin Beck to attract a large audience. The *New York Daily News* had no such doubts, calling it "a visually stunning and imaginatively devised production." The *New York Morning Telegraph* critic admitted that he loathed Brecht but still credited Anne with an exciting performance. The Associated Press critic faulted Brecht for a "one-note wail" and said "a highly skilled, stubbornly remote production" had fallen short. "Anne Bancroft gives another notable display of her emotional dexterity as the central character of this sardonic, rasping, bitter tract against war," the wire service critic wrote, echoing the overall view of most critics.

Most, but not all. For the first time in her Broadway career, Anne received an unqualified pan. Robert Brustein of the *New Republic* declared her disastrously miscast. "Anne Bancroft should probably be commended for undertaking a character beyond her years, training, and talents—but like the bravery of Courage's son, Eilif, this often strikes me as mere foolhardiness," Brustein wrote. Her makeup was unconvincing, he continued, and her performance "has the sound and gestures of a tired Jewish housewife, with no more cutting edge than Molly Goldberg." He also called Jerome Robbins not enough of a director for a play of such scope and contended that the production was intellectually spineless and too often "static and labored, and the ironies rarely register." Still, Brustein commended the production for having virtues that made it a genuinely important theatrical occasion.

Harold Clurman of the *Nation* was only slightly less cutting in his critique of the star's performance. "Anne Bancroft, who plays Mother Courage, is a charming actress with a heart-warming smile and a generous honesty of spirit," he wrote. "She is too contemporary, too locally urban, too young, too soft to do much more than indicate the part." He took issue with several aspects of the staging, arguing that Robbins had not been original enough and should have stayed with Brecht's staging or followed his own concept. Like other criticism, including a review in *Time* that described Anne's performance as "more often the folksy Bronx matriarch than the flinty earth mother," Clurman's review lauded the play and called the production impressive while urging readers to see it in spite of any shortcomings.

What were theatergoers to make of these divergent opinions? There were certainly raves to promote in advertising. Word of mouth would be harder to finesse. Preview audiences had been divided: some were enthralled and others did not like the play's form. Over time ticket sales would rise or fall depending on whether people told their friends that they had enjoyed a dynamic, intelligent show or felt like they had sat through a lecture.

Presenting the play as an Anne Bancroft vehicle could help. One bit of promotion came on her Sunday night off when she appeared again on CBS television's *What's My Line?* A major boost could come in California the next night, April 8, with the Academy Awards ceremony at the Santa Monica Civic Auditorium. Anne was up for the best actress award, one of five nominations for *The Miracle Worker*. Rather than jet back and forth between the coasts and miss a performance, she remained with the play. Besides, she did not think she would win. Her competition was formidable: Katharine Hepburn in *Long Day's Journey into Night*; Geraldine Page in *Sweet Bird of Youth*; Lee Remick in *Days of Wine and Roses*; and Bette Davis in *What Ever Happened to Baby Jane?*

That night, the previous year's Oscar winner for best actor, Maximilian Schell, opened the envelope and announced Anne's name to exuberant applause from the industry audience. In her absence, Joan Crawford came to the podium and accepted the Oscar with a personal message from the winner. "Miss Bancroft said, 'Here's my little speech, dear Joan: There are three reasons why I deserve this award: Arthur Penn, Bill Gibson, Fred Coe.' Thank you." (Not one to avoid publicity, Crawford later presented the award to Anne at the Martin Beck Theatre at the end of a performance.) It turned out to be a middling night for *The Miracle Worker*. Penn and Gibson did not win, and their film had not been a best picture nominee. Yet there was another bright spot: Patty Duke won for supporting actress and became the youngest performer at that time to receive the award.

Anne had joined Mel Brooks and her press agent, Lillian Picard, at her Greenwich Village brownstone just before the best actress category came up. She was not the favorite to win—Bette Davis was among those who thought she was nearly certain to win her third Oscar—and the room was quiet until Schell announced Anne's name. "I cried and I laughed and I shouted and the doorbell started to ring and the wire services were on the phone," she remembered. "There were photographers parked across the street. I never thought I'd win. I didn't think I had a chance." A picture of Anne on the phone, in tears of joy, ran in newspapers the next day. Millie Italiano's award room was getting another trophy.

In a more reflective and quiet mood, Anne pondered how she thought the Oscar would change her. "I'll be much easier to live with," she said. "It's very important to a certain part of you. What is it going to do to me professionally? Ask me that in a couple of years. All I know is that as soon as you conquer one thing—only then do you begin to see what's next in life." The validation from her peers obviously pleased her. The only thing lacking in her career was an unqualified hit with movie audiences. Typically, she focused on what she could do next.

Each night the eighteen cast members of *Mother Courage* introduced themselves at the beginning of the play, another way Brecht sought to divorce the audience from any sense of reality. When she declared "I am Anne Bancroft" during the first performance after her Oscar victory, the audience rose to its feet and gave her an ovation that one observer said lasted four minutes. "In that salute," the Broadway columnist Earl Wilson wrote, "Anne Bancroft ascended the heights and took her place alongside Ethel Barrymore, Gertrude Lawrence, Helen Hayes, and the other immortal ladies of Broadway."

If the box office was the measure, however, Anne was experiencing her first Broadway stumble. Sales had been faltering and the producers hoped, naturally, that the Academy Award would reenergize interest in the show. To help entice more people to the Martin Beck Theatre to see the Academy Award winner at work, Anne as well as Cheryl Crawford and Jerome Robbins agreed to take only half of their weekly share of the box office if that money was put toward publicity. A newspaper ad for the play carried her picture—as her beautiful self, not as Mother Courage—alongside the image of an Oscar with a bold headline proclaiming, "Annie Won It, and We've Got Her!"

Ticket sales were better for a time, but during the third week in April they plummeted. Window sales were falling off, and half of the balcony seats were empty. Advised by a business associate to close the play, the producers held out for a little more than a week before announcing on May 1 that the Saturday, May 11, performance of *Mother Courage,* its fifty-second, would be its last. The *Chicago Tribune* concluded, "Oscar doesn't mean much at the theater box office."

The negative reviews for the show had made Anne angry, a reaction that surprised her because she thought she was beyond caring that much about what critics thought. Yet she had her own reservations about the show and did not necessarily remember it fondly. Years later, when the actor Austin Pendleton told Anne that he had been moved by *Mother Courage,* she told him, "Well, you were just reacting to the power of the material."

"That material is not easy to do," Pendleton said as he looked back on the production. "It's hard stuff. It doesn't yield its secrets easily." He had seen Anne's previous Broadway work and admired her talent. *Mother Courage* did not change his assessment. "I couldn't get out of my seat at the end," he said. "That's not a disaster. That's the mark of a powerful show. But it was regarded by the people involved in it as a disaster, including by Annie, I think." In some ways, the appeal she had developed in her previous shows worked against her. "People came to see Anne Bancroft, and it wasn't the kind of play associated with her," Pendleton said. "And the idea on Broadway of a three-hour ironic tragedy . . . it played by different rules than a Broadway play would in those days, even today."

Whatever disappointment she felt over the public apathy that doomed the show, Anne contended publicly that the effort had been worth it. "I didn't expect *Courage* to be a popular play, but I wanted to do it anyway," she told a reporter not long after it had closed. "I wanted to go into it the way some Hollywood people want to go into a marriage. They know it won't last, but they want the experience anyway. I feel the function of an actress is to enrich as well as to entertain her audience. Actually, I don't see how you can do one without the other." Their gracious tone aside, her words overlooked the fact that her rejuvenated career had suffered its first setback. Coming on the heels of the Academy Award, it was a reminder of the tenuous nature of stardom and how wrestling with a challenging role was often its only reward.

The relatively short run of *Mother Courage* left Anne searching for work sooner than she had expected. Not only was she not earning money as she had planned that spring and summer, the play had brought her less than $30,000 after several months devoted to meetings, research, rehearsals, previews, publicity, and performances. She had earned more than three times the money for her last film in about half the time. "I never worry about what I will do for an encore," she said at the time. It was not bravado. Plenty of projects were coming her way with little effort on her part.

Earlier in the year Anne had been sought to play the psychiatric nurse in *Captain Newman, M.D.*, Gregory Peck's first film since his Oscar-winning performance in *To Kill a Mockingbird;* the part eventually went to Angie Dickinson. Ray Stark suggested that the director John Huston consider Anne for the role of the seductive hotel owner in his adaptation of Tennessee Williams's play *The Night of the Iguana*, including her along with Lana Turner, Sophia Loren, and Geraldine Page for a part ultimately played by Ava Gardner. Anne's name came up again in connection with another Huston project, a film based on the novel *The Lonely Passion of Judith Hearne*. (A film of the novel did not appear until 1987.)

Would her next role come in a film or on the stage? Television was a possibility—Anne cared more about the role than the medium—but most of the anthology programs were off the air by the fall television season in 1963. It seemed unlikely that a star of her newfound prominence would be interested in undertaking a weekly series or even a guest role on an established show. Besides, a standard thirty-episode commitment was hardly what she wanted in her career. (The made-for-television movie was just emerging as an entertainment hybrid.) Whether on film or on television, Anne had not been before a camera in a dramatic part in nearly two years. She was finding that the caliber of female roles was no higher than it had been for the last few years.

One project intrigued her with its promise of a multidimensional character. Columbia Pictures was backing a film that would reunite the producer and director of the art-house hit *Room at the Top* (1959), which followed a social climber and the people he uses along the way. Its realism and treatment of social and sexual mores drew controversy and audiences as well as several Oscar nominations, including a best actress award for Simone Signoret. *Room at the Top* was a leading example of the "new wave" of social realism in British films, inspired in part by the French and Italian films of the late 1950s. They were far removed from what Hollywood was selling and American audiences were buying at the end of the decade:

epics (*Ben-Hur*), comedies (*Some Like It Hot, Pillow Talk*), thrillers (*North by Northwest*), and Westerns (*Rio Bravo*).

For their second picture together, the director Jack Clayton and producer James Woolf were preparing an adaptation of the best-selling novel *The Pumpkin Eater*. Published in Britain in 1962 and in the United States the following year, Penelope Mortimer's story is told by a disturbed woman dealing with a crisis in her marriage. If *Room at the Top, This Sporting Life,* and other British films of the period supported the "angry young man" movement in British arts, *The Pumpkin Eater* would explore the disappointments in a woman's life as seen by a woman. Not that a woman would be hired to adapt Mortimer's novel; the task went to Harold Pinter, playwright, screenwriter, and future Nobel laureate.

Anne read the novel at her agent's suggestion and found the emotional and artistic connections she needed. "I felt deeply about the woman," she said. "I did not think of her as English—only that she was a universal character. And I thought the book had an immediate, dramatic quality which made one see its film possibilities at once." For her, the story was enriching and enlightening, qualities sorely lacking in most of the scripts she had been reading. Mortimer's unnamed narrator could be the kind of role she had been searching for.

Much as she had for the stage production of *Two for the Seesaw,* Anne set out to win over Jack Clayton. The director had considered Deborah Kerr and Ingrid Bergman for the leading character in *The Pumpkin Eater,* named Jo in Pinter's screenplay. Both Kerr and Bergman had box-office appeal that Anne could not yet match. Kerr was a more obvious choice, given that the story is told by a British woman and would retain its London setting—and that Kerr had starred in Clayton's previous film, *The Innocents,* a generally well-received psychological thriller. A disadvantage for the veteran actresses may have been their ages. The character Jo would be portrayed from her late twenties to around forty, a feat certainly easy to achieve for Anne, then thirty-two. Kerr was ten years older than Anne, and Bergman was older by sixteen years.

Yet Clayton's initial reaction to the possibility of Anne Bancroft as Jo was lukewarm at best. For one thing, he paused at the idea of casting an Italian American from New York in the role of a middle-class Briton. If he had seen *The Miracle Worker,* he did not remember what Anne looked like. Still, Clayton advised her agent that she was being considered for the part, along with a dozen or so others. That was not what Anne wanted to hear.

She sent a cable to Clayton telling him that she was the only one who could play the role, then sent stills from *The Miracle Worker* as requested. They did not help her cause—Clayton could not make out her features behind the dark glasses, the bruises, and the splattered mud—and he asked for more.

Unwilling to risk rejection by transatlantic mail, Anne decided to send herself across the ocean instead. She booked a flight to London to plead her case in person. "The first second I set eyes on her I agreed with her," Clayton said later. "No one but Anne could play this role. You'd never know it from *The Miracle Worker,* but she's beautiful." Even with two Tony Awards and an Oscar, Anne still had to sell herself aggressively. The experience reinforced her belief that having determination in life meant using it.

Clayton laid out one demand: Anne had to come to London a month before the thirteen-week shoot began at Shepperton Studios to learn a British accent. The caveat surprised her, but it did not deter her—the Actors Studio sessions, which nurtured her studious approach to developing a character, probably made this homework assignment easier to accept. Anne left for London in August 1963 and began her lessons. In time she was practicing her accent on shopping trips. "I fooled every shopkeeper in town," she said, "until we got around to the bill." At that point she had to spread her cash on the countertop and ask for help in deciphering the value of pennies, shillings, crowns, pounds, and guineas. "I can speak with the accent," she said, "but I'll never understand British money."

Anne had more to study than the British accent. Several psychiatrists had read Harold Pinter's script at the behest of Clayton, and the director gave Anne their analyses of Jo and her problems. The doctors' combined report opened her eyes to what the "official" view of Jo would be: a neurotic hysteric who cannot combine her romantic fantasies with reality. The result, they concluded, was reactive depression, a type of clinical depression affecting those who have undergone stressful life events. Anne had no training in psychiatry, using instinct and life experience in addition to the script to get inside the head of a character. Her years in analysis, however, would have given her respect for and some insight into such a diagnosis.

In Pinter's screenplay, a middle-aged Jo wanders about her home before her life unfolds with a flashback to a happier time when she is playing with her brood of children and first meeting Jake, the screenwriter who is to become her third husband. Amid a narrative that moves around in time, Jo slips into depression as she realizes Jake is unfaithful and not interested in having a child with her. She has an abortion and undergoes sterilization only to find that Jake's latest mistress is pregnant. Her own affair with her former husband drives Jake from her. By the film's end Jo and Jake and their children are together once more at a country house, the adults seeming to have accepted each other's flaws. A Clayton scholar, Neil Sinyard, sees the final scene as an expression of the film's theme, which he describes as "the shared moments and habits and memories that bind a married couple together even in their times of tension, betrayal, and breakdown."

Jo's violent reaction to her husband's infidelity—a forty-five-second brawl in their living room that took nearly three days to film—brought comparisons to Anne's nightly battle with Patty Duke in *The Miracle Worker*. She told reporters that she had enjoyed being the aggressor; her costar Peter Finch admitted being cowed during the filming. "I had to remind myself she was only acting," he said. "Thank heaven she was only acting. I thought she was going to kill me." In stark contrast was an earlier scene in which Jo, contemplating her personal failings and the emerging fissures in her latest marriage, quietly but tearfully breaks down in the food market at Harrod's department store. At that point in her career, Anne had not had such a showcase for her talents or a film with such layers and depth. Moreover, *The Pumpkin Eater* was unusual for the time in examining such issues almost solely from a woman's perspective.

With marriage the subject of *The Pumpkin Eater*, Anne's status as a woman pondering her second marriage came up in interviews. "I thought, 'This could happen to me,'" she told a reporter when discussing Jo's problems. "There's something depressingly universal about the woman in the film. She's got everything and she's got nothing." She recalled her marriage to Martin May, saying that they were very much in love—"or so I thought"—and that May's contention that she cared more about her career than their marriage had shocked her. "I thought we were happily married," she said, a statement completely at odds with her previous reflections.

When it reached theaters in November 1964, *The Pumpkin Eater* received mixed reviews even as nearly every critic singled out Anne for a brilliant performance. "Explosive and superlative in content and cast," said the *Los Angeles Herald-Examiner*, which predicted another Oscar nomination for its female star. *Time* said the film had stretched her talents "to astonishing breadth," and *Cue* called her acting "magnificent." Those less entranced tended to side with the *New Republic,* which called Anne's role "principally one of dreary noble suffering" and faulted the basis of the film as "a plush-lined ladies' novel." The *Hollywood Reporter* offered a backhanded compliment by calling the film an "art-house soap opera." In Clayton's country, the film was considered by many a masterpiece of British cinema, whereas others thought Clayton had followed "new wave" directors instead of establishing his own style. As Neil Sinyard would later write, "The battle lines over the film were drawn: artistry or artiness, profound or pretentious." For Anne, it was a battle to savor, a far cry from whether *The Girl in Black Stockings* was worth seeing.

Hobbled at the American box office in part by its status as an art film, *The Pumpkin Eater* earned a little more than $1 million in rentals but still drew a number of awards. The Academy of Motion Picture Arts and Sciences again nominated Anne as best actress, the film's only Oscar nomination. (Julie Andrews as Mary Poppins won that year.) As one might expect, *The Pumpkin Eater* fared better outside the United States. It was nominated for seven awards by the British Academy of Film and Television Arts (BAFTA), including best picture, and won awards for Anne (her second BAFTA honor after an award for *The Miracle Worker*), Harold Pinter, the cinematographer Oswald Morris, and costumes. The Golden Globes, presented by Hollywood's foreign press, named Anne best actress in a drama, and she was the best actress winner at the Cannes Film Festival, along with Barbara Barrie for the drama *One Potato, Two Potato.*

The Pumpkin Eater provided Anne one of her best roles, even if it would be seldom screened in the years ahead. Jack Clayton directed just four more feature films in his eclectic career, including the Robert Redford version of *The Great Gatsby* (1974). He declined the opportunity to direct Anne in a film adaptation of the William Gibson play *Golda,* telling her in 1978 that he did not see how he could do justice to the material. When the National Gallery of Art in Washington, D.C., sought her reflections on Clayton for a retrospective of his work in 1995, the year of his death, Anne recalled him fondly. "Jack Clayton's films are marked by a deeply felt personal vision. He never copied anyone, and never repeated himself as so many film makers are inclined to," she wrote. "Unlike most commercial Hollywood filmmakers, he didn't tell stories about heroes. Instead he looked for the heroism in unconventional people—a tougher, but higher aspiration." In Clayton, a filmmaker who selected projects carefully and looked for those with personal meaning, Anne had found a rare artistic soul mate.

Following the *Pumpkin Eater* shoot, Anne returned home in late 1963. Her visit to London had been a professional success, but there had been low moments, too. One night in October she arrived at her apartment in London's Mayfair district to discover it had been burglarized. Missing were furs and jewelry worth about $4,200 (about $33,000 in today's money). The next month, as Britons stood with Americans in grief over the assassination of President John F. Kennedy, Anne joined the actors Gary Merrill and Eli Wallach for a British television tribute in which they read excerpts from speeches of the late president. On a happier note, she had been able to visit her friend Patricia Neal, who had been working in Britain on a film of her own.

Awaiting Anne in New York was Mel Brooks. Ever since they had begun dating, reporters had been asking if her views on getting married again had changed. In the spring of 1963 she had told Sidney Fields of the *New York Mirror* that neither she nor Brooks was in a hurry. "When two people have both had bad marriages, they're inclined to move slowly," she said. Pressed on the matter, she told Fields: "Look, I've got love. That's enough, isn't it? What else would you want out of life?"

As if to answer her own question, that fall Anne was telling the press that she hoped to marry Brooks soon. She was quick to point out that marriage would not mean an end to her acting career. "I don't see how I can stop," she said. "I have a lot of energy and I must create. Perhaps when I have babies they will take up my energy, and if I have to stop for the sake of my family then of course I will." Whatever its effect on her as an actress, she was now talking about marriage as a matter of when, rather than if.

7

Something More Than Money

When a film or theater project failed to ripen, the loss could be measured in time as well as money. The producer and director Fred Zinnemann devoted nearly two years to his effort to adapt James Michener's sprawling novel *Hawaii* for the screen. In late 1963 he had sounded out Anne for the leading role of a female missionary who accompanies her husband to the Pacific islands in the nineteenth century. The director of *From Here to Eternity, High Noon, The Nun's Story,* and *The Sundowners*—all Oscar nominees for best picture—could not solve the script problems he encountered. *Hawaii* would eventually be filmed, but with a different director, George Roy Hill, and a different star, Julie Andrews.

As the arc of her career continued to rise in the mid-1960s, Anne would have unrealized projects of her own. Prominent among them was the Actors Studio Theatre production of Anton Chekhov's play *The Three Sisters.* Directing the play had been a preoccupation of the Studio's guru, Lee Strasberg. After the Studio established its own theater in 1962, a Strasberg-guided production of *The Three Sisters* seemed inevitable. Indeed, the following year the project was under way as the theater's sixth production, and Anne told the press that she would follow up *The Pumpkin Eater* with the Chekhov play.

Strasberg had a dream cast in mind. Geraldine Page would play Olga, the oldest of the sisters, Kim Stanley would play Masha, and Susan Strasberg would appear as Irina. The role of Natasha, the sister-in-law who transforms herself from an insecure figure of pity into a vicious schemer, would go to Anne. It did not turn out that way. Page told David Garfield, the Studio's historian, that Anne wanted to play Masha or not appear at all. (The role of Masha had long been the favorite of actresses interested in

Chekhov's work.) When the production began its brief run in June 1964, the cast featured Page and Stanley along with Barbara Baxley as Masha and Shirley Knight as Irina.

Punctuating a relatively quiet winter and spring for Anne—she had not married Mel Brooks as she had hoped—was the annual Academy Awards broadcast. As last year's best actress winner, she had agreed to hand out the best actor award. There was another reason for Anne and Mel Brooks to go together to the ceremonies in Santa Monica on April 13, 1964. He had conceived and written the script for one of the animated short subjects up for an award, *The Critic*. Brooks had also provided the voice for the humorous take on how a member of the audience reacts to an abstract movie. It won, too, but the golden statuette went to the film's producer and director. At the end of the night there was still just one Oscar between them.

If Anne had longed to appear glamorous to the public, she was just that when she walked across the stage of the Santa Monica Civic Auditorium to the tune of "I'll Take Manhattan." Her hair in a bouffant updo, she wore a white gown with evening gloves and dangling earrings. Her sparkling smile grew wide with delight when she announced the winner was Sidney Poitier for *Lilies of the Field*. The first African American actor to receive an Oscar for a leading role, Poitier bounded to the stage and accepted the statuette from Anne as they exchanged a brief hug. Given the time—the civil rights movement was in full bloom—it was a historic moment.

That summer the New York columnist Dorothy Kilgallen linked Anne to another Broadway musical in the making. *Do I Hear a Waltz?* reached the stage the following year, but not with Anne. Drawn from an Arthur Laurents story best remembered as the basis for the Katharine Hepburn movie *Summertime*, the musical boasted a score by Richard Rodgers and lyrics by Stephen Sondheim. It would run for 220 performances.

The second half of 1964 was far more eventful for Anne. In early August, she and Mel Brooks took out a marriage license in New York. Two days later, on August 5, they appeared at City Hall and were married by a deputy city clerk with a stranger serving as a witness. "Nobody even recognized me," Anne said. She had used her real name, which might account for why the news of her marriage did not reach the press for nearly a week. A sign of her standing with the public compared to her new husband's was the headline for a short item inside the *New York Times*: "Comedian Weds Anne Bancroft." Their wedding dinner that night was spaghetti for two that Anne cooked at her place.

In the years ahead the public would think of Anne Bancroft and Mel Brooks as one of Hollywood's oddest couples—the serious Italian American actress and the zany Jewish American comedian. In fact, they had quite a bit in common from the very beginning. Both were New Yorkers who loved the city, and both had grown up with a desire to perform. Both had worked in live television, were devoted movie fans, had close ties to the theater, and had undergone psychoanalysis. Anne wanted a strong man in her life, and Brooks had a take-charge personality. He was thirty-eight and she thirty-three at the time of the second marriage for each; they knew well the strains that their profession could place on their relationship. A sense of humor bound them together, too.

As an actress, Anne was far better known to the public than Brooks. Writers in the field of entertainment rarely received the audience's attention. That would change for Brooks, but at the time of their wedding he was working hard just to keep working. He had followed his 2,000-year-old man comedy album with the book for *All American,* a musical comedy starring Ray Bolger and directed by Joshua Logan that had run briefly on Broadway in 1962. Brooks would be turning more of his attention to movies and television as he and Anne began their life together.

"He was sort of a musical comedy schnook," the playwright William Gibson remembered. "He was also a charming guy, very funny, but he said to me, 'When I grow up I want to be a writer like you.' That was his attitude." Most people did not consider comedy to be serious business. Often lost amid the nonstop wisecracks was Brooks's intellect, another one of his qualities that Anne found attractive. That he adored her was never in doubt.

A break in their honeymoon came all too soon. Just two weeks after her marriage, Anne traveled to Los Angeles to appear in a new one-act play written for television by William Inge. She must have thought it was exceptional to warrant leaving her new husband for what would be a weeklong stay in Los Angeles.

A Pulitzer Prize winner for the drama *Picnic,* Inge had followed that success with other stage hits of the 1950s, notably *Bus Stop* and *The Dark at the Top of the Stairs.* Small-town America remained a favorite setting of the Kansas-born playwright, and he tried to develop a television series featuring people who lived in such places. CBS initially sponsored Inge's efforts but ultimately did not care for a show that lacked high drama.

Television had found plenty of success with low comedy, in the guise of *Petticoat Junction* and *The Beverly Hillbillies,* and with action-packed series like *Bonanza* and *Gunsmoke.* "Doesn't TV realize," Inge asked, "that character stories are the one place left for TV drama to turn?" After parting ways with CBS, Inge went to NBC with an hour-long drama set in a small midwestern town. The network agreed to air the program on the last remaining anthology series, *Bob Hope Presents the Chrysler Theatre.*

"Out on the Outskirts of Town" explores the relationship between a former debutante and her new husband, a onetime baseball star who is losing his mind over real and imagined personal failures. Their clash of personalities—a beautiful, cultured woman versus an unrefined ballplayer—help fuel the drama. This fictional marriage also descends into violence, an aspect of the role that drew Anne to the project. "It's marvelous," she said of the Inge script. "A woman who can love a man who beats her up. I can understand such women." She also wanted to work with its director, Frank Corsaro, who had brought the script to her in the first place.

Corsaro's background matched the pedigrees of the script and its star. His eight Broadway productions at that point in his long career included *A Hatful of Rain* and *The Night of the Iguana.* They had wanted to work together again in spite of the falling-out with Norman Mailer during the Actors Studio effort a few years earlier to bring his Hollywood novel *The Deer Park* to the stage. "Out on the Outskirts of Town" would be their only fully realized collaboration, and the experience that left Corsaro wishing there had been more.

"She was very brilliant and vivid and actually the kind of actress one sees more in foreign films," Corsaro recalled. "Her Italian background was very perceptible in her flashy temperament. She always made everything she did vivid." She brought no temperamental attitude to her work, he added, and their brief time together was nothing but positive and made Anne a favorite of his. "She was simply capable of enjoying all the elements that go around acting—improvising, that kind of thing."

The company had just six days to film "Out on the Outskirts of Town." A tight schedule was typical in a television production, and every minute counted on the set at Universal Studios. At one point the set manager warned Corsaro that their work was nearly over for the day. He was left with five minutes to accomplish a complicated scene. As Corsaro remembered the moment, he called Anne over as if to give her some direction.

"Would you do me a favor—and the show?" he asked in a conspiratorial tone.

"What?"

"In about three minutes you'll have some kind of indisposition—you know, the equivalent of a fainting spell. I don't want to go on with the scene now. I'd rather take it up fresh tomorrow."

Anne replied, "Oh, great—I'd be happy to do that."

On cue, Anne had her spell. "I think the man watching could smell something, but couldn't pin it down." Corsaro remembered. "She played it absolutely straight. She just sat there, worn out, and the thing was accomplished the next day. She had a very impish sense of humor."

Inge's play called for Anne and her costar Jack Warden to slug it out—and they went at it with too much gusto. Amid their brawl Anne fell and hit her head on the floor with such force that she was briefly unconscious. When she came to, she asked, "Did you get it?" Unfortunately, all that realism was for naught—the camera had missed the shot.

The cast included another Actors Studio alumna, Lane Bradbury, who had appeared in *The Night of the Iguana* production directed by Corsaro. She had marveled at Anne's devotion to working through her exercises under Lee Strasberg's gaze and was more than a little in awe of her. "I was excited to be doing that," Bradbury said of the Inge play, "and knowing that I would be working with somebody where I would have a real person to work with and against—not against in a bad sense."

Anne did not disappoint Bradbury, whose respect for her colleague was a testament to just how much Anne had become a force in the acting community. "Annie was out there as the character and as a foil or a lover or whatever," Bradbury said. "She was there, available, to be worked with. I can't ask any more from an actress or an actor than that. And I know that I'm going to be the best that I can be because I'm working with somebody that's the best that they can be."

During the television production Anne stayed in touch with her husband. A reporter was on hand when Mel reached her by phone during a noontime breakfast and interview at the Universal commissary. "She blushed and sparkled above her poached eggs and lapsed into pink and fluffy honeymoon thoughts," Cecil Smith of the *Los Angeles Times* noted. Anne apologized for the interruption but admitted, "I really never thought I would be like this again."

"Out on the Outskirts of Town" aired on November 6. Those familiar with how she had appeared in *The Miracle Worker* and *Mother Courage* may have been astonished that it was the same woman. Her wardrobe included a flimsy nightgown and a luscious mink coat, which gave Anne a glamorous look she had not enjoyed since her earlier years in Hollywood. Though she had looked beautiful in *The Pumpkin Eater,* the film was still weeks away from release.

Some reviews the next day deemed her role as written to be superficial, but Anne once again drew plaudits. "An exciting theatrical experience," wrote the *New York Daily News.* "She squeezed out every last drop of drama." Television's top critic, Jack Gould of the *New York Times,* thought William Inge had failed in his effort. "Anne Bancroft did not disappoint the viewer but Mr. Inge did," Gould wrote. He labeled it a "pedestrian melodrama," trite and strewn with cliché-ridden dialogue. Calling the program an "off night" for its producer, Gould said that he hoped Anne would return to television "in a vehicle worthy of her time."

As it turned out, NBC had scheduled "Out on the Outskirts of Town" to air just a week after Anne's other television appearance that fall. *Perry Como's Music Hall* was not the kind of television show Gould had in mind. The series' fall premiere aired live from Detroit on October 29 and featured Anne as well as the actor Stanley Holloway and the pianist Victor Borge. Usually elegant while appearing relaxed, Como came onstage with a crooked tie. Holloway flubbed his opening song cue, and the show ran short when a musical number had to be cut to prevent it from running long. "Nobody seemed to be trying too hard," the *Boston Globe's* critic Percy Shain wrote, "except maybe actress Anne Bancroft, who was a little out of her element as a gaily bedecked song-and-dance gal, but who gave it the old razzle dazzle effort nevertheless." Such a notice would hardly advance Anne's desire to appear in a Broadway musical.

The end-of-year holidays coincided with another break from work. Except for promoting *The Pumpkin Eater,* Anne had apparently left herself free of any film or theater obligations at least through the early months of 1965. Scripts filled her home and offers were abundant and diverse, and she remained highly selective. She felt lucky if she found one good script a year.

"If I am going to do something in which I will be engaged for more than a year, it has to mean more to me than money," Anne said. "If getting what I want means not appearing regularly, that doesn't worry me. In every other profession you can make your mistakes in private. In acting it has to be right out in public." It was neither arrogance nor inflated ego at work, just experience and a strong sense of herself.

Mel Brooks was busy that February trying to get a writer-director deal at Universal Studios. Like most writers, he understood that directing was a way to protect his script. Making a movie with his wife was on the table as he pursued a contract with Universal, at least according to a newspaper report. Working together would be one way for them to solve the problem presented by careers that often called for long periods of separation. Yet their styles were so different that coming up with a script he could direct and a role she would want would not be easy.

Anne was in a hair salon in New York when she learned that the previous night, February 17, her friend and *Miracle Worker* costar Patricia Neal had suffered the first in a series of strokes while at home in Southern California. She lay in critical condition at the University of California at Los Angeles Medical Center. Just thirty-nine years old, she was three months' pregnant with her fourth child.

Neal had begun work that week on a new film, *7 Women*. She had been in Hollywood since 1949, had won a best actress Oscar for *Hud* (1963), and had recently completed the war epic *In Harm's Way* with John Wayne. Filming on MGM's back lot, *7 Women* would have to shut down or find a new star immediately to protect its $2.1 million budget. The producer, Bernard Smith, contacted Anne the next day and asked her to consider rescuing the film.

While given little time to assess the script about Christian missionaries in 1930s China, Anne agreed in spite of mixed emotions. "I really couldn't say 'no' to accepting the part—for Pat's sake," she said later. "I think she would rather have me replace her than anyone else." It was all arranged rather quickly: Anne would fly to the West Coast that weekend for wardrobe fittings and be ready to join the production at midweek. She would receive $50,000 for the role. It was a bargain for MGM and Smith, who had agreed to pay Neal $125,000. Getting a replacement meant reshooting just two days' worth of scenes in which Neal had appeared.

Awaiting Anne on the *7 Women* set was the crusty, cranky, and brilliant John Ford. The director's best-regarded films were already ingrained in Hollywood history and American popular culture: *Stagecoach, The Grapes of Wrath, How Green Was My Valley, Fort Apache, The Quiet Man, The Searchers,* and several others spanning four decades. A filmmaker since 1917 and the winner of four Oscars, Ford was seventy-one and his skills as well as his career were in their twilight. For years his age had been showing in his health—he was nearly blind in one eye, partially deaf, and an alcoholic prone to benders. His most recent films were throwbacks in style and substance, more suited to decades past than the dawn of the new cinema that heralded the likes of Arthur Penn and Jack Clayton. Anne had never fared particularly well under the industry's older directors. There was no reason to think that she would do better in Ford's enfeebled hands.

The film was not being shot in the sort of stunning locations that had established the visual splendor of Ford pictures like 1949's *She Wore a Yellow Ribbon*. Instead, it used old Asian sets from *The Good Earth* (1937) and *Dragon Seed* (1944) on a soundstage, which made it look more like a cheap television series than a major motion picture. Had Ford cast his film with an eye toward realism—not his forte—he would not have had stock company players such as Mike Mazurki, a Ukrainian Jew, and Woody Strode, an African American, made up with slanted eyes to appear as Chinese warlords. The film had the feel of a Western, though the besieged settlers were missionaries and the rampaging savages bent on rape and murder were Mongolian bandits. Anne would later say that she was the movie's John Wayne. After seeing her dressed in a leather jacket, the *Chicago Tribune* thought she was more like Randolph Scott.

Ford had been offering a mea culpa of sorts with his most recent films, focusing on the kinds of characters who had received shoddy treatment as stereotypes over the course of his long career. *Sergeant Rutledge* (1959) was a Western about the "buffalo soldiers," black cavalry troops who had fought in the nineteenth-century Indian wars. *Cheyenne Autumn* (1964), a retelling of the historical Trail of Tears saga, followed a Native American tribe as it tried to survive under white rule yet retain its dignity. If Ford was making up for decades of marginalizing blacks and Native Americans, he may have seen *7 Women* as an opportunity to present female characters as more than soul mates, helpmates, hellions, or hookers. Breaking through all the years of Asian stereotypes he had put on the screen would have to wait.

Ford was no feminist, however, and his story of a doctor clashing with a missionary had more to say about what it meant to be a Christian—a favorite Ford theme—than what it meant to be a woman. The story takes place at a remote Christian outpost with six women, one of them married and pregnant, and the peasants who work for them and seek their protection. A new doctor arrives, and to everyone's surprise the doctor is a woman—a tough-talking woman who smokes and drinks and has a cynical view of the world. Dr. Cartwright almost immediately challenges the prim and proper mission leader, Agatha Andrews. After the mission is called on to care for cholera victims, the Chinese soldiers protecting the Christians depart and a warlord, Tunga Khan, and his bandits take over. Dr. Cartwright makes a deal with the warlord, promising to give herself to him if she is allowed to deliver her colleague's baby. Later she arranges for the safe passage of the missionaries. Dressed in Chinese clothing for her assignation with Tunga Khan, Dr. Cartwright poisons their wine and offers a final, fatal toast.

The cast was promising enough. Joining Anne were Margaret Leighton as Agatha Andrews and Sue Lyon, Flora Robson, Mildred Dunnock, Betty Field, Anna Lee, and Eddie Albert, who played the lone white male. Neither John Ford nor Bernard Smith had been able to get the stars they really wanted for the missionary doctor (Ingrid Bergman or Jennifer Jones) and the mission leader (Katharine Hepburn or Rosalind Russell).

The production brought in Asian actors for minor roles. One of them was twenty-year-old Irene Tsu, who marveled that an entire village had been constructed inside a building. "The stage was so big," she remembered. "A dozen horses would be charging onto that soundstage. Fifty, sixty, eighty people were there—extras, actors—the whole village, and chickens and ducks and pigs. Everything was there." And there was John Ford, without question the man in charge. "Most people were pretty scared," Tsu said. "He was a real phenomenon—a tyrant, you know, on the set."

Other accounts also suggest a set at turns tense and cordial, the tone depending on Ford's mood. An accordion playing a tune like "Bringing in the Sheaves" or "Red River Valley" signaled his arrival each morning. Ford could be exceedingly polite to some and bullying to others. His longtime practice was to select a member of the cast or crew to belittle during the shoot; this time the role of scapegoat fell to Eddie Albert, the likely victim on the set of a movie with which Ford sought to show an affinity for directing women. "He put him down and made sarcastic remarks to him," Anna Lee told Ford's biographer Joseph McBride. "Eddie stood it very well."

Ford hosted an afternoon tea each day, and Irene Tsu watched in fascination and some horror as he sipped his tea and chewed tobacco at the same time. Mumbling between sipping and spitting, Ford could be difficult for Tsu to understand. "And all of a sudden I heard, 'I'm talking to you!' and he yelled at me," she said. "And I really didn't know what he was saying to me at all. I just kept quiet." She was frightened to the point of tears.

"I felt a hand grab my hand under the table, and it was Anne Bancroft," Tsu said. "And she whispered to me, 'Feel my hand. My hand is sweating.' She was as nervous as me. That was the greatest thing—to have somebody do that to me, that she would be so kind." The moment became their private bond for the rest of their work together. "We would have a little thing going," Tsu said. "She would wink at me sometimes when we would be passing on the set or something."

Ford seldom missed an opportunity to display his power. When he staged a scene featuring the major cast members at a dining table, Betty Field interrupted to ask a question. Ford responded by getting up and going home. The next day, accompanied by the strains of "Red River Valley," he returned and asked his cast and crew, "Are we ready to work this morning?" Seeking to make amends, Field began, "Mr. Ford, about yesterday . . ." With that, Ford got up and went home again. Besides a tongue-lashing from her costars, Field received a warning that she would be replaced if she ever spoke up to Ford again.

Shocking a young actress to get a performance was not beyond the man often hailed as Hollywood's greatest director. One day Ford decided to prepare Irene Tsu for a scene in which her character would be taken from the village by a bandit on horseback. He wanted her to register fear about her abduction.

"Ford comes over and he's got this eye patch over his eye as usual and he's chewing something," Tsu recalled. "And he says, 'Well, that guy there, he's going to grab you and take you away, kill your mother and father, and he's going to fuck you.' I'd never heard anybody talk like that to me. I was really scared, but that was his direction to me. He liked to stir up the fear in people. I guess he got what he wanted—I was terrified."

Anne could read people as well as situations and probably made every effort to stay in Ford's good graces. Asked by a reporter how she liked working with him, she said with a laugh: "He's quite a man. It's always nice to have a man around." Ford probably knew that Bancroft had a temper herself and did not want to set it off. Old and tired, he had only so much fight left in him, especially for a project that he wanted to get over with soon after it had begun. Whether or not he knew it, 7 Women would be his last feature film.

As filming at MGM drew to a close, Anne looked ahead to the prospect of another film with Arthur Penn, *The Chase,* and four different stage productions. First would be *The Devils,* an adaptation of an Aldous Huxley novel. Next would come the French writer Jean Genet's political drama *The Screens* and, surprisingly, a return to *Mother Courage and Her Children* as an off-Broadway production. Finally, she would join Penn for a new play, a thriller being written by Frederick Knott, the author of the stage hit *Dial M for Murder.*

If it sounds like an impossibly busy slate, it turned out to be just that. Penn would film *The Chase* later that year without her; by then Jane Fonda had the leading female role. The Knott play would spend months undergoing revisions and not open on Broadway as *Wait until Dark* for nearly a year; when it did, Lee Remick was the star. Neither *The Screens* nor a *Mother Courage* revival would see a prime New York venue for years. The French play was a particularly ambitious work: it had more than fifty roles and a five-hour running time. Eventually, only *The Devils* remained in her lineup. Such a hodgepodge of projects showed that Anne's competing desires were again at work. She enjoyed making contemporary dramatic films with strong female characters but also felt the pull of the stage, whether it was a suspenseful story set in a Greenwich Village apartment or an intellectually challenging work with a foreign pedigree.

The Devils may have presented Anne the best combination of fresh material, compelling drama, and change of pace. It would certainly be far removed from the clunky Old East melodrama she was finishing at MGM. She signed up for the play in early May and made plans for weeks of rehearsals, then tryouts in Boston in October, and a Broadway opening in mid-November. In the meantime, she had found a movie script worth filming over the summer. Part of it would be shot in Los Angeles, giving her some time on the West Coast with Mel Brooks. He was working on a television series aiming for a fall premiere on NBC, a secret-agent spoof called *Get Smart.*

As John Ford's career in films came to a close, the director Sydney Pollack's was just beginning. He had studied acting in New York with Sanford Meisner, one of the great teachers of his generation who had developed his own views of Stanislavsky techniques. Meisner's definition of good acting was "living truthfully under imaginary circumstances," an approach Anne could cherish. Pollack acted in plays and live television productions in the

1950s, then moved into directing television series. His work won Emmy Awards, including one for himself, and provided the résumé he needed for feature films. By 1965 scripts were coming his way, one of them for what would become *The Slender Thread*.

The idea for a movie about a suicide hotline volunteer dealing with a disturbed caller came from an article in *Life* magazine. The writer, Shana Alexander, had chronicled a suicidal woman's effort to reach out for help as she decided to take an overdose of pills. Alexander's husband, the television writer and producer Stephen Alexander, set about developing a movie based on his wife's article. Not surprisingly, it became a mostly fictionalized version of the *Life* piece. In the film, Inga Dyson, a housewife, calls the crisis clinic in Seattle after she has taken an overdose of sleeping pills. A college psychology student, Alan Newell, must keep her on the phone while authorities try to trace the call. Flashbacks reveal why Inga has fallen into despair.

"It seemed like a big television show, which was one of its faults," Sydney Pollack told the film scholar William R. Taylor. "It didn't seem too ambitious to try the first time out." Handling the adaptation was Stirling Silliphant, who was looking for his own stepping-stone to regular work in feature films after writing scores of television scripts. Unlike John Ford in *7 Women*, those involved with *The Slender Thread* were eager to establish themselves in films.

The role of Inga was a natural for Anne, even though she might have paused at playing another wife in marital and emotional crisis so soon after *The Pumpkin Eater*. The script provided a psychological depth to the character that was unusual in movies. It also placed its female lead in a modern world full of complications at home and in society. Inga's plight could easily be seen in feminist terms: a woman whose life is based on her limited roles as wife and mother is destroyed when those roles are undermined. Absent other identities, she could believe that there was no reason to go on living.

With the film set to begin production that summer, Anne would have only a brief respite following *7 Women*. As much as she bemoaned her absences from home and husband, she needed to work. The new project would pay her $200,000, almost certainly the biggest paycheck of her film career to that point. She also may have realized that the Ford movie could not be allowed to stand for months on end as the most recent example of her talents.

Sharing top credit as Alan Newell and earning the same pay as his costar was Sidney Poitier, their pairing coming just a year after Anne had handed him an Oscar for *Lilies of the Field*. Poitier had been extremely busy ever since—*The Slender Thread* would become the last of his four movies released in 1965. He was a top star in Hollywood and the only black movie star at the time, but his role in *The Slender Thread* never made reference to his color and had no overt connection to race relations. As Stephen Alexander knew, casting Poitier would make a subtle statement. "We felt a Negro explaining the meaningfulness of life would add a drama dimension to the picture," Alexander said. With the civil rights movement in high gear and rioting in the Watts neighborhood of Los Angeles that summer, anything Poitier did on the screen carried a racial dimension.

Poitier himself saw the project as breaking barriers, in this instance the taboo of suicide. "I hope we will deal with other subjects where we have had a dark cloud of ignorance and fear," he told a reporter during filming. "I hope we can go on to explore politics more dimensionally, and race, and the intricacies of relationships between men and women. Of course, it's the artist's job to make this interesting and entertaining."

The events in Shana Alexander's magazine article had taken place in Seattle, and the company filmed half of the movie there. The city had never played such a central role in a film. Sydney Pollack made the most of the fresh location with aerial shots from a helicopter and lots of local color featuring the University of Washington, Golden Gardens Park, the Elliott Bay waterfront, and other landmarks. Location shooting had its benefits and its risks. When Anne waded into the bay from the Golden Gardens beach for a scene, she suddenly found herself struggling to stay above water. The lower half of her wet suit, worn under her wardrobe, had become saturated and was pulling her under. Pollack and other members of the crew had to rush to rescue her.

The woman depicted in the *Life* article, called Nell J. to protect her privacy, agreed to speak with Anne. The actress already had a conception of the character's emotional life, based on the article and the screenplay and on her own experiences, and meeting Nell J. did not change that basic approach. But Anne did learn more about the woman's mind-set. "She is charming, literate, and interesting, but, being aware of her background, I also realized she was terribly intense," Anne said. "She seemed to be very inside herself. She speaks softly. I can use that. I asked her what she was thinking about when she tried to take her life. She came up with things that were so terrible they made my images seem totally unimportant. Then I had to dig within myself for more important images." One could imagine Lee Strasberg nodding with approval.

The nature of the story meant Sidney Poitier and Anne never shared a scene—throughout the movie they speak to one another only on the phone. Nearly all of Poitier's scenes were shot on the crisis clinic set built at the Paramount studios in Los Angeles. Anne was on the other end of the line, speaking to him from her dressing room. "Anne Bancroft was simply fantastic," he would write in his autobiography. While Poitier could use his voice, face, and body to register his thoughts and emotions for the camera, Anne had only her voice. Then again, she had the run of Seattle in the film's flashbacks.

Working in the Pacific Northwest coincided with a bout of the flu for Anne, and it stuck with her throughout the filming of *The Slender Thread*. She returned to New York and took refuge on Fire Island for several weeks to recuperate, rest, and prepare for *The Devils*. Not only did the lack of cars and restricted access to telephones appeal to her, but the island's beach was her favorite in the region. From their house was a view of the bay on one side of the island and a view of the ocean on the other.

"If I stayed home I couldn't get any rest," she told Hedda Hopper before leaving Los Angeles for the East Coast. Work was not out of bounds at the beach, but it would be on her terms. She had enjoyed the comedy writer Lucille Kallen's humorous novel *Outside There, Somewhere!* and sought to have it turned into a play for her. That someone would not be her husband. Not only did Mel Brooks want to write original scripts, but a bored housewife juggling work at home while writing for television was not his kind of character.

In her interview, Hopper broached two subjects that Anne would not have enjoyed discussing. One was the rumor that she was pregnant—not true, she assured Hopper—and the other was that she and Mel were having domestic problems as their first anniversary approached. That one surprised her. "You shouldn't believe everything you read," Anne told Hollywood's legendary gossip columnist. Yet she may have given credence to such whispers by admitting that neither of them was easy for the other to live with.

"I'm a moody person," Anne said. "When I'm in a bad mood anything can make me angry. If I'm in a good mood nothing bothers me. I'm hard to live with and so is Mel hard to live with. But my husband is one of the funniest men who ever lived. Sometimes I laugh at him until tears roll out of my eyes." This would become a theme common to most of the public comments Anne made about her marriage—she and her husband had problems like any other married couple, but he made her laugh like no one else.

Their plan for the rest of the year called for Mel to join her at the beach until rehearsals began for *The Devils* and he was needed back in Los Angeles for his *Get Smart* TV series. Then he would return home to New York on the weekends, Anne believing that long separations were not good for their marriage.

That fall *The Devils* shaped up to be the most intricate, demanding, and involved stage production Anne had yet undertaken. Aldous Huxley's novel *The Devils of Loudun* had been published in 1953, the same year that Arthur Miller's play *The Crucible* also turned to fear over satanic possession and witchcraft trials as metaphors for the anticommunist hysteria of the era. The playwright John Whiting adapted the novel on a commission from the Royal Shakespeare Company, which staged the play in London's West End in 1961. The Arena Stage in Washington, D.C., brought the play across the Atlantic with a 1963 production. The Actors Studio Theatre hoped to present the Broadway debut with Anne in the leading female role. That plan eventually fell through, and the producer Alexander H. Cohen picked up the play for Broadway.

Cohen had been producing shows for twenty-five years and had a taste for popular entertainments as well as highbrow star vehicles. One of his greatest successes had been the previous season's production of *Hamlet* with Richard Burton, which had grossed a record $1.25 million. "What's good will succeed if you've got the seats," Cohen said. "You must equate art with seats." To that end he sought the nearly 1,800-seat Broadway Theatre for his $175,000 production of *The Devils* and predicted that it would break even after ten weeks. To help reach that goal, he raised the top ticket price to $9.40 (at the time a movie ticket cost about a dollar).

Selling tickets meant casting stars in the top two roles. The difficulty of finding two actors of sufficient dramatic skill as well as star power had kept Cohen from bringing *The Devils* to Broadway any sooner. At one point he had Richard Burton on board but no female lead of similar renown. When Dorothy Tutin agreed to repeat her Royal Shakespeare Theatre triumph, Cohen had no male star to put up against her. Hiring Anne solved half of

Cohen's casting problem. The solution to the other half was Jason Robards Jr., by then a veteran of eight Broadway shows, numerous televisions appearances, and a handful of films. He had forged a reputation for drama since the 1950s with *Long Day's Journey into Night, The Disenchanted, Toys in the Attic,* and *After the Fall.* He showed his talent for comedy with *A Thousand Clowns* and had recently finished a film version of that show.

For his director Cohen turned to Michael Cacoyannis, who was forty-three when he began rehearsals for *The Devils.* Born on the Greek island of Cyprus, he had been an actor but turned to writing and directing movies in the 1950s. Cacoyannis was virtually self-taught and established himself as the first internationally known Greek filmmaker. He wrote and directed the drama *Zorba the Greek* with Anthony Quinn and Alan Bates, a huge hit in 1964 with audiences in the United States and elsewhere. His first Broadway effort, Terrence McNally's *And Things That Go Bump in the Night,* opened in April 1965 but closed after two weeks. Nevertheless, Cacoyannis promised to bring cinematic energy and spectacle to Cohen's expensive production.

The Devils returned Anne to the seventeenth century, the same period she had explored as Mother Courage. She would depict the hunchbacked mother superior of a French convent who has found herself lusting for Father Urbain Grandier, a libertine but also a vocal opponent of Cardinal Richelieu's government. Her character, Sister Jeanne, accuses Grandier of bewitching her even though she has never been in his presence. The charges create an opening for the Catholic Church and the French government to rid themselves of a major critic. History had provided the basis of Huxley's novel and Whiting's play. Grandier was indeed put on trial for witchcraft, then burned alive at the stake after refusing to confess while having his legs crushed. His views against celibacy among priests—he put his opposition into practice with local women—provided more historical support for the sex and violence central to the drama.

Joining Anne and Jason Robards for the first day of rehearsals on September 10, 1965, were those assigned to the play's two dozen speaking parts. Another two dozen performers would join the company for other roles. They faced a script divided into fifty-three scenes to be played out on a set featuring ramps, platforms, pillars, stairs, and ladders. "I don't go for the easy," Cacoyannis said as he explained the relationship of the stage set to the drama. "I wanted to have this dimension of man being diminished by space and in certain moments to make man grow in relation to other people or the objects around him. Spatially you have to be able to go from scene to scene without long blackouts, by the creation of areas. This play could not be done without levels." Besides, he liked material that demanded a large canvas.

For Anne's role as the sexually hysterical Sister Jeanne, Cacoyannis offered in part this observation: "The truth is that a nun, within the framework of her life, is practical and direct in her dealings with God." For the cast as a whole, he warned about a common pitfall in playing historical dramas. "It's extremely dangerous to analyze from the outside," he said. "It has to come from within. Don't fall into the trap of two-dimensional evocation of history."

Looking back at the Broadway production, the actor Michael Lombard did not remember any special challenges in spite of its size and scope. "When you have Jason and Anne and a play that's not terribly complicated, it didn't seem to me to be a particularly difficult show to do," he said. "She was a gorgeous person. She had a great sense of humor. She was very warm and friendly—and talented." One scene called on Lombard, playing a monk, to carry Anne up a staircase. "She was sorry to have me do this and was full of apologies," he remembered. "However, she was very slight and I was thirty-one and strong and it was my pleasure." She would remember Lombard when it came time for her to cast a project of her own.

The nun's role was physically as well as emotionally demanding for Anne. Not only did she have to appear as a hunchback, she had to fly into a fury that would appear to be fueled by demons. Whether it was the lingering effect of the summertime flu or simply the draining of her seemingly inexhaustible energy, she missed several performances during tryouts in Boston. *The Devils* sparked high praise from the *Boston Globe* that boded well for the New York opening on November 16, 1965.

Three raves from critics in New York suggested that Cohen and Cacoyannis had achieved their goal. "A stunning play, one of the finest of our age," wrote Howard Taubman of the *New York Times*. After saying that Robards had made Grandier "a piercing figure of fear, remorse and courage," he turned to the female star. "Anne Bancroft's prioress is particularly affecting as she recalls her childhood and its loneliness. A lost tenderness lights up her eyes. In her bursts of hysteria she communicates the hint of hollowness," he wrote. "Is the prioress play-acting or is she whipping herself into a frenzy so that she actually sees the orgiastic visions? One is never sure, and that is dramatically right."

At the *New York Journal-American,* John McClain recommended *The Devils* for its majestic set and magnificent acting even though he found the story itself depressing. The *National Observer* called the production "theater at its best" and said it had filled its huge set with "what can only be described as intimate pageantry." In spite of a few flaws, the Washington-based weekly concluded that it was "too fine a play, too rich and rewarding an experience, for anything less than the loudest of cheers."

Nearly all the other critics gave *The Devils* something far, far less than cheers. They found fault in numerous aspects of the production, including the fact that it was so cinematic in its presentation and pacing, as if the theater itself were being sullied by the unusual sweep Cacoyannis had brought to the Broadway Theatre. Walter Kerr of the *New York Herald-Tribune* led the way when he dismissed it as "a play of massive height and width, and no depth at all." The *New York Daily News's* critic John Chapman said that *The Devils* struck him as "something after the fruity movie formula" devised by the early Hollywood directors D. W. Griffith and Cecil B. DeMille and followed by the more modern filmmakers George Stevens and John Huston. "All one does, in this sure-fire recipe for gulling the masses," Chapman wrote, "is to mix equal quantities of wide-screen, spectacle, religion and sex."

The naysayers tended to criticize Jason Robards as well as Anne for their performances. "Neither seems possessed of God, merely bedeviled by life," wrote *Time.* "Bancroft's hysterical frenzies are technically expert, but they are turned off and on, spigot fashion, as if willed rather than suffered." Overacting was a charge leveled at Anne by more than one critic, a curious complaint given that her character was a hysteric with visions of demonic possession. "A good tasteful director could have improved this performance considerably," the *New Republic* judged. Writing for the *New York World-Telegraph,* Norman Nadel concluded that Anne had been miscast and was not at all convincing in her role.

Pointing out that Broadway was offering an elaborate drama with sex and violence and even frightening moments with two respected stars leading the way did not exactly taint the box office. *The Devils* performed well in its unusually large venue, as Cohen had hoped when he booked the Broadway Theatre. The advance sales were healthy enough for the show to weather even widespread critical caterwauling and continue on track for a run at least through the spring.

In mid-December, as *The Devils* entered its second month, Paramount released *The Slender Thread*. Critics in general were nonplussed with Anne and Sidney Poitier's new film. Many thought it was too much like a television program, a connection they could not help making given Sydney Pollack's and Stirling Silliphant's credits. Few critics were as taken with the acting as Kate Cameron of the *New York Daily News,* who called the drama "a tour de force for Poitier and Bancroft, enabling them to show off their well-grounded histrionic talents." Others found the dialogue too theatrical if not melodramatic. Another consistent strain in the reviews was the feeling that at ninety-eight minutes the movie had been padded for theatrical releases. Pollack's lively camera angles annoyed critics instead of dazzling them, and the pacing of the film seemed more appropriate for the home screen.

In other words, *The Slender Thread* was too much like a television show in some ways and not enough like a television show in others. Looking back, Pollack agreed with those who referred to his "restless camera," saying that a dose of Dramamine might be needed to watch it. In the end, however, the movie had cost just $1.8 million (and brought in about as much) and was an acceptably average piece of entertainment. The following year Pollack directed *This Property Is Condemned* with Robert Redford and Natalie Wood as he established a long career that would include the 1980's hits *Out of Africa* and *Tootsie*. Working with Poitier helped Silliphant get the assignment to write 1967's *In the Heat of the Night,* which won him a screenwriting Oscar.

Far worse for Anne than critical yawns over her new movie was the accident she suffered on the Broadway Theatre stage. On the evening of December 29, she fell off a ladder and injured her back, a turn of events that must have triggered unhappy memories of the horseback accident on *The Last Hunt* a decade earlier. The damage was bad enough to warrant taking her to Lenox Hill Hospital. Zoe Caldwell had been her standby and came from dinner to replace her.

The play's management soon had more reason to worry. With the new year came a transit strike that severely restricted movement in and out of Manhattan. Essential travel did not include an evening at a Broadway show, and many theater companies began playing to empty seats. Transit workers stayed off the job with no agreement in sight, and Anne remained in the hospital for a week. Cancellations and refunds ate away at the sizable advance sales for *The Devils,* some $300,000. When doctors informed Alexander H. Cohen that his star would be hospitalized for at least another ten days, he decided to close the play on January 8, 1966, after its seventy-fifth performance.

Adding insult to the injury Anne nursed into the new year, *7 Women* opened in some markets shortly after *The Devils* closed. MGM knew it had a turkey on its hands and put the film in some theaters in the first few months of 1966 before dumping it in New York that spring on a double bill with a minor crime-caper movie. A dearth of advertising, promotion, and pride from MGM signaled that the public could see two mediocre films for the price of one. Most critics warned audiences that John Ford had lost his touch. "A disaster . . . definitely to be missed," said the *New York Daily News*. A rare rave came from the *Los Angeles Herald-Examiner* ("outstanding performances, gripping suspense"), but more common was the kind of needling *Time* delivered in saying that Ford had apparently believed that "the trick of making an Eastern is to change the road signs and trade his Indians for Mongolian invaders." His career ended with a whimper, another great director who made one film too many. In general, critics treated Anne's presence in *7 Women* as if the whole affair had been beneath her.

Discussing the movie many years later, Bernard Smith was not inclined to acknowledge his own failings as a producer and looked elsewhere for the sources of faults in *7 Women*. Although Anne had come to the rescue after Patricia Neal's stroke, Smith told Ford's biographer Scott Eyman that casting Anne turned out to be a mistake. "We got the wrong girl," he said. The role of the doctor needed an austere woman, he said in retrospect, not a New York Italian. Ford was unhappy with Anne, too, saying later that he could not get her "to expand." He would also list the movie as among his best, a ridiculous assessment that spoke to his anger over its drubbing—"They are all communists, those critics"—and his ornery nature.

Anne had often complained that her earliest Hollywood directors did not give her direction and left her to fend for herself on the soundstage. How Ford articulated what he meant by "expand" probably was not along the lines of the discussions of character motivations she would have had with directors such as Arthur Penn, Jack Clayton, Sydney Pollack, and Michael Cacoyannis. Ford's direction was mostly about physical movement, not internal emotion, which Anne had found so rewarding at the Actors Studio. At the time she was not willing to share any misgivings about *7 Women* with the press. Neither was Ford, who told reporters that he thought Anne was "great" in the role. Everyone knew how to play the publicity game.

The year that had been one of Anne's busiest professionally—two movies and a major play—had ended on a sour note that would continue well into the coming months.

8

And Here's to You, Mrs. Robinson

Anne approached her thirty-fifth birthday, in 1966, with a modest outlook for her life and career. She felt content to pursue just one or two major projects a year, perhaps a play or a film or both, while devoting the rest of her time to family, friends, and other pursuits. She wanted to have children and may have been leaving her calendar open to the time she would need for a baby. In the interim, Anne would make the most of being a generous and loving aunt to her sisters' children.

She could be happy in the kitchen, too, although her interest in cooking was more about pleasing her husband than herself. Mel Brooks enjoyed Chinese food and Anne learned how to cook the dishes he liked. She remained almost painfully thin, food apparently still more of a source of fuel than a treat. Another domestic pursuit was redecorating their Greenwich Village home by selecting paints, fabrics, and antiques and refinishing furniture. Anne also lavished attention on the many tropical plants she had raised from seeds, noting for a visitor that as an Italian she came from a long line of farmers. It did not sound like the life of an award-winning actress who could have filled her days and weeks with one role after another.

A mature viewpoint on life had come to her with age, Anne believed, not that she would be any less committed to the movies or plays or television productions she agreed to join. "I simply found myself working only when the role was exactly what I wanted," she said, "with time and emotion left for other things in life." Existing for footlights and cameras was not what she wanted as middle age neared. At the same time, Mel's career had received enough of a boost from *Get Smart* that he could look ahead to writing a screenplay for a feature film that he hoped to direct. Anne apparently felt no need to match her husband job for job.

Some of the career possibilities for Anne would have excited her fans. Peter O'Toole spoke of wanting Anne to appear with him on the stage in *The Merchant of Venice* and *The Taming of the Shrew*. The Royal Shakespeare Company wanted her to come to London and play Lady Macbeth opposite Paul Scofield, an offer Anne reportedly turned down because it would have meant so much time away from her husband. Although she maintained an interest in appearing in a musical, she had no yearning for Shakespearean drama or comedy. Modern women with modern problems had a greater hold on her interest and understanding.

That Anne did not appear in more films did not escape notice. Bosley Crowther of the *New York Times* wondered in print why audiences did not see more of intelligent screen actresses, naming Anne among a handful of examples that included Geraldine Page, Eva Marie Saint, Joanne Woodward, and Lee Remick. "What in the world is the reason for this peculiar and wasteful restraint?" he asked. Part of the answer, he suggested, may have been in the uneasy relationship between box-office attraction and lush maturity in actresses. Having a life beyond a Hollywood career did not enter into Crowther's musings, perhaps because an accomplished actress in her mid-thirties was not expected to want both—at least not in the reckoning of a sixty-year-old man. Pursuing her career on her terms, she would take on another role when she found something worth her time and energy.

Following her accident at the Broadway Theatre and the closing of *The Devils*, Anne did not work professionally for the first half of 1966. The opportunity to join her favorite collaborators, William Gibson and Arthur Penn, brought her back to the stage—not on Broadway but nearly 150 miles by car north of the Manhattan theater district. Gibson was president of a reorganized regional theater company in Stockbridge, Massachusetts, now called the Berkshire Theatre Festival. The organization was preparing for its inaugural season, and the playwright and director George Tabori was serving as its artistic director. The first production that summer would be Thornton Wilder's Pulitzer Prize–winning comedy, *The Skin of Our Teeth*, directed by Penn, like Gibson a Stockbridge resident. Anne would star as Sabina for a two-week run beginning in late June.

Top pay for the performers in the eighteen-member ensemble was $250 a week. "We were able to get good actors," Penn remembered, "because we were offering four weeks of rehearsal, and they came up there." Among the cast for *The Skin of Our Teeth* was Estelle Parsons, who had been an understudy in *Mother Courage and Her Children* and had had a few more substantial roles in plays before joining the Berkshire troupe. Others included twenty-eight-year-old Frank Langella, who had drawn praise in off-Broadway productions, and twenty-four-year-old Peter Maloney, who was hired as stage manager for the production and as stage manager in the play itself.

As part of his duties as the stage manager, Maloney called Anne to arrange for her to ride by limousine for the nearly three-hour trip to Massachusetts. He would be taking the bus. "She said, 'No, no. I am not going to ride in a limousine up to Stockbridge by myself. You are going to ride with me.' She insisted she would not ride alone in the limousine," Maloney said. "I think, looking back on it, it was probably some expression of insecurity on her part. She wanted to be with somebody who was going to be part of the show and wanted to hear what I had to say about it all. It was just wonderful. She seemed to be more interested in me." One topic of discussion was his recent marriage to a classmate from Syracuse University, the pairing of a Roman Catholic man and a Jewish woman that was similar to Anne and Mel's mixed union. "She wanted to know all about that," he said.

Anne stayed in Lenox, Massachusetts, at Wheatleigh, a Gilded Age estate turned hotel whose grounds had been designed by Frederick Law Olmsted. In contrast, rehearsals for the play were in the second floor of a barn on the Berkshire Theatre property. It was still cool enough in June that Maloney had to rent kerosene heaters to warm up the barn and later the theater. That summer Mel Brooks was a frequent visitor to Wheatleigh as well as Anne's dressing room in the theater basement.

The Skin of Our Teeth had been considered avant-garde when it was first produced on Broadway in 1942. It remained a challenging production a quarter century later: its optimistic view of mankind was set amid ample evidence of the species' failings. Thornton Wilder focused on a twentieth-century New Jersey family, Mr. and Mrs. Antrobus, their two children, and their world-weary maid, Sabina, while touching on biblical themes, mythology, war, and the end of the world. At times the actors address the audience directly, even telling them that some cast members must be replaced because of illness and having the stage manager conduct auditions for their replacements. When the play won a Pulitzer Prize for drama, the *New York Times* referred to Wilder's use of "new and unusual stage techniques."

Under Arthur Penn's direction, unusual techniques were again at work as the cast approached the script from a unique angle. "Arthur was an interesting artist," Peter Maloney recalled. "He had a real commercial instinct, and yet he had a desire to break the commercial rules. He was seldom allowed to, especially in the theater, which is such a labor-intensive area of art. There's not a lot of time for experimentation. People have to learn their lines, hit their marks, and get the play up." As Penn said at the time, four weeks of rehearsals was an attraction to actors—and to himself as a director.

Penn tried a technique he was not allowed to use as a commercial director bringing a play to Broadway. He gathered Anne and the rest of the cast in the Berkshire barn to read the play and break down the text into beats, those actions the actors would fulfill physically but also what they would be thinking and what they would be trying to achieve in their performances. Maloney would note all the beats in the margins of his master script.

"About three days into the rehearsal period, Arthur had me collect all the scripts from all the actors," Maloney said. "And for the next couple of weeks we were not allowed to use Thornton Wilder's lines. We ran improvised scenes, acts, and eventually the whole play, repeatedly, improvising it. It was not just careless improvising or totally free improvising. We had to stay within the limits of the story and within the limits of those objectives we had isolated and pointed out during the first few days of rehearsals." If people got off track, Penn would have Maloney shout out a prompt to bring them back.

Anne gained the revitalization she sought by following Penn's instructions. "It led to a deeper understanding of what was in myself and what I had to bring to the part. We worked it a thousand different ways," she said later. "It led to a broadening of myself so that I realized I had many more choices than I thought I had as an actress." Only then did the cast learn the lines of the play word for word. Maloney, for one, thought the lines came easily after so much thought about what lay behind them. Central to Penn's technique was building the actors' confidence and allowing the cast to make the characters their own while still being faithful to the text.

The Berkshire Theatre Festival production of *The Skin of Our Teeth* at the four-hundred-seat Stockbridge Playhouse drew guarded praise from the *Boston Globe*'s critic Kevin Kelly. He thought the show lacked crackle: it started slowly and did not really find itself until the third and final act.

He laid part of the blame on the design of the theater's stage, a "pseudo-semi-three-quarter arena" that did not accommodate the play. "Illusion, even Wilder's raffish brand of illusion, doesn't fit easily within its dimensions." Kelly said the performances were winning, by and large, however; none was better than Anne in a shrewd interpretation of the Antrobus maid. "When Sabina erupts into fury," he wrote, "Miss Bancroft's dramatic power is mesmerizing."

A compliment of sorts came in a letter of complaint to the theater. The writer noted that she and her mother had attended a performance in which Anne had repeatedly diverged from the script by speaking to the audience and even refused at one point to continue. The writer wanted her money back. Instead of a refund, she received a copy of the play. "We were doing exactly what Wilder wrote," Maloney said. Even though they were performing an abstract work, the cast under Arthur Penn's direction had made the moment seem real.

For Anne, the production of *The Skin of Our Teeth* was significant in two ways. It was her only professional work for a twelve-month period; she would not appear before an audience for another six months after the short run at Stockbridge. Yet it was just the kind of experience she longed for—working with a director and with fellow performers she trusted, all sharing the emotional and intellectual excitement that came with creating. She also was following her goal of throwing herself into a project that suited her while enjoying life away from acting.

For years Anne had been looking for a stage musical to show off her talents as a singer. Though she had been a guest several times on Perry Como's television variety show and had sung briefly in *Mother Courage and Her Children*, headlining a Broadway musical would have challenged her vocal abilities. Producers and directors may have doubted whether she could sing with the strength and consistency required for a show playing up to eight times a week. The team behind *Funny Girl*, as an example, did not think she could handle their score. More than one good singing voice had faltered under the unyielding demands of a starring musical role on Broadway.

As far as other venues for her musical ambitions, a motion picture seemed unlikely. In the 1960s the studios preferred either major stars who could be dubbed, such as Natalie Wood in *West Side Story* and Audrey Hepburn in *My Fair Lady*, or Broadway stars like Julie Andrews who could sing and draw people to the box office. Original musicals were dying out as studios grew averse to risking millions on a script and a score that might not find favor with the public. Musical tastes were changing, too. The tune-filled movies without a Broadway pedigree tended to feature rock music, a trend fueled in the mid-1960s by the Beatles' movies *A Hard Day's Night* and *Help!*

Television presented Anne with her best opportunity for musical comedy. Having enjoyed a six-month break after *The Skin of Our Teeth*, she accepted an offer for a show that was as close to a Broadway production as she was likely to get. In the 1966–67 season ABC was producing an original musical now and then for its hour-long anthology series, *ABC Stage 67*, airing at ten o'clock on Thursdays. Critics had not been impressed with the three musicals presented so far, but the network decided in January to move ahead with another, "I'm Getting Married," and scheduled it for mid-March 1967. The people behind the words and music could not have been more accomplished. The lyrics and the book were written by Betty Comden and Adolph Green, the team who had Broadway hits in the 1940s and 1950s such as *Wonderful Town* as well as the script for the MGM musical *Singin' in the Rain*. The composer was Jule Styne, who had followed *Gypsy* and *Funny Girl* with more Broadway shows and popular tunes.

"I'm Getting Married" was a two-character show about a woman who is engaged but has second thoughts. In a series of fantasy sequences in which she appears as different characters, she ponders her future and ultimately decides that she is marrying the right man at the right time. Comden and Green described the female role as "a young American girl on the brink of a big step in her life—marriage." Five original songs would carry the hour of light entertainment from a pair of writers who believed in happy endings as well as marriage itself. (Both were married, just not to each other.) There would be little in the way of plot, which would make the show more like a character study with music. In keeping with the production's simplicity and to enhance its intimacy, a pair of pianos instead of an orchestra would accompany the characters.

Whether she knew it or not, the show Anne chose for her musical comedy debut bore more than a passing resemblance to a production already playing on Broadway. *I Do! I Do!* had premiered the previous December and was on its way to a 560-performance run at the 46th Street Theatre. When it opened, Mary Martin and Robert Preston—the only two in the cast—played a couple whose marriage is explored across a half-century of highs and lows. The connection did not end there. The lyricist Tom Jones and composer Harvey Schmidt had rejected the producer David Merrick's effort to improve their score with four songs ordered from Comden and Green—songs that ended up in "I'm Getting Married."

Anne felt that "I'm Getting Married" was right for her. "It's not too dramatic and I was very anxious to sing," she said. "It's light and just perfect for television." Having been married not once but twice, she could relate to a character who has doubts about marriage. She thought that the theme was real even if it would be told through elements of fantasy. "It shows all the torture a girl goes through before getting married," she said. "I remember going through it myself, both times."

Her costar was the comedian and comic actor Dick Shawn. He had begun his career as a singer and dancer and had worked in nightclubs and stage musicals. By the time he joined Anne he had appeared on television and in movies, most notably *It's a Mad, Mad, Mad, Mad World,* and had replaced Zero Mostel in the Broadway musical *A Funny Thing Happened on the Way to the Forum.* Their director for the television show was Gerald Freedman, who had been an assistant to Jerome Robbins on *West Side Story* and *Gypsy* and later directed Broadway musicals and wrote the book and lyrics for a show. Several years earlier he had directed Anne in *The Alligators* at the Actors Studio.

With just a week or so to put together the special, the group worked quickly but was not rushed, Freedman remembered. "Betty, Adolph, and Jule were around but not interfering," he said. "Jule had written his score and it was set. Nothing could be more fun and creative than working with Betty and Adolph. They were the best and loved the chemistry of Anne and Dick."

As Freedman recalled, the Broadway musical veterans were excited to be working with Anne in part because of her status as the star of a hit movie. "She was always prepared, had good questions, showed up and did her job. She was a pro," he said. "She was intense, but that was a good thing. She was focused, didn't waste time, ready to work. But she was also fun and playful. She never pulled a star thing. She loved Dick and he made her laugh. She loved to laugh." Although he was known best as a crazy comedian, Shawn impressed Freedman as a good musician and a talented actor.

"They had fun with each other, they had sexual chemistry. Both of them brought that to the work," Freedman said. "They stimulated each other and worked off of each other moment to moment. That was special about them. I don't remember directing them so much as saying that was great, maybe not this, a little more of that. Guiding them, not telling them what to do."

In the eyes of television critics, all the talent behind "I'm Getting Married" went to waste. When the show aired on March 16, 1967, it drew groans in newspaper columns. A common jab was the familiarity of the material, given that it was so similar to a show then on Broadway. Saying that the ABC show "lacked a life of its own," Percy Shain of the *Boston Globe* faulted Comden and Green's script as having "tried too hard to be clever and not hard enough to be human." George Gent at the *New York Times* decided that Jule Styne's music was part of the problem and dismissed the show as "a witless pastiche that committed the unpardonable sin of show business: it was incredibly dull." Anne and Dick Shawn were ideal for their roles, wrote Aleene MacMinn of the *Los Angeles Times*, but ill-served by recognizable material and undistinguished words and music. Her colleague Hal Humphrey would list "I'm Getting Married" among the worst television shows of 1967.

Anne's musical debut and potential rocket to Broadway had landed with a thud. Most telling was that none of the critics had much to say about her singing. Her low, throaty voice—a chest voice, in musical terms—had been "acceptable," according to the *Boston Globe* review, which praised her acting in the different fantasy characters as a tour de force. Like any performer, she needed good material to shine, and the television original had failed to provide it, at least by the standards of television critics.

Her television director, for one, did not believe that a full-blown musical was beyond her talents if she had set that as a goal. "She may have been intimidated. It wasn't a special voice, but she was musical and could sing," Gerald Freedman said in hindsight. In the years ahead Anne would appear in more television specials with music, but singing would never become a focal point of her career. "I think she did musicals just to fill out her repertoire," Freedman said. "She never fancied herself as a singer." Could Anne have carried a Broadway musical? "Her personality would have been enough," he said. "She didn't have a special voice like Ethel Merman or Mary Martin. Voice was not her excellence. She just sold herself. It wasn't her voice that was remarkable. It was Anne Bancroft that was remarkable."

The reviews for "I'm Getting Married" appeared while Anne worked on her next film. She had agreed to star in a comedy based on a novel that had received little attention when it was published in 1963—so little, in fact, that its producer, Lawrence Turman, bought an option on the film rights for $1,000 with a purchase price of $20,000 if a film ended up being produced. His initial investment seemed endangered when he sought studio backing to hire a screenwriter. No one besides Turman was interested in this odd story about an aimless young man who stumbles into an affair with a much older woman.

Guiding *The Graduate* throughout its four-year odyssey from unheralded novel to movie screens was Larry Turman. A former agent, he had already produced four films, most notably a 1964 adaptation of the Gore Vidal play *The Best Man,* starring Henry Fonda, when he read a *New York Times* review of Charles Webb's first novel. In the October 1963 review the *Times* critic thought the sardonic comedy was a fictional failure because of unanswered questions about its hero's psychological motivations and a preposterous climax involving a runaway bride. Yet he commended the book for using dialogue brilliantly and predicted that it would arouse talk and controversy, two qualities that caught Turman's attention. After reading the novel, the producer became determined to see *The Graduate* made into a film.

Turman's initial efforts to find a writer for the screenplay met with a lack of interest. After he saw the Broadway play *Barefoot in the Park,* a Neil Simon comedy that had opened in 1963, he thought the director Mike Nichols would have the insight and style needed for *The Graduate* to make the transition from page to screen. He was already familiar with Nichols's cutting sense of humor, having been a fan of his comedy work with Elaine May in nightclubs and on television. Turman sent the novel to Nichols's agent, then came up with an offer he delivered in person: a fifty-fifty partnership to make a movie from Webb's story.

At the time Nichols had never directed a movie but had established himself as the most-sought-after director in the American theater. He had cowritten and performed in a popular Broadway show in the 1960–61 season, *An Evening with Mike Nichols and Elaine May,* directed by Arthur Penn. Then he directed *Barefoot in the Park* in 1963 and the comedy *Luv* in 1964. Nichols quickly accepted Turman's offer, but it would take many more months for Turman to secure the financing needed to begin a production.

In the meantime, Nichols directed another Neil Simon stage hit, *The*

Odd Couple, in 1965. Still, none of the major studios was interested in a Nichols-Turman production of *The Graduate.* Turman could not attract even the minor studios. Finally, on the promise of a movie made on a low budget, the producer Joseph E. Levine decided to back the venture. He did not care for the book, either, but was willing to bet that Nichols would come up with a hit for his Embassy Pictures, then a distributor of low-grade foreign films. Levine and Embassy could use the respect that would come with the Nichols name.

The initial screenplay, written by the novelist Calder Willingham, failed to capture the tone that Nichols and Turman sought. On Nichols's advice, Turman hired Buck Henry, a comedy writer and Mel Brooks's cocreator of the TV series *Get Smart.* With a new screenplay under way, Nichols accepted the assignment of directing Elizabeth Taylor and Richard Burton in the film version of the Edward Albee play *Who's Afraid of Virginia Woolf.* Released in 1966, it set new standards for adult material in an American film and became one of the year's most popular films. The movie went on to earn thirteen Academy Award nominations. By the time the major roles for *The Graduate* were cast, in early 1967, it was clear that Nichols had passed his film debut with flying colors.

Turman had considered a number of actresses to play the story's older woman, Mrs. Robinson. "It was a very unusual role," he remembered, "and very showy in its own quiet way." Prominent were sexy stars of the 1940s and 1950s: Ava Gardner, Rita Hayworth, Ingrid Bergman, Lana Turner, and Susan Hayward. Younger actresses like Anne Bancroft were on his mind, too, along with her frequent acting rivals Geraldine Page and Patricia Neal. With an eye toward casting against type, Turman sent the novel to Doris Day, but her manager-husband, Martin Melcher, rejected it out of hand. Mike Nichols met briefly with Ava Gardner, who doubted her own ability to play the part. Patricia Neal had not quite recovered from the stroke she had suffered two years earlier.

Anne was the only one to receive an actual offer from Turman and Nichols. She made the most sense from the standpoint of age alone, considering that the sexy stars of the previous generation were in their late forties or early fifties. The others on Turman's list were in their early to mid-forties, about the age of Mrs. Robinson, and did not carry their years that well. Anne, at thirty-five, was the youngest and making her look a few years older would be easy, if she would be willing to take the part in what appeared to be a low-budget sex comedy that sounded almost dirty to some.

"Everybody was telling me it was beneath me and that I shouldn't do it," Anne told the talk show host Charlie Rose in 2000. "I read the script and I loved the script. I thought it was absolutely wonderful. I couldn't wait to do it." When he looked back decades later, Mike Nichols also remembered Anne being warned that it was too risky, especially given her standing as the saintly Annie Sullivan of *The Miracle Worker*. Those who thought that were ignoring her role in *The Pumpkin Eater* and her recent stage work—and inventing a concern about her professional persona that Anne almost certainly did not share. When the writer Sam Kashner recounted the making of *The Graduate* for *Vanity Fair* in 2008, he reported that Mel Brooks persuaded his wife to take the part because he liked the script by his friend Buck Henry.

For the production itself, Anne provided star quality at a good price. She was paid $200,000, the same amount she had received for *The Slender Thread*. "She was a wonderful professional who ended up being very lucky, smart, good casting on our part—and very good for her as well," Turman said. "She's a strong woman, which is one reason she was good for the picture, good for the role. She plays a strong, troubled woman in the story." The budget for *The Graduate* would grow to $3 million, but Anne would remain the biggest name associated with the film, except for the director. She was a safe choice, too. Nichols knew what she was capable of doing with the role, and they had a personal history—besides sharing a friendship with Arthur Penn, the two had dated at one time.

Scores of young actors were considered to play the hapless title character. Several underwent screen tests, Robert Redford and Charles Grodin among them. In the end, Nichols and Turman decided that twenty-one-year-old graduate Benjamin Braddock would be played by a relative unknown, Dustin Hoffman, then twenty-nine. He had been impressive in stage work in New York and brought the kind of sweet goofiness to the part that Turman wanted. With the help of makeup, lighting, and good acting, Anne and Hoffman would appear to be a generation apart, not separated by just six years.

Anne and Mel rented a house in Beverly Hills with a friend from the *Skin of Our Teeth* cast, Frank Langella, and his girlfriend as Langella prepared to star in a Mark Taper Forum production of *The Devils*. Mel, by then deep into his first feature film project, visited on weekends and any other time he could get away from New York. On most nights during the week Anne would join Langella and his girlfriend for dinner, which made the separation from Mel more tolerable.

When rehearsals began in March 1967 on a soundstage rented at Paramount studios, they reflected Mike Nichols's theater experience and echoed the Arthur Penn approach that Anne had found so rewarding. Devoting three weeks to going over the script, developing characterizations, and blocking scenes was unheard of for a Hollywood film, let alone one with a small budget. Anne joined other leading players for a first reading of Buck Henry's script: William Daniels and Elizabeth Wilson as Benjamin's parents; Gene Hackman as Mr. Robinson; and Katharine Ross as Elaine Robinson.

The screenplay before them closely followed the plot of Webb's novel. A recent college graduate, Benjamin Braddock returns home uncertain what to do with his life. The wife of his father's partner, Mrs. Robinson, initiates an affair with the young man she has known nearly all his life. Their awkward relationship grows tense when his parents pressure him to go out with the Robinsons' daughter, Elaine. He falls in love with her, then loses her when he tells her about the affair. At the last moment, he crashes Elaine's church wedding and wins her back, the couple escaping the angry Robinsons and other guests by boarding a city bus, their future uncertain but one they can face together.

The first read-through of the script by all the actors provided at least one surprise: Anne's reading came off as flat and with little life to it. "Maybe I was so unsophisticated at that point in time that I expected her to give an inflection," Larry Turman said in looking back. "Well, she didn't bother— and it didn't affect her performance."

Anne probably had not yet decided just what kind of performance to give at that point and wanted guidance. She went up to Mike Nichols that first day and asked if he liked her character. "No," he replied. "She's much too sweet." When she asked what he thought Mrs. Robinson was like, Nichols told her he could not say but that he could suggest how the seductress sounded. In a flat tone, he spoke one of Mrs. Robinson's early lines: "Benjamin, will you drive me home, please?"

Anne responded immediately: "Oh, I know what that is. That's *anger*."

Recalling the exchange many years later, Nichols said: "She was such a great actress. Even in that one moment . . . it was done. She knew all about it. She was ready to play Mrs. Robinson."

Improvisation was part of Nichols's method for putting actors in touch with their characters. Much of those exercises centered on the two families, the Robinsons and the Braddocks, and how they had spent time together when the children were younger. In doing so the actors developed a sense of how the younger characters related to their parents and to each other. Plenty of time was spent learning their lines, too, and both Dustin Hoffman and Katharine Ross later said they could have taken the show on the road by the time rehearsals ended.

Had they done so, Gene Hackman would not have been part of the troupe. Early on Nichols realized that Hackman, though sixteen months older than Anne, looked too young to be Mr. Robinson and replaced him with Murray Hamilton, who was eight years Anne's senior. If people questioned Nichols's judgment on the cast change and other matters, they had only to reflect on how his first movie had turned out. The Academy Awards ceremony came on April 10, not long after *The Graduate* began production, and *Who's Afraid of Virginia Woolf* won five Oscars that night, including best actress for Elizabeth Taylor and best supporting actress for Sandy Dennis. During the awards ceremony, Anne accepted the award on behalf of Taylor, who was filming in the south of France. Nichols himself did not win the director's award that evening (it went to Fred Zinnemann for *A Man for All Seasons,* the year's best picture), but the message was clear: his new company of players was in good hands.

Nichols continued to build all aspects of *The Graduate* around the theme of the empty consumerism that had marked Mrs. Robinson's life and now threatened Benjamin's future. "It all says a very specific thing: if you live in a world of objects you become an object," he told a reporter. "The only way to save yourself is passion, which he finally develops for a young girl." At that moment *The Graduate* was Mike Nichols's passion, and he attended to every detail. He asked the pop duo Simon and Garfunkel for two of their songs, "The Sound of Silence" and "Scarborough Fair," for the film, in addition to one original. They reworked a composition called "Mrs. Roosevelt" into the more appropriately titled "Mrs. Robinson." Nichols sought a monochromatic look for the production and designed shots that put Dustin Hoffman amid water—at one point he is framed by an aquarium—to give a visual emphasis to a character feeling adrift.

When it came to Anne's character, Nichols pictured a natural predator. He encouraged the production designer Richard Sylbert and costume designer Patricia Zipprodt to think of Mrs. Robinson as a jungle animal. Sylbert gave the Robinsons' den a jungle motif—he thought of it as her lair—while Zipprodt considered a jungle feline look for Mrs. Robinson's wardrobe. Zipprodt came up with a tiger print lamé sheath gauzed over by

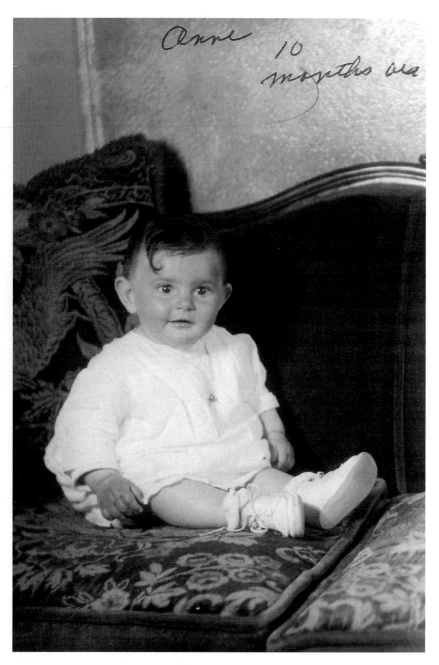

Anna Marie Italiano at ten months, 1932. (Courtesy JoAnne Italiano Perna)

Anne with her mother, Millie, and older sister, JoAnne, circa 1933.
(Courtesy JoAnne Italiano Perna)

Anne, about thirteen years old, with her younger sister, Phyllis, and their aunt Mary Madonna, circa 1944. (Courtesy JoAnne Italiano Perna)

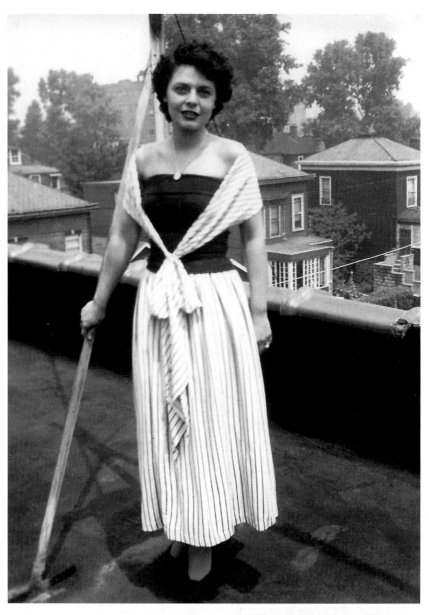

Seventeen-year-old Anne Italiano on the rooftop of her family's apartment building on St. Raymond Avenue in the Bronx, circa 1948. (Courtesy JoAnne Italiano Perna)

Anne and her father, Mike Italiano, in their Bronx neighborhood, circa 1950.
(Courtesy JoAnne Italiano Perna)

Anne and the actor John Ericson, who were engaged for a brief time in 1951–52. (Courtesy JoAnne Italiano Perna)

Twenty-year-old Anne Bancroft (far right) joins her father, her manager, Mort Millman, and her mother outside Santa Monica Superior Court in 1951, when a judge approved her contract with Twentieth Century-Fox. (Courtesy JoAnne Italiano Perna)

Richard Widmark and Anne Bancroft listen to the director Roy Ward Baker on the nightclub set of *Don't Bother to Knock* (1952), her first film. (Twentieth Century-Fox/ Photofest)

As a starlet in Hollywood in the early 1950s, Anne posed for publicity photos that emphasized her figure. (Courtesy JoAnne Italiano Perna)

Goliath carries Anne amid screaming carnival-goers in *Gorilla at Large* (1954), a movie she would view as the nadir of her early Hollywood film career. (Twentieth Century-Fox/Everett Collection)

Anne and her husband Marty May on the day of their marriage (the 1954 ceremony) at her childhood parish in the Bronx. (Corbis)

Anne's hair and makeup were lightened for her role as the object of mountain man Victor Mature's affections in *The Last Frontier* (1955). (Columbia Pictures/Photofest)

In another break from playing contemporary urban characters, Anne appeared as an Apache woman in *Walk the Proud Land* (1956) with Audie Murphy. (Universal Pictures/Photofest)

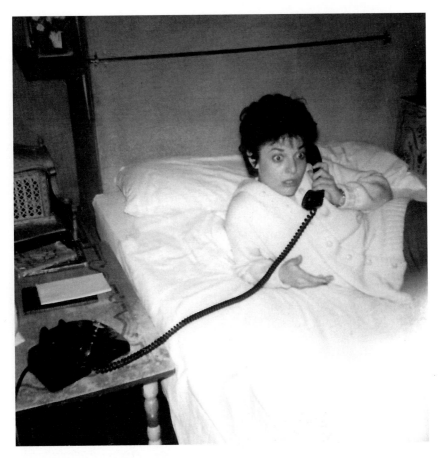

On the set of the Broadway play *Two for the Seesaw* (1958), Anne is in character as the kooky Gittel Mosca. (Courtesy JoAnne Italiano Perna)

Anne and Henry Fonda in *Two for the Seesaw*, the two-character play that made her an overnight star on Broadway. (Everett Collection)

Torin Thatcher, Anne, and Patty Duke in *The Miracle Worker* (1959). The nightly battle between Annie Sullivan and Helen Keller was a Broadway sensation. (Everett Collection)

Anne with the producer Fred Coe and the director Arthur Penn on the set of the film version of *The Miracle Worker* (1962). (AP)

Relaxing on Fire Island in 1962, Anne reads a script amid the critical success of the film version of *The Miracle Worker.* (Courtesy JoAnne Italiano Perna)

Following a performance of *Mother Courage and Her Children* in 1963, Joan Crawford presents Anne with the Oscar she won for *The Miracle Worker.* (Photofest)

Anne plays the disturbed wife of a philandering husband (Peter Finch) in *The Pumpkin Eater* (1964), a role that brought her a second Oscar nomination. (Columbia Pictures/Everett Collection)

Sidney Poitier received an Oscar for *Lilies of the Field* from Anne in 1964. The ceremony offered fans a rare glimpse of Anne in a glamorous setting. (AMPAS/Photofest)

Anne Bancroft and Mel Brooks meet the press in August 1964 to announce their marriage, the second for both. (Photofest)

Anne appears as a troubled nun in the Broadway play *The Devils* (1965).
(Everett Collection)

The producer Bernard Smith and the director John Ford share a laugh with Anne during *7 Women* (1966), Ford's final feature film. (MGM/Everett Collection)

Anne and Dustin Hoffman in the seduction scene in *The Graduate* (1967). The huge financial and critical success forever set her in the public's mind as the sexy Mrs. Robinson. (Everett Collection)

Frank Langella, Anne, and the playwright William Gibson during the Broadway production of Gibson's play *A Cry for Players* in 1968. (AP)

In a skit for her Emmy-winning TV special in 1970, Anne plays the wary bride of Dick Shawn. (CBS/Everett Collection)

Robert Shaw (standing) and the director Richard Attenborough with Anne on the set of *Young Winston* (1972), her first film after a five-year absence. (Columbia/Everett Collection)

Anne faces off with Jack Lemmon in Neil Simon's *The Prisoner of Second Avenue* (1975), one of her few comedies. (Everett Collection)

Anne and Shirley MacLaine play friendly rivals in *The Turning Point* (1977). Both were nominated for Oscars for the film, which introduced ballet to millions of moviegoers. (Twentieth Century-Fox/Everett Collection)

Anne meets Golda Meir in Tel Aviv in June 1977 as she prepares to play the former Israeli prime minister in *Golda* on Broadway. (Photofest)

Anne directs Dom DeLuise in *Fatso* (1980), her only feature film as writer and director. She also played DeLuise's sister in the comedy. (Twentieth Century-Fox/Everett Collection)

Max von Sydow and Anne play a psychiatrist and his patient in *Duet for One* (1981). The drama closed in two weeks, a rare Broadway flop for Anne. (Everett Collection)

A remake of a World War II-era comedy *To Be or Not to Be* (1983) offered the comic actor Mel Brooks and his wife the opportunity to work together. (Twentieth Century-Fox/Everett Collection)

In *Agnes of God* (1985), Anne plays a mother superior dealing with a psychiatrist (Jane Fonda) who is investigating a death at her convent. The role brought Bancroft her fifth and final Oscar nomination. (Everett Collection)

The film version of the two-character play *'night, Mother* (1986) reached movie theaters with two Oscar winners, Anne Bancroft and Sissy Spacek. (Universal Pictures/Everett Collection)

The author Helene Hanff and Anne on location in New York during filming of Hanff's memoir, *84 Charing Cross Road* (1987). (Everett Collection)

Anne Bancroft and Jane Alexander play patient and nurse in a 1989 Los Angeles production of Manuel Puig's surreal play *Mystery of the Rose Bouquet.* (Everett Collection)

Anne found starring roles in made-for-TV movies like *Homecoming* (1996), with Kimberlee Peterson. She plays the cranky grandmother of a group of abandoned children. (Showtime Networks/Everett Collection)

In her final film, *The Roman Spring of Mrs. Stone* (2003), Anne appears as an Italian countess turned procurer who introduces a younger man (Olivier Martinez) to a fading American actress. (Showtime Networks/Everett Collection)

Anne played mostly character roles in films after turning sixty. She appears as a U.S. senator in *G.I. Jane* (1997) with Demi Moore. (Everett Collection)

Mel Brooks and his wife attend the seventy-fifth-anniversary gala for *Time* magazine at New York's Radio City Music Hall in 1998. (AP/Mark Lennihan)

Max Brooks and his son, Henry, join Mel Brooks for Mel's Hollywood Walk of Fame ceremony in 2010, five years after Anne's death. (Everett Collection)

A portrait of Anne shot during the *Graduate* era. (Everett Collection)

a black chiffon cage dress. She also worked on a Chanel suit for Anne, black with leopard trim and a little leopard hat. At times Nichols's attention to detail annoyed Zipprodt, a theater veteran working on her first film. She was forced to search again and again for just the right leopard coat and had to go to the trouble of obtaining real jewelry from Harry Winston's when Nichols would not settle for imitations.

For Nichols, the key to understanding Mrs. Robinson came in the hotel room scene in which Benjamin tries to communicate on a more personal level with the woman he has been sleeping with. Not only does it become clear she does not want to talk about herself, but the little she does say suggests that her life is as empty and meaningless as her marriage and their affair. Benjamin manages to get her to reveal that she was an art student in college when she became pregnant and had to get married, though she had earlier expressed no interest in talking about art.

"I guess you kind of lost interest in it over the years, then," Benjamin says.

"Kind of," Mrs. Robinson says.

Ahead of that day's work, Nichols explained to Anne that Mrs. Robinson is thinking about how she gave up her whole life for financial security and is sad about it. But when they shot the scene, Anne gave the last line a bland reading. "And I said, 'Annie, what about the beautiful insight, the very heart of your character?'" Nichols recounted later. "And she said, 'Oh, I'm sorry, I forgot.' And then she did it beautifully. She just simply forgot."

Staying in touch with that underlying sense of anger and sadness in Mrs. Robinson was crucial for Anne's performance. "I can understand how a woman living with such an empty inner life could turn to alcohol and sex," she said not long after the movie opened. "There was such a delicate balance in *The Graduate* that I had to keep a straight line. If I took one step away from that line I would make her a caricature. And if I stepped the other way I would have made her a tragic character." In the scene, her face relayed the sadness behind the line "Kind of" far more than the two words. "Part of Annie's genius is that you're sort of on Mrs. Robinson's side," Nichols said, "partly because she's so much fun and partly because . . . I don't know. She's a beautiful woman and you feel for her."

With more distance from the film, Anne offered an even deeper analysis of Mrs. Robinson. "I think she had dreams. She had dreams and the dreams could not be fulfilled because of things that had happened," she told Charlie Rose in their 2000 interview. "And so she spent a very conventional life with this conventional man in a conventional house, you know. Even though it was in Beverly Hills, it was still a very conventional life. And meantime, all the dreams that she had had for herself, you know, and the talent—she probably was a gifted artist, you know. I thought that she was. And none of that could happen anymore." She later cited her years of self-reflection—confronting her own anger—as helping her relate to Mrs. Robinson's empty inner life. Carrying that anger for months on end while shooting the film was emotionally and physically draining for her.

A taskmaster as well as a perfectionist, Mike Nichols would not be hurried and usually called for several takes of each scene. Delays were common. Patricia Zipprodt was amazed at the amount of time Nichols would spend choosing Benjamin's wristwatch or having the character's blue blazer taken apart and reassembled because of a few wrinkles. Everyone waited as Nichols made sure Dustin Hoffman's collar was raised an eighth of an inch. To Zipprodt, some of his demands seemed more like whims.

One scene was reshot at no small expense after Nichols came up with a better idea for staging it. When Benjamin and Mrs. Robinson rendezvous in a hotel room for the first time, he impulsively kisses her. Nichols decided that a conventional kiss was not enough. He did the scene again with Benjamin giving Mrs. Robinson a kiss on the lips just after she has taken a long drag from a cigarette. Her eyes communicate a sense of panic or discomfort as the kiss continues. He pulls back and she exhales a large plume of smoke—a bit guaranteed to get a laugh from the audience. Why guaranteed? Because Nichols and Elaine May had performed a similar gag in their skit about two teenagers making out in the front seat of a car, and he knew it would work.

If Nichols saw the smoking kiss as just a funny moment amid a scene of awkwardness, Anne had her own reading of what it really meant—at least to her. "What I was thinking at the time was how inadequate a kiss was for this woman," she said. "That woman needed a lot more than a kiss. She was not after romance. She was after being devoured. To lose the terrible rage that she lived with, to turn it into something else." Her Los Angeles housemate Frank Langella remembered a less thoughtful reaction to Nichols's direction, saying that at the time Anne merely dismissed the bit as "a stupid idea."

Bedroom scenes in The Graduate called for Anne to appear in just a bra and slip. Revealing so much of her body made her more than uncomfortable. "I thought I'd die," she said. "I chased everyone off the set. Once Mike knew how upset I was about making these scenes, he put up screens. I had thought it would be easy to do those undressed scenes." The script also called for a naked Mrs. Robinson to trap Benjamin in her daughter's room when she makes her pitch for having an affair with him. "When I got to the day I had to do it, I couldn't do it," she told Charlie Rose. "I just couldn't do it. And, of course, that sort of left Mike up a creek." A body double was engaged for the glimpses of Mrs. Robinson's naked body and breasts.

Anne was already sensitive about how she appeared in the film. To give her face more years, Nichols had her lit rather harshly. At one point she threw a brush at a mirror and yelled at him, "You made me look terrible!" She may have been too close to the realization that she was getting older and did not appreciate how attractive she would appear in the film—and working too hard to enjoy much of anything about the production. Nichols, on the other hand, often had to walk away from a scene he was shooting, afraid that his laughter over how well Anne and Dustin Hoffman worked together would ruin the take.

The months Anne spent on *The Graduate* were not a period she would recall with fondness. As often happened with work she found stressful, she felt ill part of the time—she suffered another bout of pneumonia and, by some accounts, experienced dark moods amid a series of painful menstrual cramps that practically immobilized her. During the filming of the melee outside the church she fainted in the intense Southern California heat and was sent home for the day. Whatever her mood, Anne managed to put her performance first. "She was not an effusive person. She was a consummate professional, no nonsense, did her work," Larry Turman recalled. "She had the type of nature, personality, that was probably less warm and fuzzy and trying to please as most conventional actors are." Only she could know how much the troubles of Mrs. Robinson colored her frame of mind during those months. Nichols would bestow on her the ultimate accolade from one who pursues excessively high standards: "Everything she does is perfect."

Regardless of the difficulties Anne endured while making *The Graduate*, Mike Nichols won her over as a director. Long before shooting had been completed, she decided to work with him again. She agreed—perhaps too quickly, given how worn out she would become—to join the cast of a Nichols-directed revival of the play *The Little Foxes* set for October 1967 at New York's Lincoln Center. Principal photography on *The Graduate* ended in early August, meaning Anne enjoyed only a short break from work. Mel had been busy too, directing his first feature film, *The Producers,* from his own script. He created a farce about a disreputable Broadway producer who sets out to stage a show guaranteed to close in one night so he can pocket his investors' money. *The Producers* relied on a modest budget of about $1 million as Mel shot the film in New York over the summer. Joining the star, Zero Mostel, were Gene Wilder, who had met Mel while appearing with Anne in *Mother Courage and Her Children,* and Dick Shawn, her recent television costar. It would not be the only time that Anne and Mel's professional connections would cross.

Mike Nichols seemed as tireless as Anne in spite of the many months he had labored on the Paramount lot shooting *The Graduate.* Even during rehearsals in Manhattan for *The Little Foxes,* he managed to find time to oversee the final touches on his new film as it neared a December release. In its tale of greed and deception among members of a genteel Southern family in 1900, *The Little Foxes* offered one of the most memorable female characters in American drama. Tallulah Bankhead had played the scheming Regina Giddens in the original Broadway production in 1938, and Bette Davis had the role in the highly regarded 1941 film version. Anne continued her run of working with outstanding talents when Nichols cast George C. Scott, Richard Dysart, E. G. Marshall, William Prince, Maria Tucci, and Austin Pendleton. He had hoped to have Margaret Leighton lead the cast, but some members of Actors Equity fussed enough over the idea of a British actress playing Regina that Anne was brought in, and her *7 Women* costar took the supporting role of Regina's sister-in-law.

When the twenty-seven-year-old actor cast as Regina's nephew arrived at Lincoln Center for rehearsals, two women stopped him for directions to the stage door of the Vivian Beaumont Theater. One of them asked, "Are you Austin Pendleton?" He was, he responded, and then he asked, "What's your name?"

"She said, 'Anne Bancroft,' and she had a twinkle in her eye, feeling the humor of that moment," Pendleton remembered. "And from that point on we were friends." Though he had not recognized her, the Ohio-born actor certainly knew who she was, having seen every Bancroft Broadway performance since *Two for the Seesaw* a decade earlier. Anne had changed in appearance, of course, and in his eyes not in a bad way. "She was growing even more beautiful," he said. "The face had more outline to it than in the earlier years, more distinctiveness. The cheekbones were more prominent, the shape of it was different."

Rehearsals were freewheeling for the first several days, Pendleton remembered, as Mike Nichols allowed the cast to try different interpretations of Lillian Hellman's characters. A similar approach had marked rehearsals for *The Graduate* earlier that year. Back then Nichols had enjoyed an effective collaboration with the screenwriter Buck Henry and did not feel constrained by Charles Webb's novel. Directing the first major revival of *The Little Foxes,* however, came as its famously tart playwright was not only very much alive but still a strong presence in the theater community—and in the Vivian Beaumont Theater itself.

"Lillian Hellman began coming to rehearsals," Pendleton said. She thought the correct template for her play had been the Bette Davis film, directed by William Wyler, and she sought that kind of icy, contained performance in Anne's version of Regina. "Anne started out early in rehearsals bringing a passionate heartiness to it that I loved," Pendleton said. "But then Lillian came in three, four days in and put the kibosh on that."

Anne may have seen Regina as a more outwardly passionate, angry woman trying to outwit the powerful men in her life. Nichols knew well how she could communicate anger and disappointment in ways both subtle and fiery. While she was charming and funny with her colleagues during rehearsals, at least as Pendleton remembered, Anne faced the challenge of delivering what the playwright wanted and not necessarily what the director had hoped to bring out.

"I think the thing that Mike had cast her for turned out to be the thing that Lillian didn't want," Pendleton said. "So all of a sudden she's playing in the first New York revival of a classic American play, one of the legendary American roles, and everybody's unhappy with what she's instinctively doing and what Mike's encouraging her to do. So that must be very frightening."

Nichols could hardly be expected to ignore the person who had created the characters. As Hellman observed rehearsals and constantly criticized his choices, Nichols began to take a more traditional approach to the material. His giving in to her demands may have been one reason Hellman later told an interviewer that they had gotten along just splendidly. "He had to confine himself more and more to Lillian's ideas," Pendleton said of

Nichols, "but he directed with great sharpness." Years later, in 1981, Pendleton himself directed a revival of *The Little Foxes* with Elizabeth Taylor as Regina. Hellman was on hand again, at seventy-five, to direct the director. "I said, 'You know, Lillian, I liked Mike's production of that more than the movie,' and Lillian said, 'If you had told me that at our interview, you would never have gotten this job.'"

During the Lincoln Center production, Pendleton had his own problems with Mike Nichols—and it took Anne's intervention to rescue him. The first run-through of the play brought notes from the director to everyone but Pendleton, who naively thought he alone had pleased Nichols. Instead of praise, the director told him, "How can I give notes on a performance that is wrong from beginning to end?" With no idea how to characterize the part to the director's liking, Pendleton assumed he would be fired and expressed his dismay to Anne before leaving the theater.

The next day Anne invited Pendleton into her dressing room. "I've figured out what is driving him crazy," she said. "It's the way you walk." She explained: Pendleton was a smart person and thought of himself as a smart person, and when he walked he led with his head. On the other hand, his character, Leo, is dumb and takes pride in the affair he is carrying on in Mobile with a woman of ill repute. Therefore, when Leo walks he should lead with his groin, not his head. Anne offered an example of how Pendleton should walk and urged him to think of nothing but how he should walk onstage with his pelvis first.

While it might have seemed like a minor change, Pendleton found that he was processing the character differently, in terms of Leo's feelings and how he encounters the world through his body. The new approach even affected his speech rhythm. Pendleton applied Anne's advice to his performance. "And Mike said, 'I see that our talk has had an effect, and I'm very happy about that.' From that point on I was fine," Pendleton said. "She saved my job." He had been surprised that Anne had cared enough to help him—and the memory of her generosity never ceased to move him.

One night during the play's run, Anne provided a glimpse of what might have been had Lillian Hellman not reined in Nichols and insisted on a contained performance in which Regina's ambition and fire were not allowed out in the open. In the third act, after she has killed her husband and is in danger of being cut out of the business deal she has sought, Regina turns on her brothers and declares, "You'll do no more bargaining in this house." Anne let her instincts guide her that one time. "It was wildly passionate," Pendleton recalled. "There was rage. She was so charged with it that her voice came close to breaking, without diminishing the rage." After the performance, her costar E. G. Marshall joined Pendleton in Anne's dressing room to tell her that she had been brilliant. "Well," she said, "Mike told me I was never, ever to do anything like that."

The revival of *The Little Foxes* opened on October 26, 1967, to mostly positive notices but several uncomplimentary ones. Critics who called it a worthwhile production or even an outstanding one outnumbered those who found fault in Hellman's play and in Nichols's direction. "The present production is a model of casting," *Time* magazine wrote. "Anne Bancroft's congealed contempt, George Scott's rasping arrogance, Margaret Leighton's wounded bird cries—all these file on the nerves as director Mike Nichols expertly dovetails scenes of explosive malignance." Walter Kerr of the *New York Times* found the production "brilliant," but his colleague Clive Barnes suggested it was a magnificent presentation of a mediocre work. "Anne Bancroft, as the wicked sister, with iron instead of bone in her skeleton, a huskily musical voice that hums a dance of death, and a smile so icy that you expect almost to hear it melt, leaves, helped by her director, a series of unforgettable visual and aural images," Barnes wrote.

Among those unfavorably impressed was *Newsweek* magazine's Jack Kroll. "Mike Nichols has directed an 'all-star cast' in a version that tries for effects rather than depth or balance, and makes an intelligently calculated play seem like an obvious melodrama." Citing performance after performance as off-kilter, Kroll dismissed Anne's Regina as "glossy and beautiful and much more the Dragon Lady than a strong Southern woman dehumanized by the rapacity all around her." Martin Gottfried's notice in *Women's Wear Daily* rejected Hellman's play outright and contended that Nichols had failed to disguise its obvious faults. He thought the cast was abysmal and said that Anne's Regina "could as well have been a saloon's singer-owner in a cheapie Technicolor Western." Writing for the *Nation,* Harold Clurman thought Anne was wrong for the role and found even less merit in George C. Scott's performance. He offered kinder words for others in the cast but closed with a backhanded compliment: "For a wide audience in New York and on the road the production works and will 'pay off.'" In other words, the rubes could look forward to an enjoyable evening.

Whatever the merits of his opinions, Clurman correctly predicted the production's popularity with theatergoers. Within a week of its opening,

The Little Foxes had sold out the remaining performances for its seven-week run at Lincoln Center. When the show moved to the Broadway theater district's Ethel Barrymore Theatre on December 19, Anne and George C. Scott left the cast as planned, and Margaret Leighton and E. G. Marshall assumed their roles. Not only had she garnered another round of praise for her performance, but Anne had also led the cast of a New York play considered a financial success for the first time since *The Miracle Worker.*

Just days after Anne completed her work in *The Little Foxes,* movie theaters in New York, Los Angeles, Chicago, and elsewhere began showing *The Graduate.* Critical reaction was overwhelmingly favorable. "The year's most brilliant film," wrote the *Washington Post*'s Richard L. Coe. Bosley Crowther, the film critic of the *New York Times* for nearly thirty years, wrapped up his career at the newspaper with "a hearty salute" to a movie he called "funny and sharp" and comparable to the first film by the writer-director Preston Sturges, perhaps the best satirist at work in Hollywood in the 1940s. "It is deftly sophisticated without in any way being above or con-descending to the mass audience's intelligence and taste," Crowther wrote. "And its cinematic style is energetic, aggressive, and full of surprises."

Crowther found both Anne and Dustin Hoffman superb, a view shared by most. "A dazzling performance," the *Boston Globe*'s George McKinnon wrote of Anne. Of all the performances, Clifford Terry of the *Chicago Tribune* wrote, "the sharpest is that by Miss Bancroft, bitchily con-vincing as the suburban Circe, whether displaying her assertiveness in as small a way as being the one to command a martini from the waiter, or revealing all her matrimonial boredom-bitterness in a sigh or a sneer." In the *Chicago Sun-Times,* Roger Ebert wrote that Anne, "in a tricky role, is magnificently sexy, shrewish and self-possessed enough to make the seduction convincing" in what was "the funniest comedy of the year." The relatively few negative comments tended to center on Nichols's directing ("an alarmingly derivative style," wrote *Time*) and a story that some believed turned melodramatic. Praise was commonplace, however, and none surpassed that from Stanley Kauffmann of the *New Republic,* who cited the film's cinematic skill, its intent, and its ability to connect with people in calling it "a milestone in American film history."

Word of mouth coupled with such reviews fueled a tremendous turn-out of moviegoers across the country. People just kept going to see it, many of them more than once. And there was the music. Simon and Garfunkel's songs were another part of the film's appeal, so much so that "Mrs. Robinson" spent three weeks in June 1968 at Number 1 on the *Billboard* pop chart, and the soundtrack album was at the top for nine weeks. Simon and Garfunkel's music went on to win three Grammy Awards, including record of the year for "Mrs. Robinson." It all meant that Anne's performance carried a musical dimension even though she never sang a note.

By the end of 1968, *Variety* deemed *The Graduate* the year's top-earning film. In its list of movies and rental figures—the money the studios earned as opposed to box-office sales—Mike Nichols's second film earned a staggering $39 million in its first year. Far down in second place was *Guess Who's Coming to Dinner* at $25.1 million, followed by a reissue of *Gone with the Wind* at $23 million and *Valley of the Dolls* at $20 million. Considering its negative cost of just $3.2 million, Larry Turman's yearslong effort to make a film from Charles Webb's novel ended with a huge payoff. Turman and Nichols each owned a 13 percent share of the film and enjoyed a success that was more than artistic. As was the way of the movie business at the time, Anne and Dustin Hoffman had only their salaries to show for their work—and the career-fueling buzz that came from starring in a movie practically everyone would see.

Higher ticket prices, more movie theaters, and more ticket buyers would eventually drive older movies out of the public perception of what constituted the most popular films of all time. When inflation was taken into account, *The Graduate* remained near the top of the list a half century after its release as measured by domestic revenue. In 2015 the website Box Office Mojo placed the film at Number 21, with an adjusted gross of $695 million, which made it the highest-ranking comedy on its list of two hundred films. Only three other films released in the 1960s—*The Sound of Music, Doctor Zhivago,* and *Mary Poppins*—brought in more dollars.

The Graduate would gain a place in the history of American film for reasons other than popularity. It was among a new wave of motion pictures that were different from those made during the medium's first seven decades. Not only were they technically modern and thematically sophisticated, but they also were much more realistic and ambitious in how they sought to depict human endeavors and emotions. The censorship code that had guided filmmakers since the 1930s had aimed to make every film suitable for general audiences, particularly children. Its authority had been withering throughout the 1960s in the face of foreign films and independent productions that stretched the boundaries for sex, violence, and language. By 1968 American audiences were more than ready to be treated like grown-ups. That year the Motion Picture Association of America, the studios' trade organization, instituted a ratings system to fend off government censorship while allowing filmmakers unprecedented leeway to determine the content of their movies. The film historian Mark Harris would point to *The Graduate* as well as *Bonnie and Clyde,* directed by Arthur Penn the same year, as among the groundbreaking films of the new Hollywood.

Anne gained a legacy of her own from *The Graduate.* Her insightful portrayal of a sexy older woman seducing a man young enough to be her son would stay with her for the rest of her life, even overshadowing her Oscar-winning performance in *The Miracle Worker.* The incredible popularity of the film, coupled with the Simon and Garfunkel tune, would create an unbreakable link between her and Mrs. Robinson. Seldom would a newspaper or a magazine story about Anne not mention *The Graduate,* regardless of the subject at hand. For many years she resented the inordinate amount of attention paid to that one role. In time, though, she would reconcile herself with the idea that for many people it was her most memorable portrayal if not necessarily what she believed represented the wide range of her talents.

With the success of *The Graduate,* Anne's film career finally gained the only component it had been missing—a blockbuster. She had earned the respect of critics and peers long before Mrs. Robinson appeared onscreen. The only question remaining as *The Graduate* filled theaters week after week in 1968 and beyond was how she might turn its success in her favor. She could quickly sign on to one or more films at an enhanced salary to make the most of any box-office power she had earned. She could seek roles in high-profile movies of the era or decide to appear in smaller, independent productions for which she could demand a share of ticket sales. She might even be able to use her newfound appeal with audiences to star in a musical. Five years after Anne had returned to films, what lay ahead of her could have appeared almost limitless.

Indeed, what would Anne Bancroft the movie star do in her film career over the next five years? The answer was surprising: almost nothing.

9

Turning to the Stage, Leaving the Movies Behind

Even as *The Graduate* renewed interest in her talents, Anne continued to limit her professional activities in every medium. She declined to join the cast of a Western starring Gregory Peck, *The Stalking Moon,* an understandable choice given her unhappy history with the genre. Eva Marie Saint took the part instead. There was talk about Anne's joining Natalie Wood in a film version of *I Never Promised You a Rose Garden,* a novel about a young woman's battle with schizophrenia and the therapist who treats her. The pairing never happened, and the production stalled for nearly a decade.

Before 1968 was over producers would sound out Anne for Broadway-bound productions—or at least use her name in columns to promote their efforts. Elliot Martin, a producer, tried to interest her in the screenwriter Charles Bennett's play about a sexually frustrated, manipulative drunk; it was never produced. More promising was a musical version of the Oscar-winning Bette Davis film *All about Eve.* Although its producers claimed that Anne was considering the adaptation under way with an eye toward a spring opening, not until March 1970 did the curtain rise on *Applause—* starring Lauren Bacall. It would win Tony Awards in four categories, including best musical and best actress. If Bacall could handle the score, surely Anne could have done so.

More and more offers were coming Anne's way because of the hit status of *The Graduate,* some of them probably fueled by an awards season in which peers and critics alike recognized her portrayal of Mrs. Robinson as one of the year's top female performances. She won the Golden Globe for best actress in a musical or comedy and was nominated for best actress by the British film academy and, for the third time in six years, by the Academy of Motion Picture Arts and Sciences. On Oscar night in April 1968, Katharine Hepburn won for *Guess Who's Coming to Dinner.* (Anne would lose the British award to Hepburn, too.) The only Oscar winner for *The Graduate* was its director, Mike Nichols. The year's best picture award went to *In the Heat of the Night.*

Anne's missing out on a second Academy Award did not slow the offers that came to her from across the globe. She had been around long enough to know that box-office receipts more than the quality of her performance were responsible for all the attention. It was as though her work in films meant more now that there was money behind it. To some degree she found the idea insulting. Yet it was not professional pique alone that caused Anne to be absent from movie screens for five years. She insisted that she would not work for the sake of working. If high quality was what she sought, the realities of Hollywood meant that she would be swimming against a strong current of mediocrity. Good scripts were hard to come by, and good scripts with leading roles for women were even harder to come by. Scarcer still were good scripts with leading roles for women over the age of thirty-five.

The evidence could be found in the pages of *Variety.* Of the top films at the box office in 1969, for example, most were male-oriented action movies like *Butch Cassidy and the Sundance Kid, True Grit, On Her Majesty's Secret Service,* and *The Wild Bunch.* Stark dramas like *Midnight Cowboy* and *Easy Rider* revolved around male characters. At the same time, Anne's competition was fierce. Barbra Streisand starred in *Hello, Dolly!* while Ingrid Bergman played the older woman in the comedy *Cactus Flower.* Maggie Smith was the title character in the British drama *The Prime of Miss Jean Brodie.*

A little nepotism might help an actress seeking a starring role. Jean Simmons had an Oscar-nominated lead in the drama *The Happy Ending,* written and directed by her husband, Richard Brooks. Joanne Woodward costarred with her husband, Paul Newman, in the racing film *Winning,* a product of his own film company. Anne's husband was in the business, too, but she was unlikely to find a starring role in the male-oriented scripts written by Mel Brooks. Over the next few years the movies that the studios backed and audiences patronized were no better at presenting mature women in leading roles.

From her perspective, Anne did not want to play the same type of character no matter how much money she was offered. "I have this thing about reaching out, about trying to expand and develop, to do something," she said a year and a half after *The Graduate* was released. "Who wants to be cast always and forever in the role you played last? I'd be playing Mrs. Robinson from now until my life ended unless I took initiative and stretched myself. I have to prove to me, to myself, that there's more within me than just Mrs. Robinson. Or Gittel. Or Annie. Or even that mad, mad nun in *The Devils*."

Not every film was right for her and she knew it. The London-based American director Joseph Losey had been trying for years to film the novel *The Go-Between*. He could not raise the money, not even after Harold Pinter had written the screenplay and Julie Christie had agreed to star. Losey believed that if he could get Anne to join the cast, the money would follow. He asked Pinter to put in a transatlantic call to Anne, whom he knew from *The Pumpkin Eater*. According to Pinter's account, he described the plot to her—in the Edwardian drama, a woman from an aristocratic British family suspects that her daughter is having an affair with a farmer—and Anne was immediately interested. She had only one question: Who was playing the daughter? "I said, 'Julie Christie,'" Pinter recalled. "There's this great pause across the Atlantic and she said, 'You want me to play Julie Christie's *mother*?'" When the movie was shot in 1970, the mother was played by Margaret Leighton.

Being selective—some would say picky—came with an obvious drawback for an actress approaching middle age. If Anne did not work, she could not build on her career. If she did not take advantage of the success of *The Graduate*, it would eventually dissipate as other actresses demonstrated their own popularity with moviegoers. Moreover, if getting good roles was tough for an older woman, time would only make it more so for Anne as other actresses joined her in the over-thirty-five club. Retirement was an option—many actresses left the business once they were out of their twenties and thirties—but Anne had not lost her desire to perform.

There would be two other outcomes from not working, one of them a reputation for turning down acting offers. In time Anne would be seen by some as hard to please, if not difficult, when it came to enticing her with a role. To those in her profession who shared her belief in committing only to roles that mattered to her, it was an enviable stance. Few working actors had the financial resources or artistic standing to wait for just the right assignment. A lack of press coverage was another result of her absence from the movies, a plus for her personally but a negative for columnists and entertainment writers who relied on celebrity goings-on for their reports. As Anne worked less, there was less reason for her to agree to interviews. She was not keen on submitting herself to reporters to begin with—she often found interviews becoming too personal as well as long and tedious—and Mel Brooks encouraged his wife not to make herself so available to the press.

Rejecting movie script after movie script and declining interviews would not leave Anne idle. She also had the theater and television to consider. In the meantime, she had her home in Greenwich Village, her beach house on Fire Island, and her usual pursuits with friends and family. There was also a newfound pleasure—seeing her husband's film career begin to take off. By the early months of 1968 the first Mel Brooks feature film, *The Producers,* had opened in a few theaters. Word of mouth soon turned it into a cult hit, then all kinds of moviegoers were catching on to the joys of its subversive humor. A second Brooks movie seemed likely even if the box office was low.

One other factor probably played a part in Anne's decision to curtail her professional pursuits after *The Graduate.* She seldom spoke of it, but acting took a toll on her emotionally as well as physically. She usually lost weight while working on a film—she told a reporter in 1968 that she weighed 110 pounds and was a size eight—and she cited the odd hours as having an effect on her eating habits. She acknowledged that retaining Mrs. Robinson's anger had been difficult, even more demanding than playing the neurotic mother in *The Pumpkin Eater.* Developing such characters and staying in touch with their fraught emotions led her to isolate herself in certain ways for weeks or months. "I'm always lonely when I work," Anne told a reporter. "You're going through a very private inner experience that requires personal strength. I accept this loneliness, but it's one of the big fears of going back to work." Facing such loneliness and fear, she had to believe that a role would be worth it to her.

In a repeat of the summer she had enjoyed two years earlier, Anne appeared at the Berkshire Theatre Festival in July 1968 in a new play by her friend William Gibson. Having the star of *The Graduate* in the Massachusetts summer theater at the height of the film's popularity was a coup. It also was another sign of her loyalty to Gibson. Anne had agreed to lend her name to a play that had not been staged before and one in which her role was not the focal point. For his part, Gibson provided the kind of secure and creative atmosphere that she craved.

A Cry of Players is set in an English town during one autumn in the 1580s and follows Will, a twentysomething romantic who wants more from life than his conventional circumstances can offer. An educated man, Will works for his father's tannery, is married to a woman, Anne, nearly a decade his senior, and has a daughter and newborn twins. His rebellious nature has led him to poach fish and game, carry on an affair with a local girl, and flout local authority. When a company of traveling actors comes to town to put on a show, he considers joining them even though it would mean leaving his family and abandoning any effort to become a teacher. Will must determine who he is and whether he should pursue this other existence—a "to be or not to be" moment, one might say.

Not coincidentally, a line in *Hamlet* gave Gibson's play its title. The melancholy Dane asks, "Would not this, sir, and a forest of feathers—if the rest of my fortunes turn Turk with me—with two Provincial roses on my razed shoes, get me a fellowship in a cry of players, sir?" Is Gibson presenting the seminal event in the life of William Shakespeare? To those who assumed that young Will was the Bard himself, Gibson would say, "There's nothing in the play to contradict that conjecture." In fact, biographers know relatively little about Shakespeare's life in the eight-year period after his wife, Anne Hathaway, gave birth to their twins in the town of Stratford and before records show his plays were appearing in London theaters. Gibson filled in those "lost years" with his imagination.

A Cry of Players was not meant to look or sound as though it was an Elizabethan drama. In production notes Gibson stated, "The people in it have not yet discovered the fork, they live in filth, and wear rags not unlike those of, say, Appalachia; their songs are crossed by the rhythms of our time." The playwright saw the basic story as contemporary in nature: a rebellious young man with the heart of an artist considers leaving a constricting small town for the freedom of the big city. It may have been another reason Anne found Will's wife to be a character worth her time and energies. Not only was the mixture of contemporary theme and period drama a change of pace for her, but Anne would appear as a sexually charged wife and mother yet not one burdened with quite the same angst as other characters she had already played.

Gibson had been writing and revising *A Cry of Players* for more than twenty years and was tinkering with it even as Anne and the rest of the cast arrived in Stockbridge that summer. With eighteen principal characters and a half dozen other actors as townspeople, the play did not seem to Gibson to be suitable for Broadway, given the economies many producers were seeking at the time. The Berkshire Theatre Festival's Stockbridge Playhouse was a natural home for Gibson's first play since *The Miracle Worker.*

Unexpectedly, the initial production of *A Cry of Players* gained an additional venue. After Gibson complained in the *New York Times* that Lincoln Center did not seem interested in American writers, its theater director contacted him and eventually offered to bring his new play to the Vivian Beaumont Theater. Scheduled for a November opening, the Gibson play would appear in repertory with a revival of *King Lear* starring Lee J. Cobb and directed by Gerald Freedman. It seemed fitting that *A Cry of Players* would alternate with one of Shakespeare's most celebrated works.

The director and acting teacher Gene Frankel guided both presentations of *A Cry of Players.* He had established a reputation in off-Broadway venues since the 1950s and was drawn to works with social and political dimensions. He had won Obie awards for directing the seventeenth-century Ben Jonson comedy *Volpone,* the mid-twentieth-century feminist play *Machinal,* and the 1958 French drama of racial prejudice *The Blacks.* Frankel was an Actors Studio alumnus who warned his students that "talent is not enough—you must have courage, the courage to travel to those dimly lit spaces where the talent tells you to go." His background and outlook seemed to fit with Anne's and the kind of theater Gibson was trying to achieve in Stockbridge.

Frank Langella, a close friend since *The Skin of Our Teeth* and their house-sharing days in Los Angeles, appeared as Will. Anne Hathaway, as drawn by Gibson, was an earthy, sensual character called on to pull at her husband's emotions, suffer his insulting behavior, and display the sexuality that had won him over and kept him close to her. Nevertheless, the play revolves around Will's dilemma. He is the center of attention, no more so than when he is placed in stocks for poaching a deer and then whipped bloody before a crowd of townspeople.

In the cast as one of the players who comes to Will's town was twenty-two-year-old Peter Galman, fresh out of the American Academy of Dramatic Arts and earning his union card from Actors' Equity with the role. As he remembered the production, he and others in the large cast were excited at the prospect of appearing with Anne. "We were all a little nervous, I think, because the magnitude of her celebrity had reached a point where there were going to be great expectations," he said. In addition, Frank Langella's star was on the rise, and the new play was from the author of *Two for the Seesaw* and *The Miracle Worker.* "It made us all feel that it was going to be a very special event. And it was," Galman said. "I was certainly glued to the whole rehearsal process to see how these pros worked."

Anne and the other members of the cast gathered for rehearsals in a wooden building near the theater while the set was being built. "I was in love with her from the first moment," Galman said. "I walked up to her and said, 'You remind me of my sister,' and she smiled and asked me a little about my sister in Chicago, so we had a nice chat." Anne dressed in the same outfit each day. "She came in with rehearsal black, with rehearsal pants on, every day, like a dancer would wear, something that you can move in easily," Galman said. "And I thought, well, that's the way actors come to work. They are prepared for anything and everything."

When it was called for, Anne could flex her star muscle. That July was unusually hot, and the rehearsal hall was not air conditioned. "It was a steam bath," remembered Ray Stewart, then thirty-six and cast in a featured role. "Several actors were wearing bathing suits—really. We were suffering. After about a week of this—it never let up—Anne told the producer, 'You know, we really can't work like this. You've got to air-condition this place.' And he said, 'Oh, that won't work. Forget it.' And she said, 'I think you'll find a way,' and walked out."

Anne and Stewart returned for rehearsal early the next morning to find a truck with a large air-conditioning unit parked outside. Pipes connected the unit to the building's interior, which had cooled down considerably. The producer told Anne that a handful of workmen had labored all night on the project and were asking if they could meet the star of *The Graduate*. Grateful to be cool, Anne went outside to say hello, then rejoined Stewart a short time later. As Stewart recalled, "I said, 'Well, that's the least you could do.' And she said, 'Well, I would have fucked all of 'em.'"

"This was, like, the second day I had met her," Stewart said. "I didn't know her at all. Well, that's the moment I fell in love." For the rest of rehearsals and the run of the play in Stockbridge and New York, he detected not a trace of diva about her. "She was Annie Italiano. She was just a good old girl who grew up on the streets of New York."

Gene Frankel's rehearsals were conducted in a far more traditional manner than Arthur Penn's improvisational exercises for *The Skin of Our Teeth*. Both Stewart and Galman watched Anne as she developed her character with the aid of notes kept in her bound script. "She had her head in that book," Stewart said. "I never saw anyone study like she did." According to Galman, now and then Anne would put a check mark next to a line that she felt she had finally gotten right or had understood. Stewart observed her drawing little pictures in the margins of her script—familiar images such as a head or an arrow or a star. "She was mapping out her performance visually," he said. "They were hooks to connect you to what was coming."

There was a great deal of back-and-forth about Anne Hathaway's lines and where the emphasis should be and what meaning they would have, Galman said. "I think they didn't want to create a character that was a harridan but someone who was passionate about her family yet understanding of the man's intellect," he said. If Anne had doubts about whether Anne Hathaway was coming off as strident in the script, Frankel did not seem to offer much in the way of help or reassurance, at least in Galman's view. "I think she probably needed a much stronger hand," he said. "I don't know if the director was able to set her at ease enough with it." Galman never thought that Anne seemed miserable, just working through the process of realizing the character and putting her own interpretation on it. "She was wonderful—wonderful in the role," he said. "She had such presence and such strength and passion, such command of herself onstage."

The response to the first preview performance of *A Cry of Players* ahead of its two-week run at the Stockbridge Playhouse suggested that audiences understood who was at the center of the play. Theater protocol called for the star of the show to take the final curtain call and enjoy the closing blast of applause. Anne took the last bow after the first performance, but the audience had clearly favored Frank Langella in his star-making turn as Will. Those in charge decided that he should go last from then on.

Langella went to Anne's dressing room before the second performance to protest a management decision that had placed him above her, the star and an actress far more accomplished. According to his memoir, Anne was realistic about the situation if obviously unhappy. "That's the way it's gonna be, Frankie," she told him as she put on her makeup and brushed her hair. "You got the bigger hand last night. It's your show, and I'm gonna look like the gracious star giving it up to the new guy. Now get the fuck out of here and let me get dressed."

"So on she sailed, took her bow, turned, and flung both her arms out to the wings and presented me with a giant smile to the audience," Langella wrote. "There was no price to pay in our friendship, and a valuable lesson to be learned in how to understand and survive the playing field." There were ironic echoes of *Two for the Seesaw*—the younger performer overshadowing the established star.

The drama critic of the *Boston Globe*, Kevin Kelly, called *A Cry of Players* "a magnificent play" and "uncommonly beautiful." He was particularly taken with its heartbreaking love scenes. "Miss Bancroft, alternating between love and rage, struggling to comprehend what is beyond her comprehension, is perfect as Anne," Kelly wrote. Frank Langella, he noted, had the more complex role and offered his own memorable performance, "almost always in command."

Once the production began its public performances, the company as a whole saw little of Anne except on the stage. With the Penn and Gibson families living nearby, Langella in the cast, and Mel Brooks visiting when he could, she did not lack for friends. During rehearsals she had politely declined to join the actors who went out for drinks. "She was very much to herself," Peter Galman remembered. "She was kind of shy, kind of modest, and maybe just kind of protective in that way that you're protecting your own creative spirit within." Not that Anne was anything other than professional and pleasant, he said, "but I was too puppy dog to bother to really become a friend, I guess."

Much of the Berkshire company regrouped that fall for the Lincoln Center run in repertory with *King Lear*. Gerald Freedman, who had guided Anne in "I'm Getting Married" for ABC television, approached her with the idea that she play Lear's eldest daughter, Goneril, meaning she would alternate between supporting Langella's Will in *A Cry of Players* and flattering Lee J. Cobb's mad king. She turned him down and also declined his invitation to play Lear's youngest daughter, Cordelia. He hoped that she would reconsider and accept the role of Goneril, but she would not.

"I think it scared her, in a way," Freedman remembered. "That's a hell of a part and you'd be compared with all the important actresses of the twentieth century. She didn't have the desire to compete at that level. She played around in rehearsal and in private with classical plays of that nature, but she wasn't comfortable doing it. I think she would have grown into doing it."

To some degree Anne's refusal to join the production surprised

Freedman because she would slip into the theater during *Lear* rehearsals and watch Cobb, her costar in *Gorilla at Large* all those years ago. Sharing a stage with Cobb in such a high-profile production might have intimidated her, Freedman thought. "She was a brave actress, always, but the demands of the text were something she wasn't familiar with," he said. "I would have loved to help her, and I know she would have been a memorable Goneril. She and Lee would have had such chemistry. But doing both *A Cry of Players* and *Lear* would have been a huge undertaking." William Shakespeare and Lee J. Cobb aside, Anne may well have thought that she would court disaster in trying to maintain the emotional and physical energy required for two draining and different roles played in rotation.

Freedman had a sense that Anne was not happy with Gene Frankel, which might have made taking on more work with *King Lear* a wrong move for a different reason. "The director was not on top of his game. I think she felt she had enough to deal with at the time," Freedman said. "Gene was not a great director. He was a director and he had a reputation in New York but didn't really do any important work. He just wasn't up to it. He wasn't up to Anne. I think she enjoyed me because I met her at her level and we traded ideas about it. I never felt her resist me. But that wasn't true on *A Cry for Players*. That wasn't a happy experience for her."

After preview performances at Lincoln Center, Anne and Frank Langella would join Frankel and William Gibson in Ray Stewart and Tom Sawyer's dressing room for a drink. Stewart and Sawyer served as bartenders and kept a bottle of Bombay Sapphire Gin on hand for Anne. "If something didn't work like it should, they would discuss what could we do here," Stewart said. "It was a very deep, creative discussion." Often Mel Brooks would join them as they sought to work out any problems in the show.

Anne could not complain too much about the New York notices for her work in *A Cry of Players*. When it opened at the Vivian Beaumont Theater on November 14, 1968, several critics expressed doubts about the play as written—they did not believe that William Gibson had delivered on the premise of presenting a believable young Shakespeare—but nearly all lauded the performances of Anne and her costar. "The drama, for all its moving moments, seems just a little hollow," wrote the *New York Post*'s critic Richard Watts Jr., who still recommended the production as a valiant effort that was frequently successful. Clive Barnes of the *New York Times* wrote: "Its virtue is theatricality, its vice is obviousness, and its saviors are

Frank Langella; Anne Bancroft; the director, Gene Frankel; and the entire Lincoln Center Rep. As I left, the cheers were swelling in the auditorium. It is a joyful noise welcome in the house."

Among those not won over by the play, Walter Kerr of the *New York Times* said the dialogue sounded like what Gibson might have written twenty years ago before he did better work and dismissed the production as "soft, squishy, and overstuffed." John Simon, writing in *New York* magazine, acknowledged that its leading actress had a presence, but not much more. "Anne Bancroft gives yet another of her crowd-pleasing performances: clever but insuperably commonplace," he wrote. "Under her blurry Irish brogue—meant to gloss over something even less appropriate—she carries her dual legacy of Bronx and Broadway wherever she goes." Simon joined those who said that *A Cry of Players* was among the better efforts in a poor theater season.

An unexpected problem during one performance gave Anne a fit—of suppressed laughter. She had suggested to Ray Stewart that he try a spray-on makeup to turn his hair gray instead of the liquid he was using, the spray needing only to be brushed out instead of washed out each night. In the final dramatic minutes of the show, another actor shoved Stewart, as called for in the script, and his head snapped back. "A white cloud rose above my head like Hiroshima and started to settle on my dark costume," Stewart said. "This is right in front of Anne. She had her back to the audience. It was one of the most horrifying experiences I ever had onstage." When he lined up with the featured actors for the curtain call that night, Anne walked past him and whispered, "I wet my pants . . ."

The Shakespeare of William Gibson's mind was as close to the Bard as Anne would come during her career. During her long absence from movies, she declined Charlton Heston's invitation to join him in a film version of *Antony and Cleopatra* that he planned to direct in Spain. (The role went to Hildegard Neil.) Good judgment led her to turn down the movie adaptation of Gore Vidal's satirical Hollywood novel *Myra Breckinridge,* a work that was practically pornographic in print and went on to earn an X rating and blistering reviews when it reached the screen with Raquel Welch. The writer-director Garson Kanin wanted her to costar with Jack Lemmon in a Los Angeles revival of the stage comedy *Idiot's Delight,* a Pulitzer Prize winner from 1936, which was far more in line with her tastes. Her name also was bandied about during the lengthy gestation period for a film version of the Broadway musical *Mame;* it would not go before the cameras for many years (and starred Lucille Ball when it did).

Anne took a break from accepting any work during the first half of 1969—with one notable exception. She flew to London in April to appear on an episode of NBC's variety show *Kraft Music Hall* hosted by the British comedians Peter Cook and Dudley Moore. She sang "Limehouse Blues" and "Scarborough Fair," and Mel Tormé provided a medley of love songs. The British satirists performed send-ups of two popular movies, the modern-day horror film *Rosemary's Baby* and, yes, *The Graduate.*

April was also the month of the Academy Awards, and Mel Brooks had been nominated for best original screenplay for *The Producers.* Anne remained in New York because, Frank Langella recalled, she was scared that Mel would not win and she could not face that prospect. The competition was indeed formidable. Besides *The Battle of Algiers* and *Hot Millions,* there was *Faces,* written by Anne's drama school classmate John Cassavetes, and *2001: A Space Odyssey,* written by Stanley Kubrick and the science fiction master Arthur C. Clarke. Comedy won out over international, personal, and interstellar angst, and Mel bounded up to the stage to receive the award from Frank Sinatra and Don Rickles. The Brookses were now a two-Oscar family.

A few months later Anne returned to Stockbridge, Massachusetts, for another summer stint with William Gibson and Arthur Penn. Gibson's new play for the Berkshire Theatre Festival—actually, it was less a play than a recitation—would be the most unusual material Anne had yet attempted. Gibson had devised from the letters and diaries of John Adams and his wife, Abigail, a text creating a portrait of their marriage amid the boiling American Revolution. The tumultuous period of independence was already playing out on Broadway in the musical *1776,* which had opened that March and prominently featured the same Founding Father whose legacy had so impressed Gibson. He wrote some material to bridge events, but the words from the future president and first lady were their own.

"I really don't know what we have here," Gibson told the *New York Times* in spring 1969 as plans were announced for a Stockbridge Playhouse staging of *John and Abigail.* He had planned to experiment with the material with a few actors, treating it more like a workshop. "But the thing grew," he said, "and it was decided to give it a production as a regular part of the summer schedule." Anne had already agreed to play Abigail Adams, her faith in her friend rising above any concerns over what sounded like an unsettled script. Joining her as John Adams was James Broderick, a stage and television actor who had recently finished filming *Alice's Restaurant* for Arthur Penn.

Penn was the artistic director at Berkshire that summer but was not going to direct *John and Abigail* himself. The initial plan was to put the production in the hands of Frank Corsaro, the Broadway veteran who had directed Anne in the NBC television show "Out on the Outskirts of Town." Corsaro bowed out unexpectedly, however, and two of the weeks that had been set aside for rehearsals went by as Gibson and Penn considered a replacement. They found one in Frank Langella. Though he lacked Corsaro's experience, Langella knew his way around after two previous summers in Stockbridge and understood the goals that Gibson and Penn shared for the Berkshire theater program.

"Bill's play is a great challenge," Anne said at the time. "I've never done anything like it, just two characters talking all night long, almost nonstop, and all of it taken from the correspondence between John and Abigail." Of course, she had done something like it—Gibson's *Two for the Seesaw* twelve years earlier—but she had never been so hemmed in by historical fact. Gibson's new play also had Anne and James Broderick create and imagine a gallery of other characters. "And we have to place ourselves in the history, all that," she said. "It's very hard, very tricky concentration, but stimulating." To her, the Berkshire program offered one of the few places she could try out different approaches as an actor. By then she found New York lacking in that kind of creative nurturing and discovery, which suggests that her days at the Actors Studio were in the past.

Unfortunately, *John and Abigail* presented more problems than Anne had dealt with in her previous Berkshire summers. Besides the unusual nature of the material and the change from an experienced director to a relative novice, Anne had only what Gibson had written to develop her sense of Abigail Adams. There was no time to throw herself into research—and no one like Abigail Adams to talk to—and it left her feeling less well prepared than she had been when she played that other real-life character, Annie Sullivan.

A sign of deeper problems was Gibson's ongoing revision of the script. At one point he added another character to the cast, played by Ray Stewart, a Berkshire veteran, to smooth out the transitions. "I was dressed in a colonial officer's costume," he said, "and I would come in between certain scenes and paint the picture." They decided that the new character was not the answer and tried a chorus. "The fact that they added this, took it out, added a chorus, expanded it . . . it was a bit of a mess," Stewart said. In the meantime, Anne's voice became so raw during rehearsals that she insisted that the production be cut back to five nights a week. It was no wonder that her vocal cords were taking a beating—the play was running three hours with two intermissions.

"Three dull hours," the Boston Globe's Kevin Kelly wrote in a review of John and Abigail that he presented as a tongue-in-cheek missive to the couple. He found Adams's letters to be boring and James Broderick's reading, which he described as a dry monotone, to be without any sense of characterization. "But Miss Bancroft sparks everything she grazes," Kelly wrote. "She creates a wonderfully winning Abigail." Aiding her, he believed, were letters that were far more dramatic than her costar's. "I can't even tell you how disappointing the evening was," he wrote. "And so damn long!"

William Gibson would have agreed. Decades later he told Gary English, a drama professor and director, that they all thought it had indeed been a mess. "They basically had never found a kind of theatrical ring to it," English said in recounting a discussion with Gibson. "I got the impression from him, although I don't know that he ever really said so, that they didn't have a lot of time to work on it." As English heard the story, there was no finger-pointing or anguish or broken friendships. "They'd worked on it, they'd tried to make it work, and it didn't. And that was that," he said. "Frank Langella, Annie Bancroft, and Gibson all went over to his house and got drunk and laughed themselves silly because they thought it was so ridiculous."

Anne had never been in such a fiasco, and one can imagine what she endured each night. There was little for her to do but look ahead. Besides, she had a movie obligation waiting—not hers, but her husband's. Much as Abigail Adams had supported John during his trying time, Anne was about to do the same for Mel.

The producer of The Producers, Sidney Glazier, capitalized on good word of mouth for the first Mel Brooks movie to raise money for the second. Mel decided to adapt a Russian satirical novel from the 1920s and wrote The Twelve Chairs, a movie about the madcap efforts of three men—a young scoundrel, a former aristocrat, and a greedy priest—to find a chair containing a fortune in gems hidden in its cushion. Mel chose to film in

Yugoslavia, an economical move that would reduce the budget to a tenth or so of what it would have been in the United States. Besides providing cheaper labor and accommodations, Yugoslavia offered locations that may have been the best possible substitute for postrevolutionary Russia outside the Soviet Union.

The British actor Ron Moody, who had starred as Fagin in the film version of the musical *Oliver!* the year before, signed on as the aristocrat. Mel hired Anne's *Cry of Players* costar Frank Langella to be the young scoundrel. For the role of the priest Anne suggested that Mel consider a chubby comic actor she had seen on Dean Martin's television variety show. Mel did and ended up casting Dom DeLuise, the beginning of a long professional association between the director and actor and a deep friendship between the Brooks family and DeLuise and his wife, Carol Arthur, also an actor. Mel put himself in *The Twelve Chairs* as the aristocrat's former lackey and used local actors and townspeople to enhance the film's Eastern European look.

Shooting in and around Belgrade was scheduled for several months in the latter part of 1969. Anne was not one for long separations from her husband and felt the urge to join him on location. Nothing suggested it would be a comfortable getaway for her or even a vacation from stress. "We wasted entire days because of the language barrier," Frank Langella said when the film came out the next year. "The physical discomfort was unbelievable, and I almost gave up on movie-making before we were through." What would there be for Anne to do except suffer along with Mel? For years she had managed to find ways to accommodate both her career and her husband's. Now a choice was before her: be there for Mel as he worked nonstop for months in Yugoslavia or remain at home, perhaps even working, in New York. It was just the kind of emotional tug-of-war that bedeviled her for so much of her life.

Then an idea clicked in her mind. She had been asked again and again to return to television in another special, and she suddenly realized that a show cobbled together from sketches and musical numbers would not have the same hold on her time as a movie or a play. Was it practical for Anne to do a television special in New York and still be with Mel as he worked on a movie set in Eastern Europe? She was determined to try, deciding as she often did that she could have everything she wanted if she worked hard enough.

Martin Charnin, a Broadway performer turned composer and lyricist who also worked in television, conceived an hour-long showcase for Anne's talents as a singer and dancer and to give her an opportunity to display her comic skills. "The idea that really got me was that wonderful one of doing all these different kinds of women in a man's life," she said. As the show developed into a dozen or so segments, Anne would appear as a bride going down the aisle, a medieval lady dancing with armor-clad knights, a sultry woman embracing her lover by firelight, a glamorous matron, and a kooky lady dancing away the decades but trying to keep up with changing styles. There would be a few dramatic moments, but most of the show was light and infused with comedy and music.

With sketches and songs in hand, Anne joined her husband in Yugoslavia. She watched the dailies with Mel, offered suggestions to Frank Langella and Dom DeLuise, and generally cheered people up. "She was a great and loving pal throughout the shoot," Langella said. Anne also made time for rehearsing material written for her television special. She returned to New York to work with the company, then flew back to Belgrade to prepare some more on her own. "When she wasn't rehearsing or shooting, she wanted to be with Mel, so that meant a constant check of airline and train arrivals and departures in Yugoslavia," said Joe Cates, the special's executive producer. "That was kind of hectic, I must admit." In time her efforts to have it all would pay off.

Annie, the Women in the Life of a Man gave its star an incredible range of characters to play. Some of its music came from standards such as Jule Styne and Frank Loesser's "I Don't Want to Walk without You, Baby," Cole Porter's "Ev'ry Time We Say Goodbye," and Irving Berlin's "Change Partners." Among a few newer tunes was Stephen Sondheim and Richard Rodgers's "Stay" from their 1965 show, *Do I Hear a Waltz?* In a somber nod to the ongoing war in Vietnam, Anne played a mother reading a letter from her son, a World War I soldier, as the sketch went into an antiwar song, "Maman," from the 1967 show *Mata Hari* with lyrics by Martin Charnin.

Of the sketches focusing on laughs, one featured Anne as a clueless if trendy young woman auditioning for a musical. She does not get the cleverness behind the lyrics of George and Ira Gershwin's "Let's Call the Whole Thing Off," pronouncing the word pairs "potato/potato" and "tomato/tomato" the same way. In another comic turn, she tells her psychiatrist that she has a nightmare in which she hosts a party for the Peruvian singer Yma Sumac and introduces her to the other guests, among them Ava Gardner,

Ida Lupino, Mia Farrow, Uta Hagen, and Oona O'Neill. This leads to lots of tongue twisters—Yma, Ava . . . Yma, Uta . . . Yma, Oona . . .

The male supporting cast included people from Anne's past. Playing her father in the bridal sketch was John McGiver, the character actor who had been her high school drama teacher. Dick Shawn, her betrothed in the TV show "I'm Getting Married," was again her groom. Lee J. Cobb, her *Gorilla at Large* costar, was the psychiatrist in the Yma Sumac sketch. Also on the roster were Jack Cassidy, the talk-show host and producer David Susskind, the comedian Dick Smothers, the opera singer Robert Merrill, and the dance instructor Arthur Murray.

The medieval sketch with the dancing knights and the Arthur Murray sketch were choreographed by Alan Johnson, a Broadway veteran who had choreographed the "Springtime for Hitler" number in Mel's film *The Producers*. In spite of Anne's limited experience as a dancer, she was terrific to work with, he remembered. "When you work with dancers, you count in counts of eight to help them memorize it," Johnson said. "She never counted. She really sort of just absorbed it. You told her where to go and what it felt like and she got it immediately. I kept thinking she does this as well as acting—she's acting the dance. What she knew as an actress, what she was as an actress, she brought to singing and dancing. It was all the same art—very unusual."

It would be difficult to find any other show Anne performed in her career, whether onstage, in the movies, or on television, that received such unqualified praise. The dean of television critics, Jack Gould of the *New York Times,* called the CBS special airing on February 18, 1970, a tour de force for its star and a milestone for the televised variety show. "Rightfully, she should be the toast of the country by tomorrow morning," he wrote. "Miss Bancroft sings like an angel of feeling, engages in hilarious sketches with a genuinely fresh twist, dances with the spirit of the Fred Astaire era and the modern jump, recites poetry ranging from a somewhat serious vein to a tongue-twisting gag and does it all with an easy modesty that is totally disarming." The critic at the *Washington Post,* Lawrence Laurent, told readers her special was "easily the finest entertainment hour of this television season."

The Academy of Television Arts and Sciences honored *Annie, the Women in the Life of a Man* with two Emmy nominations. In winning for outstanding variety or musical program/variety and popular music, Anne and the producers beat out specials starring Frank Sinatra, Jack Benny, Bill

Cosby, and Burt Bacharach. Its second award was for writing. One of those winners was Thomas Meehan, who thirty years later would coauthor with Mel Brooks the book for the stage musical version of *The Producers*. Among the numerous writers providing additional material for her special had been two important men in her own life, Mel and William Gibson.

For Anne and Mel, their first project together—even if he had just a small hand in it—had been a smash. She had pulled off the seemingly impossible balance of being a supportive spouse and a career woman through sheer willpower. "It was absolutely perfect," she said later. "It worked out fine and it kept my marriage together. I was very happy."

Anne did little press ahead of the special, adding to her new reputation for not granting interviews. "She values her time off," the executive producer Joe Cates explained to Jerry Shnay, who wrote about television for the *Chicago Tribune*. "And when it is her own time, she wants to be with her husband." Shnay reported that the word going around was that Anne refused to be interviewed unless she was allowed to read the story and edit it before it was published. No self-respecting journalist would abide by that condition. Rex Reed, a critic and profile writer known for revealing portraits of celebrities as well as a nasty streak, claimed that Anne was the only person who had turned him down for an interview and never relented. "She kept making excuses about family illness and things," Reed said. "Then I met her husband once at a cocktail party and he told me she was the most neurotic lady he'd ever been married to." That kind of hurtful barb explained in part why Anne and Mel avoided interviews unless they were promoting their work.

The role that finally brought Anne back to the big screen would place her in the most ambitious historical film to reach movie theaters in 1972. After the success of 1969's *Easy Rider* and 1971's *The Last Picture Show*, many studios and filmmakers were favoring inexpensive, intimate dramas that could reap major rewards at the box office. Going against the trend was Carl Foreman, the screenwriter for *The Bridge on the River Kwai* and the screenwriter and producer for *The Guns of Navarone*, both hugely popular war movies. Foreman had been trying for a decade to launch *Young Winston*, a film about Winston Churchill's early years as a war correspondent and elected official. Developing the project in 1970, Foreman hired the actor and director Richard Attenborough to oversee filming of what Attenborough would call an "intimate epic"—one budgeted at a hefty $6 million.

Foreman hoped to persuade Attenborough to play Lord Randolph Churchill, the future prime minister's father, a task the actor was not eager to accept if he was to direct the film. They would eventually look elsewhere among the ranks of British actors. The role of Churchill's mother allowed them to bring an American flavor to the film while remaining historically accurate. Lady Randolph Churchill was a Brooklyn-born American, Jeanette "Jennie" Jerome, the daughter of a nineteenth-century financier. That she was considered one of the era's most beautiful women would have made the part attractive to almost any actress. Her life carried whiffs of scandal—her husband died of syphilis and she was romantically linked to many men.

Attenborough knew from the first whom he wanted alongside Lord Randolph. "Jennie, his American wife, in my view cried out for one actress alone—Anne Bancroft," the director said. The American studio handling the picture thought he was wasting his time. "When I said I wanted Anne Bancroft," Attenborough said, "the big brass at Columbia Pictures said, 'Forget it—we've offered her dozens of pictures—she's turned them all down.'" He sent Anne the script anyway, then flew to New York to meet her at the Regency Hotel.

"She came through the revolving doors and I knew at once that, come hell or high water, she had to pay Jennie," Attenborough said. When Anne had wanted to star in *The Pumpkin Eater,* she had to campaign for the role. This time, she was the one who needed coaxing. She explained that she had not been able to make a connection with the character. "In this particular instance," Attenborough said, "she was enthusiastic about the script as a whole but felt that there were elements in her role about which she was very uncertain." Whatever his arguments were that day, she turned him down.

Attenborough returned to London disappointed but hopeful that revisions in the script already being undertaken by Carl Foreman would lead Anne to a change of heart. She read the new version of the script but even then retained her doubts. "After several phone calls," Attenborough said, "she was convinced that she had found the understanding she required to create a true characterization, which for her had always been an essential before accepting any offer." To the surprise of the executives at Columbia Pictures, Anne had agreed to make their film her first since *The Graduate.*

Appearing as the young Churchill would be Simon Ward, a thirty-year-old actor with stage and television experience but little film work.

Robert Shaw would play Lord Randolph Churchill. By then Shaw had been in films and television for a quarter century and had gained international recognition for supporting roles in the James Bond film *From Russia with Love* (1963), *Battle of the Bulge* (1965), and *A Man for All Seasons* (1966), for which he had received an Oscar nomination for his performance as Henry VIII. He was a novelist and a playwright, gregarious and outspoken but intense and volatile. Shaw would make the most of his relatively few scenes as a father who seldom spoke to his son and usually berated him when he did.

Nearly all of Anne's scenes would be either with Robert Shaw or with one of the three actors who played Churchill at ages seven, thirteen, and nineteen and up. Shaw would not have ingratiated himself with Anne on two points of their craft. "When I am directed by a fellow actor, we don't have to waste a lot of time communicating," he told a reporter, a compliment aimed at Richard Attenborough. "God spare me from directors who want to sit down with me and discuss the character. I can't play an essay on their theories." He also did not share her interest in looking inward. "Anne Bancroft became very annoyed with me because of my feelings about psychiatry," he said with a chuckle. "I was afraid analysis would take away what little talent I had left." They did share at least one outlook when it came to the business of acting. "Nothing destroys an actor faster than working in junk," Shaw said. That was a sentiment Anne could cheer.

The film covered events in the first twenty-five years of Churchill's life, yet the billing would feature Shaw first and Anne second; Ward would receive "and as" credit. Lady Randolph was not meant to be the focus of *Young Winston*, of course, yet the role was a grand way for Anne to reintroduce herself to moviegoers. She aged from her mid-twenties, when Winston leaves home for boarding school, to her late forties, when he returns from the Boer War a hero and wins a seat in the House of Commons.

Changes in Anne's physical appearance were negligible and she was beautifully coiffed and dressed throughout the film. She had several pivotal scenes in which she demonstrates Lady Randolph's inattention to her young son, deals with her husband's thorny temperament and madness brought on by his fatal illness, and witnesses her son's coming of age as a soldier and statesman. The behavior that caused so many tongues to wag was only hinted at. Churchill's biographer William Manchester described the real Lady Randolph as "a beautiful, shallow, selfish, diamond-studded panther of a woman." Only the character's beauty truly stands out, a flaw in the film that even Anne could not overcome. Then again, the movie was about young Winston and not his mother.

Attenborough spent nearly six months filming *Young Winston*. The production used Shepperton Studios outside London as its base and shot at locations associated with Churchill's life—for example, the Harrow School, Chartwell House, the Royal Military Academy Sandhurst, and Blenheim Palace. A stretch of railway in the Welsh countryside stood in for South Africa. Outside Britain, Morocco was used for some battle scenes representing skirmishes in India and Sudan. Most of the scenes featuring Anne were filmed at Shepperton over the course of several weeks in mid-1971.

Richard Attenborough could be sympathetic as well as empathetic to his players. Educated at the Royal Academy of Dramatic Art, he had been in the movies for thirty years. *Young Winston* was just his second film as a director, but he had already learned to be resourceful and, when necessary, a bit devious. In a key scene young Churchill and his mother have a tense if quiet clash over a speech he would give in Parliament that had the potential to wreck his blossoming career. Attenborough began the scene with Anne and Simon Ward late one afternoon and resumed shooting the next morning.

"Unfortunately for the moment we were all in high spirits," Ward said later. "Dickie, who can direct during any kind of chaos, suddenly blew up at the man serving tea, accusing him of rattling the cups on purpose. He put on such a tirade that we all went rigid with anxiety. Then he ordered the scene to be shot." Afterward, Attenborough went around the set apologizing, explaining that his temper tantrum had been in the service of putting Anne and Ward in the tense mood he needed for the scene.

Young Winston was released in Britain in the spring of 1972 and in the United States that fall. Many American critics found much to admire in the film. "A superior biographic movie" that featured a perfect performance by Anne, wrote Kevin Kelly of the *Boston Globe*. Arthur Knight of the *Saturday Review* complimented Carl Foreman for conceiving "the action film in which the action is subordinate to the gradual emergence of the central character" and praised the cast for making their characters into human beings. "A rousing adventure story that touches the heart and stirs the intellect," wrote Judith Crist of *New York* magazine. "A glowing and inspiring work." Others were underwhelmed and pointed to exciting

moments and a dignified portrait of Churchill but not a particularly compelling film. Vincent Canby of the *New York Times* dismissed *Young
Winston* as "a big, balsa-wood monument" that moves at a "lumbering
pace." Anne and Robert Shaw were such interesting actors, Canby said,
"you wish it were about them." More than one critic thought Anne had
little to do. Gary Arnold of the *Washington Post* wrote, "While Miss
Bancroft looks faintly ludicrous as she flashes monotonous anxious expressions, I'm not sure anyone could shine in this rather uptight and conventional conception of Jennie Jerome."

As one might expect of an unabashed celebration of Winston
Churchill, the film drew more praise and attention in Britain than the
United States. The British film academy nominated it for six BAFTA
awards, including those for Anne and Robert Shaw in their leading roles
and for Simon Ward as most promising newcomer. In a sign of its perceived shortcomings even in Britain, the film was not a best picture or best
director nominee and won only for costume design. At the Academy
Awards, *Young Winston* received just three nominations—for art direction, costume design, and adapted script—and no Oscars in the year dominated by *The Godfather* and *Cabaret*. The highest honor the film earned
was the Golden Globe for best foreign film in English.

Columbia Pictures had rolled out *Young Winston* as a "road show"
release in the United States, meaning that it played in major cities with
reserved seating, higher ticket prices, one or two screenings a day, and an
intermission. The public, however, did not respond to the movie as if it
were an event. Initial film rentals were disappointing, reaching $2.1 mil-
lion to place well outside the top fifty on the annual *Variety* rental chart. By
comparison, the top movie of 1972, *The Poseidon Adventure*, brought in
$40 million, followed by *Deliverance* and *The Getaway* at about $18 million
apiece. Though *Young Winston* fell short of the level of a David Lean epic,
Richard Attenborough would reach that height with *Gandhi* in 1982. For
Carl Foreman, *Young Winston* was his last major film production.

In terms of scope, *Young Winston* was the only motion picture epic
that Anne had appeared in since *Demetrius and the Gladiators* nearly
twenty years earlier. She would never again grace such a lavish film production. Only with the rise of the television miniseries would she take
the opportunity to play supporting roles in historical epics. The contemporary drama remained her venue of choice. Without question, however,
she had returned to the movies on her terms—in a respectable film and

in a role that was radically different from the one she played in *The Graduate.*

Her break from her profession after *Young Winston* included a trip in August 1971 with Mel and some of their friends to the French Riviera. A month later, on September 17, she turned forty years old. So much had happened since her birth in the Bronx: singing atop a picnic table, school plays, drama lessons, live television, Hollywood, marriage and divorce, Broadway, and a return to the movies and television. There had been honors, too, among them two Tony awards, an Oscar, and an Emmy. For most people a fortieth birthday is a time to take stock in the past and consider the future. As that milestone approached for Anne, there was one role she had longed to play at least once, yet it appeared to be out of her reach. But, to her surprise, it was not. She was about to become a mother.

10

Motherhood and More Roles to Follow

Ideas for stories could come from anywhere and at any time. Sumner Arthur Long was trying to make a career as a writer in Hollywood when he was walking along the street and a woman caught his eye. She was in her fifties, very pregnant, and beaming. He thought to himself, "I wonder what her husband said when . . ." Some years later, in 1962, Long finished that thought with the play *Never Too Late,* a comedy about a middle-aged woman who discovers to her delight—and her husband's shock—that she is going to have a baby. A Broadway hit, *Never Too Late* played on the notion that a baby late in life could bring with it uncertainty, humor, and love.

Surprise, at least to some extent, accompanied the diagnosis that Anne, age forty, would be having a baby in spring 1972. "She never thought she would get pregnant," her longtime friend David Lunney remembered. "It was like a cartoon thing—she came home from the doctor and said, 'Guess what, honey?' And he said, 'What?' 'I'm pregnant.' And she had Max."

There was more to it, of course. The prospect of giving birth at her age carried a degree of risk. As a woman passes her mid-thirties, the chances increase for miscarriage, birth defects, and genetic disorders. Anne listened to the warnings—and the predictions that this could be her last chance to give birth. She decided to forgo the increase in risk of miscarriage that came with amniocentesis, the medical test that would show whether the baby carried any abnormalities in its chromosomes that would lead to birth defects. She was determined to have her child.

And she did. On May 22, 1972, a healthy boy, Maximillian Michael, was born to Anne and Mel in New York City. "She was thrilled to death to have Max," said a close friend, Bobbi Elliott. "My God, that was the high-light of her life." Elliott and her husband, the musical director Jack Elliott, were raising three children, one of them a daughter just a few years older than Max. Even before Max's birth, Bobbi Elliott and Anne talked about the challenges facing a mother. Anne was naturally curious and worked diligently at anything she cared about, traits that helped her as an actress, and she wanted to know everything when it came to raising a child.

"She was very fearful. She was very worried that she wouldn't be the most perfect mother in the world," Bobbi Elliott said. "She was always wor-ried about that, as she was terribly worried that she wouldn't be the perfect person onstage. People in show business . . . they're terribly insecure. And that was one of the most endearing qualities about her."

During her pregnancy and for the first year after her son's birth, Anne shifted her focus away from her acting career. She had no interest in com-mitting herself to the late hours and potentially long run that a play would demand, and she declined to be cast in films for the time being. She also avoided discussing her son with reporters, offering only a banal com-ment—"We are doting parents"—or evading questions about her new-found role as a mother. When a *TV Guide* writer in 1974 asked Anne about Max, then two, her demeanor immediately darkened. "I'm sorry, didn't someone explain? We do not discuss him publicly, ever," she said. "Mel and I are adamant. Our work is public, our other life is not, that emphatically includes our son. Oh, look, our time, this world, it's too full of maniacs, of hostility." It was a point difficult to argue with, even coming from enter-tainers who sought public attention.

Many years later, when Max was an adult, Anne felt more comfortable sharing her thoughts about her late-in-life pregnancy. "I tried very hard to become a mother," she said in an interview published in 2000. "I didn't realize I had a lot of conflict about it. I knew it would be a tremendous responsibility. On the other hand, I wanted it. I needed it."

Being able to afford household help and other comforts made life eas-ier, if not easy, for Anne. "It was quite a thing for her. She was bowled over," her younger sister, Phyllis Italiano, would confide to an audience at a screening of one of Anne's movies. "She would say to me, 'You never told me it would be this constant.' . . . I remember her hanging diapers out on Fire Island and her looking at me across at the other house with almost tears in her eyes."

Producers and directors still came calling. Where Anne landed on the list of sought-after actresses at the time—Shirley MacLaine, Jane Fonda, Dyan Cannon, Angela Lansbury, Colleen Dewhurst, and Geraldine Page— indicated that she remained a leading choice for major films. Given a chance to say no, Anne usually did. Two of the roles she passed up in the early 1970s turned into career milestones for the actresses who accepted them: the mother in *The Exorcist,* played by Ellen Burstyn, and the head nurse in *One Flew Over the Cuckoo's Nest,* played so effectively by Louise Fletcher that she won an Oscar. The producer David Susskind adored Anne and wanted her for *Alice Doesn't Live Here Anymore,* a drama about a widowed mother who tries to get a fresh start in life as a singer. Warner Bros. made it clear, however, that backing the movie would be contingent on casting Ellen Burstyn. She won the role and an Academy Award.

As far as the actor-writer-producer-director Jerry Lewis was concerned, any list of actresses could be boiled down to two. When his book *The Total Filmmaker* came out, he told *Newsday* that George C. Scott was his idea of the "total actor"—working from within, technically oriented, and capable of being soft, sentimental, and devastatingly vulnerable. "Let's say an order came down from God and He said that no more actors allowed but two," Lewis mused. He would choose Scott and Paul Newman. What about actresses? "Anne Bancroft and Streisand," he replied. "That's all we need." Whether Anne would be interested in working was another matter.

Her absence from movie screens coincided, happily, with the break her husband needed to breathe life into his own career. The first two Mel Brooks films, *The Producers* and *The Twelve Chairs,* had their fans but did not draw enough people to the box office to avoid being considered flops. Mel had been working on a script that would parody the Western and began directing the production for Warner Bros. in the first half of 1973. *Blazing Saddles* was an enormous hit, reaching Number 6 on the *Variety* list of film rentals for 1974.

As *Blazing Saddles* filled theaters, Mel directed a film he had written with Gene Wilder, who would play the title role in *Young Frankenstein.* The parody of the classic horror films of the 1930s came out near the end of 1974 and scored an even greater success for Mel. It was the fourth-most-popular film on the *Variety* list for 1975, behind *Jaws, The Towering Inferno,* and *Benji.* Since both his movies were released in the same year, Mel ended up with Oscar nominations in two different categories for two different films: in music/song for *Blazing Saddles* and for cowriting *Young*

Frankenstein with Wilder. A supporting actress in both films, Madeline Kahn, drew a nomination for her comic work in *Blazing Saddles.*

Mel's name and face were becoming familiar to moviegoers, in no small part because he was an indefatigable promoter of his work and himself. Soon, more and more people around the country were aware that the wisecracking talk-show guest who was behind two of their favorite comedies was also, inexplicably to many, the husband of that eminently serious and respected actress Anne Bancroft. By then she had returned to work herself, but her projects were not finding the positive reception that had greeted her husband's.

Not long after the Brooks family celebrated Max's first birthday, in May 1973, his mother went back to work. Deciding that she could afford to take the time for one project a year and still be a mother and wife, Anne agreed to costar with Jack Lemmon in the movie version of a Neil Simon play, *The Prisoner of Second Avenue.* The production would be based in Los Angeles at Warner Bros., the same studio where Mel was making *Blazing Saddles.* Some location work was on the schedule, but it was in New York, the play's setting. For her first film since *Young Winston,* Anne had chosen a production that would make it easy to be with her son and husband most nights.

Convenience was not the only reason *The Prisoner of Second Avenue* was an attractive movie project for Anne. It was a high-quality enterprise in every way. The stage production had opened on Broadway in November 1971 with Peter Falk and Lee Grant under the direction of Mike Nichols. It ran for nearly two years and received Tony awards for Nichols as director and Vincent Gardenia as featured actor and a nomination for best play. The story presents a harried middle-aged couple living in a New York high-rise and dealing with the less pleasant aspects of life on the Upper East Side. Aside from losing his job amid a recession, Mel Edison has to cope with noisy neighbors, a garbage strike, a heat wave, a water shutoff, and burglars. His wife, Edna, bears the brunt of his tirades and goes back to work herself, becoming the breadwinner after Mel suffers a nervous breakdown. He recovers, but they remain prisoners in their own city.

While Simon adapted the play for film—he called it a serious comedy or a funny drama—he worried that moviegoers across the country would not be in sync with the New York theater audiences that had made the play popular. "*The Odd Couple* and *Barefoot in the Park,* both true comedies, were successful in both mediums," he wrote in a memoir. "The darker my plays became, however, the more lackluster the results when they were transferred to the big screen." An open question was whether ticket buyers in rural and suburban America would connect with the travails of high-pressure life in New York.

As Anne knew only too well, movie studios wanted movie stars instead of Broadway stars to make their films more appealing to the general public. Her star status was not in doubt after *The Graduate,* and she got the screen role over Lee Grant, her *Two for the Seesaw* replacement. With Jack Lemmon playing Mel, the film gained another Oscar winner and a veteran of the Simon movies *The Odd Couple* and *The Out-of-Towners.* Edna would be Anne's first character in a script by Simon, who had worked with Mel Brooks as part of the writing staff for Sid Caesar's television show back in the 1950s. Their director would be Melvin Frank, an accomplished comedy writer since the 1940s who had turned writer-director in the 1950s. The previous year he had scored a success with *A Touch of Class.*

The character Mel Edison was the prisoner of the title, meaning that Jack Lemmon was the film's lead. All the events turn on Mel's urban angst, but Edna gets in a few zingers of her own. The screenplay had bolstered the role of Edna and made her much more a part of the overall story. Anne had not played such a comic role in films before and, for the first time, was onscreen as an average New York housewife concerned with such things as keeping up the apartment and doing the shopping—and dealing with a manic husband. She also did not have to be so concerned about her Bronx accent showing.

Warner Bros. conducted a sneak preview for the film in August 1974, then held back on a national release for months. Another hint of a production in trouble was a *Variety* review that appeared in its December 25 issue. "The film is more of a drama with comedy, for the personal problems as well as the environmental challenges aren't really funny, and even some of the humor is forced," the entertainment trade journal said. "The Warner Bros. release may therefore perform erratically." The *Variety* critic also suggested that Lemmon was playing a character that he had done before and that Anne was less familiar to moviegoers in a comedic role. As far as the material, "Simon's comedy is no better and no worse than it was in the '60s; the trouble is, it's now the '70s." In short, Anne's new movie was stale and she was out of place in it, and, worse from a studio perspective, it probably had limited appeal. Nearly three more months went by before the movie opened.

The Prisoner of Second Avenue earned better reviews than the *Variety* forecast would have suggested when it finally went into release in March 1975. One of the best appeared in *New York* magazine, where Judith Crist recommended the film and singled out Anne, "all too rarely on screen," for bringing "a resilient, resourceful, wise, and witty woman to life on screen, and how sweet—and rare—it is!" Anne provided "a quietly beautiful portrayal," wrote Charles Champlin of the *Los Angeles Times,* "bright and sympathetic, and the measure of Miss Bancroft's confidence as an actress is that, like the wife she plays, she is sustaining rather than competing." Taken as a group, the reviews were decidedly mixed, some mildly recommending the movie and others suggesting that it was a travesty. When the reviews were more positive than negative, Anne was among the praiseworthy elements. A negative review tended not only to criticize Neil Simon and Jack Lemmon but question why Anne had wasted her talents along with theirs. In the meantime, just $2.2 million in rentals placed it well outside the top fifty films of the year, lining up with the *Variety* prediction of erratic commercial results.

Anne went back to the well of her previous success—television—for what was supposed to be her annual project for 1974. In an effort to repeat their triumph of several seasons before, many of the talents who had worked on *Annie, the Women in the Life of a Man* reassembled for an ABC television special aimed at a Thanksgiving audience. It would be called *Annie and the Hoods.* "The concept's just the same," she said. "I do lots of different characters again, different moods." Martin Charnin returned as producer and even directed this time. The all-male supporting cast included Alan Alda, Jack Benny, Tony Curtis, David Merrick, Robert Merrill, Carl Reiner, Gene Wilder—and Mel Brooks. It would be the first time Anne and her husband appeared together on any screen, large or small, and it was conveniently taped in Los Angeles, where most of the cast lived. One notable exception was Merrick—the Broadway producer flew the three thousand miles from New York just to appear in a sketch in which Anne auditions for him by riding into the room atop an elephant and performing "Some Sunny Day" with other singers and dancers.

As part of her preparation for the show's musical segments, Anne worked with Nancy Lunney, a vocal coach and accompanist who was married to her childhood friend David Lunney. The Christopher Columbus High classmates had reconnected when David and Nancy Lunney moved to Los Angeles. David's daily drive to work at the American Film Institute took him near Anne and Mel's home, and one day he pulled over and knocked on their door, the beginning of a new phase in their friendship. Their daughter was nearly the same age as Max, and the two families began socializing.

Nancy Lunney had never heard Anne sing until she began working with her ahead of *Annie and the Hoods*. "She was very musical, and she loved to sing," Lunney remembered. "It was not a polished voice. She sang the way she talked. She certainly carried a tune very well. She was certainly very musical, but it wasn't a skilled voice. Maybe she had complete control over it, but it didn't sound like it." Can such a voice be appealing to an audience? "I think so," Lunney said. "I love actors who use their acting abilities. They are using the words as well as their voices to convey something. They're not singers, but they sing it better than anybody."

In working with Anne, Nancy Lunney followed her lead and would accompany her on piano as she practiced songs. "I didn't feel like I was teaching her. I really felt like I was accompanying her in every sense of the word. We worked on what she wanted to do." In Lunney's experience, actors who were not great singers needed to draw on other resources. Anne was in that group. "Instead of vocalizing the way a trained singer would vocalize, the way she'd vocalize was she sang the song 'Broadway Melody,' and we'd keep raising the key a half a tone, and she'd sing it a half-tone higher, and a half-tone higher, and a half-tone higher—that was the way we'd vocalize."

Annie and the Hoods played off the idea of "hoods" as different stages in a woman's life—bachelorhood, adulthood, motherhood, likelihood, unlikelihood, and so on. Anne appears as a dozen or so characters in the sketches, even one placed on a pedestal by a chauvinist (Tony Curtis) but eager to climb down. For the concept of motherhood, she is in a baby's room with a crying newborn. Apprehensive at first, she embraces the infant and begins to sing "The Nearness of You." In contrast to that tender moment, she plays a gum-chewing bimbo named Bambi Levine in a sketch with Carl Reiner as a British television interviewer. Bambi is the unlikely fiancée of Prince Charles, "the envy of every girl in the world," Reiner says. "Yeah," Anne responds, "I got the big one."

For adulthood, Anne and Gene Wilder play a couple who consider books on the stock market and French cooking sexy bedtime reading. In the parenthood sketch she reads Ogden Nash poetry with Alan Alda. Reprising the most memorable segment of the other show, the Yma Sumac sketch, Jack Benny appears as the silent therapist listening to his patient's bizarre dinner party nightmare. This time the guests are at Jilly's Restaurant in New York and include Lily Tomlin, Willy Brandt, Rollie Fingers, Mollie Parnis, Polly Bergen, and Wally Schirra. The introductions giving her bad dreams: "Jilly, Willy. Rollie, Mollie. Polly, Wally . . ."

In a nod to her role as performer and the contributions of the writers, Anne told *TV Guide:* "Look, the material's hysterical, but it's not mine. I just work here. I have nothing to do with the thinking." One of those who did, the writer Gail Parent, remembered a positive experience working on Anne's special. "She was so beautiful and so graceful and so funny," Parent said years later. "When you get a professional like that it's such a gift— they're so good. And she was great, a great actress."

Drawing the most attention in the press was the pairing of Anne and Mel, another sign of his newfound celebrity. In their sketch depicting a woman who has discovered her husband cheating—other womanhood— she is called on to serve Mel a martini when he comes home and to sere- nade him with "Guess Who I Saw Today." Asked in an interview why they had not worked together before, Anne said they had not found the right vehicle. "Mel, as you know, does those way-out comedies like *Blazing Saddles* and they don't usually have big parts in them for women," she said. "But if he ever came up with something he wanted me to do, I would jump at the chance." It would not take too long for Mel to come up with that something.

What did Anne think about the relationship of the material to the women's movement? It was rare for her to get into public discussions of political and social issues, but *Annie and the Hoods* raised the question. "The movement does one bad thing," she told *TV Guide.* "It can force women out into the marketplace who'd really prefer to stay home with the kids in the kitchen. Otherwise, it's leading to pure freedom, which I've been fanatical about since I was a kid."

In television it could be difficult to catch lightning twice. The critical reception for *Annie and the Hoods* was decidedly negative, almost the opposite of the acclaim the other show had received. *Variety* contended that the hour-long special was dull and even embarrassing. "Her flair for song-and-dance performance, a pleasant surprise in the first special, was pushed beyond its limitations this time out," the trade journal wrote. Though *Newsweek* wrote approvingly of the show, the *New York Times* deemed it a dud that "sank slowly in a swamp of mediocrity." The *Los*

Angeles Times blamed the writing, and the *Chicago Tribune* said, "There was no laugh track and you could hear the silence across America." She would appear in several television movies in the years ahead, but Anne never again made a television special highlighting her comedic and musical talents.

One job a year quickly became two when Anne went almost directly from her television special to another close-to-home project. The movie's simple title, *The Hindenburg,* pretty much said it all—and for those who did not know the true story behind it, the poster would feature an exploding airship. On May 6, 1937, the German dirigible had just completed a transatlantic flight when it crashed in flames while docking in Lakehurst, New Jersey. Newsreel cameras recorded the event, and the radio broadcaster Herb Morrison's eyewitness description—"Oh, the humanity!"—became a classic. What precisely caused the airship's hydrogen tanks to ignite and kill thirteen passengers and twenty-two crewmen was never determined, which gave the screenwriter plenty of room to imagine a tale of mystery and sabotage.

The *Hindenburg* promised to be different from *The Prisoner of Second Avenue* in almost every way. While it too was a high-profile film cast with accomplished colleagues, the real stars were the special effects—namely, a twenty-five-foot scale model of the airship. The movie itself was a drama almost devoid of humor, which was appropriate since it featured one of the great aviation disasters of the twentieth century. The production carried a budget approaching $15 million, a hefty sum at the time. It would be shot almost entirely at Universal Studios, which assured Anne of another easy commute. One of the reasons she declined the role of Nurse Ratched in *One Flew Over the Cuckoo's Nest* may have been its location shooting in Oregon.

The disaster movie as a genre found a receptive audience in the early 1970s. Though movies had featured natural and man-made calamities now and then since the silent era, Hollywood quickly followed the popular 1970 film *Airport* with the cruise ship disaster *The Poseidon Adventure* in 1972, the high-rise fire disaster *The Towering Inferno,* and another entry with the simple title *Earthquake,* both in 1974. Each had featured a perilous event with a lengthy period of mayhem from which to draw its drama. The *Hindenburg* disaster was over in thirty-four seconds, which meant that the 125-minute film being shot at Universal would need to build suspense about the cause of the disaster and develop more empathy than usual for its victims.

The producer and director Robert Wise spent two years developing *The Hindenburg*. "I was caught up by the whole mystery of what that might have been about, what it cost in human lives, and, very frankly, about the romance of flying on one of those big dirigibles," he said. "My biggest problem was, could I make it work? Could we make the blimp real?" He met with Universal's matte painting specialist and decided that he could show a scale model cruising through the skies and capture the unique feeling of airship travel that had disappeared with the disaster nearly forty years earlier.

The veteran filmmaker who had won Oscars for *West Side Story* and *The Sound of Music* rejected the idea that his new film was part of a genre synonymous with special effects, all-star casts, and melodrama. The attention paid to the special effects for *The Hindenburg* undercut his argument. In addition to the scale model of the airship, the production featured replicas of the gondola, passenger areas, and interior sections of the airship. Re-creating the explosion and crash—the newsreel footage would be intercut with the movie scenes—stretched into ten minutes for the film's exciting climax.

Heading the cast was George C. Scott, playing a German security official trying to discover if there was indeed a plot to sabotage the Nazi government's technological pride and joy. Billed below Scott and the title, Anne was "also starring" in the film as "The Countess." In true disaster film form, the rest of the cast included notable actors: William Atherton, Roy Thinnes, Gig Young, Burgess Meredith, Charles Durning, Richard Dysart, Robert Clary, and René Auberjonois. Three members of the cast had appeared with Anne on the stage—Scott and Dysart in *The Little Foxes* and Auberjonois in *A Cry of Players.*

Except for Scott's investigator, Anne's Countess was the most visible passenger aboard the ill-fated airship. The beautiful widow is all but fleeing Nazi Germany and secretly planning to make a new start with her daughter, who is in boarding school in the United States. Her backstory, which includes a relationship with Scott's investigator, is one of several bits of intrigue meant to give *The Hindenburg* the air of an Agatha Christie story in which the suspects undergo scrutiny as the crime unfolds.

Scott's character was based on a real person, but Anne's was wholly invented by Nelson Gidding, who was writing his fifth screenplay for Wise.

"We had no idea that we would have a part for a female star of the stature of Anne Bancroft," Wise said. "But this character, as Nelson wrote it, became so intriguing that people who read the script got fascinated by the relationship between these two characters. We decided to make it a more substantial part without blowing the whole thing up too much."

In a smaller supporting role was thirty-three-year-old Colby Chester, a Connecticut native who was carving out a career in films and television. Appearing with three Oscar-winning performers—Scott, Anne, and Gig Young—and other respected actors under the direction of Robert Wise was his most prominent assignment yet. "My experience on that film was almost starry-eyed," Chester recalled. "I'd done a lot of television by then, but the thought of working with Anne Bancroft and George C. Scott was just about as much of a fantasy as I could imagine, especially her because she was so beautiful and so sexual—and surprisingly so small." At six-feet-two he towered over the five-feet-five actress.

When they were not shooting a scene, the actors sat in director's chairs in a large circle—all except for George C. Scott, who stayed in his trailer and exuded a sense of disdain for the entire enterprise, Chester remembered. (In a sour mood, Scott told the press that he was done with acting after this job.) Members of the cast would be called to perform a scene, rehearse it a few times, and then shoot. In the meantime, some of the actors would tell stories—Gig Young in particular enjoyed reminiscing—and Chester remembered Anne talking about her husband and their young son and their friend Frank Langella. A few times Anne and other members of the cast grabbed lunch together at the studio commissary.

"What impressed me about her was she was just an actress. She was on the set, she was there to do her job, there was none of this sort of star treatment going on. She was who she was, and you could tell when she wanted to be left alone," Chester said. "It was certainly not a great part for her, and it surprised me in a way that she was cast in it. She was featured, but she certainly wasn't integral to the story. I had the feeling she made some good money on it and hadn't worked for a while and decided to do it."

In front of the cameras, Anne was all business. In one of the production's few location shoots, the cast traveled to the Burbank airport for a scene in which the passengers go through German customs before boarding the airship. When the Countess is interrogated by Nazi officials to the point of insult, she takes umbrage and declares that her host in Boston is with a prominent bank—"and I can assure you, Major, he is *not* the doorman!" The scene over, Colby Chester walked up behind Anne and asked, in a takeoff on the clueless *Get Smart* delivery of Don Adams, "Was he a bank *guard?*"

"She turned to me and her demeanor changed completely," Chester said. "And she looked at me and she said, 'You must never, ever interrupt an actress while she's working.' That just about reduced me to the size of a flea. And I know she didn't mean to be harmful, but I understood exactly what she meant when she said it because she was a serious actress. After that I never ever attempted to break a conversation with her unless she said something to me." Fortunately for the young actor, Anne did not carry a grudge and playfully called him "college boy" during the shoot.

Chester could not help observing Anne as she took a moment to prepare for a scene. "You could tell that it was really far more serious work to her than, say, it was to me or some other actors that were on the set," he said. "I think we just kind of went there and spoke our lines and that was that. I could see her definitely thinking and working on it. I think it was so unfortunate that that sort of talent was wasted in that movie."

Robert Wise was businesslike and seemed more concerned with coordinating the special effects, as Chester recalled, and had little to do with the actors. *The Hindenburg* was one of Wise's late-career films that focused on technology, coming after *The Andromeda Strain* and before *Star Trek: The Motion Picture*. When Wise reminisced about the film, he focused on the technical challenges, particularly how he made the final explosion look realistic without harming the stuntmen fleeing the controlled flames. "Nobody got hurt," he said. "We lost a couple of cameras, but we got great footage." His comments gave the impression that working with the actors was not as memorable.

Unlike Mike Nichols or Arthur Penn, Wise did not spend a great deal of time rehearsing his cast and exploring interpretations of the characters. "One of the problems with rehearsing for films is that very often you have a large cast that start on the picture at different times on the schedule. I do try, at least, to sit down with the main cast and read through the script to hear the words and to get a sense of the characters," Wise said at the time he was making *The Hindenburg*. "I'm not one of those directors who feel they have to keep everybody stirred up to get the best out of them." He may well have thought that the cast he had assembled needed little direction, given their experience and the lack of complexity in their roles.

For Colby Chester, working with the star of *The Graduate* was the highlight of making the film. "She was Mrs. Robinson, so you could imagine me, a red-blooded American man coming on the set, and here is this woman who every guy my age at the time *The Graduate* came out wanted to have as a sex teacher. That part of her was definitely there. She just really sort of exuded that," he said. "The one thing I learned from her was respect for acting. She really was respectful of her talent and the craft. She was the real deal."

Most critics thought *The Hindenburg* gave its cast only cardboard characters to play amid admittedly sophisticated special effects. Kevin Thomas at the *Los Angeles Times* called it a "thinking man's disaster epic" compared to its predecessors. "Unfortunately, the people aren't nearly so interesting as those in the first films," he wrote. "We don't get to know these people well enough to become deeply involved in their fates." *Variety* dismissed it by citing "dull and formula scripting, a lack of real empathy and phone-in acting [that] shoot down some good though unspectacular special effects." Acknowledging the genre as a guilty pleasure, Vincent Canby of the *New York Times* wrote, "I wouldn't have missed a single foolish frame of it." Moviegoers turned out in force for a time and brought the film slightly more than $14 million in rentals in its first year, enough to put it at Number 10 in the annual box office list but still a financial disappointment considering its sizable budget.

Leading a cast meant enjoying the praise or shouldering the blame that came with a film. In a change of pace, Anne decided to lend her prestige to a project in which she would play only a supporting role. More to the point, her name would not shine brighter than any other in the credits. The medium was television, but not a one-hour drama like those she had done early in her career or a light and funny show like her musical comedy specials. A television program aimed for an Easter audience could not be light and funny with the title *Jesus of Nazareth*.

The Italian director Franco Zeffirelli planned an all-star miniseries based on the Gospels of the New Testament. *Jesus of Nazareth* would be an epic by television standards, a six-hour presentation over two nights costing about $12 million. Zeffirelli had been working in Italian films since the end of World War II and gained attention in London and New York as a stage director. His first film as a director was 1967's *The Taming of the Shrew*, starring Elizabeth Taylor and Richard Burton. His next, *Romeo and Juliet*, was an international hit in 1968 and an Oscar winner for its cinematography and costume design as well as a nominee for best picture and director. His 1972 film about Saint Francis of Assisi, *Brother Sun, Sister Moon*, did not draw as much attention, and he had not directed another film when he began preparing *Jesus of Nazareth*, a two-year undertaking.

Zeffirelli vowed from the beginning that he would present the life of Christ without mythology and would adhere closely to the Gospels while making a drama that captured the time and place. "People don't want to see the real Jesus," he said. "They want to live in a dreamland with him. They don't accept that he was a man, so they make of the cross a pretty symbol to hang around the neck rather than realize that it was an element of torture." In pursuit of that goal, he sought an authentic look for the miniseries and replaced the colorful splendor found in Cecil B. DeMille's biblical epics with simple garments worn by people living in dusty villages.

Like DeMille, Zeffirelli understood the value of casting stars to attract an audience. He hoped that prestige rather than money—he was not paying much—would be enough of an incentive. His first catch was Laurence Olivier, who had read the opening and closing for *Romeo and Juliet*. He readily agreed to take the role of Nicodemus, a witness to the crucifixion who helps bury Jesus. Other stars followed, among them a handful of other Oscar winners: Ernest Borgnine, Anthony Quinn, Rod Steiger, and Peter Ustinov. Also in the series were Michael York, Christopher Plummer, James Mason, Claudia Cardinale, James Earl Jones, Valentina Cortese, Stacy Keach, and Donald Pleasence. Each star would be paid $30,000 a week, no more and no less.

For the role of fallen woman turned follower Mary Magdalene, Zeffirelli cast Elizabeth Taylor. Before too long Taylor dropped out of the project, saying she was unwell, and Zeffirelli turned to Anne. "But I realized I was asking the impossible. She is an actress who works seldom—by choice," he said later. "She doesn't like to be away from home. . . . She demands prohibitive fees mainly to discourage requests and remain at peace." To his surprise, Anne accepted, telling Zeffirelli that the figure of Mary Magdalene had always fascinated her. The key may have been that Anne respected Zeffirelli as a director, and his project promised to surround her with professionals she admired. "There's little money," she said, "but never mind. I can earn more in other projects less exciting than this one, which at least will give me satisfaction in playing the role." As he assembled his gallery of stars, Zeffirelli believed that God himself had a hand in guiding their efforts.

Anne would not be making a cameo—the term for a fleeting appearance of a star in a production—but instead be playing a character essential to the story. *Jesus of Nazareth* would be filmed on location instead of in a studio lot, which meant significant time away from home for her. By the mid-1970s the Holy Land sites had taken on too many of the trappings of the twentieth century. Instead of shooting there, Zeffirelli planned to divide filming between Morocco, with its fortress-like villages and an undeveloped countryside that could be used for Joseph and Mary's trip to Bethlehem, and Tunisia, with its low, white buildings. The production was based in the Tunisian city of Monastir and made many side trips to the Moroccan and Tunisian interior.

Then a complication arose, one of Anne's own making. At home in Los Angeles, she tripped over a sofa and broke a toe. Confined to bed, she picked up a script that the agent-turned-producer Freddie Fields had sent to her. The script was for a movie, *Lipstick,* in which a high-fashion model is raped and seeks justice in the court system, then takes the law into her own hands. Anne's days of playing a model were long gone, but Fields was offering her the supporting role of the prosecutor. She had never played a lawyer before, yet the logic that went into building a legal argument and formulating a cross-examination caught her attention. "It was the most interesting thing I'd been sent in years," she said. She had not played such a supporting role since her first years in Hollywood.

Anne faced a dilemma: *Lipstick* was to be filmed at the same time as *Jesus of Nazareth* and would put a strain on her commitment to raising her son. "That's my first responsibility," she said around that time, "and believe me nothing is more demanding than a child." Two roles, two continents, conflicting desires. Just as she had when the choice was between Mel in Yugoslavia and her television special in New York, Anne decided she could have both by breaking up her scenes in *Lipstick* with flights to the miniseries set. "I had all the jet lag to contend with," she recalled. "At times it was gruesome. I would catch a cold in L.A., recover, fly to North Africa and catch a cold, recover and fly back." How she would manage to find time for her son and husband or rationalize her decision was not something she discussed publicly. Her choice, however, was one that a growing number of women faced if they wanted a career as well as a family.

The major challenge Zeffirelli faced was casting Jesus, which he called "the world's trickiest role." He sought a British actor around thirty but considered asking for Al Pacino or Dustin Hoffman. One can imagine the wisecracks that would have followed had the stars of *The Graduate* been reunited as Jesus and the forgiven seductress. Wisely, Zefferilli recognized that a relatively unknown actor would be needed for a television program aiming for a worldwide audience that could number four hundred million. He chose Robert Powell, an experienced actor not well known outside Britain, saying, "The spell of Jesus is in his eyes."

Anne would not appear in *Jesus of Nazareth* until about midway through its six hours. The script called for her to play Mary Magdalene as a prostitute, although that aspect of her character was not specified in the Gospels. In her first scene, Mary Magdalene drives away curious young boys outside her home and returns to a man who has obviously spent the night and later puts coins in her hand. From him she first hears of the young man from Nazareth. In later scenes, Mary Magdalene joins those listening to Jesus on a hillside, receives his forgiveness for her sins, watches as he is put to death, and tells the disciples that he has risen. With the exception of Jesus' mother (played by Olivia Hussey), Anne's was the most prominent female role in the international cast.

In writing about the making of *Jesus of Nazareth,* Zeffirelli described an extraordinarily emotional set the day they filmed the removal of Jesus' body from the cross. Robert Powell, Olivia Hussey, and Anne were among those who spent hours rehearsing while the crew set up cameras and prepared special effects to darken the sky and simulate rain. All was ready to begin filming at sunset. The scene was going well as Hussey threw herself onto Powell's body; but then, in the middle of her performance, an extra stepped in front of one of the cameras. Another problem was discovered— the lens of a camera had been soaked in the downpour. "We had to do it all over again," Zeffirelli said.

By the time everyone was ready once more, the director found Hussey near a state of nervous breakdown brought on, he believed, by tension, exhaustion, and a glass of cognac. She did not seem to be able to control herself and was on the ground screaming and laughing as if possessed. He tried to bring her to her senses, for her own good as well as for the good of Powell and Anne and others standing by, but he could not.

"We decided, however, to carry her there, almost like a sack, and place her in front of the camera," Zeffirelli said. "Miss Bancroft, suddenly overcome seeing Olivia stumbling, laughing, shouting, falling to her knees, lost control and began to slap her, shouting: 'That's enough. We can't go on like this. You are ruining everything, you are being irresponsible!'"

The scene unfolded as it had before, and Powell was again removed from the cross and laid on the ground. "Finally, we were able to drag in Olivia and throw her on the body of Jesus," Zeffirelli said. "She lay there, trembling." Viewing the footage later, the director found the image—Mary clasped to her dead son as if they were asleep in the rain—so effective and moving that he kept it in the program.

When Anne flew back and forth between North Africa and Los Angeles in the fall of 1975 and the early months of the following year, *Jesus of Nazareth* was closer to the beginning of its production schedule than its end. The NBC miniseries would not air in the United States until Eastertime in April 1977. By then Anne had completed three other films, including *Lipstick,* and begun to contemplate a return to the New York stage.

In terms of her feature film career, *Lipstick* marked a significant departure for Anne. It was the first "issue" movie in which she appeared and the first time she accepted the special billing "and Anne Bancroft." The small if showy role of an assistant district attorney prosecuting a rape case suggested that she was willing to appear in movies in which she was not the main attraction or even the leading female—a wise move given that it would be increasingly difficult for her, at forty-five, to find films in which she would be the sole star. In other words, her career was heading on a trajectory familiar to actresses her age.

The issue at the heart of *Lipstick* was not rape itself but how the victim and the accused were treated in the criminal justice system. The director, Lamont Johnson, had paired potent personal dramas with social issues in acclaimed and controversial television movies: interracial relationships (*My Sweet Charlie*), homosexuality (*That Certain Summer*), and capital punishment (*The Execution of Private Slovik*). "In most cases," Johnson said in reviewing his career, "I've chosen projects that have to do with an individual who has faced seemingly insuperable obstacles to deal with an extraordinary challenge." As far as a television venue for *Lipstick,* its nudity and sexual violence would have kept it off the airwaves. In other hands it would have been ripe for an exploitation film instead of an issue-driven drama.

In the film, Chris McCormick, a fashion model, meets her teenage sister's music teacher, Gordon Stuart. Young Kathy has a crush on Stuart and persuades Chris to invite him to their apartment to listen to his electronic compositions. Chris is polite but uninterested in his work, which Stuart takes as an insult. He binds her to her bed and rapes her. After charges are filed, Assistant District Attorney Carla Bondi warns Chris that prosecuting the case will lead to her being abused in court when Stuart's attorney disputes her testimony and attacks her character. That is exactly what takes place, and Stuart is acquitted. When he attacks Kathy, Chris takes justice into her own hands by tracking him down and shooting him. In a voice-over at the end, Carla Bondi argues in defense of Chris that justice had to be achieved outside the system—and Chris herself is acquitted.

A bit of stunt casting brought the fashion model Margaux Hemingway, then twenty-one, and her thirteen-year-old sister, Mariel, to the production. Neither had been in a film before but gained attention in part because of their link to Ernest Hemingway, their grandfather. Chris Sarandon followed his appearance as the man wanting a sex change in *Dog Day Afternoon* the previous year with the pivotal role of Gordon Stuart. Anne's key scenes come when Carla Bondi explains to Chris what is in store for her and when Bondi confronts Stuart on the witness stand.

Freddie Fields made room in the budget for a technical adviser and hired Tobey Shaffer, a former assistant district attorney for Los Angeles County. She read a late draft of the script and pointed out ways to make it as accurate as possible while not diminishing the drama. "It had nothing to do with the plot or character development," Shaffer said. "It was really the legal things. Would this have happened? What would the dialogue be? What would the courtroom dialogue be?" As she recalled, Fields, Lamont Johnson, and David Rayfiel, the screenwriter, were receptive to her suggestions. Shaffer met with Anne to give her a sense of what a female district attorney would encounter in such a case. The former prosecutor was not meant to be a model for Anne but a guide to understanding the legal system and the people operating within it.

They visited the county criminal courts building in downtown Los Angeles one morning to see justice in action. No special arrangements were made, and Anne made no attempt to hide who she was. "Of course everyone was all over her—Mrs. Robinson and all that kind of stuff," Shaffer recalled. People were interested but respectful and let them go about their business. "We went around to different courtrooms that we could, just to get an idea and the feel of it," Shaffer said. She took Anne into courtrooms with judges whom Shaffer thought would represent the best her profession had to offer.

Anne was allowed to pick her own wardrobe for the movie but then changed several of her outfits after talking to Shaffer. "We had a whole conversation about how you'd want to present yourself," she said. "No matter what, as a woman lawyer, you walk into anything and the first thing they see is a woman. You don't say to yourself, 'Deal with it.' You say, 'How can I present myself best? How do I look professional? How do I look like I know what I'm doing?' So obviously you won't want to dress in a voluptuous way, you don't want to look like a slob who just threw a tracksuit on. It's just making yourself look presentable." In the film Anne looked pretty but not glamorous.

During rehearsals, Anne pointed out that she felt that her character should have something additional to say in a particular courtroom scene. "Anne was really tuned into it—not becoming me, but becoming a lawyer and how a lawyer thinks when you put yourself in this environment and what would you do to try to convict this guy," Shaffer said. "I very much admired that. I thought she was very smart about that." What Anne needed were rebuttal questions, Shaffer suggested, and she wrote a few lines of dialogue for her.

One point of contention between Anne and the filmmakers concerned how the rape victim, Chris McCormick, would appear in the courtroom. Anne told her friend Mimi Gramatky that the director and producer wanted Margaux Hemingway to show a little cleavage when she testified. Anne objected and pointed out that the assistant district attorney would never allow a rape victim to appear that way. In the film Anne whispers to Hemingway before testimony begins, "Button your blouse—don't let the newsmen see you that way." As Anne told the story to Gramatky, it was an unscripted moment meant to guarantee that Hemingway's blouse would be buttoned throughout the courtroom scene—and Anne would get her way.

Overall, the set was calm and quiet, according to Shaffer, and Lamont Johnson was not at all an uptight person. Anne's parents dropped by with little Max once or twice, and Mel Brooks occasionally visited, she remembered, all part of a nice working environment. "She was just a fun person—very unpretentious, just a normal person," Shaffer said. "This was her job—to be a good actress and really care that everything was done to enhance her character."

Lipstick faced the dilemma confronting other issue movies that sought to condemn what it depicted: how to capture the horror and brutality of rape without making it alluring in some way. It also had the challenging task of presenting a compelling drama that had something to say without turning preachy. The first signal that *Lipstick* was faltering may have come when its preview screening in Pasadena, California, ended in chaos. The audience of two hundred, apparently expecting a social comedy on the order of *Shampoo*, was caught off guard by the rape scenes and practically stormed the box office to demand a refund.

Freddie Fields ordered a few trims in the film but reserved the major surgery for the marketing campaign. Leaving behind a subtle approach that did not refer to rape, the new advertising featured such statements as "*Lipstick* is a film about rape." In newspaper ads, a close-up of Margaux Hemingway's face was replaced by two pictures—one of her being violated and another of her with a rifle—and the line, "Rape can turn a cover girl into a killer." Box office receipts reportedly improved once the new ad campaign was in place.

Released in April 1976, *Lipstick* appealed to moviegoers who appreciated the vengeance its female victim wrought on her attacker. Mariel Hemingway recalled in a memoir, "My father took me to New York and we sat and watched the movie in a theater on Forty-second Street where people yelled at the screen and cheered Margaux on in every revenge scene." The film placed the younger Hemingway in an impossible situation when critics tended to say her sister was no actress but that she was a natural. When she was shooting the film, she had loved being a part of it. And there was Anne, whom she remembered as "nice and supportive."

Marketing and audience clamor had no positive influence on reviews, however, and the critical reception for *Lipstick* was overwhelmingly negative. The common accusation was that the film exploited its subject rather than enlightened the public's understanding of it. There were also comparisons to 1974's revenge movie *Death Wish*, which also had been condemned as exploiting urban violence. One of the relatively few positive reviews came from Kevin Kelly of the *Boston Globe*, who called *Lipstick* "an engrossing melodrama on a hot subject." More in line with the critical consensus was Roger Ebert of the *Chicago Sun-Times*, who branded *Lipstick* "a nasty little item masquerading as a bold statement on the crime of rape." At the *Chicago Tribune*, Gene Siskel was downright angry—and particularly critical of Anne. "Under the guise of examining rape in America, *Lipstick* violates the audience, ramming unmotivated violence and cornball legal proceedings down our collective throat," he wrote. While a few other critics expressed their disappointment in Anne's performance, Siskel was damning. Her role had been "hideously written" and "oh-so-earnestly played," he wrote, then added of Anne: "She may have lost whatever it was she had. Her last three films have been horrendous."

Behind that nasty observation lay the fact that Anne's last three movies—*The Prisoner of Second Avenue, The Hindenburg,* and *Lipstick*—had not achieved the critical or popular success expected of them. Those films and *Annie and the Hoods* also had not generated the praise for her performances that had become a given. Like any performer, she was helped or hobbled by the quality of the material and the contributions of her collaborators. Anne could give it her all—there was no evidence that she had not—and still come up short. Second only to her talent and drive in the formula for success was her ability to choose roles wisely. Those next choices would determine whether she had suffered an artistic dry spell or whether her career was veering perilously off track.

11

Pulled between Home and Work

The tenth anniversary of Anne's marriage to Mel Brooks, in 1974, came between the releases that year of *Blazing Saddles* and *Young Frankenstein*. When the decade was over, Mel had written and directed two more hits— *Silent Movie* in 1976 and *High Anxiety* in 1977—and led the cast in both. Already a savvy and successful filmmaker, he was becoming a movie star. Understandably, the people who bought the tickets to Anne's and Mel's films were interested in what went on behind the scenes with these two people who seemed so mismatched and yet so happy. If tabloid reporters skeptical about their marriage conducted a hunt for gossip, they apparently came away empty-handed. Life was not only good for the Brooks family; it was also free of scandal.

When they moved to Los Angeles, Anne and Mel had leased a house on Rising Glen Road in the hills north of the Sunset Strip. They eventually bought a place in Beverly Hills on Foothill Road, a classic 1950s ranch house with high ceilings and a U-shaped swimming pool. "It wasn't like a mansion," their friend Nancy Lunney said. "It was a nice, big Beverly Hills house." Anne maintained a garden as well as a citrus orchard on the half-acre property. There were enough trees to allow Max to dream up playtime adventures, just as long as they did not involve tramping through his mother's lettuce or string beans. Someone was always on hand to help look after Max, Nancy Lunney remembered, and Frank Langella described a "huge phalanx" of nannies, assistants, and others in the employ of his friends over the years.

Anne and Mel maintained a fairly standard tone when they had to face reporters' never-ending questions about their marriage—light and humorous while evasive as far as any truly personal revelations. The talk-show host Merv Griffin, a family friend, inquired about the dynamics of their marriage when Anne appeared on a special show taped in Venice, Italy, during a celebrity tennis tournament in 1979. She playfully deflected his questions. At one point Griffin asked, "When you and Mel spend a quiet evening at home—"

Anne interrupted. "We don't."

"Ever?"

"Ever." Anne noted that they were never alone at home. There was always the housekeeper and their son. Griffin tried another tack and asked if, whenever they were alone and talked, the conversation was as animated as it would seem to be.

"I don't think we've ever really talked. You know what I mean?" Anne said. "We never sit down and say, 'Well, what did you do today?'"

Griffin asked, "How do you know the marriage is working?"

"I don't—I don't know," Anne said. "Tell me, is it? I don't even know if he likes me."

Griffin laughed. "Oh, does he like you!"

"Oh," Anne said with a smile and a laugh. "That's so nice to know."

Griffin said he thought that their household must be very emotional. Anne agreed and actually revealed a bit about their lives. "We have a child who also is very emotional," she said. "Between the three of us . . . I'm the one that backs off. The one with the Italian temperament. I'm the one that has to back off because, you know, we can't have three of us like that in the house."

It was true that Anne's temper and other emotions could appear in a heartbeat. "She was very volatile, very volatile," Nancy Lunney remembered. The woman who oversaw the Directing Workshop for Women at the American Film Institute, Jan Haag, said of her: "I always rather felt I needed to duck when Anne entered a room. Nonetheless, she was one of the really great actresses of our time." Her costar and friend Frank Langella found himself trying to "weather her storms." Another friend, Austin Pendleton, her *Little Foxes* costar, said he did not see the kind of anger Langella described or even hear about it from others, but he agreed that her displays of emotion could be sudden. "Her responses to things were emotional," Pendleton said. "It was part of what made her work so great." Alan Alda thought that her deeply felt passions were the source of some of her best acting. "Anne had a volatile temper that she could spring on you with no warning," he recalled in a memoir. "She was a Vesuvius of emotion."

Alda based a character in his film *The Four Seasons* on Anne. The woman in his 1981 movie about friendship among couples defends her emotional outbursts by declaring, "I say what I feel—I'm Italian!" Alda tried to interest Anne in playing the role, inviting her to dinner one night to pitch it to her. He realized too late that he had made the mistake of not telling her that dinner was as much about business as spending time with her. "Her reaction was an immediate lack of interest," he said. "In fact, I saw a little puff of smoke warning of an eruption, but I had only myself to blame." The part eventually went to Rita Moreno. Alda's friendship with Anne continued for years.

Anne could use her ability to tap into her anger to her advantage. Once, in renting a house from a real estate agent she did not like, she decided to channel Mrs. Robinson—"from beginning to end," she told a group of acting students. "And scared hell out of her. I got the house for two hundred dollars less and everything else I wanted. I even frightened my friend who was with me and who knew what I was really like." In fact, Anne encouraged young actors to do their daily chores as they thought their character would, telling them it was a way of preparing for a role that they could not play in real life.

"There was a dark side to her and a wonderful bright light in her, too," her friend Mimi Gramatky recalled. "It's like any wonderful actor or actress—there's a flip side to it." To Gramatky, the two sides to Anne were connected to who she was and to the profession she chose. "She would be Anne Bancroft, who was pristine and perfect, and slip right into Anna Marie Italiano, talking with her hands, and talking with the accent. That was natural for her. The other one was definitely a role she was playing," she said. "New York Italian—that was her natural state. That's who she was when she was herself. When she was doing Anne Bancroft on talk shows and stuff she was Anne Bancroft. But that was a role."

One night Gramatky was visiting Anne's house to discuss a remodeling project when Mel Brooks called. "I heard this huge argument on the phone—it was like a wonderful sort of battle on the phone with Mel," Gramatky said. "And then she came back in and she sat down and she said, 'Now, where were we?' And we went right into talking about exactly what we were talking about. It was like doing an acting exercise." A short time later Mel called back. "She played this incredible love scene with Mel. 'Of course I'll wait for you. . . . I wouldn't think of anything else but waiting for you, my darling.' I was just in stitches, it was so damn funny," Gramatky said. "And I wondered if that was what their relationship was really like."

Though Frank Langella's memoir painted a portrait of a fine actress bedeviled by a streak of narcissism, he also remembered a "loving, warm, and fiercely loyal friend." Anne showed strength and vulnerability to those she trusted, whether they were people she worked with or friends outside the business. "She was one of the first women I'd ever met in Hollywood who was incredibly supportive of women and incredibly supportive of talented women," Mimi Gramatky said. People close to her accepted whatever her flaws might have been. "She was a girlfriend," said Bobbi Elliott, who knew Anne for decades. "What's better than saying she was a girlfriend? And very much the definition of one. If you weren't feeling well one day and one of the children was sick, she'd call to find out how everyone was."

Anne was funny, too, although when it came to making people laugh, her husband drew all the attention. "In some cases, she was actually funnier than he was," Mimi Gramatky said. Not to everyone. "Mel was unbelievable," Nancy Lunney said. "It would never stop, it would never stop. And she laughed and laughed and laughed and laughed. She obviously adored that part of him." Without question Anne had her own sense of humor and a wit that made her someone to enjoy spending time with. "First of all, she was smart, and she got whatever was being said," Bobbi Elliott remembered. "That was the joy of it. You didn't have to translate anything. When somebody's smart, they usually have a good sense of humor." Her kindness toward children was another trait that endeared her to her friends. "She adored children," Elliott said. "My kids knew no more about her being a movie star . . . they just knew she was Anne. And Mel was hysterical with them. We just had a wonderful time."

The Brooks family led a quiet life by the standards of Hollywood in the 1970s—and those standards had undergone a change. Anne knew the pleasures and pitfalls of the Hollywood nightlife from her time there twenty years earlier. A different generation had taken charge when she and Mel made Los Angeles their second home. Rock and roll replaced the big band and jazz sounds of their youth. The prevalence of drugs may have been at the root of an even bigger social change in the movie community. Marijuana had become common and was being replaced as the illicit substance of choice. "Cocaine was a drug well suited to the driven, megalomaniacal, macho lifestyle of Hollywood," the journalist Peter Biskind observed in his book about the movie industry in the 1970s. Sue Mengers, one of the leading talent agents of the decade (and Anne's for a time), kept cocaine in a sugar bowl for guests at her Beverly Hills home.

That kind of scene did not attract Anne and Mel. "My parents weren't baby boomers. They were the World War II generation," Max Brooks explained in an interview while visiting Mansfield University in 2012. As he remembered, they preferred the company of friends over dinner—at their home, at a friend's home, or in a restaurant. "My parents didn't go to parties," Max said. "Their friends weren't the party crowd."

Carl Reiner and his wife, Estelle, and the Brookses were the closest of couples. Their circle of friends included Larry Gelbart, another alumnus of Sid Caesar's television show and the writer behind the television series *M*A*S*H* and the movie *Tootsie*. Gelbart and his wife, Pat, hosted a regular Saturday tennis game for years and Anne and Mel played there. Another weekend gathering place was the home of Julann Griffin, a comedienne earlier in life and later Merv Griffin's wife. The television producer Norman Lear and his wife, Frances, and Dom and Carol DeLuise were also a big part of Anne and Mel's social group.

Weekends with friends were about tennis and eating, playing charades and other games, and just talking and laughing. At times Anne would join in a three-part harmony with Estelle Reiner, Pat Gelbart, or Carol DeLuise. "Music was always going," Bobbi Elliott remembered. "And the hilarious conversations. There was always something about Mel and Larry Gelbart— they were like matches for one another. One would always light the other one up. Larry could say two words and Mel would go off for two minutes. They were really very funny."

The Reiners liked to put together a picnic for their family and their friends, taking over one of the local parks on a Sunday. The men and boys would play baseball in the morning and the women would show up with food around eleven. There would be three-legged races and other activities. The smaller children enjoyed having their faces painted, and one of the makeup artists would be Anne.

"Without question she was one of the most loving, caring, fun-loving people I knew," Bobbi Elliott said. "She was never the movie star with close friends. She was really the girl next door. That was just the most adorable thing about her. When she got onstage she was still the girl next door—with a lot of talent."

Occasionally Anne's work as an actress would slip into her social life. Julann Griffin remembered the day that Anne asked if Griffin's teenage son had seen *The Graduate* recently, though it had been years since the movie's initial release. As a matter of fact, he had. Anne thought so, she told her friend, because he was looking at her a little differently.

Just as Anne and Mel had stock answers to questions about their marriage, their son would offer his own when, invariably, someone would want to know what it was like to grow up with his famous parents. "People asking that are expecting an answer that I can't give them," Max said in the Mansfield University interview. "I think they want a sort of a quick sound bite. . . . 'Oh, it was hilarious, it was a laugh a minute, it was just funny all the time at our house.' And the truth is, that's just not the case." Dinner conversation, for example, could focus on something as mundane as the artichokes they were eating. "Literally, that's what they'd talk about. And I notice as I get older, you tend to get more obsessed about what's in front of you," he said. "That's what it was like having dinner with them." His mother liked to read science books, which may have been a link to her long-ago interest in becoming a lab technician, whereas his father read Tolstoy and other Russian writers.

What little about their lives Max was willing to reveal suggested that Anne tried to devote herself to her only child while not turning away from her passion to perform. She read to her son, for instance, but working as she did meant she was not always at home by bedtime to continue the story. "She would record the rest of the book that she was reading to me," Max recalled in an interview with *Library Journal*. "So no matter what, my mother read me to sleep every night."

When he was eight, Max found his teachers to be indifferent to his desperate pleas for help with his reading. Clowning around in class might have made him appear spoiled and lazy, perhaps even a kid just aping his famously funny father instead of doing his schoolwork. Anne took her son's anguish seriously and had him tested for a learning disorder, which led to a diagnosis of dyslexia. In the years ahead Max would spend two hours a day with a tutor. His mother had his school books recorded so that he could listen to them.

In a *New York Times Magazine* profile prompted by his own success as a writer, Max described a woman who did not take to motherhood easily and a parent who was protective, perhaps overly so. As much as Anne treasured her family life, she made room for bursts of professional activity, especially once Max was in school. Yet she did not pursue her career to the fullest extent possible. "It was hard for her to be a mom, to give up all that and to try and raise me, because she didn't have much of a mom," Max told the writer Taffy Brodesser-Akner. "But she did it. She did an amazing job." Understandably, those who met him after he had grown up compared him to his famous parents. "People expect me to be funny like my dad and maybe melodramatic like my mother," he remarked in another interview. In some ways, Max as an adult was a blend of Anne and Mel—a writer with a sense of humor and an ability to create different characters.

Finding characters that Anne and Mel could play in a movie—not an easy task—led the couple to consider a remake of the 1942 black comedy *To Be or Not to Be* in which they would reprise the roles originated by Jack Benny and Carole Lombard. Anne's friend David Lunney pitched the project as a way for Anne and Mel to work together, but it was slowed by issues over obtaining literary rights to the story, financing, and deciding on a screenwriter. In the meantime, Mel came up with the perfect role for Anne: herself.

Silent Movie gave Anne her first role in a Mel Brooks film—albeit a supporting one—and it was her first feature film to be released after *Lipstick* a few months earlier. Mel called on her to play herself in a sequence that would make fun of her sexy image. Since *The Twelve Chairs* in 1970, his movies had been less about a comic narrative than an excuse for a collection of comedic scenes—usually based on parodies of film genres—held together by a simple storyline. *Silent Movie* was a parody of moviemaking itself as well as a tribute to the sight gags that filled comedies before there was sound. The story revolves around director Mel Funn's effort to recruit Hollywood's biggest stars to appear in his next film, a dubious prospect because it would be the first silent movie in fifty years. One of those stars, naturally, is Anne Bancroft.

Maybe not so naturally, if Mel was not kidding when he described to the film critic Gene Siskel how he cast *Silent Movie*. He and his cowriters had already written the script when they started considering whom to ask to appear as the stars. Anne was offering advice on casting, too, and finally posed a question to her husband: "Well, are you going to ask me?" She said she could understand why he would not want her. After all, she had not had a runaway hit since *The Graduate* and she did not want to hurt the movie. "Well," Mel told her, "I think we'll take a chance with you, kid."

The script—the dialogue was in title cards—teemed with sight gags, kooky sound effects, and inside jokes about the movie business. Marcel Marceau, the French mime, would have the only spoken dialogue, an emphatic "Non!" uttered when he turned down Mel Funn's offer. James Caan heard about the script through the grapevine and asked to be cast.

Burt Reynolds, a family friend and one of the most popular stars of the decade, agreed to join in. When Mel and Liza Minnelli were on *The Tonight Show* together, he talked about the movie and she volunteered to take part. Paul Newman responded favorably to playing his role with a plaster cast on one of his legs and engaging in a wheelchair chase through a hospital. Brooks paid each star scale wages of $138 a day for five or so days of work.

Anne not only played up her status as a glamorous actress, but also participated in a sly joke aimed at her Mrs. Robinson image. In Mel's new movie, she appears at a nightclub in a ravishing red gown and white feather boa accompanied by four younger men. Her entourage makes its way through the club to the applause of other diners, Anne acknowledging the ovation with a smile and a wave befitting a diva. As a way of getting near her, Mel Funn and his coconspirators—played by Dom DeLuise and the pop-eyed comic Marty Feldman—pretend to be flamenco dancers. "Who are they kidding?" Anne whispers to one of her companions. "They probably want me to do their movie." Mel pulls Anne onto the floor and dances a tango with her, then spins her crashing through the kitchen doors. A change of partners turns into a cheek-to-cheek encounter with Marty Feldman. Anne matches his orbital antics by opening her own eyes as wide as possible, crossing them and then uncrossing them one by one, a trick she learned from Carl Reiner. Finally, the trio asks her if she will appear in their movie. "I'll do it!" Anne declares and jumps into their arms. They carry her off the nightclub floor—but not before banging her head into a brick wall. She had never appeared in such slapstick.

Audiences turned *Silent Movie* into a summer hit in 1976. Most critics were amused, to varying degrees, and recommended the film as a source of chuckles and smiles if not uproarious laughter. Anne's comic turn drew notice, too, as it showed her in a charmingly zany role. Coming out a few months after *Lipstick,* the comedy may have helped erase that experience from moviegoers' minds. It certainly associated her name with a hit, for a change. *Silent Movie* became the fifth-most-popular film released that year, bringing in $20.3 million in rentals. At the same time *Blazing Saddles* enjoyed a lucrative rerelease, at $13.8 million, to reach the tenth spot on the annual *Variety* list.

That year Mel achieved a sign of star status that his wife never matched. Since the 1930s the Quigley Poll had asked theater owners to list the most popular movie stars. Mel joined the top-ten list in 1976 at fifth place, just below Robert Redford, Jack Nicholson, Dustin Hoffman, and Clint

Eastwood. He returned in 1977 at seventh place and again in 1979 at tenth. Theater owners apparently did not think Anne's name brought in patrons to that degree—turning down roles and being off the screen for years at a time had its consequences. But, then, actresses in general did not fare well in the poll. In the 1960s only twenty-eight of the one hundred spots went to actresses, most often Doris Day, Elizabeth Taylor, and Sandra Dee. In the 1970s, only sixteen of the one hundred slots were filled by women, almost half the time Barbra Streisand; in four of those years she was the sole actress listed.

Mel was becoming more recognizable in public than his wife. Their friend Nancy Lunney recalled going to the movies with her husband, David, and the Brookses and waiting with Anne at the concession stand while Mel and David stood across the lobby. A young woman at the counter whispered to them, "You know who that is? That's Mel Brooks." Anne, practically deadpan, agreed that it was indeed. "And this girl kept going on and on about Mel, not knowing who she's talking to," Nancy Lunney said. "I don't think this woman, this young girl at the concession stand, really knew who Anne Bancroft was. She knew who Mel was." Did such a moment stoke a sense of rivalry in Anne? "When she was not being recognized and he was, that was difficult for her," Lunney said. "But I never sensed that she, in any way, resented what he was doing and his success."

Relatively few films at that time focused on a female protagonist and fewer still actually dealt with issues unique to women. As Anne herself would discover, there was an audience waiting for such a film—and, if she chose, she could be part of it. That film was not going to be *The Gingerbread Lady,* an adaptation of a Neil Simon play that had won Maureen Stapleton a Tony Award in 1971. In a story considered serious by Simon standards, Stapleton played an alcoholic cabaret singer trying to pull her life together. The playwright tried to interest Anne in a film adaptation in 1976, but no movie version would appear until 1981, and by then the story had been overhauled and retitled *Only When I Laugh.* The star was Marsha Mason, Simon's wife.

The movie starring Anne that would become a landmark "woman's film" actually had two men behind it. Herbert Ross, a dancer and choreographer turned Hollywood director, would conceive the story, produce the film, and direct it. The author of the original screenplay, Arthur Laurents, had a flair for creating female roles for the stage and screen. He wrote the books for the late 1950s stage musicals *West Side Story* and *Gypsy* and the screen-plays for 1956's *Anastasia,* which brought an Oscar to Ingrid Bergman, and 1973's *The Way We Were,* with Barbra Streisand and Robert Redford.

Titled *The Turning Point,* the film about two female friends in the world of ballet also reflected the contributions of Nora Kaye, its executive producer. Kaye had become an international star during her two-decade career as a ballerina and influenced the look of modern dancers. She married Herbert Ross in 1959 and together they formed a ballet troupe, she serving as its chief dancer and he providing works to perform. She retired from the stage, and Ross returned to Broadway and worked in film and television. They sought to produce a movie that showed what ballet dancers went through to create a performance, but the personal drama in *The Turning Point* was not their own. The lives that inspired the story were primarily those of Kelly Brown and Isabel Mirrow, two successful dancers who left performing, began a dance studio in Phoenix, Arizona, and raised four children. Mirrow and Nora Kaye had been friends as children in New York, and Kaye was godmother to the Browns' daughter Leslie.

"We wanted to explore the turning points and choices men and women have to make in the arts," Ross said. "We wanted to explore marriage versus career; we wanted to explore life styles and life forces. And, behind all that, we wanted to show the dancer as a metaphor for aspiration, for betterment; the dancer dedicated and striving for perfection." Seven years would pass before their idea actually became a movie.

History was against them, and they knew it. American films had seldom used ballet as a major subject. A British production from 1948, *The Red Shoes,* remained the best-known and most popular ballet drama. It was an Academy Award nominee for best picture and a winner for its art direction and music. The limited interest in two 1950s movies with ballet sequences, Charlie Chaplin's drama *Limelight* and Gene Kelly's performance film *Invitation to the Dance,* suggested that American moviegoers were still not drawn to ballet on film unless it was a part of a traditional Hollywood musical, such as *An American in Paris* (1951).

Not much had changed by the 1970s. Hollywood studios were not excited by a drama about two middle-aged women, even less when their world revolved around ballet. Herbert Ross had directed a half dozen movies by then, including the Barbra Streisand vehicle *Funny Lady* and the Neil Simon comedy *The Sunshine Boys,* but studio after studio turned down Ross and Kaye when they sought seed money for their ballet story.

A positive if guarded reception came at Twentieth Century-Fox, where the production chief, Alan Ladd Jr., agreed to provide money for Laurents to write the screenplay. Ladd had a reputation for taking chances on projects rejected elsewhere, among them *Young Frankenstein* and *Star Wars,* and he saw the possibilities of big returns from low-cost films with top talent. He also saw an untapped audience eager for films aimed at women. Around the time Fox backed *The Turning Point,* three other "women's pictures" were in the studio pipeline: Robert Altman's *3 Women,* Fred Zinnemann's *Julia,* with Jane Fonda and Vanessa Redgrave, and Paul Mazursky's *An Unmarried Woman,* with Jill Clayburgh. Ironically, all were written and directed by men.

Laurents's screenplay opens with a former ballerina, Deedee Rodgers, reuniting with her friend and onetime rival Emma Jacklin, now the prima ballerina with the American Ballet Theatre. Deedee and her husband, Wayne, had been dancers with the company but left to marry and raise a family in Oklahoma City. Their teenage daughter Emilia is a dancer, and Emma encourages her to study with the troupe. An invitation to join them follows, and Deedee accompanies her daughter to New York. Over the summer each of the women faces conflict: Emma is being pushed aside for younger dancers, Deedee feels she is being replaced as Emma becomes a mentor to her daughter, and Emilia tries to balance her desire to dance with her budding relationship with the star male dancer, Yuri. Over a drink at a bar, the old friends share regrets and trade accusations. Deedee accuses Emma of persuading her to marry Wayne when she was pregnant to eliminate her as a competitor. Emma counters that Deedee married to avoid the truth that she lacked the degree of talent to compete with her. Outside, their argument escalates into a fight that eventually reduces them to laugher and, in time, a reconciliation.

The Turning Point provided not one but two excellent roles for actresses in middle age. When it came to casting, Grace Kelly declined to come out of retirement, and Audrey Hepburn also turned down Ross. Two other Oscar-winning actresses—forty-five-year-old Anne Bancroft and forty-six-year-old Joanne Woodward—became his top choices. The wife of Paul Newman, Woodward won her Academy Award in 1957 for *The Three Faces of Eve.* Finding good roles had been no easier for her than it had been for Anne over the years, and several of her more recent films had been made with her husband as costar or director. When word of their casting reached the columnist Rona Barrett, she predicted that Twentieth Century-

Fox would take a bath on a movie with two stars who could not sell tickets. Someone heeded that advice and Woodward was dropped from the cast. Stung by the rejection, she later declared that she would never make another feature film. She held to that vow for years and concentrated on made-for-television movies, except to work with her husband.

Cast in Woodward's place was Shirley MacLaine, six years younger than Anne and a trained dancer. As a twelve-year-old she had gone backstage after a ballet performance to meet Nora Kaye, whose Brooklyn accent showed MacLaine that not all great ballerinas hailed from Russia. In the early 1960s MacLaine's popularity had won her the role of Gittel Mosca in the film version of *Two for the Seesaw* in spite of Anne's Broadway triumph. Too many forgettable films and a failed television series followed for MacLaine, but she had drawn favorable notices and sizable audiences touring in a revue built around her many talents. How she solved the studio's box-office fears was not clear—she had not appeared in a film for four years.

To her disappointment, MacLaine played the dancer turned wife and mother, while Anne was the aging ballerina. "I can't say that I identify with my character," MacLaine said when filming was under way. "At the age of twelve, I knew that settling down with a family was not the course for me. *The Turning Point* is not a woman's movie. It's a movie about the choices in life. I know a lot of men, too, who gave up their dreams to be an artist or a scientist or the guy who invented paper clips and ended up carrying a lunch pail back and forth to the factory." She tried in vain to persuade Herbert Ross to change the story, knowing from experience that a woman could have a husband and a child and still pursue a career. That was not the story Ross and Kaye wanted to tell.

MacLaine was far more outspoken than Anne and linked the scarcity of challenging film roles for women to the lack of courage in Hollywood for dealing with political issues. "Perhaps we who hold feminist attitudes have intimidated the writers. They are afraid their male chauvinism will show," she said. "It's a very small community out there and a subject like women's liberation is just too political for the Hollywoodians." Anne was silent on the subject, but, then, she avoided interviews during the making of the film.

For the roles of Russian dancer Yuri and Deedee's daughter Emelia, Ross turned to the ballet world. The coup of the film was signing up Mikhail Baryshnikov, then the principal dancer with the American Ballet

Theatre and thought by many to be ballet's greatest dancer. Joining him as the ingenue was his own dance partner, Gelsey Kirkland, and their offstage romance piqued interest in their pairing for the film. Shortly before filming was to begin, Kirkland left the production, saying she was ill. (She later wrote of her struggles with eating disorders and drugs at the time and faulted the script for being unrealistic and silly.) In her place came a new performer with the New York City Ballet, nineteen-year-old Leslie Browne, the daughter of the inspirations for the film. She had added an "e" to her last name to make it appear more feminine.

The Turning Point began filming in New York in August 1976, shooting outside Carnegie Hall, the Russian Tea Room, and other New York landmarks to establish the setting. Ross took over the Minskoff Theatre to film the ballet sequences, drawing from the repertory of the American Ballet Theatre. The budget was tight at $4 million, and Ross saved time as well as money by shooting two pas de deux each day with five cameras. The male and female dance duets would become highlights and help bring ballet a wider audience, one of the goals of Ross and Kaye. They also knew that gaining a larger audience meant placing the dance sequences in a compelling story that nonfans of ballet could enjoy.

The film company relocated to Los Angeles for most of the dramatic sequences featuring Anne and Shirley MacLaine. Ross used the plaza at Century City for the climactic fight scene between Emma and Deedee. Arthur Laurents had rejected suggestions that the fight, perhaps the most memorable scene in the movie, was comparable to the brawl between Norma Shearer and Rosalind Russell in *The Women,* an all-female drama from 1939. "They were two bitches clawing at each other physically," Laurents said. "These women aren't bitches and they end up better friends than ever before."

With Anne's help Ross drew an unrehearsed reaction from MacLaine in the scene in the bar that preceded the fight. As their characters aired out long-held grievances tinged with bitterness—in the script the women call them "hoptoads" that leaped out of their mouths—Anne responded to the most hateful accusation by throwing her drink in MacLaine's face. Ross had persuaded Anne not to tell MacLaine it was coming, and her surprise at being doused was obvious.

Ross also wanted Anne and MacLaine to battle it out on the plaza even though Anne was slighter in build than her costar. "It was late and we were about to start the fight sequence," he recounted, "and Shirley suddenly said, 'I don't want to hit Anne. She's too small and I'll hurt her.' Anne kept saying, 'Hit me, hit me, hit me.'" MacLaine still worried about overpowering her costar, but Anne made it clear she could handle herself. "Suddenly this wind blew up and the cameraman asked me if I still wanted to shoot," Ross said. "So we started and skirts and hair was flying."

As MacLaine told the story, no choreography was followed when they began their tussle. "You can't organize something like that," she said. "We just went into it and started fighting, both of us in elegant evening gowns and high heels. I was afraid of hurting her because she seemed so fragile and thin, but I was wrong. Anne could really pack a punch. And all of that was improvised." Nor did anyone expect the fight to end in laughter as they swatted at each other's rears. "That wasn't in the script," she said. "And I just started laughing because, you know, after twenty seconds I pretty well start laughing at anything. As I'm feeling her—and she was extremely fragile, but that kind of wiry fragile that you know you don't fool around with—I started laughing. And then she started laughing. And then it all broke down. And that was what the scene became about—these two old friends who couldn't really be mad for very long."

Over the years MacLaine's memories of making the movie did not suggest that a warm relationship developed between her and her costar. In an interview in 2010 she pointed out that Anne was not in her element as a ballerina. "Poor Annie had to look like she could dance," MacLaine said. "It was difficult for her to be ethereal." In her book *What If . . .* she referred to Baryshnikov enjoying her on-the-set jousting with Anne. In *Dance While You Can* she included Anne among the many fine actresses with whom she had worked, then wrote a subtle dig under a picture of herself with Anne: "Of course, because I was the real dancer they cast me as the housewife who gave it up. Anne Bancroft played herself." A woman who lived for her career and would do anything to get a role? In the parlance of *The Turning Point*, it sounded like one of those little hoptoads at work.

Anne seldom talked about *The Turning Point*, perhaps because interviewers tended to ask about *The Graduate* and *The Miracle Worker* when they brought up her films. Working with Herbert Ross might not have been a happy experience for her. In discussing the director, MacLaine described a talented man who could be pompous and insulting. (She said he had been cruel to Dolly Parton and Julia Roberts while making 1989's *Steel Magnolia*, their second film together.) "Annie was a little aloof," MacLaine said in recalling *The Turning Point*. "But with Herb Ross being the director, that was the way to go. He could be sarcastic." Whether all their efforts were worth it would not be known for at least a year. *The Turning Point* completed shooting at the end of October 1976 but was not scheduled for release until the next fall.

In the mid-1970s, as she tried to find the right balance between being an actress and being a wife and mother, Anne added to the demands she placed on herself by stretching her talents in a new direction. Not only did she want to try writing a script, but she wanted to try directing as well. Female screenwriters were hardly unusual in Hollywood, but few women were given opportunities to direct American films. Though numerous women had directed during the silent era—the film scholar Anthony Slide counted at least thirty-one—hardly any women were put in charge of major productions as talkies ushered in the golden age of Hollywood. (Slide concluded that one reason may have been that the source of directors for talking pictures was the stage, another male-dominated venue.) By the time Anne explored writing and directing, she had not yet worked with a female director.

Just around the block from Anne and Mel's home in Beverly Hills, an effort to give women the opportunity to direct was under way. The American Film Institute established its Directing Workshop for Women in 1974 in response to the growing criticism that women were largely excluded from the ranks of film directors. The AFI provided classes for its student filmmakers, but the Directing Workshop for Women was not offering classes for newcomers. "The whole idea behind the DWW was simply to give already accomplished women working in film the opportunity to direct," said its founder, Jan Haag. "Where else were they—especially the movie stars—to find that? We gave them an encouraging, non-threatening, nurturing environment in which to practice what they had already learned from working in other aspects of the film industry." The AFI provided equipment and, from the ranks of its students and volunteers, the personnel the program's participants needed to make their films.

Among the fifteen women in the initial Directing Workshop for Women, the class of 1974–75, were the producer Julia Phillips and actresses Ellen Burstyn, Lee Grant, and Margot Kidder. Most of the industry professionals chosen for the DWW were people not known outside their areas of expertise. High-profile participants like Burstyn and Grant brought the kind of attention the program needed to raise money in its first few years. "The actresses, as it turned out, were often the most talented at directing," Haag said. "No great surprise. Who had more contact with directors? Who had more hands-on opportunity to view directing and to develop a passion for wanting to do it?" Still, the number of actresses admitted to the workshop was kept to around one-third of the total in each class so that the DWW did not become celebrity-driven.

Anne's friend David Lunney, who was working at the AFI, brought information about the directing workshop to Anne to see if she would be interested in applying. They were going over the application at her home when Mel walked in, Lunney remembered. "He said, 'Well, what would she do?' And she said, 'It's a women's directing workshop, it's an application for it, I'm going to direct a film,' and he said, 'Oh, you don't want to do that.' And she said, 'What? You can't stand having two directors in the same house?' It was that flash of temper—and a joke." Anne was accepted in the second class, 1975–77, as were Randa Haines, who would later direct *Children of a Lesser God,* and the actresses Dyan Cannon and Kathleen Freeman.

The goal for the members of Anne's class was to direct two videos of twenty to thirty minutes each. The short productions, shot in black and white, would be a calling card of sorts for gaining work in film and television. Anne wrote the scripts for her two videos, *The August* and *Fatso.* Working with her was Mimi Gramatky, one of the volunteers for the workshop who was seeking experience in making films. "It was a treat to work with her," recalled Gramatky, who went on to establish a career as a production designer and art director. "She also sort of took me under her wing as a mentor and taught me how Hollywood treats women."

As Gramatky remembered, *The August* was based on an experience Anne had while appearing in *The Miracle Worker* on Broadway. Marlene Dietrich had come backstage to see her after a performance and brought along a much younger man. In Anne's story, the stage actress decides to take a young man from the stage company back to her hotel room rather than spend another night alone, although what happens after that is ambiguous. In the video, Sally Kellerman played the Dietrich character, Hope Lange the stage actress, and Carol DeLuise the actress's dresser.

The workshop offered space at AFI headquarters for building sets. At that time the institute was in the Greystone Mansion, a Tudor-style building with more than fifty rooms that had been completed in 1928 as part of the Doheny Estate. For *The August,* Anne's crew built a set for the hotel room and another for the backstage dressing room. The AFI provided a meager budget of three hundred dollars for the project, but Gramatky recalled that Mel filled in with whatever else they needed for his wife's video, not that it needed much. For example, he came up with the cash to buy a large piece of fabric on which Gramatky painted a city street to hang behind the hotel room window.

Anne was very much in charge, Gramatky said. At one point Sally Kellerman and Hope Lange were doing a scene together as Anne discussed a camera angle with the cinematographer. According to Gramatky, "Sally started to direct Hope and tell her, 'Honey, it's been a long time for you, so let me help you on this one.' And Anne heard that . . . and she said in this booming stage voice, '*Who* in this room has been an actress for twenty years? *Who* in this room has been a star for twenty years? And *who* in this room is directing the movie?' And Sally just stuck her tail between her legs and turned around and said, 'You.'"

The workshop projects brought out the same kind of intensity and single-mindedness Anne employed when she was preparing for a role. "She was the first person I'd ever met in my life who would forget to eat," Gramatky said. "She had an assistant that would bring her breakfast—it was always some fruit and a bran muffin—and remind her to eat because she'd forget. She'd get so wrapped up in something, she'd forget."

For her second video, Anne wrote an autobiographical story that touched on food and its influence on the Italian American family. *Fatso* starred Dom DeLuise as a binge eater, Doris Roberts as his sister, and Candice Azzara as the girl he falls in love with. (Anne had seen Azzara in a steak sauce commercial and asked if she would like to work on the project.) Another friend, Estelle Reiner, also had a small part. Mimi Gramatky was not sure she could stay on for the second video, needing a job to earn some money, and told Anne she did not think she could do it. "She looked at me square in the face," Gramatky said, "and delivered a line that just melted my heart: 'Oh, I really want you to do this. You have talent and I have an eye for that.' I would have followed her anywhere at that point." In time Anne and Mel hired Gramatky to restore a rental property for them and take on other design-oriented projects for their homes.

Anne had her own tricks for keeping down costs for her workshop videos. "She gave me her Saks credit card to go buy clothes for the actors," Gramatky said. Once they were done with the scene, Anne told her to return the clothes to the store. "They looked at it and said, 'We don't take returns,'" Gramatky said. "And I said, 'Oh, I'm sure Mrs. Brooks would be very disappointed,' and handed them the credit card. It said 'Mrs. Mel Brooks,' and they said, 'Oh, of course we will.'" Anne did have her standards. When they sought to shoot a scene on location at a deli, the owner offered the use of the place at no cost if Anne would autograph a picture he could hang on the wall. "And she said, 'Why would I want to have a bloody picture on someone else's wall that I don't even know?'" Gramatky recalled. "I remember thinking how strong that was—what incredible character she had in that statement."

The shooting schedule for each of the videos was about five days, as Gramatky remembered, and *The August* and *Fatso* were shot several months apart. When she began working with a student editor on the first cut of *The August,* Anne appeared surprised at how different the editor's cut was from what she had in mind. "She looked at it and said, 'Oh, my gosh! Editing is creative, too.' It was because she'd been an actress all her life," Gramatky said. "She didn't know what the process was. She really didn't know what the postproduction process was." Anne was learning more about how to make a movie, the goal of the workshop.

Anne and other Directing Workshop for Women participants screened their videos for each other. "The women all received each other's films well, out of mutual respect," Gramatky said. "They largely were interested in how people did things and what things happened because they were all learning from each other. It was a very productive and wonderful experience, I think." Dyan Cannon's short film *Number One* was nominated for an Oscar for best live-action short film made in 1976. For Anne, *Fatso* would lead to even bigger things in the years ahead.

In the spring of 1977 people across the United States awaited the initial airing of *Jesus of Nazareth.* In their reviews ahead of the opening night of the miniseries, April 3, the major television critics agreed it was visually excellent but were divided over its dramatic merits. Tom Shales of the *Washington Post* called it "one of the most visually beautiful films ever produced for television" and commended the production for achieving a "brilliant balance" between presenting the biography of Jesus and exploring the political and social context in which the story occurs. "There may never have been a religious film with so pervasive a sense of place and period," he observed. Harry F. Waters of *Newsweek* wrote: "Rarely have both the humanity and the divinity of Christ been evoked with as much passion, sensitivity and ecumenical deference as Zeffirelli has brought to the story." Among those less impressed was John J. O'Connor of the *New York Times*. "There is an admirable daring in the willingness to flirt with overripeness, an intelligence behind the artistic flirtations," he wrote. "*Jesus of Nazareth* falters occasionally, but Zeffirelli snatches it back quickly and makes us watch his intricate maneuvering, nearly always with interest."

Anne's performance as Mary Magdalene was not commended by Shales—"the only bit of casting that really seems reckless"—or by O'Connor, who found her coming close to a poor imitation of Anna Magnani at times. (He thought the only unqualified disaster among the stars to be Anthony Quinn's turn as Caiaphas, the high priest and enemy of Jesus, saying Quinn sounded like "a reject from *The Godfather*.") At the *Boston Globe*, William A. Henry III found most of the performances to be "solemn, stately and dull" in an otherwise beautiful and reverent production that lacked the zeal of the faithful. *Newsweek* was more pointed: "One doesn't know quite what to make of Anne Bancroft's Mary Magdalene, rendered with a discombobulating Bronx inflection. 'Ged owdah heah,' she screeches at her hecklers." Given the international cast, the criticism was nonsensical since none of the accents originated in the Holy Land.

That critical knock and a few others aside, *Newsweek* predicted—correctly, it would turn out—that *Jesus of Nazareth* would become an Easter staple for television. That first year viewers made it one of the most-watched television dramas of all time; it was estimated that as many as 90 million people watched one or both segments, and that about half of American television sets in use those Sunday nights were tuned in. Anne's earthy Mary Magdalene may have struck some as overdone, but the experience had vindicated her personal reasons for wanting to appear in Zeffirelli's television tapestry. The timelessness of the story ensured that it would be her most-viewed performance.

Would Anne fare better or worse playing an icon of the twentieth century? She had every reason to return to Broadway: Arthur Penn was directing a new play by William Gibson. The subject, the former Israeli prime minister Golda Meir, was larger than life. The very idea—Anne Bancroft as Golda Meir!—could sell tickets before a word was put to paper. The producer of the Theatre Guild, Philip Langner, sought $500,000 for the production, a fairly expensive tab for a straight play. "That wasn't difficult with these lovely people involved," Langner remembered. A record 297 investors readily put up the money.

Langner had tried for years to interest Meir in a play about her life. It was the stuff of drama: birth in Kiev under czarist rule, a childhood in the shadow of pogroms, emigration to Milwaukee, Wisconsin, as a young girl, marriage at nineteen followed by a move to Palestine, and a lifetime of work toward establishing a Jewish state. One of the signers of Israel's declaration of independence, Meir held various government positions and became prime minister in 1969—only the fourth woman in history to become a head of state. The greatest crisis of her five years as prime minister was the Yom Kippur War, in October 1973. She left office in 1974 but remained an outspoken advocate of Israel and one of the most admired women in the world.

Meir put off Langner's entreaties for a play about herself, believing the idea frivolous and nonsensical. She softened that view after her autobiography, *My Life,* published in 1975, became a best seller and generated attention for the cause of Israel. A play might do the same, she realized, and agreed to work with Langner and the Theatre Guild on such a production. In the effort to develop a script, Langner turned to William Gibson. "We went to him first," Langner said. "He was a wonderful playwright, and we knew him and we felt we couldn't do better than if he would be willing to write it. And, of course, when we have Golda, you can get glorious people to come along." He arranged for a meeting in May 1976 between the playwright and the former prime minister. Gibson admitted being awestruck by Meir, then seventy-eight, especially after she told a few stories from her life. Under the terms of their agreement, she would have an equal share of Gibson's royalties and veto power over the outline.

Not content to use her autobiography as his sole source, Gibson spent months interviewing people in New York and in Israel as he gathered biographical material and learned more about the nature and character of Israel, as much a character in the play as Meir herself. The spine of the story would be the Yom Kippur War, which challenged her leadership and led to the collapse of her government. Flashbacks would revisit her personal life and the sacrifices she made as a wife and mother working toward the creation and survival of Israel. Gibson eventually saw the theme as "the dream aspired to, the price paid, and the reality we settle for." He completed the play in January 1977 and gave a copy to Arthur Penn, who agreed the next day to direct it.

Gibson's approach to Meir's life carried echoes of his 1969 play *John and Abigail*. It would be nonlinear, set during the war but moving through the past. Those onstage with Meir would be unnamed, serving more as functionaries than characters as they witnessed events depicted in the script. Visuals would be central to the staging—photographs, films, maps, and dates would be projected on screens. Arthur Penn, always open to experimentation in theater and film, thought that the mixed-media presentation could prove revolutionary. Curiously, no one seemed concerned about the muddle that had emanated from Gibson's last effort to mix history and technology with nonlinear drama in telling the story of John and Abigail Adams.

Gibson always looked for a way to involve Anne in his work, and it was probably a foregone conclusion that she would be asked to play Meir. Whether she would agree depended on how she related to the character he had written. "When I read the parts about Golda's personal life," she said, "I immediately found myself crying." The military sections made her angry because she could not understand them—the details of maneuvers and deployment of aircraft did not register with her. "But I knew I wanted to do the play," she said. "It had me involved on a purely personal level." Arthur Penn explained the military aspects of the story to her satisfaction. "I could see what was happening to Golda, inside of her during the war," she said, "and I knew I felt it inside of me." What was important to Anne had less to do with grasping the policy and the politics in the play and more to do with understanding the person.

In June, Anne flew to Israel with Gibson's wife, Margaret, and spent more than a week with Meir. "The idea was that Annie would soak up some of Golda's stuff and be able to use it," Gibson told the writer Nat Segaloff. Liking her subject was not necessarily her goal. In fact, Anne dreaded meeting Meir at her suburban Tel Aviv home, in part because she was fearful of coming face to face with this world figure completely outside her realm of experience. She also was on edge just being in Israel because of the ongoing tensions and conflicts with its Arab neighbors.

"When she opened the door herself and greeted me, I suddenly was calm," Anne said later. "My anxiety was gone. I looked into her eyes and I knew. I knew we would be okay." Gibson put it a little more dryly: "Annie and Golda fell in love with each other. These politicians love actors, and vice versa, I suppose." The two did become fast friends. Meir gave a garden party for Anne and later told Gibson that there "wasn't one who didn't love her."

Meir wanted Anne to get a sense of her life and the lives of Israelis. They attended a wedding, a bar mitzvah, a diplomat's dinner, a poetry reading, a party given by Israel's national theater, and a dinner at a kibbutz. Meir took her to the Golan Heights, Galilee, and the border with Lebanon. Anne was surprised and enchanted by how Israeli life went on in spite of the shadows cast by conflict. For the Method-trained actress, the tour was also about observing her subject for mannerisms and speech patterns and asking how she dealt with problems. Did she shout when angry? What made her cry? Anne asked about little details—did she wear jewelry, had she ever worn a wedding ring? (Never.) She took note of how Meir held a cigarette, how she answered the phone, how she scratched her head.

Anne needed to find something in Meir's life that she could connect with her own. "Something that would be a clue to my playing the role so that I would have a handle to hang on to every night," she explained to the writer Margaret Croyden. "When I work, I have to find a personal image that is similar to the person I'm relating to in the play. If you don't lock into something extremely personal within yourself, the play will have gone by without your having felt anything." It was Anne's version of the Method, but the connection she found, the handle she needed for her performance, she did not reveal. It would be fair to wonder if Anne related to Meir as a woman who wanted a family life but sought something more and felt guilty about the conflicts those competing desires produced. Surely that subject came up during the many days they spent together. Meir once wrote about it: "There is a type of woman who cannot remain at home. In spite of the place her children and family fill in her life, her nature demands something more; she cannot divorce herself from the larger social life. She cannot let her children narrow her horizon. For such a woman there is no rest." Anne, so restless during much of her own life, may well have found a personal truth in Meir's observation.

When they parted, Anne told Meir, "The next time I see you I'll be you!" She left Israel having become a convert to the cause. "I'm going back to New York with a mission—to deliver that play," she told Croyden. "Through that play *Golda* we will tell the story of Israel. We will deliver Golda's message." A photograph of Anne and Meir appeared in newspapers and helped the drumbeat for the production grow louder. Advance sales would eventually approach $1 million, nearly double the production's capitalization.

The first day of rehearsals that August drew heavy coverage by local news media. "It was the noisiest sendoff in theatre annals," Gibson said, "good only for ticket sales." Once the reporters and photographers went away, rehearsals went smoothly. "Bancroft was feeling her way slowly, but I had no concern about her. She was solid," Gibson said. The company was in high spirits as it worked toward tryouts in Baltimore and Boston ahead of opening in New York.

Only later did Gibson realize that he had made a grievous error, by his estimation a fatal one. He had understood the structure of the play intuitively but had not thought through how it would be staged. The play's nature was antirealism, but Gibson and Arthur Penn proceeded to give it a realistic presentation. "Our instinct for realism was warping the entire production," Gibson said, "and none of us knew it." Philip Langner put the problem more simply. "It just had too many damn scenes. In other words, it was a great, big physical production with this scene and that scene. I've come to believe that all you need is the actors. The less scenery the better. The people in the audience get it," the producer said. "I just thought it was overdone."

Decisions were made in rehearsals and in staging that went against the grain of the play as Gibson had conceived it. For example, one of the numbered actors eventually was listed in the program as Israeli General Moshe Dayan, giving the audience the expectation of a dimensional character that the writing did not fulfill. That was true of Golda Meir herself, Gibson thought later, when Anne in makeup with a false nose, jowls, and a heavily padded costume gave a startling likeness to Meir. "Penn and I were delighted," he said, "and blind to its implications." Her step back in time to her childhood and her days on a kibbutz as a young woman might seem incompatible with her makeup, even ridiculous. In short, a nonrealistic play was being presented realistically and was becoming ever more elaborate—a recipe for disaster.

Alarms began to sound in tryouts in Baltimore, but no one listened. The audience in the small theater the production had booked brought its imagination to the bare-boned presentation—no costumes, no makeup, no set, and no visuals were employed. The response was emotional and gratifying. The reviews, however, were overwhelmingly critical. Anne's performance was praised, but the production was labeled a mishmash that was long-winded, confused, aimless, and boring. In that way, *Golda* was beginning to resemble *John and Abigail,* a production that had left people dazed and confused.

There was talk of closing the play, but Gibson and Penn thought they could make it work out of town and still get to New York if they turned to a more linear structure. Gibson decided later that they went in exactly the wrong direction and therefore many of the qualities of oil and water in the production remained. Meanwhile, Anne and others in the company worked through change after change in script and staging—the visuals were greatly reduced, even though they had cost nearly one-fifth of the budget—and the company marched on to Boston.

Awaiting them were more theatergoers who told of being moved to tears and more bad reviews, this time including a barb that Anne had been mannered and unconvincing. A literal disaster struck the next morning when an electrical fire destroyed the set and efforts to douse it left the theater seats soggy and sooty. The production moved across the street for a few days. Its pared-down performances seemed to draw a better response, though no one made the connection to the lack of bells and whistles lost in the fire. The set was rebuilt as it had been before the accident.

A more ominous development in Boston concerned not the structure or presentation of the play but Anne. She was becoming worn out and her body stocking was causing her discomfort. She did not want to appear in the last Saturday performance in Boston, and her understudy took her place. Most people sought a refund rather than pay to see someone other than the star. A production with a high break-even point could not afford to refund money regularly.

If Anne felt uncomfortable in Boston, she had even more discomfort to face in New York. The second evening performance at the Morosco Theatre was part of a fund-raiser for Israel, and Golda Meir herself was in the audience, seeing the play for the first time. Her presence affected other theatergoers and made Anne tremble onstage, according to Gibson. "When I asked an actor how it felt, he said fine till he'd looked into Bancroft's eyes," Gibson said. "I asked what did he see, and he said, 'Terror.'"

In Anne's dressing room after the performance, Meir sat in near silence as Anne removed her makeup. There was one moment of levity. When Anne took off her false nose, Meir remarked, "I wish I could." Otherwise, the atmosphere was tense. Though Meir told the press that she thought the play had been "terrific" and that she had liked it very much, an appointment was being made for the next day in her hotel room with Langner, Gibson, Penn, and their star.

Anne was late for the conference and was asked to wait downstairs as

Meir, surrounded by her retinue, launched the opening salvo. "She had to say frankly the show was false and she detested everything in Bancroft's characterization," Gibson recounted. "It was too old, feebled, stooped, limping, tearful, and shuffly with hand in pockets. And too yiddisher-momma." Meir did not put any stock in letters brought by Langner calling the play wonderful and inspiring. If she had looked and sounded like Anne, Meir said, she "could never have been elected prime minister."

When Anne joined them, Meir at first did not want to repeat her criticism, but Anne insisted on hearing it. Meir did not hold back. As Langner remembered, a key point was whether she had vacillated in some way in deciding what course to take with her life. "Golda made quite a speech, saying, 'I was never doubtful.' Anne had sort of thought of Golda being a young woman that was feeling her way, and Golda said, 'I was never feeling my way. I always knew exactly what I wanted to do.' In other words, she was a very dominant kind of woman. She was so strong-minded."

Anne listened without interruption until Meir finished, then moved her chair closer to Meir. "Now you have to be specific," she said. "On what line do I put my hands in my pockets?" They spoke for an hour before Anne left and went directly to the theater to play the matinee. "Anne was well able to take it," Langner said, "and she did a fine job of toughening herself up, her character, instead of, 'Oh, dear, will they let me do this? . . . Will I be able to do this?' Golda didn't want that at all. I remember Golda saying, 'I didn't have doubts. I didn't mess around—I did it.'"

Gibson said Anne quickly modified her take on Meir. "Grit personified, she gave a quite different performance, younger, strong, dry, simpler but valid," he said. "It was how she would act it thereafter." Even Meir was impressed. She attended another preview performance two days later and sat in tears as a noisy ovation erupted from the audience. Backstage, she told Anne, "I don't know how you did it in twenty-four hours." Anne replied, "I had forty-eight."

Meir may well have been pleased—who could say, given her previous comments and the fact that she had financial and personal reasons to want the play to succeed? But her criticism had led Anne to make changes that essentially took away the performance she had conceived, at least in Gibson's view, and resulted in the kind of compromise that he believed eroded her confidence. It was certainly possible that the personal connection on which Anne had based her characterization was part of Meir's critique. If that was the case, where was Anne to go?

The official opening of *Golda* was set for November 14, 1977. On the same day, New York theaters began showing *The Turning Point*. It drew some of the highest praise of Anne's career. The tone was set by an early notice in *Variety*, which forecast a career highlight for both Anne and Shirley MacLaine while calling their movie "one of the best films of this era." The cheers continued in the *New York Times* ("powerhouse performances"), the *Washington Post* ("enormously appealing"), and the *Los Angeles Times* ("vivid moviemaking").

Critics divided their compliments almost evenly between the stars, and Anne received her first glowing notices in years. "A brave, bravura performance," wrote Richard Schickel of *Time*. "Lined in the face, skinny to the point of emaciation, febrile in manner, she tiers the definitive portrayal of an aging star." Charles Champlin of the *Los Angeles Times* wrote, "She is dazzling to see, tough and vulnerable, wry and resilient, a woman of masks we are able to glimpse behind." Writing for *Newsweek*, David Ansen said of MacLaine's costar: "Bancroft has lately shown a tendency toward florid, great-lady-of-the-screen mannerisms, but here she has a part in which to use those mannerisms for all they're worth. Emma is a prima donna, as well as being a gifted and generous artist, and Bancroft is sensational in this tricky role." The negative comments she drew— "Bancroft is as usual unbearable," sniffed Stanley Kauffmann of the *New Republic*—were few and forgettable.

The Turning Point would end up on the top-ten lists of at least sixteen critics. The National Board of Review named it the best film of the year over *Julia* and *Annie Hall*, and Anne was honored as the year's best actress. The Golden Globes presented the film its award for best drama while giving the actress award to Jane Fonda for *Julia*. When nominations for the Academy Awards were counted, *The Turning Point* received eleven, including best actress nominations for Anne and MacLaine and supporting cast nomination for Leslie Browne and Mikhail Baryshnikov. The film was also nominated for best picture, Herbert Ross for best director, and Arthur Laurents for best original screenplay. *The Turning Point* would not be among the most popular films—it was the year of *Star Wars*—but it took in a respectable $15.4 million in rentals for seventeenth place on the *Variety* list. In terms of critical and industry acclaim, the movie rivaled *The Graduate* and renewed respect for Anne's talents.

If *Golda* could reap just half the compliments heaped on her new movie, it would be a banner year for Anne. Instead, the majority of reviews of *Golda* were scathing, especially considering the talents behind it. "When the rear-screen projections are more dramatic and involving than the play taking place in front of them," wrote Douglas Watt of the *New York Daily News*, "you're in trouble." At *Time*, T. E. Kalem wrote: "A conscientious, reverential, monumental bore. The real Golda Meir should sue." Several critics remarked on the dullness of a show stuffed with facts—"*Golda* isn't a play," wrote Martin Gottfried of the *New York Post*, "it's an assignment"—and lacking vitality. The weight of the criticism fell to its playwright, William Gibson. Anne's portrayal drew some negative comments—Watt thought she failed to capture Meir's spirit—but for the most part she was commended for bringing Meir to life. Writing for the *New York Times*, Richard Eder cited Anne's "extraordinary portrait of a leader who possessed strength amid confusion," but a mixed tone marked his review. "*Golda* is to be remembered for the spectacle of an actress overwhelmed by the character she plays, and yet able to master it almost completely," Eder wrote. "But it is also to be remembered as a very partial and superficial portrait of a historical figure and its history." Ticketholders reading the reviews faced the dilemma of seeing a play that could be dull while featuring a marvelous performance by one of the nation's best actresses.

They decided to see Anne at work regardless of the play's flaws. Advance sales and word of mouth kept the 1,009-seat Morosco Theatre nearly full. Yet by this time Anne had suffered a loss of spirit, in Gibson's estimation. She had managed to cope with all the changes, the negative reviews in tryouts, the frank critique from Meir, and the bad press in New York. Contractually, she had months more to endure. (The theater's treasurer estimated that *Golda* would need to run a full year before it would break even.) Added to all that stress was Gibson's suggestion that they restage the play, rehearsing the new approach in the daytime ahead of the evening's performances. It seemed an impossible task, given that Anne was already exhausted and depressed by so many compromises. The restaging was not pursued.

As it had in the past and would again in the future, Anne's health had the final say. She had already asked that the schedule of eight performances a week be reduced by one. Her request refused, she began canceling anyway, citing illness or other personal problems. Sales fell when ticket buyers realized that there was a chance they would lose out and come to the theater the night her understudy went on in her place. A case of strep throat put her down for two weeks at the end of January and into February, and the production was suspended. Anne would not let *Golda* end on that sour note and returned February 11 for a final ten-performance run, ending with a Sunday matinee. She could not manage the last three performances, and the play closed on Thursday, February 16.

Golda went from being a sure winner to a $500,000 loser. William Gibson readily took the blame, then and later, believing that he had not reconciled his vision for the play with the way he agreed that it be staged. When asked what went wrong, Anne did not point a finger at anyone in particular, certainly not herself. Most of her reflections were about Golda Meir's objections to how she depicted her on the stage, which suggested that the criticisms from her friend had taken a toll. "Golda wanted a digni-fied portrait—a photograph. She wanted to look perfect—while making powerful decisions. She also didn't want any jokes in the play," Anne said a few weeks after the play had closed. She defended the nuances in her por-trayal as having a basis in fact—Meir did indeed limp and keep her head down, physical traits Meir had found objectionable. Mainly, Anne blamed her bronchial illness on the cigarettes she practically chain-smoked during each performance. Asked if she would do another Broadway show, Anne said, "Not for quite some time, not until my husband goes to China or our child goes to college." In other words, she had no desire to return to Broadway.

When *Golda* had seemed like a winner back in November, Mel Brooks said that his wife should win an Oscar for *The Turning Point* and a Tony for *Golda*. He was on the right track—Anne was nominated for both awards. The night of the Academy Awards was April 3, less than two months after the play had closed. Anne remained at home, telling the press that she was too weak to attend. The odds did not favor her, especially since Shirley MacLaine had been nominated in the same category and costars tended to cancel each other out. The award went to Diane Keaton for *Annie Hall*. Anne and MacLaine were not the only nominees for *The Turning Point* to go home empty-handed. Of its eleven nominations, not one resulted in a win. It became the only film in academy history to have that many nomi-nations without winning at least one Oscar, a dubious feat matched in 1985 by *The Color Purple*.

Two months later, on June 4, the Tony Award for lead actress in a play went to Jessica Tandy for *The Gin Game*. Anne had stayed home then, too, but she had been the only nominee for *Golda*, a show the *New York Times* had branded "an artistic and financial failure." The nomination was as much an acknowledgement of Anne's courage and professionalism in a difficult production as it was a recognition of her widely lauded performance. The effort to do her part in meeting the high expectations for *Golda* had worn her down. What *Golda* did not destroy was her desire to find a new challenge once she was up to it.

12

A First-Time Director's True Calling

Anne spent part of her recovery from the physical and artistic rigors of *Golda* in the Caribbean, enjoying an island getaway that was becoming a regular retreat for the Brooks family. For much of the first half of 1978 she was out of sight, if not out of the minds of the public because of her Oscar and Tony nominations. As a sign of her standing as a woman to admire, readers of *Ladies' Home Journal* placed her in a list of women of the year published that spring. Amid categories like social responsibility, science, sports, local government, national government, business, and popular music, readers selected Anne and Cicely Tyson for performing artists.

The most prominent project linked to Anne in the months after *Golda* was a film version of the tell-all memoir *Mommie Dearest* by Joan Crawford's daughter. The 1978 book shocked Crawford's fans with its tales of child abuse and a glamorous movie star with self-destructive urges—all real and not make-believe, according to Christina Crawford. Anne would mull over the project for the next two years. At one point Franco Zeffirelli was set to direct with Anne starring. In 1980 the producer Frank Yablans told the press that Anne would indeed play Crawford, but within weeks there were reports of differences over the script. The following year it was Faye Dunaway on theater screens screeching "No more wire hangers!" in what would become a camp classic from the director Frank Perry. Anne's better judgment had prevailed.

While she kept *Mommie Dearest* simmering on a back burner, Anne focused on turning her second short video for the American Film Institute's Directing Workshop for Women into a feature-length movie. Mel Brooks had wanted to produce films that went beyond his signature comedies, and his wife's project became the first movie produced by his new company. Its name, Brooksfilms, was as close a connection to his own name as Mel wanted, rightly figuring that the public would think that any movie he produced would be a comedy. Keeping a low profile was unusual for Mel, but he was content that the industry would know the driving force behind movies coming from Brooksfilms.

Jonathan Sanger had been working for Mel and was asked to serve as associate producer and unit production manager for *Fatso*. Mel went to Twentieth Century-Fox to get the backing needed for his wife's first feature film, which was budgeted at around $3 million, a modest amount at the time. Though the studio would have wanted to continue working with Mel, it was unlikely that *Fatso* was merely a project to keep him happy. "I don't think a studio makes a movie without having a sense of the commercial possibilities of the movie," Sanger said in looking back at *Fatso*. "I think they thought it was a good idea, and he was a terrific pitchman and was able to convince the powers that be at the studio that it would be a good idea. But they had to like the script and really believe in it."

Anne's AFI short would have helped to ease any worries about her lack of experience as a director. "Normally they might be concerned with a first-timer," Sanger said, "but she was not your average first-timer. She was somebody who had a lot of experience with actors by being around sets her whole life. She relied on others for the technical aspects of the shoot, but she was certainly very involved in every detail of it." As Sanger recalled, Mel generally stayed away once the deal was set up—he had other projects in the works, too. "It was entirely Anne," according to Sanger. "I think she probably preferred it that way. She didn't need him to tell her how to direct the movie. She knew what she wanted; this was her story. He also knew her well enough to know that she was not somebody that you tell how to do anything. Not that she didn't seek advice from people. She was in charge, no question about it."

As they assembled a crew, Anne tried to hire as many women as possible, especially for jobs that were not usually filled by female workers. "That was an important thing for her," Sanger recalled. "We wound up having a very female-centric crew, very unusual for Hollywood at that time." In that spirit, Anne hired Brianne Murphy as director of photography. A woman had never been in that position on a Hollywood feature. Murphy had worked her way up and was admitted to the union in 1973 as the only female director of photography. Hiring her was a point of pride for Anne.

Fatso was a valentine to Anne's childhood in the Bronx and a celebration of her Italian American roots. "There was so much of my family in this, so much of my family," her younger sister, Phyllis, remarked after a screening of the film in 2010. "There was so much that was part of what we grew up with. What she did was, she just took our lives and put it onto film." Love and history aside, it would be labor-intensive to write and direct a film—and play a leading role. Anne knew it could be done—Mel had been directing himself for years.

The film's title refers to compulsive eater Dominick, a middle-aged man raised on food as a reward for good behavior and now suffering from a weight problem. The danger becomes clear when he attends the funeral of an obese cousin, dead before forty, his massive casket hauled to the cemetery on a boat trailer. Dom's sister, Antoinette, shares his grief and encourages him to get help. The list of foods to avoid brings tears to his eyes. When he begins to fall for Lydia, who runs a store near his card shop, he decides to join the weight-loss group Chubby Checkers. Later, he calls his "checkers" to help him get through a period of craving, but they swap so many stories about favorite foods that they end up eating everything in sight. Eventually, Dom realizes that Lydia loves him for who he is and that he too must accept his problem with food as just a part of himself. They marry and have one child after the other.

Anne was inspired in part by her sister JoAnne's struggle with compulsive eating and dedicated the novelization of *Fatso* to her. She wrote the leading role in the film for her friend Dom DeLuise—she would play his sister—but pointed out that the story was not about DeLuise, even though the fictional Dominick shared many of his traits. "I know a part of him that he doesn't wish to reveal, you know. And he never would unless you told him, look, this isn't you. This is somebody else," she said. "And he achieved everything that I asked for."

It did not come easily to DeLuise. "Dom was all over the place as an actor, in a good way," Jonathan Sanger recalled. "But she always had to make sure he was contained and wasn't being Dom but the character, the younger brother." A good-hearted, jovial man by nature, DeLuise practically burst onto the set each day with a smile and a joke or a funny comment for everyone. The role he was playing carried with it far more angst than was natural for DeLuise, who gained thirty pounds for the movie. "She wanted the humor that he had, but she didn't want him to go out of character. She wanted him to stay in that character, and that was a challenge," Sanger remembered. "He was uniquely a celebrity and the celebrity had to be pared away to get to the character of this man who had this problem and still be somebody you wanted to watch."

Other familiar faces in the *Fatso* cast guaranteed a friendly set when they began shooting at the Fox studios in spring 1979. Estelle Reiner, Carl's wife, played a customer at the card shop, and Ron Carey, a regular in Mel's films, was Dominick's brother, Frank. Michael Lombard, who had been in *The Devils* with Anne, was in a supporting role. Her sister Phyllis was one of the mourners in the opening scene and served on the crew as Anne's assistant. In a tribute to their mother's family, the siblings whom DeLuise, Anne, and Carey portrayed were christened DiNapoli.

For the role of Lydia, Anne asked Candice Azzara to appear again opposite DeLuise, reprising her role in the video short. "I just knew what she wanted," Azzara remembered. "An actor has to read between the lines. What the part says is not there. The thing is somehow, you just knew that this girl, Lydia, saw this man as the man of her dreams and she didn't see what he looked like." Azzara was not jealous of the close attention Anne paid to Dom DeLuise. "She got a performance out of him that I think is just brilliant," the actress said. "It was a serious comedy, you know? She brought out the empathy in him."

A week in New York for location shooting was part of the forty-day production schedule. "Anne's a genius when working with actors," Brianne Murphy said at the time. "Little adjustments do big, big things. Together we discover how it should be covered." Anne also tended to details, such as ordering cookies from the Bronx bakery of her youth and asking that they use the original recipe that produced larger cookies than the ones the owners were selling by then.

A warm, comfortable set where people enjoyed coming to work had been one of Anne's goals. As Jonathan Sanger remembered, she worked well with the actors, giving them enough room to develop their characters while still keeping them focused. "She relied on her instincts and her own knowledge of performance," he said. "There were very few people who could or would even want to deny her primacy in that area. When she came on and talked about performance, she knew what she was talking about." She also did not spend an inordinate amount of time on her own performance as Dom's mothering sister. "She didn't overshoot herself," Sanger said. "When she felt that she had gotten the performance from herself that she wanted, she moved on very quickly."

There was a family feeling on the *Fatso* set, which reflected the tenor of the movie. Dom DeLuise's mother was often there making sauce, and something was always cooking. "It was very different from any other movie I've been in. It was almost like a happening," Candice Azzara said. "I felt like I knew everyone there, too. I knew the characters, I knew them—we were all from an Italian background. It was almost like my family was there." Mel Brooks made a point to say that he was not overseeing his wife's first feature film. "She hasn't asked me for one bit of advice on how to shoot a scene so far," he told the columnist Maggie Daly. Besides, the film Anne had envisioned almost certainly had a different take on the subject than Mel would have employed. "Her humor is much more subtle than Mel's," Brianne Murphy said. "Anne plays things for their serious side."

When *Fatso* was released in February 1980, most movie critics were not impressed by Anne's first effort at conceiving a story and creating a feature film from it. A rare recommendation came from Kevin Thomas of the *Los Angeles Times,* who thought Anne had delivered an affectionate ethnic comedy in an appealing, modest debut as a writer and director. Those kind perceptions were not shared by other critics. "It has a few nice moments, but only a few, and that takes care of the good news," wrote Janet Maslin of the *New York Times.* "The bad news is that the story is at once sentimental and unfocused, the jokes aren't often funny, and the camera shakes every time it tries to follow the actors across a room." At least two critics gave a personal edge to their dismissal of the film. Connecting the film to Mel's production company, Stanley Kauffmann of the *New Republic* asked, "What in the world persuaded financiers to back this picture?" Gary Arnold of the *Washington Post* took the personal criticism a step further: "One trembles to imagine the commotion that must engulf the Mel Brooks residence when he and Bancroft have a spat." The film's box office was so low that it did not register on the annual *Variety* list.

Anne did not direct again, and probably not because of bad reviews and a cold box office. She had been dealing with critical notices and underperforming films for decades; they were part of the life of an actor. Being in charge, however, had been a new experience for her, and she had not enjoyed it. Some members of the cast were unprepared, Candice Azzara remembered, and Anne's frustrations were evident at times. Her sister Phyllis recalled that Anne was not happy with some of the performances but realized that, given time and budget restraints, she could do nothing about it. "It wasn't her thing to direct," Phyllis Italiano said. "She didn't like being in control." Years later, when Mel was asked why his wife did not direct another movie, he replied, "She hated the actors."

If that were the case and not an exaggeration, Michael Lombard was surprised. He remembered a warm, wonderful time on the *Fatso* set with a cast of fellow New York Italians. "If she didn't like the actors, they didn't know it," he said. "There's a big difference from being an actor to being a director. I was quite surprised that she was doing it in the first place. It never occurred to me she was going to be a director. I'm sure it was difficult. It's such a huge responsibility. You are responsible for everything as a director, and it probably was just not worth it to her. Maybe if the movie had been a big hit she would have tried again."

Jonathan Sanger also remembered Anne saying she would not want to direct another film, even though he and others encouraged her. "She said, 'Yeah, but actors are too difficult. They're just too difficult.' She said, 'When I'm acting, I'm into my own character, but if I have to deal with these people on a daily basis, I don't think I can handle that. I don't really think I necessarily want to do this again.'" Given the angst Anne often went through to find her own characterization, it would make sense that she did not want to experience that struggle tenfold when overseeing a cast. Writing was different—a writer creates every character—and now and then she would consider writing a story or screenplay.

To Candice Azzara and Phyllis Italiano, *Fatso* presented the Italian American family in all its colors. "Italians love this movie. They say, 'Oh, that's my family.' Italians relate to this movie," Azzara said. "They know everyone in the movie. They know the love for food, the love for family, the yelling and the screaming, the hitting, the getting crazy . . . it's just Italian." Italiano said *Fatso* had become a cult film for young Italian Americans. "It's the only one," she said, "that shows Italian American families as they are." If that had been Anne's goal, then she succeeded far more than reviews and ticket sales would have suggested. Along the way she found—or rediscovered—that her true calling was acting.

Sometime after she directed *Fatso,* Anne faced a crisis unlike any other in her life: she was diagnosed with breast cancer. At the time it was unusual for celebrities, particularly actresses, to announce to the world that they were undergoing treatment for any kind of cancer. Betty Ford, the wife of President Gerald Ford, had been open about her mastectomy in 1974 as a way of raising awareness of the disease and reducing the fear and ignorance surrounding it. In Anne's case, she kept her illness secret to the point that it was not reported in the press or shared with all her friends. There was a practical reason for the secrecy. Film stars had to be insured when they were cast in a movie, and a history of illness made them a financial risk that many studios simply would not accept.

Keeping private her treatment and the effect the illness had on her health also meant that Anne would not be on the receiving end of sympathy or never-ending concern—she wanted neither. Had her cancer been made public, it would have joined *The Graduate* and her marriage as subjects always brought up in interviews. She did not want to be reminded that cancer now hung over her life. Strong-willed and focused, she would not give it any more time or thought than was absolutely necessary.

Onscreen Anne appeared almost unchanged—older, of course, but still slim and attractive. In public she did not appear to be ill, which suggests that she had managed to weather the treatment she received. It was also difficult to tell what effect, if any, her illness had on her work. Taking long breaks from movies and television or the stage had been her way for years, so time out for treatment and recovery would not be noticed by friends or fans. Besides the usual goal of someone with cancer—five years without a recurrence—she simply sought to keep this aspect of her life to herself.

Work, as always, was a reward in itself—and she did not have to look far for a most promising role. *The Elephant Man* was the second film in the production pipeline at Brooksfilms. As Anne and Jonathan Sanger were checking out locations in New York for *Fatso,* Mel was considering a screenplay sent to Sanger about a nineteenth-century Englishman named John Merrick, who was known to medical history as the Elephant Man. Merrick suffered from physical abnormalities that left him with a freakishly shaped head, a curved spine, and a distorted body covered with unsightly growths. He was mentally fit, but his appearance made him an outcast. The script, based in part on two books about Merrick, followed his progress from an abused circus attraction to a patient at London Hospital and, through the care of a sympathetic physician, the toast of London society.

Mel set about making *The Elephant Man* with Sanger as producer. The script needed work and the film needed a director. An alumnus of the American Film Institute, thirty-four-year-old David Lynch, was hired on the strength of his 1977 independent film *Eraserhead,* a black-and-white horror movie about a father and his deformed child that was on its way to becoming a cult favorite. Mel and Sanger recognized that Lynch's unsettling visual style would be a good match for the John Merrick story. Lynch, Sanger, and Mel worked with the screenwriters Christopher De Vore and Eric Bergren to revise their script, and Mel eventually found a financial backer and distributor in Paramount Pictures.

Once John Hurt was cast as Merrick, there was the question of who would play the actress who befriends Merrick and helps introduce him to London society. British performers filled the cast, which on its face made choosing an American seem unlikely and even out of place. Anne was familiar with the script and Mel let Sanger and Lynch know that she was interested. One might have assumed that Mel set aside the role for his wife, but Sanger said that was not the case. "There was a real separation in their lives between her work as an actress," he said. "There was never an assumption that, 'Oh, she's my wife, she'll do it.' She was not his wife as an actress, she was 'that great actress.'" Sanger and Lynch thought Anne would be a terrific choice for Mrs. Kendal. Anne had played a Briton in *The Pumpkin Eater* and was popular with British audiences, which made it unlikely there would be a backlash in having an American in the story.

Aside from her work in the film, Anne's major contribution to *The Elephant Man* may have been pushing for Anthony Hopkins to play Merrick's doctor. She had worked with Hopkins in *Young Winston* several years earlier and judged him one of the finest actors alive. Sanger and Lynch were pondering whether to cast one of several other actors for the role, but Anne urged them to seriously consider Hopkins. "She was really a big fan of his work," Sanger said. At the time Hopkins was just starting to register with American audiences—his Oscar-winning turn in *The Silence of the Lambs* was a dozen years away. With Hopkins and Hurt starring, the veteran performers John Gielgud, Wendy Hiller, and Freddie Jones brought even more shine to the *Elephant Man* cast. What may have seemed like a highbrow horror movie was shaping up to be a prestigious production for Brooksfilms.

Anne spent a week or so on the *Elephant Man* set in London. Her role as the actress Mrs. Kendal called for just three scenes—the first in a dressing room in which Mrs. Kendal reads about Merrick in a newspaper, followed by her visit to Merrick's room at the hospital, in which they read lines from *Romeo and Juliet*. Anne's last scene came at the theater the night Mrs. Kendal invites Merrick to sit in a box and experience the wonders of the stage. It had been some time since Anne had worked with a director as green as David Lynch. "She treated David not as a first-time director who didn't know what he was doing but as the director of the movie," Jonathan Sanger recalled. "She was very respectful of David, but she liked him personally. There was a good personal rapport. She immediately warmed to him."

The same could not be said of Lynch's relationship with Anthony Hopkins. He had little patience with Lynch, a newcomer unsure of himself, in Hopkins's view, and Hopkins could hardly believe Lynch was in charge of a major production of such high quality. Then again, Anne did not allow herself to be treated like clay in the hands of her young director. "She wasn't interested in David telling her how to perform her role," Sanger said. "She knew who she was. David didn't have to say very much to get what he needed from her." Anne tried different approaches to her character and asked to do additional takes if she thought she could come up with something better.

The Elephant Man received some glowing reviews when it was released in October 1980 and was listed among the National Board of Review's top ten films. Merrick's plea—"I am not an animal! I am a human being!"—became one of the most familiar lines in movie history. The second film released by Brooksfilms garnered eight Academy Award nominations, among them best picture, best director, and best actor. It did not take home any Oscars the following year—*Ordinary People* and its director, Robert Redford, and *Raging Bull*'s star, Robert De Niro, were the big winners. *The Elephant Man* fared better with the British film academy, receiving seven nominations and three awards—for best film, best actor, and best production design. In terms of ticket sales, it garnered $26 million at theaters to rank as the twenty-fifth-most-popular film of the year (according to the modern-day online site Box Office Mojo). The general public may not have known it, but Hollywood was learning that Anne's husband could do much more than churn out crowd-pleasing comedies.

After directing and starring in *Fatso* and providing strong support in *The Elephant Man,* Anne slipped back into her familiar pattern of weighing roles and choosing what interested her while keeping close to her husband and son. The success of *The Turning Point* and the high-profile projects that followed had seemed to renew interest in Anne for various feature films and television movies, although thoughts of casting her were probably tempered by the fact that she was on the verge of turning fifty.

There was no escaping time except through retirement, but *The Elephant Man* was evidence that she could still find a place, large or small, in a top-notch feature film or television production.

Anne was on the short list for *The Fan,* a thriller about a young man's obsession with a renowned stage and film actress; the role went to Lauren Bacall. She was asked to appear as Holocaust survivor Fania Fenelon in *Playing for Time,* a television film drawn from Fenelon's memoirs. The role was offered to Jane Fonda, too, and ultimately went to Vanessa Redgrave, who won an Emmy. There was talk of casting either Anne or Irene Papas in a television movie about the opera singer Maria Callas, but the project stalled. Michael Palin, a Monty Python alumnus, considered both Anne and Maggie Smith for the leading female role in his comedy *The Missionary* and asked the longtime producer John Calley who had the bigger box-office name. "Neither meant a thing" to ticket buyers, Calley responded, and Smith ended up playing the part. Anne's name may have brought with it prestige, but standing out as a useful marketing tool remained elusive.

In between the release of *Fatso* and *The Elephant Man* and while *Mommie Dearest* was still a possibility, the producers of *Jesus of Nazareth* asked Anne to join their new TV miniseries project, *Marco Polo.* With a budget of $25 million and an air time of ten hours, the proposed biography of the explorer of China would be the most ambitious made-for-television saga yet and take more than a year to film on locations across Europe, Africa, and Asia. Playing young Marco's dying mother, Anne undertook a relatively quick piece of work that involved a trip to Venice, Italy, once filming was under way in November 1980. Though the miniseries was filled with stars—among them Burt Lancaster, John Gielgud, John Houseman, Ian McShane, and Leonard Nimoy—Anne shared her death-bed scene with only the child actor playing Marco Polo. She brought along eight-year-old Max and allowed him to watch her "die" before the camera. "He could see me do it," she said, "then get up and walk away." Critics commended the stunning scenery when *Marco Polo* aired on NBC in May 1982, but most lamented what they thought was a weakly written, banal script. People tuned in, but not in blockbuster numbers.

Speaking of China, Anne had assured the *New York Times* after the disappointment of *Golda* that she would not return to the stage unless her husband was going to China or until her son was entering college. Four years later, Mel was still at home and Max was not yet in middle school. Apparently enough time had passed that Anne considered appearing in a two-character play set for Broadway in fall 1981. The playwright Tom Kempinski's *Duet for One* had already been produced in London's West End with Frances de la Tour, his wife, and David de Keyser. De la Tour was a member of the Workers Revolutionary Party, and the Broadway producers were wary of bringing her to New York and sparking the kind of stir that greeted another party member, Vanessa Redgrave, when she was cast in movies and television.

The life of the British cellist Jacqueline du Pré had inspired *Duet for One*. She was twenty-six and at the height of her fame when, in 1971, she was struck by what turned out to be multiple sclerosis. She retired and within a few years was practically paralyzed. She died in 1987, seven years after the London debut of *Duet for One*. In Kempinski's play, Stephanie Abrahams is a violinist whose multiple sclerosis has confined her to a wheelchair. Over the course of several visits to the office of a psychiatrist, Dr. Feldmann, she reveals an anger and bitterness behind her sunny facade. Her desire to die clashes with Feldmann's efforts to prompt her to find a reason to continue living.

For the initial Broadway run of *Duet for One*, the producers first signed Ellen Burstyn. She had seen the London production and was eager to appear in the play with her Actors Studio teacher, Lee Strasberg, as the psychiatrist. Strasberg agreed to take the role if it were offered—his participation would make the production an event—and Burstyn suggested to her *Exorcist* director, William Friedkin, that he consider directing the play. In her memoir she described her disappointment when Friedkin and the producers decided that Strasberg was not right for the part and told her that they were interested in Max von Sydow instead. She left the venture feeling betrayed.

Faye Dunaway read for the part, but in July 1981 it was announced that Anne had been signed. Cast opposite her was von Sydow, the Swedish actor best known for Ingmar Bergman films and the American movies *The Exorcist* and *Three Days of the Condor*. He had appeared on Broadway once before, in a twelve-performance run of *The Night of the Tribades* in 1977. Friedkin, though an Oscar winner for *The French Connection*, had not yet directed a drama on Broadway, and his film career was in a fallow period. His three previous movies—*Sorcerer*, *The Brink's Job*, and *Cruising*—had been met with indifferent box-office returns and critical carping if not outright hostility.

Duet for One opened December 17, 1981, at the Royale Theatre. It closed just two weeks later, after twenty performances, and became the shortest run Anne would have in a Broadway show. What happened? In the years ahead *Duet for One* was not a topic that either Anne or William Friedkin was eager to discuss. Reviews provided a sense of how *Duet for One* may have gone wrong in the transfer from the West End to Broadway. A critic who had seen the London production, Jack Kroll of *Newsweek,* told his readers that the play he had liked in London was not one he liked in New York, saying that what had been humane and effective had become dispiriting. The problem he cited lay mainly with Anne's performance. She brought a steely quality to Stephanie that made her unpleasant rather than despairing, Kroll explained, and her profane outbursts were no longer evidence of spiritual pain. The change in tone, he said, revealed the weaknesses in Kempinski's play. Kroll concluded, "Under Friedkin's direction, they've overwhelmed a fragile play instead of finding the life in it." Those were the focal points of most of the reviews: the shortcomings of the play, the flawed interpretation in Anne's performance, the mild presence of von Sydow's psychiatrist, and the lackluster direction of William Friedkin.

The anger that Anne could bring to a role—quiet anger in *The Graduate* and explosive anger in *The Pumpkin Eater*—may indeed have worked against her in *Duet for One*. Audiences probably preferred their heroine to be brave if despondent rather than seething. In the hands of others, *Duet for One* rediscovered some of the success it had enjoyed in London. Besides other productions at theaters around the world, the play was shot as a made-for-television movie produced for the BBC in 1985 with the original cast of Frances de la Tour and David de Keyser. A year later, Tom Kempinski revised the story to accommodate a twenty-member cast for a feature film directed by Andrey Konchalovsky and starring Julie Andrews and, in a return to the role of the psychiatrist, Max von Sydow. Andrews was nominated for a Golden Globe for her performance.

Whatever the causes, failure brought out Anne's tendency to judge herself harshly. Her high school drama teacher, Elisa Coletti Goldberg, attended one of the last performances of *Duet for One* and visited Anne after the show. "She said when we went backstage to see her, 'Oh, I haven't done a very good job.' She was desolate about the fact that that play closed so fast. She was really feeling down, you could see, and she was disappointed in herself."

Duet for One would be the end of Anne's work in the most respected dramatic venue in the United States. She would appear on a stage again in the years ahead, but not on Broadway. In her eight Broadway shows since 1958 she had starred in four new plays, in three that had originated overseas, and in a revival of a classic American drama. She had grown into a force on the stage and had been a welcome presence there for a generation. Movies and, in time, television would now be the place to find Anne at work.

For years a remake of the wartime dark comedy *To Be or Not to Be* promised Anne and Mel just the kind of story to meld their different acting styles and film personas. It was first announced to the press as an upcoming film in 1975 with Anne's high school friend David Lunney coproducing with Mel's production company and *Prisoner of Second Avenue*'s director, Melvin Frank, writing and directing. Four years later it cropped up again in the trade press as a vehicle for Anne and Mel, now with their friend Thomas Meehan writing a screenplay based on the original film produced and directed by Ernst Lubitsch. More time passed, and the project, by then with a screenplay by Meehan and the writer and comic actor Ronny Graham, was set to begin principal photography in early 1983. Before shooting began, David Lunney and William Allyn filed suit against Mel, Brooksfilms, and Twentieth Century-Fox claiming, in essence, that they had been cut out of the project. They would end up with a credit saying that the production had been suggested by them.

Lubitsch's *To Be or Not to Be* had been a unique comedy for American audiences still reeling from the nation's entry into the Second World War. Released in March 1942, three months after the attack on Pearl Harbor, the film was a farcical yet cynical look at a theater group in Poland on the eve of the bombing of Warsaw by Nazi Germany. The radio comedian and sometime film actor Jack Benny appeared as a hammy and egotistical actor married to a popular actress, played by Carole Lombard. She has an admirer in a young pilot who schedules a rendezvous with her; he is to leave the audience for her dressing room as her husband begins Hamlet's most famous soliloquy, which both insults the husband and makes him suspicious. What could have remained merely a bedroom farce turns serious when the Germans invade Poland and the theater troupe comes under the Nazi thumb. As the performers plot to escape to Britain, Benny impersonates a Polish traitor to prevent him from revealing the identities of people in the underground movement. The film becomes a comic caper with a Hitler lookalike, then ends happily with the troupe safely in London and

Benny once again performing *Hamlet*—and another young man in uniform excusing himself from the audience just as Benny begins the famous soliloquy.

Finding laughs in the plight of Poles and turning Hitler into a comic character struck some critics, though not all, as tasteless. "A subject far from the realm of fun," wrote Bosley Crowther of the *New York Times*. "To state it is callous and macabre is understating the case." Lubitsch himself offered a rebuttal, defending the mixture of melodrama with satire or even farce in a column in the *Times*. As far as making light of the Nazi menace, he wrote, "The American audiences don't laugh at those Nazis because they underestimate their menace, but because they are happy to see this new order and its ideology being ridiculed." The film also suffered from tragic bad timing that was beyond anyone's control: Carole Lombard died in a plane crash while selling war bonds not long before its release.

Forty years later, that baggage had become considerably lighter. *To Be or Not to Be* was seldom seen outside festivals. As far as using Adolf Hitler as a comical character, the 1960s television sitcom *Hogan's Heroes* had spent six seasons making fun of clueless German soldiers overseeing a prisoner-of-war camp. Most famously, Mel Brooks himself had deflated the Nazis with the "Springtime for Hitler" musical number in *The Producers*. Throughout his career, Mel would continue to make light of Hitler as a way of diminishing him. "By using the medium of comedy," he said in 2006, "we can try to rob Hitler of his posthumous power and myths." Mel had presented the gag "Hitler on Ice" as part of his film *History of the World, Part I* two years before remaking the Lubitsch film and sharing the director's goal of turning ridicule into a weapon.

The choreographer of "Springtime for Hitler," Alan Johnson, had contributed dance sequences to *Blazing Saddles* and other Brooks movies as well as Anne's first television special. Mel was taking top billing over Anne in *To Be or Not to Be,* and he asked Johnson to be the film's director. "I think he realized it was a load, a big load, to direct and star in," Johnson recalled. The movie stayed much closer to the Lubitsch version than one would have expected, given that Mel's almost manic persona was the complete opposite of Jack Benny's quiet consternation. In this instance, however, Mel was willing to do more than play a variation of himself. "He wanted to stay very true to the movie," Johnson said. "He said, 'Okay, I won't do any Mel Brooks things. I'll be honest, I'll play the character.' And I said, 'Great, that's what's needed.' And he did, for the most part."

In spite of being the director, Alan Johnson felt constrained by Mel throughout the Brooksfilms production. "It was still Mel's movie," he said. "I'd stage something, a little bit of a scene, and he'd see it and say, 'No, no. That's terrible. Go look at the original.' He was just hateful and a little crazed." Mel also felt free to criticize the performances of others in the cast, Johnson recalled. More than once he thought about quitting but kept deciding to stay on. "It was hell," Johnson said in looking back at the production, although he admitted that he liked the way the movie turned out and enjoyed working with Anne, Charles Durning, and others in the cast.

As her husband took on his most demanding movie role yet and clashed with his hand-picked director, Anne was both costar and supportive spouse. "She was on the set all the time with him, even when she wasn't called," Johnson said. Jonathan Sanger, the associate producer of *Fatso*, remembered how different it was for Anne to be a cast member in this Brooksfilms production. "She loved just being there and just acting and not having to be responsible for anything more than doing what she was doing," Sanger said. "The tension of making the movie was not in her hands. She just had to do what she could do."

To Be or Not to Be did show how different Anne and Mel were in their approaches and abilities—different while successful. Mel would ask for numerous takes when shooting a scene, believing that he could be better if he had another chance, according to Alan Johnson. Anne did not have that problem. "I was sitting next to her on the set," the director said. "They were doing a take with Mel. And they were setting up and they said, 'Okay, take nineteen.' And she went, 'Jesus, nineteen! How come I get two and he gets nineteen?' And I said, 'Well, you know what you're doing . . .' He hated to let go of what he did."

The opening scene of the film, set in a theater, featured Mel in a tuxedo and Anne in a silver lamé gown with padded shoulders performing a snappy song-and-dance number set to "Sweet Georgia Brown"—in Polish. A friend of Mel's had translated the lyrics and taught them how to sing them, Johnson recalled. "It was a stupid idea and a funny idea—that's why he did it," Johnson said. Without question, Mel had an instinct for what would make people smile. For many moviegoers the novelty number was the highlight of *To Be or Not to Be*. Mel and Anne learned the lyrics in Polish well enough to perform it on talk shows and during get-togethers with friends.

The plot of the new version of *To Be or Not to Be* generally followed the original. One key difference was the elimination of the character in the Lubitsch version who impersonates Hitler, which allowed Mel to dress up as the Führer and help lead the troupe to safety. (According to Alan Johnson, Mel had trouble with his bridgework in the middle of a scene and went to a dentist in his Hitler costume.) The new film was in color instead of black and white, which gave it the kind of modern look that most remakes favored over their original versions. It also sought to make the scenes between the actress and her admirer a little naughtier and the drama brought on by the bombing of Warsaw more unsettling—changes Ernst Lubitsch probably would have supported since he, too, wanted a strong mixture of comedy and drama. Another difference came by turning the actress's dresser into a gay man and having him rounded up by the Nazis for being gay, a character and a plot turn that would not have been allowed in an American movie in the 1940s.

To Be or Not to Be was budgeted at $9 million and enjoyed a strong supporting cast consisting of José Ferrer, Charles Durning, Tim Matheson, and George Gaynes. The Brookses' friend Estelle Reiner had her largest film role since *Fatso,* and even eleven-year-old Max Brooks had some screen time as a member of a refugee family. His mother was at her most glamorous playing a desirable older woman wooed by a much younger man. Most of the comedy was on Mel's side of the screen. He even had his own production number, a showgirls tune titled "Ladies" he'd written with Ronny Graham. They knew their subject well, having worked together in 1952 on the Broadway revue *New Faces.* The number recognized that, in the eyes of most moviegoers, Mel was the biggest star in the movie.

Mostly favorable reviews greeted *To Be or Not to Be* when it went into release in mid-December 1983. Several critics saw it as a near carbon copy of the original, though they might have differed over whether Mel and Alan Johnson had improved on or even equaled Ernst Lubitsch's work. Those who accepted the remake on its own terms—and noted that most moviegoers would not be familiar with the story—found it amusing and entertaining to varying degrees. "Do not expect the usual Brooksian ka-ka jokes and mad non sequiturs," wrote David Ansen of *Newsweek.* "This is his warmest, most plot-bound and traditional movie." Mel remained at the center of the critical discussion, but Anne was acknowledged by many as well-suited to the Carole Lombard role and bringing to it the necessary mix of glamour and understated humor. Few found the movie in question-able taste, and those who did not recommend it were far more likely to cite limp jokes and uninspired execution than question whether Nazis were suitable subject matter for a screen farce.

As the critics weighed in and fans bought tickets, Mel and Anne engaged in the typical whirlwind of promotional interviews with print and broadcast reporters. Their marriage was especially on the minds of reporters since they were costarring for the first time. When Mel and Anne appeared together on the *Today* show, the cohost and film critic Gene Shalit asked, "Do you still love each other?"

The easy response would have been an affirmative one. Instead—amid wisecracks—Mel gave an unusually serious answer and one that sounded honest and realistic. "All we know," he said, "is that we are a raft in the ocean, and we swim to each other, and cling, because life is . . . fraught with all kinds of disaster, uncertainty, unhappiness, and at least we have each other." As far as their union itself, Mel said: "Marriage is a retail store. Somebody has to watch the register and somebody has to get the pretzels down for the kids. . . . Life is very hard. I think you need a partner that you love and who loves you to get through it successfully. And I think we were very lucky." His answer seemed rooted in his life as a poor boy whose father died when he was a child—not to mention a devotee of Russian literature who wrote the lyrics "Hope for the best, expect the worst" for the main song in *The Twelve Chairs.*

Shalit asked Anne if they were content to be with each other. "I'm more than content," she said. "I mean, when he comes home at night, when that key goes in the door, I mean, my heart's fluttering. I am so happy he's home, you know. I mean, it's like the party's going to start." When asked about her marriage, Anne would often return to the idea of the key in the door signaling the start of the party. It was a wonderful image that warmed the hearts of their fans—and it appeared to be true.

Their home life underwent a major change the following year when they moved out of their Beverly Hills home upon the completion of a house on La Mesa Drive in Santa Monica. Max, then twelve and starting seventh grade, would attend the private Crossroads School in Santa Monica, and the new home would shave miles off the commute. Anne was the driving force behind the move from Foothill Road, and the change in schools was only a pretext, her son told the magazine *Town & Country* years later. "The real reason," Max said, "is that some women really like change, mainly my mother, and some men really don't, like us. We were not happy." The new house was a mammoth affair—*Variety* reported that it had more than

13,000 square feet and six bedrooms—and practically hung over the Riviera Country Club. It also had an indoor swimming pool, an important feature since Anne swam most days for relief from the back pain she still suffered as a result of her injury from *The Last Hunt* decades earlier.

Though the La Mesa Drive house lacked the woodsy feel of their Foothill Road home, Anne turned its sloping backyard into a terraced garden. An increased interest in organic gardening and naturally raised food had followed her cancer diagnosis. She raised her vegetables without pesticides and chemical fertilizers and picked off cutworms by hand to protect her plants. "She always insisted that gardening was the only way to ensure what we were putting into our bodies," Max wrote in an essay for a book about food and family. Each evening meal featured something grown in Anne's garden. Mel tolerated this agrarian activity, his son recounted, though he remarked out of Anne's hearing that it was all part of her "Italian peasant heritage." For years after her death Mel and Max would tend her treasured garden themselves.

Max's matriculation at Crossroads School brought Anne and Mel together with other parents of middle school students. Founded in 1971, the school had a reputation for a rigorous college-preparatory curriculum with programs in music, writing, and other arts. When one of its students was fatally struck by a car while trying to cross a street, Anne and Mel helped form a parents' committee that set out to determine what could be done to keep students safe. The school administration was not happy about the safety committee, recalled Jackie Eliopoulos, a friend of Anne and Mel's whose daughter was in Max's grade at Crossroads. The committee, chaired by Eliopoulos, put together a long list of safety issues, including traffic crossings, earthquake preparedness, school science laboratories, drinking by older students, and weeklong field trips.

"No one was more tireless than Anne and Mel in investigating these things. And they were busy people," Eliopoulos remembered. "They were dedicated to improving the safety of the school, and eventually the school administrators came around." Their concerns were well-founded, she said, and Anne's could not be dismissed as the worries of an overprotective mother. "She was protective, there's no question," Eliopoulos said. "She cherished that boy. He was her only child, her much-wanted only child, and they were concerned that they do the right thing for Max." Anne did not allow him to go on a school trip because, in her view, safety issues had not been adequately considered.

The safety committee met every two or three weeks. In time, though, some members grew tired if not annoyed with Mel's penchant for making jokes. "It was hard to prevent Mel from cracking us up all the time," Eliopoulos said. Anne laughed as much as or more than anyone. Complaints from other board members led Eliopoulos to bring a kitchen timer to meetings and enforce a limit of four minutes for comments. Instead of expressing offense, Anne and Mel endorsed the idea.

Jackie Eliopoulos was an actress herself, and her husband, Ted, was an actor who went by the stage name Ted Sorel. Her father, the songwriter Sam Coslow, and her stepmother had known Mel and Anne from their days in New York. Eliopoulos and her husband became close to the Brooks family when their children attended school together in the mid-1980s. "The thing that was extraordinary about Anne was her empathy for people at all levels that she worked with," Eliopoulos said. "There was no discrimination based on stature in the business and, unfortunately, that even today exists in Hollywood to an immense degree."

Several parents on the safety committee worked in film and television, often in the technical aspects. When Anne learned that someone needed work, Mel would try to help, Eliopoulos recalled. "I was amazed at their generosity, at their understanding of the vicissitudes of life in Hollywood, which are really intense sometimes," she said. Mel hired Ted Eliopoulos for a small role in his 1987 movie *Spaceballs* when he needed work and the health insurance that came with it. Anne also offered to help the Eliopouloses make up the difference when they could not afford to have both their children attend Crossroads. It was an offer they did not accept but never forgot. "I've never encountered someone so generous in that way and so aware of other people's needs," Jackie Eliopoulos said. "In Hollywood, it's rare—very rare."

Anne's son enjoyed teasing his protective mother, remembered her friend Jonathan Sanger. "Max had a wicked sense of humor, and he knew his mother would be worried. He'd be on the edge of looking like he was doing something dangerous and make her crazy," Sanger said. "Max was always a smart kid. He knew what buttons to press to make her nervous about anything he did. She was always worried—'Oh, Max!'—she was very protective of him, but it wasn't the kind of protection that, in any way that I ever saw, that made him feel smothered." The closeness of their relationship was obvious to those who knew them.

Anne and Mel continued to spend much of their social lives with their closest friends. Going out like a normal couple often meant being interrupted by well-meaning fans and some obnoxious ones. Their evenings among friends were about entertaining each other while playing games like Dictionary (players invent a definition for an obscure word) or engaging in other laughter-inducing activities. One memorable gathering began when the television producer Norman Lear invited four couples to join him and his wife, Frances, for a weekend at a fully staffed villa in Palm Springs owned by a friend. The group—Anne and Mel, Carl and Estelle Reiner, Dom and Carol DeLuise, Larry and Pat Gelbart, and the Lears—spent nearly every moment making each other laugh. More such weekends would follow. There were games on those outings and during other social gatherings Anne and Mel attended, including charades and "pass the orange" (one person cradles an orange in the crook of his neck and passes it to another).

With the Lears as their hosts, the friends also entertained each other with an impromptu variety show that played off whatever talents a person might care to exhibit. Anne belted out a throaty version of "Some Sunny Day," a song she had sung for years. When Larry Gelbart suggested that someone eavesdrop on the "audience" witnessing this performance, Anne readily volunteered. As Carl Reiner recounted in a memoir, she reported back that the imaginary fans singled out that interesting, dark-haired girl Anne Bancroft, and were thrilled to learn that the Oscar-winning actress could sing so beautifully and was both gracious and down-to-earth.

Anne's report was a sly reflection on how she viewed her public persona and suggested that she still wished she had a career that showcased her singing. Instead, she had to settle for being one of the most respected dramatic actresses of her generation. But Anne was never content with settling for anything short of her goal at the moment—and that goal was changing.

13

Old Ladies and Liberation

One day on the set of *To Be or Not to Be,* Anne turned to the camera operator as Alan Johnson prepared another shot. "Do I need a light here?" she asked. "I want this to be the most gorgeous I've ever been because, after this, it's all old ladies!" The comment was more than just a humorous aside. Anne was acknowledging an important shift in her career—one that she could manage to a degree but was largely out of her control. No longer would she play the older woman being chased by a younger man. While attractive in her fifties, Anne would not try to sustain her Mrs. Robinson persona. Yet romance of any kind would elude most of her characters in the future, a byproduct of the sexism and ageism entrenched in Hollywood and beyond.

In a rare public admonishment of the film industry, Anne told the *New York Times* in 1984, "People don't write wonderful parts for women because women have not been given a chance to live wonderful lives that people want to write about, and because most of the writers are men." Coming from a person who avoided controversy and was publicly apolitical, her comment suggested that she had reached a point where she did not worry about any consequences from speaking her mind and venting her frustrations. At least the youth-centric attitudes in film and television production struck at men as well as women, though women fared worse. Anne was a realist, however, and she prepared to develop characters that grappled with a new set of conflicts, usually involving grown children, failing marriages, and the regrets that come with the passage of time.

"The truth is, there aren't all that many roles for someone my age," Anne said not long after turning fifty-three. "There's a lot more than there used to be, that's true. But still . . . there's a very dry spell between the very glamorous years and mother parts, but once you make the jump into the 'older women' parts, you can usually find work." That she would seek out such roles was more evidence that she put performing ahead of maintaining an image. Unlike some actresses, she was not interested in quietly fading away to avoid aging in public. Her reward came with the chance to play some of the more interesting female characters in movies in the 1980s.

To Be or Not to Be was important to Anne for another reason. She was a serious actress in the eyes of the public and critics. Nearly every role she had played since *The Miracle Worker* called on her signature dramatic intensity. Except for *Silent Movie,* no film or stage play offered her a completely comedic part. During those years she felt that she had to play certain kinds of roles because it was what was expected of her. "I didn't like that feeling. I felt entrapped by it," she said. Working on *To Be or Not to Be* was liberating for her—and not because she would be doing more comedies. Her newfound sense of freedom came in deciding that she would do what she wanted and not what was expected of her. And to her it felt wonderful.

As "old ladies" go, the female lead in the poignant comedy *Garbo Talks* was an inviting one. The story from the comedy writer Larry Grusin presents a New Yorker named Estelle Rolfe, a Greta Garbo–loving radical who battles life's injustices in her own way. At a construction site, she rides an elevator to a top floor to reprimand hard hats for their vulgar catcalls. She is charged with shoplifting for changing the price tag on lettuce that had been marked up ahead of a new batch coming in. Her eccentric behavior embarrasses her thirtysomething son, Gilbert, a mild-mannered accountant. When Estelle is diagnosed with an inoperable brain tumor, she asks her son to fulfill her dying wish to meet the famously reclusive movie star. Gilbert spends months pursuing various schemes to contact Garbo, a quest that opens his eyes to the world. He finally succeeds in finding the star, who responds to his plea by visiting Estelle in the hospital as she nears death.

The script for *Garbo Talks* had made the rounds for a few years before going into production for release in 1984. At one time there was talk of casting Elizabeth Taylor as the mother and the pop singer Barry Manilow, in his acting debut, as the son. Eventually the script came to the veteran director Sidney Lumet as he looked for a more lighthearted project to follow the heavy political drama *Daniel* (1983). He planned to shoot at such locations as the Museum of Modern Art, the Delacorte Theater in Central Park, the Gotham Book Mart, and Fire Island. The city was as much his as Woody Allen's and Martin Scorsese's—most Lumet movies were set there—and he seemed to view it as either enchanting or infuriating. In *Garbo Talks* he saw a light, fluffy story and presented the city accordingly. If the movie was his valentine to New York, as the film scholar Joanna E. Rapf has written, Lumet was all the more likely to want to turn to city-born actors to share the joy.

Anne would have seemed a perfect choice for Estelle—there would be no criticism of her accent this time. Yet Lumet paused when it came to casting her, unsure whether she was old enough for the part. "Sidney, believe me," she told him, "I'm old enough." When they met to discuss the film, Lumet got a close-up look and readily agreed. "Gee," he said after studying her face, "you really *are* old enough." The glamorous and sexy roles that understated her true age were proving hard to shake.

Lumet's partiality for people-driven dramas like *Serpico, Dog Day Afternoon,* and *The Verdict* and his careful preproduction planning and efficient shooting methods appealed to her. Long considered an actor's director, he rehearsed his *Garbo Talks* cast in a large loft ahead of filming. "If Sidney saw a take that wasn't that good," Anne remarked later, "he would say, 'Why don't we try it this way now' and he'd give you a sugges-tion." Shooting in March and April 1984 went faster than expected and helped the film come in two weeks early and well under budget.

Anne's approach to Estelle was relatively simple. She based her charac-terization mostly on one of the most passionate people she knew, Millie Italiano. "My mother doesn't even need a cause. She just gets fired up." Onscreen she was close enough to becoming Millie that even her twelve-year-old son, Max, thought she was playing the woman he called "Nanny." At the same time, Anne also compared Estelle to Gittel Mosca, the free spirit from *Two for the Seesaw.* "Maybe that's why I like this lady so much—they're a lot alike," she said. "I feel I've come full circle."

There was a bit of reality at play for Anne as she made *Garbo Talks.* Years before, she had spotted Greta Garbo strolling in the city. Anne had encountered other movie stars of her childhood, one of them Joan Crawford, a golden-age legend whom fans could walk up to and greet. "Crawford fascinated me at one point and I got to know her," she said. There was nothing approachable about Garbo. "I looked," Anne admitted, "and then looked away. I don't care who you are, you have to respond to her dignity, her need to be unapproached." At the time of the film's produc-tion, Garbo was still living in New York and occasionally drawing atten-tion when she appeared on the city's streets.

With her character confined to a hospital bed for much of the film, Anne had less to do in *Garbo Talks* than her costar Ron Silver, a Lower East Side native who was well cast as Gilbert. (In the script, Estelle named her son after Greta Garbo's favorite movie leading man, John Gilbert.) Anne made the most of her scenes, the best coming at the beginning, when Estelle dresses down the construction workers, and near the end, when Garbo appears in her hospital room. Face to face with her idol at last, Estelle links moments in her life to Garbo's films and explains how her favorite actress has been an essential part of her being. The deathbed scene was one of the reasons she took the part.

Unbroken by any cuts, the scene would run seven minutes, and Lumet wanted to shoot it in one continuous take, a single shot. At first Anne doubted whether she could remember that much dialogue. "With age your memory starts to go," she admitted. Soon, though, the idea of the camera being pointed at her for that length of time began to terrify her. She came close to telling Lumet that she could not do it. "Finally I took myself aside and said, 'You have to have the courage to do this,'" she said. "Then I just began working on it, every morning for maybe a month, until I had it." She almost always found the answer to an artistic problem in hard work.

Her monologue provided the most powerful moment in the movie and one of the highlights of Anne's film career. "That's one of the best scenes I've ever seen in my life," recalled her fellow Fox contract player Robert Wagner. "It's one of the best pieces of acting I've ever experienced." Members of the Hollywood Foreign Press Association would think so, too, and nominate Anne for a Golden Globe as best actress in a comedy or musical. (Kathleen Turner won for *Romancing the Stone*.)

Garbo Talks was the kind of film that could win the hearts of moviegoers or alienate them as treacle. In a rave review, Sheila Benson of the *Los Angeles Times* called it "so thoroughly and entirely satisfying, it's almost sinful" and praised Anne for playing her character "with bracing wit and an illuminating tenderness." Most other critics did not buy the premise as anything but a situation, and not a believable one, even if they thought there were humorous moments and good performances. "A well-acted and well-meant but empty comic drama," wrote Rita Kempley of the *Washington Post*. Her newspaper colleague Paul Attanasio was more pointed about a "fuzzy, emotionally tawdry melodrama" that offered a shameless parade of New York stereotypes. What little he liked centered on its star. "Anne Bancroft brings an engaging vivacity to her role as a woman who makes love to the world by attacking it," he wrote. Major awards and box-office receipts—a paltry $1.5 million by some estimates—were as scarce as good reviews.

If only reviews and reports from the box office were Anne's chief concerns in life. Five years had not passed since she had been diagnosed with cancer when the disease reappeared. From then on it was never far away. She would endure showers of small cancers over the years, but she managed to keep the illness at bay and continued with her life and career relatively unimpeded. Anne would tell reporters how she struggled to develop characterizations and would rail about the difficulty in finding good roles for an older actress, but the fight that mattered most remained a closely held secret. Personally and professionally, she was determined to live by her own terms.

As Anne faced her mortality far earlier than anyone might have imagined, a film adaptation of the 1982 Broadway hit *Agnes of God* came to her attention. In John Pielmeier's three-character play, a young nun named Agnes stands accused of having a baby in a convent and murdering the child. A psychiatrist who has turned away from the church is appointed by the court to ascertain Agnes's state of mind and, in doing so, finds herself trying to understand this ethereal if irrational young woman. The convent's feisty mother superior, a dual citizen in the worlds of faith and reality, suggests a supernatural answer to the mysterious pregnancy. With Amanda Plummer as Agnes, Elizabeth Ashley as the psychiatrist, and Geraldine Page as the mother superior, the play ran for nearly six hundred performances on Broadway. Plummer won a Tony Award as featured actress and Page was nominated as best actress.

The film director Norman Jewison, a Canadian-born Protestant, was attracted to what he saw in the story as the "timeless human conflict between believing what we can see and believing what we can't see or experience." An all-genres filmmaker, he had directed comedies in the early 1960s, then *The Cincinnati Kid, In the Heat of the Night, The Thomas Crown Affair,* and other dramas before overseeing the 1970's-era musicals *Fiddler on the Roof* and *Jesus Christ Superstar.* In the late 1970s and early 1980s, Jewison was directing smaller-scale, character-driven films that explored labor relations (*F.I.S.T.*), individual rights (*. . . And Justice for All*), and race relations (*A Soldier's Story*).

When Jewison decided to direct *Agnes of God*, set for release in 1985, the balance of power between the psychiatrist and the mother superior weighed heavily on his casting choices. He knew he wanted Jane Fonda to play the psychiatrist. Who could match her in strength of personality and star power? There could be little doubt that Geraldine Page would have the presence he required. Then he received a call from Anne at his Los Angeles office. She wanted to play the mother superior and persisted even after Jewison said that he would discuss it with her another time. "I'm married to a director," she told him. "I know that none of you know how to make up your minds. I'm going to help you with the decision." Jewison, when pressed, admitted that he did not see her as the mother superior of a convent. For him, Anne was still the sexy, sensual Mrs. Robinson, too young and too beautiful for the part of a middle-aged nun. "I'll be right over," she said. Just as she had with *The Pumpkin Eater*, Anne was taking matters into her own hands.

A year after she had persuaded Sidney Lumet that she was old enough for one role, Anne had to prove to Jewison that she was not too beautiful for another. Within the half hour she was in a chair in his office showing off her pale complexion, her lined face, and the dark areas under her eyes. She had worn no makeup to make the point that *The Graduate* was eighteen years in the past, and, at fifty-four, she was no longer the woman of his dreams. Not yet convinced, Jewison asked Anne to try on a nun's wimple and black veil. She practically disappeared under the garments. "I realized she would be a superb Mother Miriam Ruth," he said. The young nun at the center of the tug-of-war between faith and logic would be played by Meg Tilly, who had made such an impression the previous year in *The Big Chill*.

Filming for the $8.1 million production would take place in budget-friendly Canada, in the city of Montreal and outside Toronto. Before going on location, though, Norman Jewison brought together Anne, Jane Fonda, and Meg Tilly at a rehearsal hall in Los Angeles to go over John Pielmeier's adaptation of his play. It would be the first time Anne and Fonda—arguably the finest actresses of their generation—would spend a significant amount of time together. The play called for sparks to fly between their characters, and one could not help wondering if they would fly off-camera, too, once these strong-willed women met.

Fireworks between the two stars remained in the script. "They were both, of course, absolutely lovely to each other and very warm—and happy to work together," Pielmeier recalled. After a table reading, Jewison began blocking and doing scenes and soon moved to rehearsing Anne and Fonda's scenes together without a script. "I had the impression they liked each other and certainly respected each other very much—and enjoyed the process of working together," Pielmeier said. "Those were fun, meaty scenes to play. Actors can have a good time kind of sinking their teeth into that. They are very much give-and-take scenes. It's like two really good tennis players meeting on the court for the first time."

Jewison had set aside two weeks for rehearsals. "He rehearsed the movie script as if it were a play," Pielmeier said. "They were off-book by the end of those two weeks and were able to do a run-through, a work-through, of the movie script, certainly all of their scenes that didn't involve other actors. It was a very, very valuable process that I found fascinating. Everybody was working with the kind of discipline that you would expect in the theater—and that I had certainly not come to expect in Hollywood."

On Broadway, *Agnes of God* had been set on a bare stage. Jewison worked with Pielmeier in expanding the setting and the cast of characters to accommodate audience expectations for a feature film. One of the locations in Canada was a nineteenth-century boys' academy outside the city of Guelph in southwestern Ontario. To turn the facility into a convent, Jewison called on the production designer Ken Adam, best known for James Bond and Stanley Kubrick films. To populate it with elderly nuns, the production put out a casting call for women ages seventy-five to ninety. (Those who wore makeup were advised to remove it.) Shooting in Canada for ten weeks during the winter of 1984–85 gave the film a pensive look to match its tone.

Anne recognized *Agnes of God* as a story of sacrifice and hope. Raised a Roman Catholic, she understood the tension between faith and fact and, in Norman Jewison's view, completely identified with Mother Miriam. She also connected the story to the Bible verse John 1:29—"The next day he saw Jesus coming to him and said, 'Behold, the Lamb of God who takes away the sin of the world!'"—and to the words in the Catholic communion rite: "Lamb of God, who takes away the sins of the world, have mercy on us." In the story, the psychiatrist finds herself drawn back to faith because of Agnes's plight. "She is supposed to be sacrificed," Anne said. "And in the end, she is."

Not in the film as in the play. Instead of a monologue in which the psychiatrist notes that Agnes has starved herself to death in the confines of a hospital, the film closes with Agnes being allowed to return to the convent.

She continues to see the world through the eyes of an innocent. "That was a choice I made," Pielmeier said. "I just felt that the movie didn't take us to where I felt I could kill her off." He found himself unsatisfied with the last few minutes of the film, thinking it ended too abruptly. Still, he said, "I think it's a really terrific movie up to that point." The different ending would not change the story's compelling questions about the compatibility of faith and reason.

Issues of faith had drawn Jane Fonda, a Protestant, to make the movie after a four-year layoff from acting. "There are people who for their own reasons develop a well-defined philosophy to justify their atheism, as the psychiatrist has done in *Agnes*," she said while promoting the film. "But many more people obviously have a need to believe, some deep need to believe in something outside themselves."

There was another reason Fonda wanted to be in the cast—the opportunity to work with Anne. Under Jewison's direction, there were long scenes, some covering ten pages of script, that allowed the two titans to clash on film. "It was great locking horns with Anne Bancroft," Fonda said later. "She is a formidable adversary as the mother superior." Off-camera, they shared stories about Henry Fonda, who had died in 1982. "She found it fascinating to have a firsthand, objective report on her father as a stage actor," the *Los Angeles Times*'s film critic Charles Champlin wrote after interviewing Fonda. Anne would not have had to hide her personal feelings about her sometimes difficult costar when talking with his daughter—he had been a sometimes difficult father, too.

Most of the major critics were unmoved by *Agnes of God* when it opened in September 1985, faulting the screenplay as a philosophical muddle and drubbing Norman Jewison for a long-winded, ponderous production. "The material itself, thoroughly unsurprising on the stage, is if anything even more so on the screen," wrote Jane Maslin of the *New York Times*. The cast usually fared better—Rex Reed of the *New York Post* considered the actresses to be riveting. Years after they had sharpened their talents under Lee Strasberg, Anne and Jane Fonda could still capture a moviegoer's attention.

If *Agnes of God* was akin to a prizefight between two heavyweight champions, the members of the Motion Picture Academy thought that Anne had won the bout. The following year she was nominated for best actress for the fifth time in her career. The only other Oscar nominations for *Agnes of God* went to Meg Tilly for supporting actress and the composer Georges Delerue for his original score. On Oscar night at the Dorothy Chandler Pavilion in March 1986, Anne looked radiant in a light-colored gown and pearls, a far cry from the image of Mother Miriam that flashed on television screens as F. Murray Abraham announced her nomination. When he opened the envelope he declared, "I consider this woman the greatest actress in the English language—the winner is Geraldine Page." Anne had gotten the role Page had created on the stage, but Page had won the Oscar for *The Trip to Bountiful*. It was only fair—she had lost to Anne in 1962 and had never won an Academy Award in spite of seven previous nominations. The victory was a last hurrah of sorts for Page. The following year she suffered a fatal heart attack after a Friday night performance of *Blithe Spirit* on Broadway. Page was the first of Anne's long-standing rivals to die, an unsettling reminder that getting older meant more than being offered fewer roles.

Appearing with much younger performers like Meg Tilly was one of the pleasures that came with the "old ladies" phase of Anne's career. In *'night, Mother,* released in 1986, she shared the screen with Sissy Spacek, eighteen years her junior and an audience favorite since the horror movie *Carrie* (1976) and her Oscar-winning performance as the country singer Loretta Lynn in *Coal Miner's Daughter* (1980). That Bronx-born Anne would have given birth to Texas-bred Sissy Spacek might have put off purists, but the pairing would excite their fans.

Or would it? Marsha Norman's play had warning signs written all over its potential box office. *'night, Mother* was a two-character story set in real time at a house in the country. A shy and emotionally fragile woman in her thirties, Jessie quietly informs her outgoing, dominating mother that she is going to kill herself that evening. For the next ninety minutes Jessie and Mama wrestle over the meaning of life and death and how much a person actually controls her existence and how much one person should control another.

Spacek had seen the Broadway production with Kathy Bates and Anne Pitoniak—it won the Pulitzer Prize in 1983—and wanted to appear in a movie version. At first no one wanted to back a film that was such a downer, even though *'night, Mother* was a stage success in dozens of countries as well as the United States. A story about two women, a mother and daughter, sparring over suicide just was not the kind of material expected to draw an audience to movie theaters eager to show action films, science fiction, and comedies; those kinds of movies sold tickets, even the bad ones.

Just about the only reason the project stayed alive was Spacek's involvement. She was riding the crest of her popularity in the mid-1980s, having won the Oscar in 1981 and receiving nominations for *Missing* and *The River*. Finally, after two years of rejection by every major studio, *'night, Mother* drew the backing of Aaron Spelling. The *Charlie's Angels* and *Fantasy Island* producer was desperate to prove to the industry as well as television critics that he could do more than crank out lightweight if hugely popular television series year after year. With a bare-bones budget of $3 million, *'night, Mother* was a bargain if Spelling was in the market to buy some class.

Marsha Norman insisted that Tom Moore, the director of the Broadway production, also direct the film version of her play, even though he had yet to direct a movie. Retaining the original cast of Kathy Bates and Anne Pitoniak was not going to happen since Spacek was behind the project and Pitoniak was unknown except for her Tony-nominated performance as Mama. (Her most recent film credit was as Jane Fonda's mother in *Agnes of God*.) The question, then, was whom to cast opposite Spacek.

Several actresses as well as Anne were considered for what would have been a choice screen role for an older performer. "I don't remember anybody having any real weight except Anne, because anybody would have given anything to work with Anne Bancroft," Moore said in looking back on the film. "The question was really whether she was too young or whether she appeared too young." Anne Pitoniak was nine years older than Anne; the age difference between Pitoniak and Kathy Bates was twenty-four years, not the eighteen that separated Anne and Sissy Spacek. It did not make a difference if it meant having Anne in the role. "Ultimately, talent will out," Moore said, "whether you're the right age or not." From a box-office perspective, two Oscar winners would help win over potential ticket buyers uncertain of the entertainment value of the story.

Although she had seen the play on Broadway, Anne wanted to talk to the director before accepting the part. "When Anne came in to meet and spoke in that Bronx accent, it was very shocking," Moore remembered. "It was the last thing you expected because of course she had a very cultured voice which she used to many different effects. It was, 'Who is this person? This is not Anne Bancroft.'" Anne had not played a character as rural America as Mama and would need to focus on erasing her natural inflections to match her costar's native twang.

Everyone sacrificed something to make *'night, Mother* possible. Anne and Spacek reportedly took a third or so of their usual salaries, and Moore accepted the director's guild minimum for his work. Costumes were not much of an expense, given that the stars would be wearing the same outfits throughout the film. All the action took place at the farmhouse set. Two weeks of rehearsals—a low-cost way of working through the script—preceded ten weeks of shooting in early 1986 at the Burbank Studios, which at the time included the old movie lot of Warner Bros.

Anne needed those rehearsal weeks to become comfortable with more than the script and her character. "Anne was not easy to get to know, she really wasn't," Moore said. "She was tough, she was really tough. She knew herself, she knew what she wanted, she knew what she needed." Anne gave Moore the impression of being aloof during the first table reading of Marsha Norman's adaptation, perhaps looking for a way to get out of the film altogether. "It scared her and she didn't know if it was right for her," he said, "and to some extent I think she was looking for it not to work." As moved as she had been by the play, Anne admitted that the material and her character were beyond her own experience. She worried that she had been terribly miscast.

Reflexively, Anne sought answers to her concerns in part by reading as much as she could about people with Jessie's and Mama's problems. As she did, she looked inside herself for connections. On the surface, there would seem little in common between a New York actress and a simple country woman with her pink housecoat and optimistic bromides. The Method approach demanded that Anne find a link with the character. In doing so she invented a past for Mama that went beyond the play and screenplay, imagining at one point that Mama had accompanied Jessie on her first day at school and answered all the questions for her. That helped her understand Mama's boundless energy and how she dominated and controlled her daughter.

"Mama exists in me. She's somewhere there inside me or else I couldn't create her," Anne insisted later. "I don't pull things out of the air and stick them into me. They're inside me. And what I do is take those character traits and just pull them up." Along the way she posed questions to Marsha Norman as she tried to understand how Mama could so misread her daughter's situation. "I write characters who make mistakes and actors are reluctant to make mistakes," Norman told the *New York Times.* "Anne Bancroft is a real smart person. 'Doesn't Mama know that's a dangerous thing to say? How could I make this mistake?' she would ask. As soon as they walked off the set, Sissy would come out of Jessie, but Anne lived further away from Mama." Those character traits Anne raised from deep within herself may have been too personal for her to reveal.

To look more like Mama, Anne sought to push her strong, dark features to the background by cutting and bleaching her hair and tweezing and bleaching her eyebrows. As a result, she appeared more plausible as the mother of her pale, freckled costar. To sound like Mama (and perhaps to better match Spacek's own accent), she paid for a dialect coach out of her own pocket. Once Anne developed an accent, she retained it throughout the filming and kept it up everywhere, even at home. "That's just the way she was," Tom Moore said. On the set, Anne called on her powers of concentration. A visitor found her repeating lines to no one in particular.

Moore eventually won Anne over as the production worked through the usual initial problems. "I think he does know what he's doing," she remarked to someone at one point. "I think we can trust him." It made sense that she would rely on Moore, who could tap his intimate knowledge of the play. As they often did, rehearsals gave Anne the time to find her character and tamp down her anxieties. "I think once we started filming, she knew where she was, knew who the character was and how she intended to play it," Moore said.

Scenes were shot in chronological order, a rarity in movie production because of multiple sets, location shooting, and availability of cast members. Two actresses and a single setting made it possible—and the roller coaster of emotions playing out in real time made it essential. "You had to stay in an extraordinary state of alarm and distress for huge amounts of time," Moore said, "and I think it was very hard on both women." As he recalled, Anne liked to run through a scene again and again and build on it, whereas Sissy Spacek was more instinctual in her approach and often better in early takes. In a sign of their mutual generosity and respect, the actresses helped each other pick up where they had left off the day before by running through their lines, building up to their new scene.

Some critics had accused Anne of overacting in recent years. Only once during the filming of 'night, Mother was she asked to film a scene again—the moment when Mama realizes she is not going to be able to persuade Jessie to abandon her plan and breaks down. "She felt she had given everything because, emotionally, she had," Moore said. "But I felt, and the producers felt, too, that we had simply gone over the line. It turned into pathos." She reluctantly reshot the scene for what Moore believed was the correct emotional balance. "She accepted it," he said. "I think she thought she had done some of the best work of her career—and she may have. Sometimes there can be an extraordinary scene that just doesn't work in terms of how it's going to play out in the whole film." It was just the sort of moment for a star to exercise her power—there could be no do-over without her—but Anne trusted her director.

She could still make a point if she thought she was being directed too much. When it came time for the movie's final scene—Jessie has killed herself and Mama sets about doing what her daughter had advised her to do—Moore began explaining to Anne what the scene was all about and what Mama was feeling at that moment. He went on and on until Anne stopped him. "You know, Tom," she said, "I think I'll just pretend I had a daughter who shot herself and we'll just see what happens." Caught in the act of "doing that director thing," Moore could not help bursting into laughter—and Anne joined him.

Over the course of filming Anne and Sissy Spacek developed a bond as they revealed so much emotion while playing mother and daughter. Spacek's favorite movie was *The Miracle Worker*, and she was not disappointed to find Anne a powerhouse to work with. Anne was seldom sentimental about her costars—it was not unusual for her never to see them again once a film wrapped—but she told the *New York Times* that she and Spacek had a special relationship. Spacek had come to know Anne so vividly in the context of *'night, Mother* that she did not recognize Anne's voice on the phone once she had shed the accent she had adopted for the role.

Critics liked to harp on Anne's accent in a movie if they detected any Bronx inflections, but they found little fault with her twang in *'night, Mother*. "There will be nothing stronger than *'night, Mother* on the screen this year," Jack Kroll told readers of *Newsweek*. Less persuaded by the adaptation was *Time:* "The casting of Anne Bancroft and Sissy Spacek, who cannot help projecting intelligence and the will to prevail, is inimical to the story's cause. Still, the painful honesty of the play's psychological observations survives and remains worthy of attention." The top movie critics on television cheered the stars—"Anne Bancroft gives the performance of a lifetime," declared Dennis Cunningham on CBS—and generally lauded the play's transition to film. Among those less enamored, Janet Maslin of the *New York Times* found Anne's performance too broad in opening scenes that were overly busy. Yet, once the situation was set up, Maslin said, the movie developed "an irresistible momentum."

To help the film's prospects, Anne attended the Hollywood Foreign Press Association's annual luncheon. She posed for photos and generally schmoozed with the journalists, not her favorite activity. In due time she earned another Golden Globe nomination. The chatter ahead of the Academy Awards mentioned Anne as a possible best actress nominee. No Oscar nomination came. Sissy Spacek was nominated for the fourth time in six years—not for 'night, Mother but for her role in *Crimes of the Heart*, another Broadway adaptation. Awards tended to elude 'night, Mother that year. Marlee Matlin won both the Oscar and the Golden Globe as best actress for *Children of a Lesser God*, yet another play turned into a film.

With mixed reviews, no major awards, and little traffic at the box office, 'night, Mother faded away even if it had a profound influence on those who saw it, particularly women. In spite of her efforts to play a character so different from herself, Mama did not join Annie Sullivan, Mrs. Robinson, and other roles at the foundation of Anne's film career. "I think she was very disappointed," Tom Moore said, "and I think it came as something of a shock—that it was not being recognized for what it was." Hollywood was finding the strongest roles for women originating in Broadway dramas and comedies, practically ensuring that Anne would return to an adaptation in the future. In the meantime, male-oriented films remained the top product, not movies about women.

One such film came to Anne in an unusual way. She was sitting on the beach at Fire Island when a man she did not know walked up to her and said, "I've just read something that would be perfect for you." The next day, he found her in the same spot and handed her a book of fewer than one hundred pages before going on his way, never to be heard from again. His enthusiasm had impressed her and she began reading *84, Charing Cross Road*.

It took hardly any time at all for Anne to join those enchanted by Helene Hanff's memoir about her twenty-year correspondence with a London bookseller, Frank Doel. They never met, but in their letters they shared their passion for English literature and, along the way, the details of their very different lives in the 1950s and 1960s. Hanff, a single New Yorker with a barbed wit, was scratching out a living as a freelance writer for magazines and television while Doel bought and sold books and lived a sedate life with his wife and children. Theirs was not a story of unrequited love but of two people brought together by the power of words.

A year after Doel's death in 1969, Hanff published their correspondence to popular acclaim in Britain and the United States. The BBC dramatized their unusual friendship in a television production in 1975. A stage adaptation of *84, Charing Cross Road*—the title referred to the bookstore's address—premiered in London in 1981 and was still playing when a Broadway production opened with Ellen Burstyn and Joseph Maher. Frank Rich in the *New York Times* found the material good-natured if innocuous and the production a stage reading tricked up with a star and an imposing set. Missing, he thought, was more about the correspondents' personal lives and relationships. Rich's colleague at the *Times,* the venerable Walter Kerr, found the production far more appealing. It closed after three months.

Aside from telling a charming story, Hanff's letters resonated with Anne for a personal reason. In the author's voice she heard a school classmate she had remained close to over the years. His respect for books—and his need for and love of them—came back to her as she read *84, Charing Cross Road.* The experience was all the more poignant for Anne because her longtime friend had died recently. (The friend was probably Richard Shufflebotham, a Christopher Columbus High School drama club alumnus.) Her reaction to the book was so intense, in fact, that Mel Brooks pursued and bought the film rights for his wife and presented them to her as an anniversary gift.

A film adaptation would provide Anne a starring role and Mel's company, Brooksfilms, a low-budget project that, if handled carefully, would be a prestigious one to join *Fatso, The Elephant Man, Frances,* and *To Be or Not to Be.* Unlike a play, a movie could expand the scope of Hanff's and Doel's different worlds, showing their friends and families and life in their cities. Nevertheless, Brooksfilms faced the arduous task of convincing a studio that a movie about two middle-aged bibliophiles who never met could make for a compelling movie. Some years passed from the time that Anne first read the book until 1986, the year that *84 Charing Cross Road* went into production. (The comma was dropped from the title.)

Having Anne in the lead female role would have been half the battle to appeal to moviegoers interested in a character-driven film about ordinary people. For the part of Frank Doel, Anne and Mel went to one of their favorite actors, Anthony Hopkins. It turned out that he needed no cajoling. "I was very moved by the script when I read it," Hopkins said at the time, "despite an agent making a crack that it was about as exciting as watching paint dry." It would be the third film in which both Anne and Hopkins appeared, although they would not share any scenes. In fact, they barely saw each other during the production, which was divided between London and New York.

Chosen to direct was David Jones, a renowned stage director in Britain who had won praise three years earlier with his first film, *Betrayal.* Jones knew he did not want the characters bound to pen and paper or the movie to merely illustrate a letter with a scene again and again. "The writer Hugh Whitemore and I tried to set up a counterpoint between the content of the letters and the characters' actions on screen so that they weren't just doing the same job but passing on extra information," Jones said. The result was a quiet film, yet that was so much of the story's appeal.

Anne had not played a movie role based on a living person since *The Slender Thread* some twenty years earlier. Though she had spoken with the suicidal housewife of that story and gained an understanding of the woman's frame of mind, she did not feel a need to discuss with Hanff how she felt over the years that she wrote to Doel. "It was all there in the writing," Anne said. "I didn't want to do any imitation." On the stage in *Golda* she had discovered the perils of knowing the actual person too well.

Anthony Hopkins saw a contrast between Hanff's life and Doel's and allowed it to guide his performance. "Without signaling to the audience, I just tried to keep a hint throughout of his mortality and to suggest the story was about the sorrow of life as well as the joy and sweetness," he said. "There is a scene just before the end when Frank talks of his children growing up, leaving the nest and pursuing their careers. For me that caught very exactly the bone-aching sadness of life, the quiet pain of suburban existence when you ask after people's children and find they are gone and scattered." His subdued, melancholy portrayal of a reserved bookseller, a change of pace for the intense actor, balanced Anne's lively and spirited writer.

Columbia Pictures delayed the release of *84 Charing Cross Road* into the early months of 1987 to avoid a competing awards campaign with *'night, Mother,* but the strategy was to no avail. There were no nominations, perhaps in part because *84 Charing Cross Road* was all but forgotten by the time awards season came around again. More damaging to its prospects (it took in just over $1 million in domestic ticket sales) were the negative reviews by major film critics. Most found the film dull and unsatisfying, not at all charmed by the back-and-forth between Anne's passionate bibliophile and the quiet bookseller. Roger Ebert, himself a lover of books and London, thought the underlying idea of the film was not sound and posed a question in his review for the *Chicago Sun-Times:* "Why didn't that silly woman get on the boat and go to London ten years sooner and save herself all that postage?"

Anne received a drubbing here and there, among them a suggestion by *Time*'s critic Richard Corliss that she had overacted. "She hurls apostrophes to the walls and abuse at her typewriter. One sighs: Relax, Anne, you got the job," Corliss wrote. He concluded, "If the viewer expects little from *84 Charing Cross Road,* he will not be disappointed." One of the few critics who thought the film achieved its goal was Kevin Thomas of the *Los Angeles Times.* "A joyous celebration of the life of the imagination," Thomas wrote, and commended both Anne and Anthony Hopkins for "some of the warmest and most winning moments of their screen careers." Of the film's female star, he wrote: "What a pleasure to watch Anne Bancroft in a role that fits her like a glove."

The film had a larger following in Britain, and the British Academy of Film and Television Arts nominated Anne for best actress, Judi Dench for supporting actress, and Hugh Whitemore for adapted screenplay. The only victor among them was Anne, who took home her third BAFTA prize, having previously won for *The Miracle Worker* and *The Pumpkin Eater.* A seven-time nominee, she was clearly a favorite of British audiences.

The anticipation in Britain for *84 Charing Cross Road* was so great that it was chosen for a royal performance. Anne turned the event into a holiday for the Italiano girls, inviting her sisters, JoAnne and Phyllis, to join her. The charity event drew Prince Charles and his wife, Diana, as well as the Queen Mother and Prince Philip. Anne was in the receiving line, her sisters standing behind a barrier while the royals greeted her and numerous other celebrities. (As usual, the beautiful Diana drew the most attention.) After London, the trio visited Vienna as part of a rare international outing for Mike and Millie's daughters.

Anne again received top billing for her next movie, but *Torch Song Trilogy,* released in 1988, belonged in every way to its writer and star, Harvey Fierstein. It had won the Tony Award for best play in 1983, beating *'night, Mother* and *Plenty,* and Fierstein had won the award for best actor. The roots of the four-hour stage drama stretched back four years to a series of one-act plays at the experimental theater La MaMa and then an off-Broadway venue. The subject matter was controversial—the life and loves of a drag queen—and the production proved to be a landmark in theater in its presentation of a gay man, Arnold, who seeks love and respect. That it mixed humor and tragedy with eyebrow-raising details of gay life helped make it a Broadway hit.

Not surprisingly, years passed before a film version of *Torch Song Trilogy* was produced. Gay-themed movies were not moneymakers, and studios that showed any interest pushed to have the sexual relationships trimmed and even omitted, preferring to focus on the dramatic (and sexless) clash between Arnold and his disapproving mother. There were suggestions that major stars be cast to shore up the box office—Dustin Hoffman and Richard Dreyfuss were mentioned—and that the sexual aspects of the story be toned down. Fierstein would not hear of it.

It could not be denied that a play that ran for 1,222 performances on Broadway and toured nationally had some degree of crossover appeal. A fledgling studio, New Line Cinema, offered a budget of under $4 million for a two-hour adaptation. Though the play was trimmed for the movie production, the film still featured musical numbers with Fierstein and other performers in full drag. *Torch Song Trilogy* also retained his rendezvous in a backroom of a gay club and the stark language and humor that marked the play as a modern and unapologetic look at gay life. Paul Bogart, the main director on the 1970s sitcom *All in the Family* and a veteran of feature films, would guide the movie through its fast-paced production schedule.

Harvey Fierstein had met Anne while making *Garbo Talks,* his first movie as an actor. They did not share any scenes in Sidney Lumet's film, but they became friends and enjoyed each other's sense of humor. Having her play Arnold's mother brought a major name to the production, though it cost Estelle Getty the role she had played so effectively on the stage. By then, Getty was in the midst of a long run on the sitcom *The Golden Girls.*

Anne accepted less than her usual salary to appear in *Torch Song Trilogy,* as did Matthew Broderick. The son of James Broderick, Anne's costar in *John and Abigail* at the Stockbridge Playhouse, he had launched his New York theater career as the teenager adopted by Arnold. Now Broderick was old enough to take the role of Arnold's young lover, an interesting turn for the star of *Ferris Bueller's Day Off* and *Biloxi Blues.* He and Anne were in just one scene together in *Torch Song Trilogy,* but Broderick would work closely with Mel Brooks when he starred in the musical version of *The Producers* a dozen years later.

The stage production of *Torch Song Trilogy* and its fresh, truthful look at gay life had devastated Anne emotionally. Still, participating in the film came at some expense to her professionally. The aspects of acting that she enjoyed most were as cut back as the production's budget. "You don't have the luxury of a lot of rehearsal," she said during filming. "You have to do a lot of it at home, on your own. I certainly must be better prepared with my lines, because there's no time to work on them here."

In the film, Arnold and his mother have a bitter exchange over the losses both have suffered. Her husband of thirty-five years is dead, and Arnold's young lover has been beaten to death by homophobic thugs. She is dismissive of his loss, which pushes them to confront the shame and embarrassment she has felt over having a gay son and the sadness he endures knowing that his mother disapproves of him. As she considered how to approach a character she did not understand, Anne found a connection. "I realized every mother in the world has a child that is worriness, troubleness and sadness-making, if there is such a word," she told the *Los Angeles Times*. "So all of the underlying emotional conflicts that his mother has, I have. If a mother thinks she has no worries like this, she'd better look again. A child can break your heart, but like nobody else on Earth, they can mend it." All the fretting about her own son had ended up in the emotional reservoir she tapped for roles.

Harvey Fierstein was having the time of his life making the movie and found Anne easy to work with. Onscreen their characters were anything but merry in a series of intense scenes. "We really liked each other, so we do what actors have to do," he said. When the confrontation between Arnold and his mother moves from cemetery to apartment, the emotional level rose for the costars. "She nearly killed me thirty times during the shooting of this," Fierstein said. "She would get so angry with me. Anne Bancroft's a very intense actress." Both strained to keep tears out of their eyes as they hurled the hurtful lines that powered their final scene.

One aspect of the movie version of *Torch Song Trilogy* that put off both Anne and Matthew Broderick was the changing context since the play's debut on Broadway. AIDS had been decimating the gay community for years, yet it was not part of the story, given that it was set mainly in the 1970s. Fierstein insisted that the disease remain unmentioned so that the gay characters could be seen as people and not victims. For Anne, however, the story had lost its joy by the time the movie went into production. Broderick found it somewhat dated if even more poignant in the shadow of the AIDS epidemic. Fierstein's defense of his signature work—"Is homosexuality any less funny now? Gay humor has not changed"—may explain why *Torch Song Trilogy* continued to be staged decades later.

By the same token, the film may have come at the wrong time. Many critics faulted the adaptation for that reason, unable to separate the pre-AIDS from the post-AIDS world. Kevin Thomas of the *Los Angeles Times* thought the movie had steamrolled the life out of the play in an effort to make it more mainstream and lamented, "It's hard to believe that what once seemed so heroic and touching in one medium seems so lifeless and retrograde in another." Most reviews were mixed and not as positive as Janet Maslin's in the *New York Times*, where she wrote that the film "emphasizes the lovable at every turn, but the surprise is that it does this entertainingly and well." She was one of the few critics—Roger Ebert joined her—who praised Anne's turn as the mother. "Miss Bancroft, playing in a manner that might seem scenery-chewing in another context, is exactly right in what she does here," she wrote. "And Mr. Fierstein matches her arm-wave for arm-wave, grimace for grimace, decibel for decibel." Other critics dismissed Anne as giving another overwrought performance.

That would not be the rub that critics applied to her small role in the throwback musical comedy *Bert Rigby, You're a Fool*. Putting her new-found liberation to do as she pleased to the test, Anne accepted a part that she might not have dreamed of playing before her comic turn in *To Be or Not to Be*. It was far outside the angst-ridden roles she had been taking for most of the decade and a sea change from the blustery characters she had played in *84 Charing Cross Road* and *Torch Song Trilogy*.

Bert Rigby, You're a Fool, written and directed by Anne and Mel's friend Carl Reiner and released in 1989, showcased the singing and dancing of its British star, Robert Lindsay. A few years earlier he had been a sensation in a revival of the 1930s musical *Me and My Girl* in London's West End and repeated the role to praise on Broadway and a Tony for leading actor in a musical. Reiner wrote *Bert Rigby, You're a Fool* specifically for Lindsay. Reiner's story presents a singing and dancing coal miner stuck in a northern England town that is slowly dying. A fan of the musical stars Gene Kelly and Fred Astaire, Bert Rigby joins a traveling talent show and ends up in the United States to film a television commercial. His dreams of earning enough money to reopen a theater back home are humorously stymied at every turn.

As a closing title suggests—"lovingly dedicated to Gene Kelly"—*Bert*

Rigby, You're a Fool could have been a postwar MGM musical with its dozen or so musical numbers, several of them playing out in Bert Rigby's mind. Anne appears about midway through as the dizzy, flirty producer's wife who had once danced in Fred Astaire films. Aside from two brief musical bits with Robert Lindsay, she played just one of the many comical characters Bert Rigby encounters in his American sojourn. Her lisping character recalled the kittenish chorus girl who often showed up on the arm of a well-heeled older man during the heyday of the movie musical. If Anne had longed for a different kind of role after all the dramas, Carl Reiner gave her one.

Nostalgia was just the tone sought by Reiner, who wanted modern-day audiences to have a chance to enjoy a movie that did not turn on violence and mayhem. His good intentions were not rewarded in the year of cash-generating sequels featuring Batman, Indiana Jones, and the *Lethal Weapon* gang. Critics in general were not charmed by *Bert Rigby, You're a Fool,* among them Janet Maslin of the *New York Times,* who called the movie "extremely odd." Kevin Thomas of the *Los Angeles Times* said that it had overdosed on nostalgia and that Anne's performance was "simply appalling." (The role drew Anne her only nomination for a Golden Raspberry Award, the waggish anti-Oscar, for "worst supporting actress.") Some critics were mildly amused, but Reiner's most welcome notice may have come after he screened the movie for Gene Kelly himself. Bert Rigby's hero congratulated Reiner on a "very nice" effort. It sounded like the faintest of praise.

There would be no way to know, but audiences may have shared some of the lukewarm critical reactions (if not the outright hostility) to Anne's recent film work—not to Anne herself, perhaps, but to the all-too-familiar female characters she seemed to be playing, her turn in *Bert Rigby* excepted. They had such similar qualities, especially the histrionics and streaks of bombast, that collectively they were creating a caricature for her. If that were the case, her annual appearance on film only made the impression stronger. Her recent movies barely registered at theaters—*Torch Song Trilogy* drew a little under $5 million at the box office and *Bert Rigby* less than $100,000. As she neared the forty-year mark of her professional career, Anne's performances were becoming too easy to anticipate. Better roles and better choices—and more of both—might have been the obvious answer, just not an easy one.

14

All in the Doing

Anne cherished her role as working wife and mother, raising a son and being supportive of a husband while pursuing her own professional interests. Yet she also made a promise to herself: once Max was on his own, she would act her heart out. When that time came, in the late 1980s, seeing her son leave the nest was not at all easy as she looked ahead to the next phase of her career. Competing desires still bedeviled her, at work and at home.

"She was torn. It was a very difficult thing for her," remembered her friend Robert Allan Ackerman. "She did give up a lot in her career, then once Max went off to college, it was sort of like, 'What did I do that for? Now I have to sort of start all over again,' . . . which made her feel kind of like she had missed out on a lot of stuff, even though she loved being a mother and a wife. It was a lot of ambivalence."

Anne did not look forward to the routine demands of working on a movie or appearing in a play day after day or night after night. "She'd always refer to it as movie jail or theater jail," said Ackerman, her director in a play and two film productions. "She hated having to give up her time with her family and Mel. She'd say, 'I wonder what Mel is doing now? Mel is off having dinner with Carl and Estelle,' or whoever, 'and I'm stuck here in this prison.' But at the same time she loved it."

Over the previous ten years Anne had starred in a Broadway drama, written and directed a film, and played either starring roles or supporting parts in nine movies or television shows. As the decade closed out and the 1990s loomed, she abandoned the project-a-year guideline that she had been following while Max was at home and asked her agent to start finding more work for her. The word went out that she was available—and willing to try different things.

The dramatic work of the Argentine novelist and playwright Manuel Puig certainly qualified as different. He adapted his 1976 novel *Kiss of the*

Spider Woman into a play, then a film version became an unlikely hit in the United States in 1985 and won an Oscar for its star, William Hurt. Its blend of realism and fantasy was on display again in his play *Mystery of the Rose Bouquet*. A two-character work set in a hospital room in Argentina, the play presents a wealthy older woman, the Patient, who has been placed in a mental ward for depression. Tending her is the Nurse, who claims little experience in such matters but is assigned there because her new charge has proved so angry and difficult. In time it becomes clear that what these women tell each other about their lives is not necessarily true and that dreams—depicted on the stage—are a more reliable source. As in *Kiss of the Spider Woman,* these opposites form an unlikely bond.

A veteran of Broadway and off-Broadway productions, Robert Allan Ackerman had directed *Mystery of the Rose Bouquet* in London. The Mark Taper Forum asked him to guide the drama's American debut, set for the fall of 1989. A Brooklyn native who had been captivated by the theater as a child, Ackerman had met Anne backstage after a performance of *The Miracle Worker* when he was thirteen or fourteen. "She signed my *Playbill,*" he said. "I was madly in love with her." In the years that followed, Ackerman saw nearly all her Broadway work.

A stage production in Los Angeles appealed to Anne. It meant a run limited to six weeks and returning home to Mel every night. She probably would not have played the Patient had the production been set for a venue in New York and scheduled for an open-ended run. She would have been tempted, though, because Puig's play and his characters fascinated her. Ahead of rehearsals, Anne met Ackerman at her home nearly every day for a month. They would go into an attic room and spend hours talking about the play, eventually relating it to the psychoanalysis both were undergoing at the time as well as the relationships in their lives.

"She was so bright, really bright, and so intuitive and very perceptive about people," Ackerman said. "So very often she really could read a script and really get to the center of it and really understand it—but be the first one to admit when she didn't and become very curious. She loved to talk to people about exploring the nature of the character she was about to play, the nature of the play, the playwright. She loved that kind of exploratory work. She really soaked it up."

Ackerman came to believe that Anne felt a connection with the Patient's bitter resentment and how those feelings overwhelmed the character and threatened to destroy what was good inside her. "I think Anne was going through a period of time where she felt sort of a similar kind of—I don't know if anger is too strong a word—she was in fact not as much in touch with the loving part of herself that she wanted to be," he said. "And I think that was very much what she identified with, with that role."

Cast as the Nurse was Jane Alexander, a theater, film, and television actress with a list of credits whose quality equaled those of her costar. She had won a Tony Award for her Broadway debut in *The Great White Hope*, the first of an eventual seven Tony nominations; earned Oscar nominations for *All the President's Men, Kramer vs. Kramer,* and *Testament* as well as for the film version of *The Great White Hope*; and won an Emmy for *Playing for Time* (and would win another some years later for *Warm Springs*).

As the production began its run in November 1989, the *Los Angeles Times* theater critic, Dan Sullivan, complimented both stars of Manuel Puig's "graceful and life-affirming play." Though he noted Anne's "sharp and entertaining performance," he rapped her for being too lively for a depressed patient—and for not bothering to cover up her Bronx accent, given the setting was Argentina. Sullivan also found Alexander's performance as the Nurse to be more believable: she made the most of the subtleties of character that Puig had intended.

Years earlier the filmmaker Norman Jewison had worried about one actress overpowering the other when he considered how to cast *Agnes of God*. Without question, Jane Alexander's strength onstage was comparable to Anne's when they worked together in *Mystery of the Rose Bouquet*. At the time Puig himself called it ideal casting, particularly since he had envisioned the roles as being played by *monstres sacrés*, or sacred cows, of the theater. Looking back, however, Ackerman thought the production he directed in Los Angeles suffered by some measure because his stars came to the stage with such power.

"It was almost as if they both could have played the patient," Ackerman said. "Jane is so strong—she's *strong*. And the role of the nurse really has to be somebody incredibly submissive. Jane really could have done a beautiful job doing Anne's part." The bond that the characters form by the play's end did not take place as it had in London or in a subsequent production he directed in Japan, Ackerman thought. "The two actresses in a sense—I don't mean this in a sexual way—but they have to fall in love for the play to really work," Ackerman said, "and Jane and Anne never really found that love." Be that as it may, the production was a great success for the Mark Taper Forum, and standing ovations for its two stars were common.

If *Mystery of the Rose Bouquet* proved to be a six-week term in "theater jail" for Anne, at least she had the fulfillment that came with discovering its mysteries. In fact, she might have been satisfied to leave the production without taking the stage before an audience. As the company prepared to move from the rehearsal hall to the theater, Anne ended their last session by thanking all involved for their work and took a bow. "Good-bye, good luck to all of you," she said. "I only rehearse. I don't do performances." It was a joke wrapped around a very real feeling inside her. "She loved the rehearsal process, she loved the exploration, she loved finding the character," Ackerman said, "but she didn't necessarily love coming to the theater every night and having to do it." Manuel Puig hoped that Anne would repeat her performance in a New York production, but he wrote to a friend that she would not because of her sense of duty at home.

If she was looking for a completely different experience, Anne found one by going from a surrealistic play to a television sitcom. The commitment of twenty-four episodes a season shot over several months promised the worst kind of jail for her. British television, on the other hand, took an altogether different approach, one that appealed to her desire to be at home and with friends rather than chained to a camera. A season could be just a handful of episodes. Not only did Anne enjoy London and a popularity with British audiences, but a plane ride to her home in New York was short enough to make possible weekend visits with family and friends.

And there was the money. The budget for the sitcom in which Anne agreed to star, *Freddie and Max,* was being touted as the biggest in British television history—£2 million, or about $1.4 million. The British press reported that Anne would receive £250,000, or about $175,000, for appearing in six half-hour episodes of the Thames Television production. She also would be put up in one of London's finest hotels and allowed to fly back to New York during breaks. The production sounded promising, given that Dick Clement and Ian La Frenais, among the most successful writing teams in British television, were providing the scripts.

Comedy was not completely foreign to Anne, but she had been just a supporting player in *Bert Rigby, You're a Fool.* She was one of the title characters in *Freddie and Max.* In the series, Anne plays Maxine Chandler, a fading and nearly broke American movie star living in a suite at the Savoy Hotel. Having accepted a huge advance for her autobiography, she hires an out-of-work twentysomething assistant named Freddie Latham (Charlotte Coleman) to act as researcher, cowriter, and general gofer. The two do not see eye to eye on anything, but they come to realize that each needs the other to get by. The setup promised cultural and generational clashes as the bitchy Max issues orders to her eccentric lackey. Max's situation sounded similar to that of Ava Gardner, who spent her final years in a London flat and worked with a ghostwriter to generate a memoir for some much-needed income.

The six episodes of *Freddie and Max*, dismissed as "magnificently forgettable" by the London *Sunday Times*, came and went in November and December 1990 with little fanfare beyond the attention paid to its cost and its star. When the series aired on Canadian television, the *Toronto Star* found it to be "a rich, ribald, classy exercise in culture collision" and observed that Anne had been allowed "to chew all the scenery she wants to consume." A second season was not ordered, and Anne's only sitcom all but disappeared.

Those first two projects in her reenergized career left Anne wondering what else she could do with her newfound freedom. Neither had been wholly satisfying for her. Professionally, she had some catching up to do if she wanted to be first in the minds of casting directors. She began accepting more and more small parts in feature films while taking the occasional starring role in television movies as she rebuilt her career. Moving at a busy pace for the first time in years, she landed leading parts in a Neil Simon play adapted for television and a television drama, then supporting roles in two comedies, all released in 1992.

A television adaptation of *Broadway Bound* allowed Anne to return to Simon's world, a place that she had not visited since *The Prisoner of Second Avenue* nearly twenty years earlier. The play was the final installment of Simon's autobiographical trilogy, begun with *Brighton Beach Memoirs* and continued with *Biloxi Blues*, focusing on the young Eugene Jerome. *Broadway Bound*, set in 1948, follows Eugene as he and his older brother, Stanley, break away from their Brooklyn home to become comedy writers just as their father leaves their mother. Opening on Broadway in December 1986, *Broadway Bound* became a Tony nominee for best play and a finalist for a Pulitzer Prize (*Fences* by August Wilson won both awards). The Tony for best actress went to Linda Lavin as Kate Jerome, the role Anne would play in the television version. *Time* called the play the best of the decade, and it ran for nearly two years. Yet the money for a feature film version of *Broadway Bound* never came together as Neil Simon had hoped—film versions of his other Eugene Jerome plays had not been impressive at the box office—and he decided to settle for a television audience. *Broadway Bound* became the kind of no-frills production common to Anne's latter-day career. The cast, however, was accomplished—Anne, her old friend Jerry Orbach, Hume Cronyn, and Michele Lee; Corey Parker played Eugene and Jonathan Silverman was Stanley. The director Paul Bogart had made the most of limited resources for *Torch Song Trilogy* and would again for *Broadway Bound*. This time, he shot mostly on a huge set built at Warner Bros. to represent the Jerome house in a cold and snowy winter.

"It looked just like a house on the street in that neighborhood," Corey Parker remembered. "It was just amazing. Everything in that house was period. For an actor, it helps your imagination to become part of that world when they're creating that world all around you. Every detail was just how it might have been."

A few days of rehearsals followed an initial table reading of Simon's adaptation. "It was very relaxed," Parker said. "I think there was that feeling that you get sometimes where you know that everyone at the table is really good at what they do and is right for their roles." Anne was her usual self on the job—tough and to the point when there was little time to ease into a role. "She was Italian, that kind of old Italian," Parker said. "She did not mince her words at all. She said what was on her mind, and if she didn't like something or was frustrated about how things were going, she just put it right out there, very bluntly. Just the sound in her voice as she would start to get stronger—she would start to sound like this strong Italian woman."

That bluntness appeared, for example, when Anne was dissatisfied with Jerry Orbach's approach to a scene in which Jack and Kate argue on the stairs of their home. "He kept coming down the stairs with this very low-key note he was playing, which is tricky to do if you're fighting," Parker recalled. "I think it was after the fourth take, she blew up at him in front of everyone. She said, 'You're not giving me anything. You can't come down the stairs and give me nothing. We're having a fight, we're arguing. You've got to come down the stairs and give me something, Jerry.' He didn't say anything." Another take followed and Orbach played it the same way, but Anne had made her point. "She couldn't care less that everybody was there. It was time to work and she was trying to jolt him, to jar him away from his sort of standardized way of approaching it," Parker said.

Parker had studied with the acting teacher Herbert Berghof a generation after Anne, and he too was a member of the Actors Studio. He asked
her question after question and she answered every one, a challenging colleague who was also approachable and able to enjoy a lighthearted moment
with a younger actor. Once, in the makeup trailer as they ran lines together,
Parker decided to tease her by speaking the famous line from *The Graduate:*
"Mrs. Robinson, you're trying to seduce me. Aren't you?"

"She looked up through the mirror—she was having her makeup put
on—and she looked at me for a moment as if she was sizing me up," Parker
said. "And she said, 'I can see that, but I see Pacino more.' She didn't see me
playing the character from *The Graduate* but playing Dustin Hoffman—
and she was saying, 'You look more like Pacino than Hoffman.' She was
very playful."

Anne and Corey Parker shared the play's high point: Jerome coaxes his
mother into recounting a happy moment in her life, the time she danced
with the actor George Raft, and in showing her son how she danced she
turns into that hopeful, happy teenager again. Ahead of the scene Anne
began to recall how she had danced as a teenager, telling Parker that she
and a girlfriend would go to a dance palace together. Back at home, she
would take a chair into the bathroom and soak her sore, tired feet in the
cool water of the toilet bowl. Once again, Anne had found an emotional
connection to a character with her own experience.

"She was a very hard worker," Parker said. "She had attention to detail.
She was not an actress who just sort of sat around waiting to shoot something. She wanted to believe, she wanted to justify, to be really clear about
what she was doing and why. She had a very organic process that she
understood about how to find that. It was amazing to work with her."

If Anne were destined to play starring roles only in television productions, she could hardly do better than *Broadway Bound.* Critics at the
Boston Globe and *Washington Post* found the adaptation too housebound,
but most others thought it captured the play quite well. "Anne Bancroft is
all we could ask for as Eugene's mother, Kate," wrote *Newsday's* critic Terry
Kelleher, "embittered by her husband's involvement with another woman,
regretful for the lost dreams of her youth, yet proud of her vocation as a
homemaker who exists to feed, clothe, and comfort. This Kate doesn't
come alive only when she re-enacts her long-ago dance with a movie star;
we can feel her heartbeat whenever we look into Bancroft's eyes." In a similar tone, Lon Grahnke of the *Chicago Sun-Times* wrote: "Looking old and

tired but full of fire, Bancroft gives a brilliant reading of Kate's speech about the Primrose Ballroom on that long-ago night when she danced with George Raft. Where have you gone, Mrs. Robinson?" Around the corner, Rick Kogan of the *Chicago Tribune* summed up Anne's performance simply: "Bancroft is, as usual, wonderful."

Broadway Bound received five Emmy nominations; the only winner was Hume Cronyn for outstanding supporting actor in a miniseries or special. Anne had been nominated as best supporting actress in that division instead of best actress. Then again, she was nominated in the best actress category anyway for another low-budget effort and critical favorite. Such bountiful praise had not come her way in quite a while.

Kate Jerome was a postwar American woman finding herself adrift as time and circumstance diminished her roles as wife and mother. A similar loss of identity afflicted the title character in *Mrs. Cage,* a sixty-eight-minute contemporary drama aired by PBS's *American Playhouse.* Mrs. Cage seems anything but angry when she walks meekly into a police station to confess to a crime. A grocery store bag boy she had liked so much has been shot and killed by a purse-snatcher, yet his self-centered victim seems to care only about her purse. Mrs. Cage describes to a detective how she picked up the robber's gun, took careful aim, and shot the purse-snatcher's victim in the forehead. She spins out her story slowly, revealing not just how she came to commit the crime but how it followed the unraveling of her personal life. The detective, played by Hector Elizondo, listens as she describes a soul-sapping life as a suburban woman taken for granted by her husband and their daughter.

Adapted by Nancy Barr from her play, *Mrs. Cage* was essentially a conversation between two people in an office. When Anne found out that the producers had talked to her friend Robert Allan Ackerman about directing it, she insisted that she would take the role only if that came to pass. "That's how I got into making films, which I thought was incredibly generous of her," Ackerman said. "She just instinctively knew that I would know how to do it." To retain the element of an ongoing conversation between the two characters in a single scene while making the story cinematic, Ackerman had the characters whom Mrs. Cage refers to appear in flashbacks but mouth her dialogue as she spoke it.

Many of Anne's memorable characters shared some of Mrs. Cage's traits—among them the suicidal wife in *The Slender Thread,* the emotionally disturbed wife in *The Pumpkin Eater,* and Mrs. Robinson in *The*

Graduate. It was not by accident. "She loved complex characters," Ackerman said, "complicated women who had sort of a certain trajectory in their lives but then went somewhere that they never expected and are full of all of this kind of confusion and rage and don't feel like they've met their full potential." Anne acknowledged that she identified with Mrs. Cage's emotional life as an empty-nest mother. How deeply she felt the connection with the unappreciated wife of a prominent and respected husband she did not reveal.

Both Anne and Hector Elizondo drew critical praise and Emmy nominations for their roles, but there was a dash of disappointment in the project. Anne and the producers of *Mrs. Cage* had originally hoped that they could turn Barr's play into a feature film. No studio was interested. Nor were any of the commercial television networks or cable channels willing to finance the project. "It was so disappointing," Anne said. "I loved it so much. Everyone thought that my name would bring an offer. But it didn't help at all." The nonprofit environs of public television ended up being the perfect place for a low-budget film about a woman's rage, a telling comment about how the profit-driven mass media and the public to which they catered viewed the subject matter.

The yearlong effort to find a place for *Mrs. Cage* was fresh evidence that Anne's name brought with it a certain prestige but was not perceived as a path to box-office success. She quickly corrected those who thought otherwise. When a *New York Times* writer suggested that she, unlike Mrs. Cage, had options in life and a career that was hardly irrelevant, Anne replied tightly: "What makes you say that? I think you're quite wrong. People say I'm irrelevant all the time." In reflecting on the film industry's rejection of *Mrs. Cage,* she added: "People were saying my work is unimportant at the moment because what they want is Arnold Schwarzenegger." It was almost a return to her status in the 1950s, when she was told, "You have no name." Respect and accomplishments did not necessarily draw an audience to the theater or the living room television set.

If that was the case, then why not have some fun? Playing Nicolas Cage's dying but demanding mother in the opening scene of the comedy *Honeymoon in Vegas* was no more than a cameo by Anne for the writer and director Andrew Bergman, one of Mel's cowriters on *Blazing Saddles.* In the feature film *Love Potion No. 9,* also released in 1992, she appeared in a few scenes as a gypsy fortune teller whose magical mixture makes Tate Donovan and Sandra Bullock (in one of her early film roles) irresistible to the opposite sex. The writer, director, and producer Dale Launer filmed the clever comedy in Atlanta—a nonunion crew helped the production stay within its $6.5 million budget—and rented an old house for Anne's scenes.

Launer was directing his first studio film after finding success writing *Ruthless People* and other comedies. (He also wrote and produced *My Cousin Vinny* that year.) Unaware that Anne was rebuilding her career, he sought her for the role of Madame Ruth because he liked comedic scenes with actors not usually thought of for comedies. In fact, Launer had suggested her for the part Bette Midler played in *Ruthless People,* but the studio wanted someone with a following that would help shore up the box office. For *Love Potion No. 9,* she asked that she not be part of the advertising. "She said that would not be fair," Launer said. "I think she didn't want us to sell it as an Anne Bancroft movie, which wouldn't be right. We never even argued the point." She did receive the special stand-alone credit "and Anne Bancroft as Madame Ruth."

Anne was scheduled for just a day of work, all that was needed for her scenes with Tate Donovan. Her experiences in comedy—*Freddie and Max* in particular—may have led her to develop an overripe take on her character. After all, the over-the-top approach had worked for her husband. "I like restrained, dry comedy. And she was sort of chewing it up a little bit," Launer said. "I'm a little intimidated by her because she is kind of a little bit of a grande dame. Part of me inside said, 'Stick with your guns.' I wasn't going to be dickie about it, but I just kept trying to reel her in, reel her in." Nothing worked, and Launer was resigned to her outsize performance. When the dailies came in, a flicker ruined the scenes with Anne and a day of reshooting had to be scheduled. This time, Launer turned to a director's trick: call for take after take to wear down a performance that is over the top. Hours later, in a take shot over Donovan's shoulder, Anne gave her director just what he wanted.

"She nailed it, every single line," Launer remembered. "We get to the end, she turns to me and points to me and says, '*That* was great!' She didn't wait for me to say it. She knew she'd nailed it then and it felt right." To Launer, the flicker had been a godsend. "She was funny without going too far," he said. "I think it's a little gem of a performance." After seeing the film, Mel Brooks complimented Launer on directing a funny movie—and getting a restrained performance from his wife.

Offbeat characters like Madame Ruth—she wore a turban and walked bent over with a cane—did more than give Anne a break from dramas. They allowed her to place her aging features in a fictional context. Sixty years old when she played the fortune teller, she had never been comfortable seeing herself on the screen, and age did not ease that feeling. Dale Launer had been among the young men who saw *The Graduate* and fell in lust with Mrs. Robinson. A quarter century later, when they were shooting *Love Potion No. 9*, Anne remarked to Launer that she had seen *The Graduate* the previous evening for the first time. "I said, 'Well, what did you think?' And she said she was surprised at how pretty she was— delighted and surprised."

A year or so later, while she was making *Point of No Return* for the director John Badham, Anne declined to attend the screening of dailies. "She said that she did not like to look at herself any more on screen," Badham recounted. "This beautiful woman, whom time had rendered even more beautiful, could not make peace with what she saw on screen." If there was a sadness that came in seeing herself, as Badham thought, perhaps that guided Anne as she played character parts. If she did not seek beauty and glamour in her roles, her goal as a young actress in Hollywood, then she did not have to face their absence.

Age as well as gender stood in her way as Anne threw herself back into her craft. Leading roles in feature films for actresses over sixty were scarce in an entertainment industry eager to attract the eyes and dollars of young people. Of the fifty Oscar nominations for best actress in the 1990s, only three went to women over sixty: Joanne Woodward in *Mr. & Mrs. Bridge*, Fernanda Montenegro in *Central Station*, and Judi Dench in *Mrs. Brown*. Television offered older actresses more than feature films as it sought to fill tens of thousands of hours of programming time every year. Still, neither medium provided them much more than parts in support of younger stars and the venerable male actors who headlined action and adventure vehicles.

When a reporter asked Anne if it was difficult to be an actress in Hollywood and not be the age of Julia Roberts, then twenty-four, she laughed. "It's very difficult in every field and in every part of life not to be Julia Roberts's age anymore," she said. "My knees hurt. My hair is turning gray. There are very few good scripts, even for Julia Roberts. And it's even more difficult for me. I don't care much if it's TV or the movies. Most of the scripts I see are just not good." At that time Julia Roberts was riding the success of *Pretty Woman* and *Sleeping with the Enemy* and hailed by theater owners as the most popular actress in the movies, a laurel Anne never achieved, not even when she was being called the best actress in America.

A tough business was only becoming tougher. After *Mrs. Cage,* Anne seldom appeared as the leading actress in a film or television production. That did not prevent her from working steadily. She was an actress, first and last, and she wanted to be in front of a camera if not on a stage. More to the point, she still wanted what happened before the cameras rolled. "The pleasure and the thrill is all in the doing," she said. The process—evaluating the role, finding a personal connection, and developing a characterization—had not lost its appeal for her. There was at least one benefit in taking supporting roles: she no longer carried the burden that came with being the star. A box-office flop would not be considered an Anne Bancroft picture. Critics would throw their darts elsewhere. On the other hand, success would be easy to share with everyone involved.

She remained selective, if not as picky as she had been when she was being offered starring roles. Some of her choices may have surprised or even disappointed some of her friends, especially those who thought of her as a great Broadway actress. Not long after her death, the playwright William Gibson remarked with a touch of bitterness, "After *The Graduate,* she played decreasingly important parts and ended up playing somebody's drunken mother-in-law." His harsh judgment ignored his friend's many strong performances in the years after Mrs. Robinson, but it did point to a reality that Anne and other actresses faced late in their careers. If they wanted to perform, they had to take the best offer available.

Good timing and her reputation brought Anne some significant character roles in popular films in the 1990s. She benefited from female characters branching out into action movies, a genre that had been dominated by males. As female agents and officers of the law brandished firearms and employed martial arts to overwhelm their enemies, women were depicted as being in charge of national and international spy agencies and other arms of government or even business. Anne's image as a no-nonsense actress led to her being cast in roles that demanded a maturity and a toughness that not all her peers could deliver.

Point of No Return, one of the three movies in which she appeared in 1993, offered her such a role. In this film, directed by John Badham, a surly young criminal is recruited as a government assassin. In between her hours of physical training are sessions in etiquette run by an operative who tries to turn the street urchin into a proper lady fit for banquet halls and upscale restaurants. (Bridget Fonda played the unruly pupil, becoming the third generation of the Fonda family to perform opposite Anne.) The deadly Miss Manners of *Point of No Return* was the first of many characters to which Anne brought a sense of authority and strength. Another in that vein was the mental hospital administrator in *Mr. Jones,* a drama about a mentally ill man (Richard Gere) whose treatment for bipolar disorder at a mental institution leads to a romance with a doctor (Lena Olin). Anne's character had little to do, but by her very presence she gave the aura of being in charge.

Her role in her third film that year, the thriller *Malice,* did not present her as beautiful, glamorous or in charge. It called for a juicy if short appearance as the drunken mother of a young woman who works with an unscrupulous doctor to bilk a hospital out of millions in a malpractice suit. Anne and her *Little Foxes* costar George C. Scott were in a cast led by Nicole Kidman, Alec Baldwin, and Bill Pullman. Even an actor of Scott's prominence had trouble finding a starring gig after a certain age—and he was four years older than Anne.

Those films had not yet been released when, in March 1993, Anne appeared on the Academy Awards show to present an Oscar for screenwriting. Presenting with her was her *Graduate* costar, Dustin Hoffman. In the years since their film Hoffman had starred in three best picture winners in three different decades—*Midnight Cowboy, Kramer vs. Kramer,* and *Rain Man*—and had won Oscars for the latter two films. None was more popular than *The Graduate.* Hoffman played off that nostalgia when he and Anne presented the awards for screenwriting via satellite from New York. It seems that Anne had not completed the description of the award for a screenplay written directly for the screen, and Hoffman added, "and not previously published or produced." She turned to him and said, "Thank you," but continued to hold him in her gaze.

Her former costar looked at her not once but twice before asking, "Are you trying to seduce me?" As the reference to the line from *The Graduate* drew laughter and applause, Anne smiled and turned to the audience and said, "Not anymore." Both cracked up along with those in the room. "Oh, boy," she said after Hoffman hugged her, "are we having fun."

Anne was making good on her declaration to act her heart out, eventually playing major or minor roles in twenty different films and television programs during the 1990s following her short-lived British sitcom. Few were out-and-out comedies, which suggests that drama was still where her heart could be found. She provided the voice for Homer Simpson's psychiatrist on an episode of the animated television series *The Simpsons*, did more voice work as the Queen in the animated film *Antz*, and played a gypsy woman (again) for a cameo in her husband's horror movie parody *Dracula: Dead and Loving It*. She was laughably dramatic, but then a little scenery chewing would not be faulted in a Mel Brooks picture.

Her few starring roles were in television dramas. A small gem at sixty minutes, "The Mother" was shot in New York by the BBC and later aired by PBS on its *Great Performances* series. Part of what made "The Mother" special was its roots as an original teleplay by Paddy Chayefsky that aired live in 1954 during television's golden age, a period Anne had known well. Anne played Mrs. Fanning, a Bronx widow who, at sixty-six, wants to find work to give her life some kind of meaning. She had been a seamstress as a young woman, but her fingers are not as nimble as they used to be. She has been fired time and again but sets off on another rainy morning to try to land a position rather than move in with a daughter's family. The nation's top television critics, Tom Shales of the *Washington Post* and John J. O'Connor of the *New York Times,* could hardly have been more complimentary of Anne's performance. What could have been a character seething with anger, a specialty of both Chayefsky and Anne, instead is played with quiet determination amid tears of frustration. The emotional connection that Anne might have felt to an elderly woman trying to retain a sense of purpose was obvious.

Tenderness was at the heart of *Homecoming,* a made-for-television movie Anne shot in the summer of 1995. She played a cantankerous grandmother, Abigail, living a hermit's life on a farm outside a Maryland fishing village. When her mentally ill daughter abandons her four young children in Connecticut, they make their way to the farm with the hope that Abigail will take them in. She refuses at first—she carries too many regrets from raising her own children—but they eventually melt her selfish resolve and she decides to accept responsibility again.

The cowriter and director of *Homecoming,* Mark Jean, had worked in episodic television but not on a full-length film. Anne's finely tuned sense of talent, not to mention a strong role, led her to join his project. Though set along the East Coast, *Homecoming* was actually filmed in Ontario; Lake Erie stood in for the Chesapeake Bay and the town of Port Dover substituted for the Maryland fishing village. The various cities and towns through which the children pass on their sojourn were locations in Toronto, another way to stretch the $3.5 million budget. The production used a farmhouse for interiors, including the kitchen where many of Anne's scenes took place.

Anne's costars were four children ranging in age from their early teens on down, easily the youngest cast she had yet appeared with. "It was interesting giving direction to a six-year-old and then to Anne Bancroft," Mark Jean recalled. "She helped me elicit performances from the kids that I couldn't have gotten on my own." The youngest of the brood, William Greenblatt, could remember everyone's lines as well as his own, a talent that could lead to a perfunctory delivery. To get him to listen, Anne and Jean would change her dialogue a bit. "We got some great reactions by doing that," he said. "She was always ready to do that sort of thing to surprise him and the other kids, in cahoots with me. She was great in that respect."

Was the Oscar- and Tony-winning actress demanding of her first-time film director on their low-budget television movie? "She was demanding in the best way," Mark Jean said. "She was never demanding about things that don't matter—size of the trailer, grapes from Bolivia, or whatever. Some actors will have those kinds of requests or needs." Anne wanted the props to be correct—items in the kitchen, for instance, when Abigail went about her canning—and was attentive to wardrobe, hair, and makeup. "She was demanding in getting it right, that it was always the best it could be," he said. "Really, she raised the game of everybody around her."

One unexpected problem arose when it came time to film Anne in the little boat with an outboard motor that Abigail used to visit the harbor town. To Mark Jean's surprise, she had a phobia about boats and refused to go aboard. She explained that she had assumed a double would be used for those scenes. It took some cajoling, but eventually she relented. For the last scene, in which Abigail points the boat toward open water to take the children to her home for good, Jean assured Anne that he would call "cut" once the boat had gone just ten feet. "She was nervous about the whole thing, but she got in the boat—she was always a trouper—and she took off," he remembered. "And of course at ten feet I didn't yell cut. I just let her keep going because I knew credits were going to be rolling over that shot." He could read a message in her eyes: "Damn you . . ." Anne forgave Jean, and he later worked with Mel on a script for Brooksfilms.

Her nuanced performance was a highlight of *Homecoming.* "Like any great actress, Anne was in the moment, so it's not like she could judge herself," Jean said. "She had to lean on me to tell her what was good and what wasn't good. Nothing was ever not good, but just helping her to find the exact tenor of the scene, of the moment." *Homecoming* was well received when it aired on the cable channel Showtime—"a first-rate family film with the sharp tang of reality," wrote *USA Today*—and Anne was nominated for a Screen Actors Guild award for her starring role.

Away from television, Anne continued to accept small and sometimes showy dramatic parts in feature films. For an updated version of *Great Expectations* with Ethan Hawke and Gwyneth Paltrow, she played Miss Havisham, her decrepit mansion located in modern-day Florida instead of Dickens's London. She was a camper-driving free spirit cruising the American Southwest in *Sunchaser* with Woody Harrelson. In the feminist action movie *G.I. Jane,* starring Demi Moore, a female senator pushes the navy to consider women for all assignments, even combat, and handpicks a female lieutenant to join men training for a SEAL-like team. "Anne Bancroft was always my first choice for the senator, who's a representative of strength and intelligence and woman's rights," the film's director, Ridley Scott, said. "Anne's very good at that. She's quite capable of pulling off the tricky balance of being sympathetic while, on the other hand, being tough." *G.I. Jane* was one of the most popular movies of her later career.

Some television programs and films featured Anne as part of an ensemble cast, placing her among stars of her generation as well as younger performers who were getting prime roles. She was a centenarian looking back on her long life in the television film *Oldest Living Confederate Widow Tells All* and a woman who has given up the baby conceived during a rape in *Deep in My Heart,* another TV movie. Each brought Anne an Emmy nomination as supporting actress in a miniseries or movie. With its moving scene of reunion and redemption, *Deep in My Heart* actually won Anne an Emmy, the only one she would receive for a dramatic performance.

Anne also found time for a rare voice-over gig, providing the narration for a documentary, *Living with Cancer: A Message of Hope,* released in 1998. The hour-long film presents doctors and half a dozen cancer survivors at the Mayo Clinic discussing how cancer was not a death sentence and that more advances in treatment were expected. Its producer and director, the documentarian Fred Silverman, had thought that Anne's participation would add a strong presence to the program and was delighted when she agreed to read the narration. The subject carried personal dimensions for her. The disease had taken colleagues as well as loved ones over the years, among them her closest friend, Lydia Fields. In the hours they spent recording the narration, Anne never mentioned to Silverman that she too was living with cancer.

In movie theaters, Anne was in the ensemble cast for *Critical Care*, Sidney Lumet's satire about modern medicine. She was one of the wise elders working needle and thread while looking back on life in *How to Make an American Quilt*. Another feature film, *Home for the Holidays*, with Holly Hunter and Robert Downey Jr., presented her as a difficult mother overseeing a tense if funny family gathering at Thanksgiving.

"I've been getting good scripts, even if they don't turn into huge successes," Anne said as *Home for the Holidays* headed toward theaters in November 1995. "Even if I get more scripts, I can still only do one at a time, so the point is I need one good one." It did seem as if she was on a roll, as one good part after another drew attention and fostered a kind of resurgence for her. *Home for the Holidays*, directed by the actress Jodie Foster, would become a holiday favorite on television, helping make Anne recognizable to younger audiences who had never seen *The Miracle Worker* or *The Graduate*.

Her most famous films had become part of an older generation's memories of the movies. While she looked ahead to that next "good one," Anne was not opposed to celebrating the past. The Academy of Motion Picture Arts and Sciences was feeling the tug of nostalgia more than usual in 1998, the year the Oscars turned seventy—not much older than Anne. For Oscar night, the producers invited actors and actresses who had been awarded the golden statuette to join a "family album" on the stage as tens of millions around the world marked the passage of time.

Susan Sarandon, an Oscar winner herself, introduced the segment and joined the other recipients in rows of chairs on a tiered platform. The orchestra began playing "You Ought to Be in Pictures," and the first to be introduced was Mike and Millie Italiano's middle daughter. Members of the audience were already out of their seats and applauding when the announcer said, "Anne Bancroft—*The Miracle Worker*." She smiled broadly and blew three kisses before the camera moved on.

So many of the careers in Oscar's family were related to hers, a sign of how entrenched Anne had become in American movies. Among her costars on the stage were Sidney Poitier, Holly Hunter, Ernest Borgnine,

Robert De Niro, Jack Lemmon, and Dustin Hoffman. Also on hand was Patricia Neal, her *Miracle Worker* costar on the stage and the reason she made *7 Women*. So were Lee Grant, her standby for *Two for the Seesaw*, and Rod Steiger, who first told her about Stanislavsky, as well as her nominal rivals Ellen Burstyn and Faye Dunaway.

Fifty years had passed from the day Anne took the subway from her parents' home in the Bronx to Carnegie Hall to begin studying acting. Her goal had been to become a movie star. That night at the Shrine Auditorium in Los Angeles signaled how she had become so much more—she was a significant part of Hollywood's glorious and glamorous history.

Writing was a family thing for the Brookses. Max had majored in history at Pitzer College in Claremont, California, and studied film at American University in Washington, D.C., before setting out to write professionally. Anne took an option on a novel, *LovingKindness* by Anne Roiphe, in which a mother comes to terms with a rebellious daughter. Between acting jobs, she spent a few years trying to adapt the novel for the screen. Directing was not something she mentioned when discussing plans for *LovingKindness* in the year 2000—she would never get over her unhappy experience directing *Fatso*. "I hated directing," she had remarked a few years earlier. "I'm not fit to direct because I don't like the stress, the responsibility or forcing my vision on anyone." She did envision a role for herself in a movie version of Roiphe's book.

Mel was busy with a particular project of his own. The media mogul David Geffen had encouraged him to create a musical version of *The Producers*, a natural for musical comedy, given its setting and plot. Geffen even suggested that Mel work with Jerry Herman, who had written the music and lyrics for *Hello, Dolly!* and *Mame*. As Mel would tell the story, Anne stepped in at that point. "I won't let you do this, if they don't let you do the score," she told him. "That's the only reason to do it, the score." Mel was no stranger to coming up with words and music; he had written songs for his films *The Producers*, *Blazing Saddles*, and *High Anxiety*, among others. Anne's encouragement and insistence carried the day, and he buckled down to write the music and lyrics. He did take on a partner, Thomas Meehan, to hammer out the book of the musical. Meehan had written for both of Anne's television specials in the 1970s, the book for the musical *Annie*, and the screenplay for *To Be or Not to Be*.

Anne appeared in two new films in 2000. In the comedy *Keeping the*

Faith with Ben Stiller and Edward Norton (who also directed), she was the mother of a young rabbi falling in love with a gentile. *Up at the Villa* cast her with Kristin Scott Thomas and Sean Penn in a drama about expatriates in fascist Italy just before World War II. Promoting those films brought her to Charlie Rose's PBS talk show, a rare hour-long appearance in which she discussed her career. She was engaging, even flirty, as she revisited the usual topics—her marriage, *The Graduate,* rebuilding her career, her lack of box-office clout—but she also opened up about what troubled her and how happiness was not necessarily her foremost emotional goal.

"Being happy is a very complex thing," she said. "And truly, happiness is not what I'm looking for. I think what I'm looking for—see, that's what I found. I found what I think I'm looking for. What I think I'm looking for is a state of mind, of peace. Just peace. Doesn't even have to be happy. I don't even ask for that. I just want some—to be not conflicted anymore, to feel simple about things." She admitted that she had not found that peace yet but felt that she was on the path. What came across most during the hour was her warmth and humor. "We can never let Mel see this," she told Charlie Rose after the taping. "He can't see me having so much fun with another man."

As *The Producers* neared its Broadway opening night, set for April 19, 2001, at the St. James Theatre, Mel and Anne met for a late dinner at the restaurant Orso. She had attended the musical's tryouts in Chicago but had just flown back from Los Angeles and missed that evening's dress rehearsal at the St. James. Her most recent work had reached screens earlier in the year, the feature film comedy *Heartbreakers,* in which she had a cameo, and the four-hour television movie *Haven;* she would earn another Emmy nomination for her supporting role as Natasha Richardson's mother in this drama about Jewish refugees coming to the United States. That night at Orso, her attention was focused on Mel and his Broadway musical.

On the way to their table they ran into her *Little Foxes* costar Austin Pendleton. Later he could not help noticing from his table how Mel described the dress rehearsal to Anne and how she peppered him with questions. The buzz around Broadway already had it that *The Producers* would be a hit. "It was the loveliest thing I ever saw," Pendleton remembered. "She was so happy for him. And he was so happy that she was so happy for him. And I knew enough to know that he might not have ever even written it if it hadn't been for her."

The word around Broadway was wrong—*The Producers* was a phenomenon, not just a hit. The production, starring Nathan Lane and Matthew Broderick, became one of the most popular shows in New York and would run for more than 2,500 performances. On the night of the Tony Awards that June, Anne sat beside Mel in Radio City Music Hall as his show won award after award—a record twelve by the time *The Producers* was named the year's best musical. Three went to Mel himself, and he thanked his wife from the stage for pushing him to do it. Smiling and occasionally wiping a tear, Anne joined those cheering Mel on his big night.

The excitement sparked by her husband's success rekindled her interest in the theater. Anne had not been in a play for eleven years, not since *Mystery of the Rose Bouquet* in Los Angeles, and she had not been on a New York stage since the short-lived *Duet for One* in 1981. Spending time away from her family was no longer a problem. With *The Producers* filling the St. James Theatre every night and Max joining the writing staff of television's *Saturday Night Live* in the 2001–2 season, working in New York did not mean Anne would be alone.

That fall the director Anthony Page was preparing a production of a new play by Edward Albee, *Occupant*. Its subject was the late sculptor Louise Nevelson, at least on the surface. Albee had been a close friend of the flamboyant artist, and he saw in her life an example of how creative people had to live in order to be true to themselves. (Nevelson left the Ukraine for the United States as a child, married as a teenager to a prosperous older man, left their child to travel throughout Europe, and spent years living hand to mouth to pursue her art.) Rather than a traditional biographical drama, Albee imagined Nevelson being interviewed before an audience after her death; the *New York Times* called it "a kind of cosmic talk show." The interviewer, billed as the Man, questioned the irascible artist and, by chiseling away the errors and untruths surrounding her, uncovered the woman beneath the image she had created.

Edward Albee envisioned an unknown for the role so that there was no star to outshine Nevelson herself. Anthony Page, on the other hand, thought the play demanded a major actress and pictured Anne when he read it. Albee had known her for years but did not think she could be persuaded to return to the stage. Interestingly, Anne had never performed in an Albee drama. It would be tantalizing to think of her as the vicious, drunken Martha in *Who's Afraid of Virginia Woolf?* The director Vincente Minnelli had thought so and, at one point, sought to direct the film version with Anne and Henry Fonda. (It eventually became Mike Nichols's first film, in 1966, and starred Elizabeth Taylor and Richard Burton.) The closest Anne had come to an Albee work before *Occupant* may have been in the late 1960s, when Alan Schneider, who frequently directed Albee's plays, tried in vain to put together a film adaptation of *A Delicate Balance* with Anne, Katharine Hepburn, and Henry Fonda.

When she read *Occupant* that Thanksgiving, two months after turning seventy, Anne immediately agreed to join the Signature Theatre Company production after a Caribbean holiday with Mel. The off-Broadway venue scheduled previews to begin February 8, 2002, with an official opening for the limited run set for February 24. Anne gave a broad analysis of what she saw as the play's theme when the *New York Times* reported that she was returning to the stage. "It's about a woman fighting the traditions and conventions she was forced into in order to find her own path in life," she said. "And that's not just a problem for her or even just women. It's a problem for everyone: how do you find your own path?" Looking back at the trajectory of her life and career, she could have been describing her own journey.

Occupant was another two-character play, a format in which Anne could shine or stumble. Cast as the tenacious interviewer was Neal Huff, a thirtysomething actor appearing in his seventh off-Broadway show; he also had two Broadway productions to his credit. As it turned out, Huff's initial hurdle was related to the reason Edward Albee wanted to avoid casting a star. "My problem in rehearsal was not to be in love with Anne Bancroft," Huff remembered. "It was very difficult for me to look into that face and not want to be on the same side as her. She had so much heart, and she is so unbelievably brilliant that I really had no objectivity for the first few weeks of rehearsal. So the play didn't have any definition or form because I basically had a huge crush on Anne, like really, truly." His director as well as his costar urged him to needle her in their exchanges and be more adversarial. "Anthony was really all over me," Huff said, "and rightly so, to get a real backbone in there and really go after her." In time he took a colder approach to how the Man questioned and challenged Nevelson.

Anne had a different problem. Whether it was her age or the demands of Albee's dense script—an hour and forty-five minutes of back-and-forth—she had trouble learning her part. Outside rehearsals, she ran lines with Neal Huff and enlisted more help on her own time to memorize the play. "It was hard for Anne to put the book down in terms of memory," Huff said. "She was very worried that she wasn't going to be able to remember the play." The lines still were not sticking with her as previews approached, and she resorted to using an electronic earbud through which her cues could be transmitted from offstage as needed.

The tireless effort Anne put into rehearsals, previews, and her work away from the theater took a toll on her. Anxiety over learning her lines may have sapped her strength as well, not to mention the chill of a New York winter that never spared her. "She seemed weak, really frail," Huff said. "A force of nature, but she was really delicate, too." After just a few previews, she missed a performance, then another and another and another. "It was really going well, we were just getting our stride," Huff said. "Then she was gone." In the meantime, her standby, Kathleen Butler, filled in.

The Signature Theatre Company announced on February 14 that Anne was suffering from bronchitis and that the opening of *Occupant* was being postponed. The *New York Daily News* reported that some doubted whether she was up to the demands of the role. Artistically or physically? On the fringes some people wondered whether Anne was actually sick or just scared and wanted out. "I really never thought that," Neal Huff said, "because she was so bloody committed to doing the play." A few days later the theater company announced that Anne had developed pneumonia. Another week went by before word came that the production was suspending all performances until her return, expected on March 19.

Her absence gave rise to murmurs that she was responding to the rigors and difficulties of *Occupant* the same way she had when *Golda* ran into problems. Few people thought she would return to the Signature Theatre, but Anne was adamant. "I promise you I will be back," she assured Huff. Even if she recovered on schedule, time was running out. Another production was due to take over the theater in April, and *Occupant* would have only three weeks left if Anne returned as planned. To accommodate theater subscribers and those already with tickets, the company decided to wave off critics from its 160-seat theater. The move to allow the production to go on without reviews stirred talk that *Occupant* was not stageworthy, a charge the company denied.

In the weeks she was sidelined, Anne was not idle. She came back to the play as she had promised and, in her costar's view, in top form. "I have never, ever worked with an actor like that," Neal Huff said. "She was so unbelievably brilliant. She was not using an earbud at all. She was just on fire onstage. I've never seen an actor have the ability, to have the size to completely address everyone emotionally at the back of the house and then still have the most extraordinary intimacy with everyone." Mel Brooks led the noisy ovation his wife received upon her return. Three weeks of performances followed, but the damage was done, and there was never an official opening. The *New York Times* reported that the production had lost the theater company as much as a half million dollars. *Occupant* would not truly premiere until 2008, when the Signature Theatre Company presented a production directed by Pam MacKinnon and starring Mercedes Ruehl and Larry Bryggman.

Once again, Anne's delicate constitution had eroded her resolve. Whatever the underlying reasons, her difficulties with *Occupant* may well have ended her stage career. At seventy-plus she would not have been too old to appear in another stage production—Jessica Tandy had starred on Broadway well into her seventies and Angela Lansbury into her eighties. But given that she had left three different theater productions because of illness, twice when she was much younger, would any producer take the risk?

Ann had lined up a movie to follow *Occupant* well before her illness. When she traveled to Italy to make *The Roman Spring of Mrs. Stone* for Showtime, she was in fine form. The Tennessee Williams novel on which the movie was based had been published in 1950 and served as the foundation for a 1961 film starring Vivien Leigh and Warren Beatty. In the Williams story, Karen Stone, an actress, is retired from the stage, widowed, and emotionally adrift as she approaches her fiftieth birthday. She seeks some kind of renewal in Rome—physical and emotional—with a young Italian hustler. Anne could have been utterly convincing as Mrs. Stone had the production been undertaken fifteen or twenty years earlier. Instead, Helen Mirren would play Mrs. Stone, but Anne still had a juicy role as the Contessa, a procurer of young men for lonely or sex-starved women. She was the closest thing to comic relief in the moody film, and Anne appeared to relish playing a disreputable, cunning Italian.

The budget was tight—it seemed that all her films now had to get by on little money—and the production made the most of its $5.5 million by shooting interiors in a studio in Dublin, Ireland. It held to a tight schedule, planned for just twenty-four days. The director was her friend Robert Allen Ackerman, who with *Mystery of the Rose Bouquet* and *Mrs. Cage* would direct Anne more often in major roles than anyone except Arthur Penn.

Anne later remarked that she had never had more fun making a movie.

She was not the star and therefore was not on call every day. She loved being in Rome to shoot exteriors and identified with the Italian culture. Best of all for her, Mel was there. Instead of feeling she had been sentenced to weeks in "movie jail," she was able to work and spend time with her husband. "In Rome, it was a feast every night," Ackerman remembered. "She had a great time."

Mel flew ahead of Anne and Ackerman when the production moved to Dublin. As eager as Anne was to get there, one would have thought they had been apart for months. To her delight, Mel met their plane. "She was like a schoolgirl. He had only been gone like a day and she couldn't wait to see him," Ackerman said. "They were so close. They loved each other so much."

The Roman Spring of Mrs. Stone received Golden Globe and Emmy nominations for best television movie or miniseries. Among its five Emmy nominees were Mirren, Ackerman, and Anne. Mirren and Anne also received nominations from the Screen Actors Guild, and Mirren alone a nomination from the Golden Globes. The made-for-television film did not win any of the major awards, but Anne had once again shown her peers and her public that, even in her seventies, she could deliver a standout performance.

Conclusion

Inch by Inch, Yard by Yard

Anne's next role was not at all difficult to play. For the first time since Mel's comedy *Silent Movie,* Anne appeared as herself, this time in a cameo for the season finale of Larry David's caustically funny HBO series, *Curb Your Enthusiasm.* A story line that season was David's effort to star in the musical *The Producers.* In the episode set to air in March 2004, Mel and Anne attend opening night for the new production featuring Larry David and his costar David Schwimmer. Behind the scenes, the Brookses hope the production will fail so they can put *The Producers* and all its headaches behind them. In a twist that mirrors Mel's original story, they are horrified to discover that Larry David is a hit with the audience and the show will continue running after all.

There was more work for Anne in the new year. Her latest feature film, *Spanglish,* promised to be one of the most anticipated movies of the year. The writer and director was the Oscar winner James L. Brooks, who had followed *Terms of Endearment* with *Broadcast News, I'll Do Anything,* and *As Good as It Gets,* his most recent effort winning Oscars for Jack Nicholson and Helen Hunt. Adam Sandler and Téa Leoni were leading the cast of *Spanglish,* and Anne would appear as the alcoholic grandmother in a comically dysfunctional family.

Anne had been shooting for some weeks in early 2004 when she called her friend Robert Allan Ackerman with disturbing news. "She told me she had gone to the doctor and they had found something that was very small and she asked me not to tell anybody," he remembered. "They didn't want anybody to know about this." When *Variety* reported on March 2 that Anne dropped out of *Spanglish* because of minor surgery, there was no mention of a tumor or her long history of cancer. Mel assured the press that his wife was recuperating at home and reading scripts for projects planned for later in the year. On the set of *Spanglish,* Cloris

Leachman took her place—and ended up with a Screen Actors Guild nomination.

Anne and Mel decided to spend that summer at the home they had bought in the Hamptons, not far from her sisters, her mother, and the many friends who lived in the New York area. Their son had published his first book, *The Zombie Survival Guide,* the previous fall. Max had married the writer Michelle Kholos that year, too, and in the summer of 2004 she became pregnant with Anne's first grandchild. Anne was making plans for the rest of the year and beyond, putting the surgery behind her. "They thought it was successfully dealt with and it was finished," Ackerman said. He had been working on theater productions in Japan, and Anne was interested in joining him on a trip there in the fall.

The past was on Anne's mind that summer. She joined her friend Alan Alda and her daughter-in-law at the Southampton Writers Conference at Stony Brook University, located on Long Island's North Shore. While Michelle studied fiction, Anne and Alda attended a memoir-writing seminar taught by Frank McCourt, whose book *Angela's Ashes* had won a Pulitzer Prize. After all the years in which she had guarded her privacy, Anne's writing a memoir at seventy-two was an intriguing idea. In a book he would write long after the seminar, Alda recalled his friendship with Anne and the many years the Brooks and Alda families vacationed on the same Caribbean island, St. John. Among his fond memories was watching Anne sitting with children admiring sea glass and showing them how to enjoy the beauty of their surroundings.

Anne was one of ten people in the McCourt seminar. "She was a woman of great beauty, wit, and depth," one of her classmates, Susan Kelley, wrote in a memoir of her own. Kelley recalled being in the restroom when one of the younger members of the seminar, a woman of twenty-one, broke into tears. Anne asked her, "What's wrong?" and the young woman replied, "You're so smart and I know nothing." Anne offered a gracious response: "I'm older—a lot older."

She had another project in the works that summer, bringing the one-woman show *Squeeze Box* to New York. The writer and performer Ann Randolph had created a funny if twisted take on her job at a homeless shelter for mentally ill women and the characters she encountered. Anne and Mel had been fans since seeing *Squeeze Box* in 2002 at the Court Theater in Los Angeles. Anne helped Randolph and the director Alan Bailey prepare the show for a New York venue and even bankrolled the production.

Squeeze Box opened in late July at the Acorn Theater, and plans were afoot for Randolph and Anne to work together on a film adaptation to be produced, naturally, by Brooksfilms.

Months went by and Robert Allan Ackerman did not hear from Anne. The silence concerned him and he called her in New York. Her tone signaled the worst. "She said, 'You know, you better talk to Mel. I'm too upset to really talk about this,'" Ackerman recalled. "And he told me that it had come back." Anne was suffering from uterine cancer, and many of those who knew her had no idea how seriously ill she was or that she was sick at all.

In time Anne underwent chemotherapy. She lost her hair in the process and wore caps she knitted herself, "marvelous inventions of texture and color" according to Alan Alda's account. On a day that her sister Phyllis was helping care for her, Anne asked to go down to the ocean that she had loved for so long. She even managed a dip in the water.

Mel was overseeing the film adaptation of *The Producers* but was often absent from the set in New York to be with his wife. "It was kept pretty quiet during that period, and Mel didn't talk about it. He was very, very private about Anne," recalled Jonathan Sanger, who was producing the movie for Brooksfilms. "He didn't want to get a lot of sympathy from people on the set, so he didn't talk about it, and nobody on the set really knew what he was going through. It was all about Anne."

One day Anne visited the *Producers* set when the company was shooting scenes at a town house on Fifth Avenue. "We set up a room and she came there," Sanger said. "She seemed to be recovering, but it was during periods of very heavy chemo, I'm sure. She was really tired, but it was great to have her there. Obviously, at that point, people knew that she had been ill. They didn't really know the extent of it." Soon it became all too clear to her family that Anne was losing ground and was, in fact, dying.

During her illness Max was working, too, writing his first novel, the zombie oral history *World War Z,* and preparing for the arrival of his child. A boy, Henry, was born in time for Anne to hold him. For a time Max's life consisted of waking up in the afternoon, having dinner with his father and bringing him home to see the baby, then taking Mel back to the hospital to be with Anne before returning home to care for his son and spend all night writing. Hard work had been Anne's prescription for dealing with challenges, creative and otherwise.

Commitment, concentration, and perseverance had served Anne well in the past, but they could not overcome the cancer. She died at Manhattan's Mount Sinai Medical Center on June 6, 2005. The next evening Broadway acknowledged its loss by dimming the lights in the theater district.

Obituaries praised Anne as "one of the most versatile and resourceful actors of her generation" (*Newsday*), "a great, powerful, often joyful actress" (CNN), "fiery, funny, larger than life" (*Boston Globe*), and an actress who could appear "both tough and vulnerable" (*New York Times*). Not surprisingly, the opening to nearly every story cited her signature role in *The Graduate* and her Oscar-winning performance in *The Miracle Worker*. Also commonly reported was her unlikely pairing with Mel Brooks and how their long marriage had been a rare Hollywood love story. There was a common error in most of the obituaries, too: that her New York–born parents were Italian immigrants.

Anne was buried in Kensico Cemetery in the Westchester County hamlet of Valhalla, located about fifteen miles north of Yonkers. Her grave was near her father's; Mike Italiano had died in 2001 at the age of ninety-five. On her gravestone, beneath the figure of a grieving angel, were carved "Anne Bancroft Brooks," her birth and death dates, and the words "Cherished Actress, Beloved Wife, Mother, Grandmother, Sister and Daughter." Millie Italiano, who had seen promise in Anne's desire to perform when others did not, had survived both her husband and middle daughter and would live to 102.

Private memorials were scheduled on both coasts. In Los Angeles, Carl Reiner hosted a gathering at the film academy's Samuel Goldwyn Theater, at which Robert Allan Ackerman and others offered memories of Anne. At the St. James Theatre in New York, where *The Producers* was still playing, Arthur Penn, Mike Nichols, and Alan Alda were among those who delivered eulogies. Penn wept as he recalled how Anne became his pupil, a turning point in her conception of acting that also changed her life. Paul Simon played an acoustic version of "Mrs. Robinson."

Mel was inconsolable then and remained so for several years, refusing in interviews to ponder the question of what life was like without her. In 2014, when he performed a one-man show for HBO, he surprised some of their friends by speaking about his wife nine years after her death. Asked what he considered his greatest accomplishment, Mel answered, "Marrying Anne Bancroft." His audience showed its agreement with a round of applause.

Her unexpected death at seventy-three meant that Anne would not receive the honors accorded to living performers with careers of her longevity and acclaim. Surely she would have joined the recipients of the Kennedy Center Honors or received lifetime achievement awards from the Screen Actors Guild, the Golden Globes or the American Film Institute. By the time Mel Brooks was eighty-seven, he had received both the Kennedy Center and the AFI honors, tributes his wife no doubt would have enjoyed for the pleasure they brought him.

Perhaps more important to Anne than tributes would have been the lasting influence of her work on film. *The Graduate* remained the most popular movie in which she appeared. When the American Film Institute compiled lists of American movies by various categories, it began in 1998 with the top one hundred. In a list led by *Citizen Kane, Casablanca,* and *The Godfather,* the story of Benjamin Braddock and Mrs. Robinson placed at Number 7. *The Graduate* appeared on several other AFI lists over the years: greatest songs ("Mrs. Robinson" at Number 6), funniest films (Number 9), greatest love stories (Number 52), and top quotes ("Plastics" at Number 42 and "Mrs. Robinson, you're trying to seduce me. Aren't you?" at Number 63). Meanwhile, *The Miracle Worker* ranked fifteenth on the AFI list of most inspiring movies; it would stand as the connection to what had become a legendary stage performance. Other films featuring Anne's best-regarded performances—*The Pumpkin Eater, The Turning Point,* and *Agnes of God*—were not-so-buried treasures waiting to be discovered by future generations along with challenging films like *'night, Mother* and crowd-pleasers *84 Charing Cross Road, Homecoming,* and *Home for the Holidays.*

Over the course of her career Anne had grown to dislike interviews for the incursions they created into her private life. Yet those moments of personal trespass revealed a hard-won wisdom gained from decades of trying to balance a desire to perform with a need for a full life away from the lights. She assured the journalist Joan Goodman in 1987 that the appearance that she had it all did not mean everything was perfect. A realist and never totally satisfied with what she had achieved, she asserted that nothing was without its flaws, and everything came at a price.

"We have a motto in our family," Anne told Goodman. "'Inch by inch, life's a cinch. Yard by yard, it's very hard.' I say it to my husband at the start of every film. I had it printed on my son's T-shirt and I say it to him before every test. Take one little problem at a time." Goodman noted that Anne paused before adding, "I wish someone would say that to me."

Acknowledgments

Many people have supported my goal of presenting the life and career of Anne Bancroft, one of the great actresses of our lives. As much as I appreciate their help, their assistance does not mean they necessarily agree with my presentation or my conclusions. Similarly, any errors on these pages are my own.

I owe a special thanks to JoAnne Italiano Perna for sharing her memories of growing up in the Bronx, New York, with her sister Anne. Chatting now and then with Ms. Perna and enjoying her sharp insight and good humor have been among the benefits of writing about her younger sibling.

I am grateful to all those who spoke to me about Ms. Bancroft as a friend or as a colleague in the film, television, or theater productions in which she participated: Robert Allan Ackerman, Candice Azzara, Lane Bradbury, Dale Brown, Colby Chester, Elisa Coletti Goldberg, Frank Corsaro, Jackie Eliopoulos, Bobbi Elliott, Father Antimo Fiorillo, Gerald Freedman, Peter Galman, Bruce Glover, Mimi Gramatky, Julann Griffin, Neal Huff, Mark Jean, Alan Johnson, Philip Langner, Gene Lasko, Dale Launer, Michael Lombard, David Lunney, Nancy Lunney-Wheeler, Peter Maloney, Harry Mastrogeorge, Eugene Mazzola, Richard Monaco, Tom Moore, Corey Parker, Austin Pendleton, John Pielmeier, Doug Rogers, Grace Rosa, Jonathan Sanger, Tobey Shaffer, Fred Silverman, Ray Stewart, Inga Swenson, Irene Tsu, Lawrence Turman, and Robert Wagner. I should note that Ms. Bancroft's husband, Mel Brooks, and their son, Max, declined to participate in this project, as did her younger sister, Phyllis.

The professionals who manage our libraries and archives are the unsung heroes of a biography. For their assistance I thank the staffs of the Margaret Herrick Library of the Academy of Motion Picture Arts and Sciences; the Motion Picture and Television Reading Room of the Library of Congress; the New York Public Library for the Performing Arts; the Paley Center for Media in Los Angeles; the Cecil H. Green Library at Stanford University; the British Film Institute; and the American University Library in Washington, D.C. I also am indebted to the photo archives AP Images, Photofest, Corbis, and the Everett Collection.

Film writers, producers, and scholars have been generous with their research and advice. I am most grateful to Arthur Penn's biographer Nat Segaloff for providing transcripts of his interviews with Mr. Penn and William Gibson, and to Mike Wood of the William Inge Center for the Arts for a transcript of his interview with Mr. Gibson. For their time I thank the Jack Clayton scholar Neil Sinyard, the Roy Ward Baker scholar Geoffrey Mayer, the Gertrude Berg documentarian Aviva Kempner, and the Actors Studio historian David Garfield. For permission to quote from the unpublished writings of Jerome Robbins, I thank Christopher Pennington, director and trustee of the Jerome Robbins Foundation & the Robbins Rights Trust.

As a writer and editor for the Washington, D.C., bureau of the Associated Press, I am surrounded by journalists who have been generous with their advice and ideas. Bureau Chief Sally Buzbee has been exceptionally supportive of my project; my supervisors Carole Feldman and David Pace have also made it possible for me to find time to pursue interviews. Sandy Kozel provided much-needed guidance on broadcast interview sources. I am grateful for the many other colleagues who have offered their support and good cheer, among them Jay Arnold, Donna Cassata, Harry Dunphy, Philip Elliott, Jon Elswick, Jamie Friar, Fred Frommer, Bob Furlow, Robert Glass, Merrill Hartson, Jesse J. Holland, Lou Kesten, Will Lester, Lauran Neergaard, Eileen Putman, Jackie Quinn, Michele Salcedo, Tom Strong, Darlene Superville, and Hope Yen.

Friends and family have offered insightful observations and encouragement. I thank John Brady, Dorothy Daniel, Holly Daniel, Phillip Daniel, Russell Fortmeyer, Larry and Mary Lamb, Mark Lemke, Michael Perez, Ron Powers, Don Solosan, and Terri Utley. I am particularly grateful for the guidance provided by Jack Doulin, a veteran of the New York theater and an affable correspondent on all things Broadway. I also am thankful for Marilyn Greenwald's advice and support, for Dorothy Daniel's first reading of my initial draft, for Phillip Daniel's help with photographs, and for Alan Wild's fine-tuning of the manuscript.

My publisher, the University Press of Kentucky, has been supportive and helpful in every way. I thank the staff, in particular Anne Dean Dotson and Patrick O'Dowd, and Patrick McGilligan, the series editor. I also owe thanks to the literary agent Scott Mendel for his efforts in my behalf, and to Ann Twombly for her fine copyediting.

Finally, I want to express my gratitude to Jason Schaff, who was the editor in chief of our campus newspaper, the *Kansas State Collegian,* when I first gave daily reporting a try. Since then, I have enjoyed a long career in journalism and pursued other types of writing. I am fortunate to have had encouragement and friendship from a peer who showed me and others what it means to be a journalist and a professional writer. I dedicate this book to him with respect and affection.

Appendix

Theater, Film, and Television Appearances

Theater

Two for the Seesaw. Opened January 16, 1958, at the Booth Theatre, New York. Writer: William Gibson. Director: Arthur Penn. Producer: Fred Coe. With Henry Fonda and Anne Bancroft.

The Miracle Worker. Opened October 19, 1959, at the Playhouse Theatre, New York. Writer: William Gibson. Director: Arthur Penn. Producer: Fred Coe. With Anne Bancroft, Patty Duke, Patricia Neal, Torin Thatcher, James Congdon, Kathleen Comegys.

Mother Courage and Her Children. Opened March 28, 1963, at the Martin Beck Theatre, New York. Writer: Bertolt Brecht. Translator: Eric Bentley. Director: Jerome Robbins. Producers: Cheryl Crawford and Jerome Robbins. With Anne Bancroft, Zohra Lampert, Conrad Bromberg, John Randolph, Louis Gus, Mike Kellin, Eugene Roche, Gene Wilder, Benjamin Hammer, Barbara Harris.

The Devils. Opened November 16, 1965, at the Broadway Theatre, New York. Writer: John Whiting, based on a novel by Aldous Huxley. Director: Michael Cacoyannis. Producer: Alexander H. Cohen. With Anne Bancroft, Jason Robards Jr., John Baragrey, Albert Dekker, Shepperd Strudwick, John Colicos, Lynda Day, Tom Klunis, Richard Lynch, James Coco.

The Skin of Our Teeth. Opened June 21, 1966, at the Stockbridge Playhouse, Stockbridge, Massachusetts. Writer: Thornton Wilder. Director: Arthur

Penn. Producer: Berkshire Theatre Festival. With Anne Bancroft, Alvin Epstein, Estelle Parsons, Kathleen Eric, Frank Langella, Peter Maloney.

The Little Foxes. Opened October 26, 1967, at the Vivian Beaumont Theater, New York. Writer: Lillian Hellman. Director: Mike Nichols. Producer: Repertory Theater of Lincoln Center. With Anne Bancroft, George C. Scott, Margaret Leighton, E. G. Marshall, Richard A. Dysart, Austin Pendleton, Maria Tucci, Beah Richards, André Womble.

A Cry of Players. World premiere July 24, 1968, at the Stockbridge Playhouse, Stockbridge, Massachusetts. Writer: William Gibson. Director: Gene Frankel. Producer: Berkshire Theatre Festival. With Anne Bancroft, Frank Langella, William Roerick, Flora Elkins, Don McHenry, Dan Morgan, Jerome Dempsey, Ray Stewart, Tom Sawyer, Peter Galman.

A Cry of Players. Opened November 14, 1968, at the Vivian Beaumont Theater, New York. Writer: William Gibson. Director: Gene Frankel. Producer: Repertory Theater of Lincoln Center. With Anne Bancroft, Frank Langella, Stephen Elliott, Susan Tyrrell, Don McHenry, Robert Symonds, Jerome Dempsey, Ray Stewart, Tom Sawyer, René Auberjonois.

John and Abigail. Opened July 1, 1969, at the Stockbridge Playhouse, Stockbridge, Massachusetts. Writer: William Gibson. Director: Frank Langella. Producer: Berkshire Theatre Festival. With Anne Bancroft and James Broderick.

Golda. Opened November 14, 1977, at the Morosco Theatre, New York. Writer: William Gibson. Director: Arthur Penn. Producer: Theatre Guild. With Anne Bancroft, James Tolkan, Richard Kuss, Ben Hammer, Nicholas La Padula, Harry Davis, Sam Schacht, Vivian Nathan, Zack Matalon, Frances Chaney, Sam Gray.

Duet for One. Opened December 17, 1981, at the Royale Theatre, New York. Writer: Tom Kempinski. Director: William Friedkin. Producers: Emanuel Azenberg, Ray Cooney, Wayne M. Rogers, Ron Dante, Tommy Valando, and Warner Theatre Productions Inc. With Anne Bancroft and Max von Sydow.

Mystery of the Rose Bouquet. Opened November 16, 1989, at the Mark Taper Forum, Music Center of Los Angeles County. Writer: Manuel Puig. Director: Robert Allan Ackerman. Producer Gordon Davidson. With Jane Alexander and Anne Bancroft.

Edward Albee's Occupant. In previews beginning March 17, 2002, at the Peter Norton Space, Signature Theatre, New York. Writer: Edward Albee. Director: Anthony Page. Producer: Signature Theatre. With Anne Bancroft and Neal Huff.

Film

Don't Bother to Knock. 1952. Director: Roy Ward Baker. Writer: Daniel Taradash, from a novel by Charlotte Armstrong. Producer: Julian Blaustein. Released by Twentieth Century-Fox. With Richard Widmark, Marilyn Monroe, Anne Bancroft, Donna Corcoran, Jeanne Cagney, Lurene Tuttle, Elisha Cook Jr., Jim Backus.

Treasure of the Golden Condor. 1953. Director: Delmer Daves. Writer: Delmer Daves, from a novel by Edison Marshall. Producer: Jules Buck. Released by Twentieth Century-Fox. With Cornel Wilde, Constance Smith, Finlay Currie, Walter Hampden, Anne Bancroft, George Macready, Fay Wray, Leo G. Carroll, Konstantin Shayne.

Tonight We Sing. 1953. Director: Mitchell Leisen. Writers: Ruth Goode, Sol Hurok, Harry Kurnitz, George Oppenheimer. Producer: George Jessel. Released by Twentieth Century-Fox. With David Wayne, Ezio Pinza, Roberta Peters, Anne Bancroft, Tamara Toumanova, Isaac Stern, Bryon Palmer, Jan Peerce.

The Kid from Left Field. 1953. Director: Harmon Jones. Writer: Jack Sher. Producer: Leonard Goldstein. Released by Twentieth Century-Fox. With Dan Dailey, Anne Bancroft, Billy Chapin, Lloyd Bridges, Ray Collins, Richard Egan, Bob Hopkins, Alex Gerry, Walter Sande, Fess Parker.

Demetrius and the Gladiators. 1954. Director: Delmer Daves. Writer: Philip Dunne, based on a character created by Lloyd C. Douglas. Producer: Frank Ross. Released by Twentieth Century-Fox. With Victor Mature,

Susan Hayward, Michael Rennie, Debra Paget, Anne Bancroft, Jay Robinson, Barry Jones, William Marshall, Richard Egan, Ernest Borgnine.

Gorilla at Large. 1954. Director: Harmon Jones. Writers: Leonard Praskins, Barney Slater. Producer: Robert L. Jacks for Panoramic Productions. Released by Twentieth Century-Fox. With Cameron Mitchell, Anne Bancroft, Lee J. Cobb, Raymond Burr, Charlotte Austin, Peter Whitney, Lee Marvin, Warren Stevens.

The Raid. 1954. Director: Hugo Fregonese. Writer: Sydney Boehm, from a story by Francis Cockrell based on a novel by Herbert Ravenel. Producer: Robert L. Jacks for Panoramic Productions. Released by Twentieth Century-Fox. With Van Heflin, Anne Bancroft, Richard Boone, Lee Marvin, Tommy Rettig, Peter Graves, Douglas Spencer.

A Life in the Balance. 1955. Directors: Harry Horner and Rafael Portillo. Writers: Robert Presnell Jr. and Leo Townsend, from a story by Georges Simenon. Producer: Leonard Goldstein for Tele-Voz S.A. and Panoramic Productions. Released by Twentieth Century-Fox. With Ricardo Montalbán, Anne Bancroft, Lee Marvin, José Pérez, Rodolfo Acosta, Carlos Múzquiz.

New York Confidential. 1955. Director: Russell Rouse. Writers: Clarence Greene and Russell Rouse, suggested by the book by Jack Lait and Lee Mortimer. Producers: Clarence Greene and Edward Small for Challenge Pictures. Released by Warner Bros. With Broderick Crawford, Richard Conte, Marilyn Maxwell, Anne Bancroft, J. Carrol Naish, Onslow Stevens, Barry Kelley, Mike Mazurki.

The Naked Street. 1955. Director: Maxwell Shane. Writers: Maxwell Shane and Leo Katcher, from a story by Leo Katcher. Producer: Edward Small for Fame Productions. Released by United Artists. With Farley Granger, Anthony Quinn, Anne Bancroft, Peter Graves, Else Back, Sara Berner, Jerry Paris.

The Last Frontier. 1955. Director: Anthony Mann. Writers: Philip Yordan and Russell S. Hughes, from a novel by Richard Emery Roberts. Producer: William Fadiman. Released by Columbia Pictures. With Victor Mature,

Guy Madison, Robert Preston, James Whitmore, Anne Bancroft, Russell Collins, Peter Whitney, Pat Hogan.

Walk the Proud Land. 1956. Director: Jesse Hibbs. Writers: Gil Goud and Jack Sher, based on a book by Woodworth Clum. Producer: Aaron Rosenberg. Released by Universal-International. With Audie Murphy, Anne Bancroft, Pat Crowley, Charles Drake, Tommy Rall, Robert Warwick, Jay Silverheels, Eugene Mazzola, Anthony Caruso.

Nightfall. 1956. Director: Jacques Tourneur. Writer: Stirling Silliphant, from a novel by David Goodis. Producer: Ted Richmond for Copa Productions. Released by Columbia Pictures. With Aldo Ray, Brian Keith, Anne Bancroft, Jocelyn Brando, James Gregory, Frank Albertson, Rudy Bond.

The Restless Breed. 1957. Director: Allan Dwan. Writer: Steve Fisher. Producer: Edward L. Alperson for Edward L. Alperson Productions. Released by Twentieth Century-Fox. With Anne Bancroft, Scott Brady, Billy Miller, Leo Gordon, Jay C. Flippen, Marilyn Winston, Scott Marlowe, Rhys Williams, Marty Cariosa, Evelyn Rudie.

The Girl in Black Stockings. 1957. Director: Howard W. Koch. Writer: Richard Landau, from a story by Peter Godfrey. Producer: Aubrey Schenck for Bel-Air Productions. Released by United Artists. With Lex Barker, Anne Bancroft, Mamie Van Doren, Ron Randell, Marie Windsor, John Dehner, John Holland.

The Miracle Worker. 1962. Director: Arthur Penn. Writer: William Gibson, based on his play. Producer: Fred Coe for Playfilm Productions. Released by United Artists. With Anne Bancroft, Patty Duke, Victor Jory, Inga Swenson, Andrew Prine, Kathleen Comegys.

The Pumpkin Eater. 1964. Director: Jack Clayton. Writer: Harold Pinter, from a novel by Penelope Mortimer. Producer: James Woolf for Romulus Films. Released by Columbia Pictures. With Anne Bancroft, Peter Finch, James Mason, Janine Gray, Cedric Hardwicke, Rosalind Atkinson, Alan Webb, Richard Johnson, Maggie Smith, Eric Porter.

The Slender Thread. 1965. Director: Sydney Pollack. Writer: Stirling Silliphant, from an article by Shana Alexander. Producer: Stephen Alexander for Athene Productions. Released by Paramount Pictures. With Sidney Poitier, Anne Bancroft, Telly Savalas, Steven Hill, Edward Asner, Indus Arthur, Paul Newlan, Dabney Coleman.

7 Women. 1966. Director: John Ford. Writers: Janet Green and John McCormick, from a story by Norah Lofts. Producers: Bernard Smith and John Ford for Bernard Smith Productions and John Ford Productions. Released by MGM. With Anne Bancroft, Sue Lyon, Margaret Leighton, Flora Robson, Mildred Dunnock, Betty Field, Anna Lee, Eddie Albert, Mike Mazurki, Woody Strode.

The Graduate. 1967. Director: Mike Nichols. Writers: Calder Willingham and Buck Henry, from a novel by Charles Webb. Producers: Lawrence Turman for a Mike Nichols/Lawrence Turman Production. Released by Embassy Pictures. With Anne Bancroft, Dustin Hoffman, Katharine Ross, William Daniels, Murray Hamilton, Elizabeth Wilson, Buck Henry.

Young Winston. 1972. Director: Richard Attenborough. Writer: Carl Foreman, based on a memoir by Winston Churchill. Producer: Carl Foreman for an Open Road–Hugh French presentation. Released by Columbia Pictures. With Simon Ward, Anne Bancroft, Robert Shaw, Jack Hawkins, Ian Holm, Anthony Hopkins, Patrick Magee, Edward Woodward, John Mills.

The Prisoner of Second Avenue. 1975. Director: Melvin Frank. Writer: Neil Simon, based on his play. Producer: Melvin Frank. Released by Warner Bros. With Jack Lemmon, Anne Bancroft, Gene Saks, Elizabeth Wilson, Florence Stanley, Maxine Stuart, Ed Peck.

The Hindenburg. 1975. Director: Robert Wise. Writer: Nelson Gidding, from a screen story by Richard Levinson and William Link, from a book by Michael M. Mooney. Producer: Robert Wise. Released by Universal Pictures. With George C. Scott, Anne Bancroft, William Atherton, Roy Thinnes, Gig Young, Burgess Meredith, Charles Durning, Richard Dysart, Robert Clary, René Auberjonois, Peter Donat, Colby Chester.

Lipstick. 1976. Director: Lamont Johnson. Writer: David Rayfiel. Producer:

Freddie Fields for Dino De Laurentiis Co. Released by Paramount Pictures. With Margaux Hemingway, Chris Sarandon, Perry King, Anne Bancroft, Mariel Hemingway, Robin Gammel, John Bennett Perry.

Silent Movie. 1976. Director: Mel Brooks. Writers: Mel Brooks, Ron Clark, Rudy De Luca, and Barry Levinson, from a story by Ron Clark. Producer: Michael Hertzberg for Crossbow Productions. Released by Twentieth Century-Fox. With Mel Brooks, Marty Feldman, Dom DeLuise, Sid Caesar, Harold Gould, Ron Carey, Bernadette Peters, Burt Reynolds, James Caan, Liza Minnelli, Anne Bancroft, Marcel Marceau, Paul Newman.

The Turning Point. 1977. Director: Herbert Ross. Writer: Arthur Laurents. Producers: Arthur Laurents and Herb Ross for Hera Productions. Released by Twentieth Century-Fox. With Anne Bancroft, Shirley MacLaine, Tom Skerritt, Mikhail Baryshnikov, Leslie Browne, Martha Scott.

Fatso. 1980. Director: Anne Bancroft. Writer: Anne Bancroft. Producer: Stuart Cornfeld for Brooksfilms. Released by Twentieth Century-Fox. With Dom DeLuise, Anne Bancroft, Ron Carey, Candice Azzara, Michael Lombard, Sal Viscuso, Delia Salvi, Robert Costanzo, Estelle Reiner.

The Elephant Man. 1980. Director: David Lynch. Writers: Christopher De Vore, Eric Bergren, and David Lynch, from books by Frederick Treves and Ashley Montagu. Producer: Jonathan Sanger for Brooksfilms. Released by Paramount Pictures. With Anthony Hopkins, John Hurt, Anne Bancroft, John Gielgud, Wendy Hiller, Freddie Jones.

To Be or Not to Be. 1983. Director: Alan Johnson. Writers: Thomas Meehan and Ronny Graham, based on a screenplay by Edwin Justus Mayer. Producer: Mel Brooks for Brooksfilms. Released by Twentieth Century-Fox. With Mel Brooks, Anne Bancroft, Charles Durning, José Ferrer, Tim Matheson, Jack Riley, Ronny Graham, Lewis J. Stadlen, George Gaynes, George Wyner, Christopher Lloyd, Estelle Reiner.

Garbo Talks. 1984. Director: Sidney Lumet. Writer: Larry Grusin. Producers: Burtt Harris and Elliott Kastner. Released by MGM/UA. With Anne Bancroft, Ron Silver, Carrie Fisher, Catherine Hicks, Steven Hill, Howard Da Silva, Dorothy Loudon, Harvey Fierstein, Hermione Gingold.

Agnes of God. 1985. Director: Norman Jewison. Writer: John Pielmeier, from his play. Producers: Norman Jewison and Patrick Palmer for Columbia Pictures and Delphi IV Productions. Released by Columbia Pictures. With Jane Fonda, Anne Bancroft, Meg Tilly, Anne Pitoniak, Winston Rekert, Gratien Gélinas, Guy Hoffman, Gabriel Arcand.

'night, Mother. 1986. Director: Tom Moore. Writer: Marsha Norman, from her play. Producers: Alan Greisman and Aaron Spelling for Aaron Spelling Productions. Released by Universal Pictures. With Sissy Spacek, Anne Bancroft.

84 Charing Cross Road. 1987. Director: David Jones. Writer: Hugh Whitemore, from a book by Helene Hanff and a play by James Roose-Evans. Producer: Geoffrey Helman for Brooksfilms. Released by Columbia Pictures. With Anne Bancroft, Anthony Hopkins, Judi Dench, Jean De Baer, Maurice Denham, Eleanor David, Mercedes Ruehl, Daniel Gerroll.

Torch Song Trilogy. 1988. Director: Paul Bogart. Writer: Harvey Fierstein, from his play. Producer: Howard Gottfried for Howard Gottfried/Ronald K. Fierstein Production. Released by New Line Cinema. With Harvey Fierstein, Matthew Broderick, Anne Bancroft, Brian Kerwin, Karen Young.

Bert Rigby, You're a Fool. 1989. Director: Carl Reiner. Writer: Carl Reiner. Producer: George Shapiro for Clear Productions and Lorimar Film Entertainment. Released by Warner Bros. With Robert Lindsay, Robbie Coltrane, Cathryn Bradshaw, Jackie Gayle, Bruno Kirby, Corbin Bernsen, Anne Bancroft.

Honeymoon in Vegas. 1992. Director: Andrew Bergman. Writer: Andrew Bergman. Producer: Mike Lobell for Castle Rock Entertainment and New Line Cinema. Released by Columbia Pictures. With Nicolas Cage, James Caan, Sarah Jessica Parker, Pat Morita, Johnny Williams, John Capodice, Robert Costanzo, Peter Boyle. Cameo: Anne Bancroft.

Love Potion No. 9. 1992. Director: Dale Launer. Writer: Dale Launer. Producer: Dale Launer for Penta Pictures. Released by 20th Century Fox. With Tate Donovan, Sandra Bullock, Mary Mara, Dale Midkiff, Hillary B. Smith, Anne Bancroft, Dylan Baker, Blake Clark, Bruce McCarty.

Point of No Return. 1993. Director: John Badham. Writers: Robert Getchell and Alexandra Seros, based on a film by Luc Besson. Producer: Art Linson. Released by Warner Bros. With Bridget Fonda, Gabriel Byrne, Dermot Mulroney, Miguel Ferrer, Anne Bancroft, Olivia d'Abo, Richard Romanus, Harvey Keitel.

Malice. 1993. Director: Harold Becker. Writers: Aaron Sorkin and Scott Frank, from a story by Aaron Sorkin and Jonas McCord. Producers: Harold Becker, Charles Mulvehill, and Rachel Pfeffer for Castle Rock Entertainment and New Line Cinema. Released by Columbia Pictures. With Alec Baldwin, Nicole Kidman, Bill Pullman, Bebe Neuwirth, George C. Scott, Anne Bancroft, Peter Gallagher, Josef Sommer, Tobin Bell.

Mr. Jones. 1993. Director: Mike Figgis. Writers: Eric Roth and Michael Cristofer, from a story by Eric Roth. Producers: Debra Greenfield and Alan Greisman for Rastar Productions. Released by TriStar Pictures. With Richard Gere, Lena Olin, Anne Bancroft, Tom Irwin, Delroy Lindo, Bruce Altman, Lauren Tom.

How to Make an American Quilt. 1995. Director: Jocelyn Moorhouse. Writer: Jane Anderson, based on a book by Whitney Otto. Producers: Sarah Pillsbury and Midge Sanford for Amblin Entertainment. Released by Universal Pictures. With Winona Ryder, Ellen Burstyn, Anne Bancroft, Jean Simmons, Dermot Mulroney, Claire Danes, Maya Angelou, Alfre Woodard, Lois Smith, Kate Nelligan, Kate Capshaw, Rip Torn, Jared Leto, Adam Baldwin.

Home for the Holidays. 1995. Director: Jodie Foster. Writer: W. D. Richter, from a short story by Chris Radant. Producers: Jodie Foster and Peggy Rajski for PolyGram Filmed Entertainment and Egg Pictures. Released by Paramount Pictures. With Holly Hunter, Robert Downey Jr., Anne Bancroft, Charles Durning, Dylan McDermott, Geraldine Chaplin, Steve Guttenberg, Cynthia Stevenson, Claire Danes, Emily Ann Lloyd, Zack Duhame, Austin Pendleton, David Strathairn.

Dracula: Dead and Loving It. 1995. Director: Mel Brooks. Writers: Mel Brooks, Rudy De Luca, and Steve Haberman from a story by Rudy De Luca and Steve Haberman. Producer: Mel Brooks for Brooksfilms.

Released by Gaumont and Castle Rock Entertainment. With Leslie Nielsen, Peter MacNicol, Steven Weber, Amy Yasbeck, Lysette Anthony, Harvey Korman, Mel Brooks. Cameo: Anne Bancroft.

Sunchaser. 1996. Director: Michael Cimino. Writer: Charles Leavitt. Producers: Michael Cimino, Judy Goldstein, Arnon Milchan, Larry Spiegel, Joseph S. Vecchio for Appledown Films Inc., Joseph S. Vecchio Entertainment, Monarchy Enterprises B.V., Regency Enterprises, Regency Entertainment, Vecchia. Released by Warner Bros. With Woody Harrelson, Jon Seda, Anne Bancroft, Alexandra Tydings, Matt Mulhern, Talisa Soto, Richard Bauer.

G.I. Jane. 1997. Director: Ridley Scott. Writers: David Twohy and Danielle Alexandra, from a story by Danielle Alexandra. Producers: Roger Birnbaum, Demi Moore, Ridley Scott, and Suzanne Todd for Caravan Pictures, First Independent Films, Hollywood Pictures, Largo Entertainment, Moving Pictures, Scott Free Productions, and Trap-Two-Zero Productions Inc. Released by Buena Vista Pictures. With Demi Moore, Viggo Mortensen, Anne Bancroft, Jason Beghe, Daniel von Bargen, John Michael Higgins, Kevin Gage, David Warshofsky, David Vadim.

Critical Care. 1997. Director: Sidney Lumet. Writer: Steven Schwartz, from a novel by Richard Dooling. Producers: Sidney Lumet and Steven Schwartz for ASQA Film Partnership, Live Entertainment, Mediaworks, and Village Roadshow Pictures. Released by Avid Home Entertainment. With James Spader, Kyra Sedgwick, Helen Mirren, Anne Bancroft, Albert Brooks, Jeffrey Wright, Margo Martindale, Wallace Shawn, Philip Bosco, Colm Feore, Edward Herrmann.

Great Expectations. 1998. Director: Alfonso Cuarón. Writer: Mitch Glazer, based on the novel by Charles Dickens. Producer: Art Linson. Released by 20th Century-Fox. With Ethan Hawke, Gwyneth Paltrow, Hank Azaria, Chris Cooper, Anne Bancroft, Robert De Niro, Josh Mostel, Kim Dickens, Nell Campbell.

Antz. 1998. Directors: Eric Darnell and Tim Johnson. Writers: Todd Alcott, Chris Weitz, and Paul Weitz. Producers: Brad Lewis, Aron Warner, and Patty Wooton for DreamWorks Animation. Released by DreamWorks

Distribution. With Woody Allen, Dan Aykroyd, Anne Bancroft, Jane Curtin, Danny Glover, Gene Hackman, Jennifer Lopez, John Mahoney, Paul Mazursky, Sylvester Stallone, Sharon Stone, Christopher Walken.

Up at the Villa. 2000. Director: Philip Haas. Writer: Belinda Haas, based on a book by W. Somerset Maugham. Producer: Geoff Stier for October Films, Intermedia Films, and Mirage Enterprises. Released by USA Films. With Kristin Scott Thomas, Sean Penn, Anne Bancroft, James Fox, Jeremy Davies, Derek Jacobi.

Keeping the Faith. 2000. Director: Edward Norton. Writer: Stuart Blumberg. Producers: Stuart Blumberg, Hawk Koch, and Edward Norton for Spyglass Entertainment, Touchstone Pictures, and Triple Threat Talent. Released by Buena Vista Pictures. With Ben Stiller, Edward Norton, Jenna Elfman, Anne Bancroft, Eli Wallach, Ron Rifkin, Milos Forman, Holland Taylor, Lisa Edelstein, Rena Sofer.

Heartbreakers. 2001. Director: David Mirkin. Writers: Robert Dunn, Paul Guay, and Stephen Mazur. Producer: John Davis and Irving Ong for Davis Entertainment. Released by MGM. With Sigourney Weaver, Jennifer Love Hewitt, Ray Liotta, Jason Lee, Anne Bancroft, Jeffrey Jones, Gene Hackman, Nora Dunn.

Delgo. 2008. Directors: Marc F. Adler and Jason Maurer. Writers: Patrick J. Cowan, Carl Dream, and Jennifer A. Jones, from a story by Marc F. Adler, Scott Biear, and Jason Maurer. Producer: Marc F. Adler for Electric Eye Entertainment and Fathom Studios. Released by Freestyle Releasing. With Freddie Prinze Jr., Chris Kazan, Jennifer Love Hewitt, Anne Bancroft, Val Kilmer, Malcolm McDowell, Michael Clarke Duncan, Louis Gossett Jr., Eric Idle, Burt Reynolds, Kelly Ripa, Sally Kellerman.

Television

Studio One. "Torrents of Spring." April 17, 1950. CBS. 60 minutes. Director: Franklin J. Schaffner. With Louise Allbritton, John Baragrey, Anne Marno (Anne Bancroft).

Studio One. "The Man Who Had Influence." May 29, 1950. CBS. 60 minutes. Director: Franklin J. Schaffner. With Stanley Ridges, Robert Sterling, King Calder, Robert Pastene, Julian Noa, Frank McNellis, Anne Marno (Anne Bancroft).

The Goldbergs. "The Mother-in-Law." October 15, 1950. CBS. 30 minutes. Director: N/A. With Gertrude Berg, Eli Mintz, Arlene McQuade, Philip Loeb. Anne Marno (Anne Bancroft) plays a newlywed neighbor.

Studio One. "Letter from Cairo." December 4, 1950. CBS. 60 minutes. Director: Lela Swift. With Charlton Heston, Anne Marno (Anne Bancroft), Annette Erianger, Dean Harens, Gloria Stroock, Cecil Parker.

Lux Video Theatre. "A Child Is Born." December 25, 1950. CBS. 30 minutes. Director: Fielder Cook. With Fay Bainter, Gene Lockhart, Alan Shayne, Anne Marno (Anne Bancroft).

Suspense. "Night Break." February 6, 1951. CBS. 30 minutes. Director: N/A. With Anne Marno (Anne Bancroft), E. G. Marshall.

Ford Theatre Hour. "The Golden Mouth." February 23, 1951. CBS. 60 minutes. Director: Franklin J. Schaffner. With John Forsythe, Anne Marno (Anne Bancroft), Henry Hull, Gerald Mohr.

Studio One. "Wintertime." April 2, 1951. CBS. 60 minutes. Director: Paul Nickell. With Patric Knowles, Anne Marno (Anne Bancroft), Dennis Patrick, Leni Stengel.

Danger. "The Killer Scarf." May 1, 1951. CBS. 30 minutes. Director: N/A. With Anne Marno (Anne Bancroft), Gregory Morton.

The Adventures of Ellery Queen. "The Chinese Mummer Mystery." May 10, 1951. DuMont. 30 minutes. Director: N/A. With Lee Bowman, Anne Marno (Anne Bancroft).

The Goldbergs. Title N/A. May 14, 1951. CBS. 30 minutes. Director: N/A. With Gertrude Berg, Eli Mintz, Arlene McQuade, Philip Loeb. Anne Marno (Anne Bancroft) returns as a newlywed neighbor.

Kraft Television Theatre. "Stranglehold." June 13, 1951. NBC. 60 minutes. Director: N/A. With Gene Lyons, Enid Markey, Marilyn Monk, Anne Marno (Anne Bancroft).

Suspense. "A Vision of Death." July 31, 1951. CBS. 30 minutes. Director: N/A. With Jerome Cowman, Henry Hull, Anne Marno (Anne Bancroft).

Danger. "Murderer's Face." August 14, 1951. CBS. 30 minutes. Director: N/A. With Anne Marno (Anne Bancroft), Robert Pastene.

Big Town. "Comeback." September 6, 1951. CBS. 30 minutes. Production information not available.

Armstrong Circle Theatre. "Flame-Out." September 18, 1951. NBC. 30 minutes. Director: N/A. With Anne Marno (Anne Bancroft), Leslie Nielsen, Stephen L. Christian, Robert Baines.

The Web. "The Customs of the Country." September 26, 1951. CBS. 30 minutes. Director: N/A. With Joseph Anthony, Anne Marno (Anne Bancroft), Peter Cookson, Gene Gross.

Lights Out. "The Deal." October 22, 1951. NBC. 30 minutes. Director: Laurence Schwab Jr. With Tom Ewell, Joseph Wiseman, Anne Bancroft, Martin Gabel.

Omnibus. "The Capital of the World." December 6, 1953. CBS. 60 minutes. Director: Yul Brynner. With Anne Bancroft, Sal Mineo, John Marley, Mario Gallo, Leslie Nielson.

Kraft Television Theatre. "To Live in Peace." December 16, 1953. NBC. 60 minutes. Director: Harry Herrmann. With Anne Bancroft, Ray Danton, Florenz Ames, Fred Stewart.

Lux Video Theatre. "A Medal for Benny." November 25, 1954. NBC. 60 minutes. Director: Buzz Kulik. With Anne Bancroft, Selmer Jackson, Rick Jason, J. Carrol Naish, Jay Novello, Nestor Paiva, George Chandler, Ralph Dumke, Byron Foulger.

Your Favorite Story. "The Waltz." December 26, 1954. Syndicated. 30 minutes. Director: Peter Godfrey. With Anne Bancroft, Peter Graves, Warren Stevens, Dabbs Greer.

Lux Video Theatre. "Forever Female." June 23, 1955. NBC. 60 minutes. Director: Buzz Kulik. With Anne Bancroft, Fred Clark, Anita Louise, Jeanette Miller, Maidie Norman.

Lux Video Theatre. "Hired Wife." February 23, 1956. NBC. 60 minutes. Director: Earl Eby. With Anne Bancroft, Lex Barker, Joseph Kearns, Alexander Campbell.

Lux Video Theatre. "The Corrigan Case." June 21, 1956. NBC. 60 minutes. Director: James P. Yarbrough. With Anne Bancroft, Steve Brodie, Mae Clarke, Virginia Vincent, Charles Davis, Ann Baker, Frances Bavier.

Climax! "Fear Is the Hunter." July 12, 1956. CBS. 60 minutes. Director: Buzz Kulik. With Anne Bancroft, Steve Cochran, Chuck Connors, Albert Dekker, Philip Coolidge.

The Alcoa Hour. "Key Largo." October 14, 1956. NBC. 60 minutes. Director: Alex Segal. With Anne Bancroft, Alfred Drake, Victor Jory, John Marley, J. Carrol Naish, Lorne Greene.

Playhouse 90. "So Soon to Die." January 17, 1957. CBS. 90 minutes. Director: John Brahm. With Richard Basehart, Anne Bancroft, Sebastian Cabot, Torin Thatcher.

Playhouse 90. "Invitation to a Gunfighter." March 7, 1957. CBS. 90 minutes. Director: Arthur Penn. With Hugh O'Brian, Anne Bancroft, Gilbert Roland, Pat O'Brien, Ray Collins, Milton Parsons.

Lux Video Theatre. "The Black Angel." March 28, 1957. NBC. 60 minutes. Director: Norman Morgan. With Anne Bancroft, Gordon MacRae, John Ireland, Lyle Talbot, H. M. Wynant, Naomi Stevens, Burt Mustin.

Climax! "The Mad Bomber." April 18, 1957. CBS. 60 minutes. Director:

Buzz Kulik. With Anne Bancroft, Dane Clark, Jim Backus, Theodore Bikel, Estelle Winwood.

The Alcoa Hour. "Hostages to Fortune." July 7, 1957. NBC. 60 minutes. Director: John H. Secondari. With Anne Bancroft, Rip Torn, Charles Cooper, Joe De Santis, Charles Korvin, Harold Vermilyea.

Zane Grey Theater. "Episode in Darkness." November 15, 1957. CBS. 30 minutes. Director: John English. With Anne Bancroft, Dewey Martin, Phillip Pine, John Anderson.

The Frank Sinatra Show. "A Time to Cry." February 21, 1958. ABC. 30 minutes. Director: N/A. With Anne Bancroft, Lloyd Bridges, Ray Teal, John Archer.

Bob Hope Presents the Chrysler Theatre. "Out on the Outskirts of Town." November 6, 1964. NBC. 60 minutes. Director: Frank Corsaro, from a script by William Inge. With Anne Bancroft, Jack Warden, Fay Bainter, Lane Bradbury, Paul Fix, Tom Holland, Meg Wyllie.

ABC Stage 67. "I'm Getting Married." March 16, 1967. ABC. 60 minutes. Director: Gerald Freedman, from a script by Betty Comden and Adolph Green. With Anne Bancroft and Dick Shawn.

Annie, the Women in the Life of a Man. Special. February 18, 1970. CBS. 60 minutes. Director: Walter C. Miller. With Anne Bancroft, Mel Brooks, Jack Cassidy, Lee J. Cobb, John McGiver, Robert Merrill, Arthur Murray, Dick Shawn, Dick Smothers, David Suskind.

Annie and the Hoods. Special. November 27, 1974. CBS. 60 minutes. Director: Martin Charnin. With Anne Bancroft, Alan Alda, Jack Benny, Mel Brooks, Tony Curtis, David Merrick, Robert Merrill, Carl Reiner, Gene Wilder.

Jesus of Nazareth. Two-part miniseries. April 3 and 10, 1977. NBC. Six hours. Director: Franco Zeffirelli. With Robert Powell, Anne Bancroft, Ernest Borgnine, Claudia Cardinale, Valentina Cortese, James Farentino,

James Earl Jones, Ian McShane, Donald Pleasence, Christopher Plummer, Fernando Rey, Ralph Richardson, Peter Ustinov, Michael York, Olivia Hussey, Cyril Cusack, Ian Bannen, Ian Holm, James Mason, Laurence Olivier, Anthony Quinn, Rod Steiger.

Marco Polo. Four-part miniseries. Premiered May 16, 1982. NBC. Ten hours. Director: Giuliano Montaldo. With Ken Marshall, Denholm Elliott, Tony Vogel, David Warner, F. Murray Abraham, Leonard Nimoy, and guest stars Anne Bancroft, Burt Lancaster, John Gielgud, John Houseman.

Freddie and Max. Six-episode sitcom. 1990. Thames Television. 30 minutes. Director: John Stroud. With Anne Bancroft, Charlotte Coleman, Ian Congdon, Richard Pearson, Flaminia Cinque.

Broadway Bound. TV movie. March 23, 1992. ABC. Two hours. Director: Paul Bogart, from a script by Neil Simon. With Anne Bancroft, Hume Cronyn, Corey Parker, Jonathan Silverman, Jerry Orbach, Michele Lee, Marilyn Cooper, Pat McCormick, Jack Carter.

American Playhouse. Mrs. Cage. May 20, 1992. PBS. 68 minutes. Director: Robert Allan Ackerman. With Anne Bancroft and Hector Elizondo.

Oldest Living Confederate Widow Tells All. TV miniseries. May 1 and 3, 1994. CBS. Four hours. Director: Ken Cameron. With Diane Lane, Donald Sutherland, Cicely Tyson, Anne Bancroft, Blythe Danner, E. G. Marshall, Gwen Verdon.

Great Performances. "Paddy Chayefsky's 'The Mother.'" October 24, 1994. PBS. 60 minutes. Director: Simon Curtis. With Anne Bancroft, Joan Cusack, Stephen Lang, Katherine Borowitz, Adrian Pasdar, Mary Alice.

The Simpsons. "Fear of Flying." December 18, 1994. Fox. 30 minutes. Director: Mark Kirkland. With guest stars Anne Bancroft, Ted Danson, Woody Harrelson, Rhea Perlman, John Ratzenberger, George Wendt, Pamela Hayden.

Homecoming. TV movie. April 14, 1996. Showtime. One hour, 45 minutes.

Director: Mark Jean. With Anne Bancroft, Kimberlee Peterson, Trever O'Brien, Hanna Hall, William Greenblatt, Bonnie Bedelia.

Deep in My Heart. TV movie. February 14, 1999. CBS. Two hours. Director: Anita W. Addison. With Anne Bancroft, Lynn Whitfield, Alice Krige, Cara Buono, Gloria Reuben, Jesse L. Martin, Kevin O'Rourke, Peter MacNeill.

Haven. Two-part miniseries. February 11 and 14, 2001. CBS. Four hours. Director: John Gray. With Natasha Richardson, Colm Feore, Henry Czerny, Sheila McCarthy, Sebastian Roche, Robert Joy, Tama Gorski, Daniel Kash, William Petersen, Hal Holbrook, Martin Landau, Bruce Greenwood, Anne Bancroft, Kenneth Welsh.

The Roman Spring of Mrs. Stone. TV movie. May 4, 2003. Showtime. Two hours. Director: Robert Allan Ackerman. With Helen Mirren, Olivier Martinez, Anne Bancroft, Rodrigo Santoro, Brian Dennehy.

Curb Your Enthusiasm. "Opening Night." March 14, 2004. HBO. 30 minutes. Director: Robert B. Weide. With guest stars Anne Bancroft and Mel Brooks as themselves.

Author's note: Not all Anne Bancroft's appearances as Anne Marno were cited in television listings or other contemporaneous sources, which makes a complete account of her early television work impossible. This list does not include her appearances on documentaries, talk shows, game shows, news programs, and awards shows.

Notes

1. The Girl from St. Raymond Avenue

1 "I wanted to see how it felt" (Funke and Booth, *Actors Talk about Acting II,* 204). Bancroft's blind rollercoaster ride is also described in the opening of the article "Who Is Stanislavsky?" *Time,* December 21, 1959.

2 "I didn't know what he meant at first" (Funke and Booth, *Actors Talk about Acting II,* 205).

2 "Whatever it was in me" (Bancroft to Prairie Miller, Rotten Tomatoes, March 24, 2001).

3 "the best actress on Broadway" (*New York Daily News,* October 20, 1959).

3 "She may not be the most beautiful woman" (*Saturday Evening Post,* December 9, 1961).

3 "She was quick to anger" (Robert Allan Ackerman, interview by author, January 18, 2016).

3 "Know what creates a miracle?" (*Los Angeles Times,* May 19, 1962).

4 "In America you speak English" (JoAnne Italiano Perna, interviews by author, April 15, 2014, and March 1, 2015).

5 "They were a typical Italian family" (Father Antimo Fiorillo, interview by author, December 11, 2013).

6 "No one had to coax" (*New York Times,* February 9, 1958).

6 "When I was a kid" (*Boston Globe,* November 27, 1960).

6 "The neighbors used to take me" (*New York Times,* February 9, 1958).

7 "When life bothers you" (Perna interview).

7 "My mother is the fire" (*New York Times,* February 9, 1958).

7 "Whenever I couldn't find her" (*McCall's,* May 1962).

7 "Momma, I could do that" (ibid.).

7 "Born with the veil" (Perna interview).

8 "I want to be an actress" (*Time,* December 21, 1959).

8 "Mr. McGiver gave us a brief description" (Richard Monaco, interview by author, January 25, 2014).

9 "We would stop and ask him" (ibid.).

9 "Anne and I had our first boy-girl kiss" (David Lunney, interview by author, January 12, 2014).

9   "Dick, next time, make believe you kiss my cheek" (Monaco interview).

9   "We couldn't walk down the halls" (ibid.).

9   "I wasn't any good" (*Los Angeles Examiner*, March 6, 1955).

10 "That was a drama club thing" (Dale Brown, interview by author, January 21, 2014).

10 "Until my teens" (*Baltimore Sun*, May 26, 1966).

10 "Did I act?" (*Northeast Woman Sunday Times*, December 25, 1983).

10 "She brought down the house" (Lunney interview).

10 "It was the introduction of the Dior New Look" (ibid.).

11 "She had become rather elegant" (Brown interview).

11 "Anne was so beautiful" (Grace Milo Rosa, interview by author, December 27, 2013).

11 "Our drama club clique" (Monaco interview).

11 "If I were doing a play" (Elisa Coletti Goldberg, interview by author, December 28, 2013).

12 "She gave us a show" (ibid.).

12 "I was young" (ibid.).

12 "She was pissed" (Lunney interview.

12 "I squelched ambition" (*Los Angeles Times*, May 19, 1962).

12 "I'll show them" (Lunney interview).

12 "Everything that she did in school" (Monaco interview).

13 "Some dreams, some pipe dreams" (*Viva*, December 1973).

13 "The dream, the theater, is what she wanted" (*Los Angeles Times*, October 14, 1984).

14 "Very pretty" (American Academy of Dramatic Arts booklet [hereafter cited as AADA booklet] commemorating Anne Bancroft, 2007).

14 "Anne has a good combination" (ibid.).

14 "Since the studio was basically for news" (Monaco interview).

15 "We hated Hollywood" (Carney, *Cassavetes on Cassavetes*, 15).

15 "Crude, but there are possibilities" (*New York Times*, July 30, 1952).

15 "The only compliment I ever heard" (Harry Mastrogeorge, interview by author, January 26, 2014).

15 "Absolutely none" (ibid.).

15 "the greatest teacher" (Carney, *Cassavetes on Cassavetes*, 16).

15 "Our little cadre wasn't like that" (Mastrogeorge interview).

16 "She had such a healthy" (ibid.).

16 "She forced me to come on Sunday" (ibid.).

16 "We would always be in rehearsal" (ibid.).

16 "I sat there and thought" (ibid.).

17 "It was the greatest school" (AADA booklet, 2007).

17 "I had no money for malteds" (*Time*, December 21, 1959).

2. Television Nights and Hollywood Days

18   "Television in the early fifties" (Miner, *Worthington Miner*, 2).

19   "Live television was the closest thing" (Kisseloff, *The Box*, 234).

19   "the most exciting television" (*New York Times*, March 13, 1949).

20   "They move four cameras" (typescript dated April 13, 1953, Bancroft files, Herrick Library, Academy of Motion Picture Arts and Sciences [hereafter cited as AMPAS]).

20   "For me, it's opening night" (*Washington Post*, May 3, 1950).

20   "Welcome Home—The Star" (*Cosmopolitan*, February 1960).

20   "Anne had fantastic vitality" (*Saturday Evening Post*, December 9, 1961).

21   "There was a little bit of tension" (Lunney interview).

22   "She had a warm voice" (*Yoo-hoo, Mrs. Goldberg!* 2009 [DVD]).

23   "They'd been around with each other" (Lunney interview).

24   "an engaging chapter" (*Boston Globe*, May 15, 1951).

24   "refreshing" (*Billboard*, May 12, 1951).

24   "Well-rehearsed and well-acted" (*Boston Globe*, June 14, 1951).

24   "She came in and we, meaning me and my agent" (Doug Rogers, interview by author, April 30, 2014).

25   "I didn't even know" (*Los Angeles Times*, October 14, 1984).

25   "In the editing of it" (Rogers interview).

26   "Twentieth Century-Fox on this side" (Funke and Booth, *Actors Talk about Acting II*, 197).

26   "It was the most thrilling thing" (*Northeast Woman Sunday Times*, December 25, 1983).

27   "Where are the subways?" (production notes for *Don't Bother to Knock*, AMPAS).

27   "Bancroft was the only name" (*Los Angeles Times*, May 18, 1958).

28   "I couldn't have reached" (*Los Angeles Times*, July 26, 1953).

29   "We had a hell of a time" (Spoto, *Marilyn Monroe*, 198).

29   "I found that Richard Widmark" (undated typescript, Gould Papers, AMPAS).

30   "She was a revelation" (Dixon, *Collected Interviews*, 146).

30   "Another bonus for her" (Baker, *Director's Cut*, 73).

30   "Come on, will ya" (Dixon, *Collected Interviews*, 146).

30   "except to give it its stupid title" (Baker, *Director's Cut*, 66).

30   "She was good news" (ibid., 73).

30   "lands a Sunday punch" (*Los Angeles Times*, July 31, 1952).

30   "scores brightly" (*Variety*, July 9, 1952).

30   "We all went to see it" (Rosa interview).

31 "Although she looks" (production notes for *Treasure of the Golden Condor,* AMPAS).

31 "He was always urging me" (undated typescript, Gould Papers, AMPAS).

32 "Miss Bancroft comes over effectively" (*Hollywood Reporter,* January 16, 1953).

32 "the tastiest corn in a blue moon" (*New York Times,* May 23, 1953).

33 "opulent, star-spangled, two-hour film concert" (*Time,* March 2, 1953).

33 "A magnificent piece of entertainment" (*Hollywood Reporter,* January 26, 1953).

33 "impresses favorably (*Variety,* January 26, 1953).

33 "a Technicolored musical extravaganza" (*Newsweek,* February 23, 1953).

34 "They make you look so wonderful" (undated typescript, Gould Papers, AMPAS).

34 "The script said 'Laugh'" (*TV Guide,* November 23, 1974).

34 "It never occurred to me" (*Family Weekly,* March 31, 1968).

34 "I had no desire to be anything more" (*Boston Globe,* July 7, 1969).

3. Stuck in a Low-Budget Rut

35 "one of television's loveliest" (*Variety,* June 8, 1953).

35 "Hollywood was the ideal place" (*Baltimore Sun,* May 26, 1966).

36 "There was a lot of drinking" (*Films in Review,* January 1980).

37 "a warmly appealing femme lead" (*Hollywood Reporter,* July 17, 1953).

38 "In the next breath" (*Los Angeles Times,* July 26, 1953).

39 "There are more people" (*Los Angeles Times,* July 24, 1954).

40 "diverting and persuasively acted" (*Hollywood Reporter,* April 30, 1954).

40 "melodramatic muck" (*New York Times,* June 12, 1954).

40 "Anne Bancroft makes a gorgeous" (*Hollywood Reporter,* April 30, 1954).

41 "They did not know what to do" (Robert Wagner, interview by author, May 22, 2015).

41 "I used to see her around on the lot" (ibid.).

42 "It seemed that relationship" (Lunney interview).

44 "artful suspense" (*Los Angeles Examiner,* July 28, 1955).

44 "generally slack and uninspired" (*New York Times,* July 28, 1955).

44 "I don't remember" (*Los Angeles Herald-Examiner,* May 31, 1964).

45 "All he did was" (Funke and Booth, *Actors Talk about Acting II,* 199).

45 "showing continuing progress and talent" (*Variety,* February 15, 1955).

46 "We all struggled" (Granger and Calhoun, *Include Me Out,* 178).

46 "Her voice isn't very pleasant" (Orrison, *Written in Stone,* 49).

47 "The story is so disordered" (*New York Times,* December 8, 1955).

48 "a long, smooth bore" (*Hollywood Reporter,* December 7, 1955).

49 "I hope it gets by" (*Huron [S.D.] Daily Plainsman,* July 28, 1955).

49 "Not an easy thing to do" (Granger, *Sparks Fly Upward,* 336).

4. A No-Name Actress Starts Over

51 "We just came" (*New York Times,* February 9, 1958).

52 "I played all kinds" (Eugene Mazzola, interview by author, January 11, 2014).

52 "Not all the extras were good horsemen" (ibid.).

52 "As you can imagine" (ibid.).

53 "Things are shaping up" (*Washington Post,* February 7, 1956).

54 "a wild and terrifying experience" (*Boston Globe,* December 6, 1956).

54 "is not sleep-inducing" (*New York Times,* January 24, 1957).

54 "As the Indian widow" (*Los Angeles Times,* August 2, 1956).

55 "Miss Bancroft doesn't have much to do" (*Los Angeles Mirror,* July 18, 1957).

55 "Decorative and understanding" (*New York Times,* January 24, 1957).

55 "She seemed just another pretty girl" (*Los Angeles Herald-Examiner,* June 17, 1962).

55 "She always said her tits" (William Gibson, interview by Nat Segaloff, June 11, 2006).

56 "He wanted me" (*Los Angeles Times,* October 14, 1984).

56 "Through analysis" (Funke and Booth, *Actors Talk about Acting II,* 197).

57 "He helped me" (*Los Angeles Times,* June 26, 1974).

57 "All my life" (Funke and Booth, *Actors Talk about Acting II,* 198).

57 "She worked from 4 A.M." (*Los Angeles Times,* February 14, 1957).

58 "That marriage lasted three years" (*Northeast Woman Sunday Times,* December 25, 1983).

59 "I was Gittel" (publicity profile distributed for *'night, Mother,* 1986, AMPAS).

59 "I knew that's what the character" (ibid.).

59 "Where's the john?" (*Time,* December 21, 1959).

59 "The best Gittel yet" (Gibson, *Seesaw Log,* 17).

59 "How was the coast?" (ibid., 18).

59 "My mind blinked" (ibid.).

60 "She dug the lingo" (Gibson interview by Segaloff).

60 "Gittel on the hoof" (Gibson, *Seesaw Log,* 18).

60 "That was the first time" (*Saturday Evening Post,* December 9, 1961).

61 "I've had some roles lately" (*Los Angeles Times,* April 18, 1957).

62   "After the first act" (Fonda and Teichmann, *Fonda: My Life*, 255).

62   "If he said I didn't have it" (*Hollywood Citizen-News*, March 30, 1963).

62   "You must stay" (ibid.).

62   "On the third TV show I ever did" (*Time*, December 21, 1959).

63   "I defined the task" (Gibson, *Seesaw Log*, 23).

63   "Start it rolling" (Fonda and Teichmann, *Fonda: My Life*, 255).

65   "It was the emotional life" (Funke and Booth, *Actors Talk about Acting II*, 201).

65   "He gave her no answers" (Gibson, *Seesaw Log*, 36).

66   "Henry Fonda was not a risk taker" (Gene Lasko, interview by author, January 27, 2014).

66   "I asked Fred" (Gibson interview by Segaloff).

66   "He clearly made it known" (Arthur Penn, interview by Nat Segaloff, November 19, 2005).

66   "She didn't know very much" (*Saturday Evening Post*, November 20, 1965).

67   "Anne took a hell of a beating" (*Saturday Evening Post*, December 9, 1961).

67   "I can't follow this guy!" (Gibson, *Seesaw Log*, 40).

67   "Hank was wanting" (William Gibson, interview by Michael Wood, William Inge Center for the Arts, December 2004).

67   "I can't kiss her" (Arthur Penn, interview by Nat Segaloff, June 10, 2006).

67   "You think I'm right for it?" (Gibson, *Seesaw Log*, 76).

68   "I lost my temper" (Fonda and Teichmann, *Fonda: My Life*, 259).

68   "He made a lot of money" (Gibson interview by Segaloff).

68   "Jesus! I never expected" (Fonda and Teichmann, *Fonda: My Life*, 259).

68   "a wonderfully straightforward actor" (*New York Times*, January 17, 1958).

69   "Henry Fonda has never given" (*New York Journal American*, January 17, 1958).

69   "It has style" (*New York Times*, January 17, 1958).

69   "An absorbing, affectionate, and funny delight" (*New York Daily News*, January 17, 1958).

69   "a whale of a hit" (*New York Mirror*, January 17, 1958).

69   "A runaway hit" (*New York Journal American*, January 17, 1958).

69   "an attractive young actress" (*New York Times*, January 17, 1958).

69   "The young actress, who seems" (*New York Herald-Tribune*, January 17, 1958).

69   "the birth of a new star" (*New York Mirror*, January 17, 1958).

5. One Miracle Happens, and Then Another

71   "How does it feel" (*New York Post*, January 23, 1958).

71 "She was so wonderful" (Wagner interview).

71 "I don't want to read them again" (*New York World-Telegram*, January 17, 1958).

72 "He was really upset" (Afdera Franchetti, interview by Howard Teichmann, October 3, 1980, box 56, folder 1, p. 12, Howard Teichmann Papers, Library of Congress).

72 "I'm not putting her down" (Henry Fonda, interview by Howard Teichmann, June 22, 1980, box 56, folder 6, p. B9-4, Howard Teichmann Papers, Library of Congress).

73 "I didn't steal the play" (*Chicago Tribune*, October 31, 1965).

73 "Anne was really pissed" (Lunney interview).

73 "That turned out" (Penn interview by Segaloff, June 10, 2006).

74 "I can't keep a good thing to myself" (unidentified periodical advertisement hand-dated October 28, 1958, Bancroft file, New York Public Library [hereafter cited as NYPL]).

75 "I never dreamed" (*New York Post*, May 22, 1959).

75 "I'd bang my vocal cords" (Funke and Booth, *Actors Talk about Acting II*, 213).

75 "This is oversimplifying" (*New York Times*, February 5, 1978).

76 "You are not a personality" (*Washington Post*, September 15, 1963).

76 "These were the sweetest words" (ibid.).

76 "Lee tries to make you" (*New York Times*, February 18, 1982).

76 "At the Studio I learn" (*Washington Post*, September 15, 1963).

77 "bright and funny" (Manso, *Mailer*, 239).

77 "It was obvious" (ibid., 250).

77 "Finally he and Annie" (ibid., 252).

77 "You know what you can do" (ibid.).

77 "It was a strange thing" (Mailer, *The Last Party*, 297).

78 "The Actors Studio was like a gymnasium" (Inga Swenson, interview by author, April 18, 2015).

78 "It was very brave of her" (Lane Bradbury, interview by author, December 4, 2013).

78 "She was very funny" (Lunney interview).

78 "I didn't want to use up" (*Chicago Tribune*, October 31, 1965).

79 "Like falling off a log" (Gibson interview by Segaloff).

80 "Her business in life" (Penn interview by Segaloff, November 19, 2005).

80 "Before I could understand" (*Cue*, October 17, 1959).

81 "The most important thing" (ibid.).

82 "She played Annie Sullivan" (Gibson interview by Wood).

82 "He gave her an Irish accent" (ibid.).

82 "All over the world" (ibid.).

82 "What I felt from Annie" (Duke and Turan, *Call Me Anna*, 68).

83 "Helen would refuse to do it" (Penn interview by Segaloff, November 19, 2005)

83 "They were building it themselves" (ibid.).

83 "The two of us" (Duke and Turan, *Call Me Anna*, 73).

84 "There were eighteen" (ibid., 76).

84 "Well, my little dear" (ibid.).

84 "Anne Bancroft gives a glorious performance" (*New York Times,* October 20, 1959).

84 "powerful, hair-raising, spine-tingling, touching" (*New York Herald-Tribune,* October 20, 1959)

84 "Illuminating and often exciting" (*Wall Street Journal,* October 21, 1959).

84 "Magnificent theatre" (*New York Daily Mirror,* October 20, 1959).

84 "Anne Bancroft and little Patty Duke" (*New York World-Telegram,* October 20, 1959).

84 "Forceful theatre" (*Saturday Review,* November 2, 1959).

84 "If there was ever the slightest" (*New York Journal-American,* October 20, 1959).

86 "She had a sense of play" (Gerald Freedman, interview by author, September 7 and 11, 2015).

86 "I asked Annie" (Gibson interview by Segaloff).

87 "the three most important men" (*Los Angeles Mirror,* June 26, 1961).

87 "If they'd gone with any of those" (Lasko interview).

88 "I'm Mel Brooks" (*New York Mirror,* April 7, 1963).

88 "Just like that" (ibid.).

88 "He started following me around" (*New York Post,* March 11, 1967).

88 "You got a brilliant diamond" (Lasko interview).

89 "It was all pure business" (Swenson interview).

89 "It's not a good part" (ibid.).

89 "She was a barrel of fun" (Lasko interview).

89 "I didn't hold back" (Penn to Segaloff, November 19, 2005).

90 "It didn't register" (ibid.).

90 "clumsy and cluttered" (*New Republic,* June 4, 1962).

90 "has finally brought Arthur Penn" (*New York Times,* May 13, 1962).

90 "an unvarnished, often painful film" (*Chicago Tribune,* August 16, 1962).

90 "what is quite possibly the most moving" (*Time,* May 25, 1962).

6. A Challenging Role's Only Reward

92 "I want to do something" (*New York Journal-American,* November 5, 1961).

93 "That was a fight" (Garfield, *A Player's Place,* 153).

94   "I can't blame Hollywood" (*Washington Post,* May 20, 1962).

95   "Mel is so wonderful" (*American Weekly,* August 5, 1962).

95   "I was walking in the neighborhood" (ibid.).

97   "a great living contradiction" (Brecht, *Brecht Collected Plays,* 323).

98   "She said that she couldn't read it" (Jerome Robbins, notes on *Mother Courage,* NYPL).

98   "I wanted to get a part" (*Newark Sunday News,* May 5, 1963).

98   "She was heartbroken" (Robbins, notes on *Mother Courage,* NYPL).

99   "When I thought" (ibid.).

99   "One thing Annie has in her favor" (ibid.).

99   "I felt they would have quite a time" (*Newark Sunday News,* May 5, 1963).

100   "It was a change of pace" (Freedman interview).

100   "The audience for the first time" (*New York Post,* April 15, 1963).

100   "Listen, miss" (*New York Mirror,* April 7, 1963).

101   "austere but honorable production" (*New York Herald-Tribune,* April 14, 1963*)*.

101   "a different theater experience" (*New York Times,* April 11, 1963).

101   "a visually stunning" (*New York Daily News,* April 1, 1963).

101   "one-note wail" (Associated Press, April 5, 1963).

101   "Anne Bancroft should probably be commended" (*New Republic,* April 13, 1963).

101   "Anne Bancroft, who plays Mother Courage" (*Nation,* April 13, 1963).

102   "more often the folksy Bronx matriarch" (*Time,* April 5, 1963).

102   "Miss Bancroft said, 'Here's my little speech'" (Oscar speech database, AMPAS).

103   "I cried and I laughed" (*Baltimore Sun,* November 15, 1964).

103   "I'll be much easier" (*Chicago Tribune,* May 5, 1963).

103   "In that salute" (*New York Post,* April 10, 1963).

104   "Oscar doesn't mean much" (*Chicago Tribune,* May 3, 1963).

104   "Well, you were just reacting" (Austin Pendleton, interview by author, July 20, 2014).

104   "That material is not easy to do" (ibid.).

104   "I didn't expect *Courage*" (*New York Sunday News,* June 23, 1963).

105   "I never worry" (ibid.).

106   "I felt deeply" (*New York Times,* October 6, 1963).

107   "The first second" (*Boston Globe,* November 17, 1963).

107   "I fooled every shopkeeper" (*Los Angeles Times,* October 4, 1964).

108   "The shared moments" (Sinyard, *Jack Clayton,* 126).

108   "I had to remind myself" (*Life,* November 20, 1964).

108   "I thought, 'This could happen to me'" (*Los Angeles Times,* November 28, 1963).

108   "Explosive and superlative" (*Los Angeles Herald-Examiner,* November 21, 1964).

108   "to astonishing breadth" (*Time,* November 13, 1964).

108   "magnificent" (*Cue,* November 14, 1964).

109   "principally one of dreary noble suffering" (*New Republic,* December 19, 1964).

109   "art-house soap opera" (*Hollywood Reporter,* October 23, 1964).

109   "The battle lines" (Sinyard, *Jack Clayton,* 110).

109   "Jack Clayton's films" (Anne Bancroft to National Gallery of Art, fax dated August 16, 1995, Clayton Papers, British Film Institute).

110   "When two people" (*New York Mirror,* April 7, 1963).

110   "I don't see how" (*Washington Post,* September 15, 1963).

7. Something More Than Money

112   "Nobody even recognized me" (*Washington Post,* December 20, 1964).

113   "He was sort of a musical comedy schnook" (Gibson interview by Segaloff).

114   "Doesn't TV realize" (*Los Angeles Times,* October 18, 1964).

114   "It's marvelous" (*Los Angeles Times,* August 21, 1964).

114   "She was very brilliant" (Frank Corsaro, interview by author, July 10, 2014).

115   "Would you do me a favor" (ibid.)

115   "Did you get it?" (*Life,* November 20, 1964).

115   "I was excited to be doing that" (Bradbury interview).

115   "Annie was out there" (ibid.).

115   "She blushed and sparkled" (*Los Angeles Times,* August 21, 1964).

116   "An exciting theatrical experience" (*New York Daily News,* November 7, 1964).

116   "Anne Bancroft did not disappoint" (*New York Times,* November 7, 1964).

116   "Nobody seemed to be trying" (*Boston Globe,* October 30, 1964).

116   "If I am going to do something" (*Washington Post,* December 20, 1964).

117   "I really couldn't say 'no'" (*Newark Evening News,* March 8, 1965).

119   "The stage was so big" (Irene Tsu, interview by author, July 14, 2014).

119   "He put him down" (McBride, *Searching for John Ford,* 670).

120   "And all of a sudden" (Tsu interview).

120   "Are we ready to work" (Moonjean, *Bring in the Peacocks,* 239–40).

120   "Ford comes over" (Tsu interview).

120   "He's quite a man" (*Los Angeles Herald-Examiner,* April 3, 1965).

121   "living truthfully" (Meisner and Longwell, *Sanford Meisner on Acting,* 15).

122   "It seemed like a big" (Taylor, *Sydney Pollack,* 23).

123   "We felt a Negro" (Goudsouzian, *Sidney Poitier,* 237).

123   "I hope we will deal" (*Los Angeles Times,* June 27, 1965).

123   "She is charming" (publicity release for *The Slender Thread,* AMPAS).

123   "She seemed to be very inside herself" (*Los Angeles Times,* July 24, 1965).

124   "Anne Bancroft was simply fantastic" (Poitier, *This Life,* 269).

124   "If I stayed home" (*Chicago Tribune,* October 31, 1965).

124   "I'm a moody person" (ibid.).

125   "What's good will succeed" (*Washington Post,* October 27, 1965).

126   "I don't go for the easy" (*Los Angeles Times,* December 27, 1965).

127   "The truth is that a nun" (*New York Times,* September 11, 1965).

127   "When you have Jason" (Michael Lombard, interview by author, July 17, 2014).

127   "A stunning play" (*New York Times,* November 17, 1965).

128   "theater at its best" (*National Observer,* undated clipping in Bancroft file, NYPL).

128   "a play of massive height" (*New York Herald-Tribune,* November 17, 1965).

128   "something after the fruity movie formula" (*New York Daily News,* November 17, 1965).

128   "Neither seems possessed of God" (*Time,* November 26, 1965).

128   "A good tasteful director" (*New Republic,* December 18, 1965).

129   "a tour de force" (*New York Daily News,* December 24, 1965).

129   "restless camera" (*Saturday Review,* January 8, 1966).

130   "A disaster" (*New York Daily News,* May 5, 1966).

130   "outstanding performances" (*Los Angeles Herald-Examiner,* January 6, 1966).

130   "the trick of making an Eastern" (*Time,* May 13, 1966).

130   "We got the wrong girl" (Eyman, *Print the Legend,* 522).

130   Ford on not getting Bancroft "to expand" (ibid., 523).

130   "They are all communists" (Peary, *John Ford Interviews,* 107).

131   Ford calls Bancroft "great" (*Chicago Tribune,* June 3, 1965).

8. And Here's to You, Mrs. Robinson

132   "I simply found myself working" (*Family Weekly,* March 31, 1968).

133   "What in the world" (*New York Times,* January 23, 1966).

133   "We were able to get good actors" (Penn to Segaloff, June 10, 2006).

134   "She said, 'No, no'" (Peter Maloney, interview by author, August 24, 2015).

134   "new and unusual stage techniques" (*New York Times,* May 4, 1943).

135   "Arthur was an interesting artist" (Maloney interview).

135   "About three days into the rehearsal" (ibid.).

135   "It led to a deeper understanding" (*New York Times,* December 21, 1969).

136   "pseudo-semi-three-quarter arena" (*Boston Globe,* June 26, 1967).

136 "We were doing exactly" (Maloney interview).

137 "a young American girl" (*New York Times,* March 12, 1967).

138 "It's not too dramatic" (*New York Post,* March 11, 1967).

138 "Betty, Adolph, and Jule" (Freedman interview).

138 "She was always prepared" (ibid.).

138 "They had fun with each other (ibid.).

139 "lacked a life of its own" (*Boston Globe,* March 17, 1967).

139 "a witless pastiche" (*New York Times,* March 17, 1967).

139 "acceptable" (*Boston Globe,* March 17, 1967).

139 "She may have been intimidated" (Freedman interview).

141 "It was a very unusual role" (Lawrence Turman, interview by author, September 15, 2015).

142 "Everybody was telling me" (*Charlie Rose Show,* April 25, 2000).

142 "She was a wonderful professional" (Turman interview).

143 "Maybe I was so unsophisticated" (ibid.).

143 "No. She's much too sweet" (Mike Nichols in commentary track, fortieth anniversary DVD of *The Graduate).*

143 "She was such a great actress" (ibid.).

144 "It all says a very specific thing" (*Los Angeles Times,* February 5, 1967).

145 "And I said, 'Annie'" (Nichols commentary track, *The Graduate).*

145 "I can understand" (*Los Angeles Herald-Examiner,* June 7, 1968).

145 "Part of Annie's genius" (Nichols commentary track, *The Graduate).*

145 "I think she had dreams" (*Charlie Rose Show,* April 25, 2000).

146 "What I was thinking" (*Los Angeles Times,* August 17, 1997).

146 "a stupid idea" (Langella, *Dropped Names,* 257).

147 "I thought I'd die" (*Los Angeles Herald-Examiner,* June 7, 1968).

147 "When I got to the day" (*Charlie Rose Show,* April 25, 2000).

147 "You made me look terrible!" (Nichols commentary track, *The Graduate).*

147 "She was not an effusive person" (Turman interview).

147 "Everything she does is perfect" (Nichols commentary track, *The Graduate).*

148 "Are you Austin Pendleton?" (Pendleton interview).

149 "Lillian Hellman began coming" (ibid.).

149 "I think the thing that Mike" (ibid.).

149 "He had to confine himself" (ibid.).

150 "How can I give notes" (ibid.).

150 "I've figured out" (ibid.).

150 "And Mike said" (ibid.).

150 "It was wildly passionate" (ibid.).

150 "Well," she said, "Mike told me" (ibid.).

151 "The present production is a model" (*Time,* November 3, 1967).

151 "brilliant" (*New York Times,* November 5, 1967).
151 "Anne Bancroft, as the wicked sister" (*New York Times,* October 27, 1967).
151 "Mike Nichols has directed" (*Newsweek,* November 6, 1967).
151 "could as well have been" (*Women's Wear Daily,* October 27, 1967).
151 "For a wide audience in New York" (*Nation,* November 20, 1967).
152 "The year's most brilliant film" (*Washington Post,* December 31, 1967).
152 "a hearty salute" (*New York Times,* December 31, 1967).
152 "A dazzling performance" (*Boston Globe,* December 22, 1967).
152 "the sharpest is that by Miss Bancroft" (*Chicago Tribune,* December 24, 1967).
152 "in a tricky role" (*Chicago Sun-Times,* December 26, 1967).
152 "an alarmingly derivative style" (*Time,* December 29, 1967).
152 "a milestone in American film history" (*New Republic,* February 10, 1967).

9. Turning to the Stage, Leaving the Movies Behind

156 "I have this thing" (*Boston Globe,* July 7, 1969).
157 "I said, 'Julie Christie'" (Gussow and Pinter, *Conversations with Pinter,* 148).
158 "I'm always lonely" (*Los Angeles Herald-Examiner,* June 7, 1968).
159 "There's nothing in the play" (*New York Times,* May 26, 1968).
159 "The people in it" (Gibson, *A Cry of Players,* iii).
160 "talent is not enough" (*New York Times,* April 22, 2005).
160 "We were all a little nervous" (Peter Galman, interview by author, September 24, 2015).
161 "I was in love with her" (ibid.).
161 "It was a steam bath" (Ray Stewart, interview by author, September 26, 2015).
161 "I said, 'Well, that's the least'" (ibid.).
162 "She had her head in that book" (ibid.).
162 "She was mapping out" (Galman interview).
162 "I think they didn't want" (ibid.).
162 "That's the way it's gonna be" (Langella, *Dropped Names,* 255).
163 "a magnificent play" (*Boston Globe,* July 26, 1968).
163 "She was very much to herself" (Galman interview).
163 "I think it scared her" (Freedman interview).
164 "She was a brave actress" (ibid.).
164 "The director was not on top" (ibid.).
164 "If something didn't work" (Stewart interview).

164 "The drama, for all its moving moments" (*New York Post*, November 15, 1968).

164 "Its virtue is theatricality" (*New York Times*, November 15, 1968).

165 "soft, squishy, and overstuffed" (*New York Times*, November 24, 1968).

165 "Anne Bancroft gives yet another" (*New York*, December 2, 1968).

165 "A white cloud rose" (Stewart interview).

166 "I really don't know" (*New York Times*, April 20, 1969).

167 "Bill's play is a great challenge" (*Boston Globe*, July 7, 1969).

167 "I was dressed" (Stewart interview).

168 "Three dull hours" (*Boston Globe*, July 5, 1969).

168 "They basically had never found" (Gary English, interview by author, September 25, 2015).

169 "We wasted entire days" (*Chicago Tribune*, February 14, 1971).

170 "The idea that really got me" (*Viva*, December 1973).

170 "She was a great and loving pal" (Langella, *Dropped Names*, 260).

170 "When she wasn't rehearsing" (*Chicago Tribune*, February 15, 1970).

171 "When you work with dancers" (Alan Johnson, interview by author, November 2, 2015).

171 Description of *Annie, the Women in the Life of a Man:* Ken Mandelbaum of Broadway.com provides details for video clips from the special (fannetastic.com; click on "Experience").

171 "Rightfully, she should be the toast" (*New York Times*, February 18, 1970).

171 "easily the finest entertainment hour" (*Washington Post*, February 18, 1970).

172 "It was absolutely perfect" (*Viva*, December 1973).

172 "She values her time off" (*Chicago Tribune*, February 15, 1970).

172 "She kept making excuses" (*Washington Post*, April 26, 1970).

172 "intimate epic" (*Times* [London], July 8, 1972).

173 "Jennie, his American wife" (ibid.).

173 "When I said I wanted" (*Chicago Tribune*, June 27, 1971).

173 "She came through the revolving doors" (*Times* [London], July 8, 1972).

173 "After several phone calls" (ibid.).

174 "When I am directed" (*Boston Globe*, November 26, 1972).

174 "Anne Bancroft became very annoyed" (ibid.).

174 "Nothing destroys an actor faster" (ibid.).

174 "a beautiful, shallow, selfish" (Carnes, *Past Imperfect*, 176).

175 "Unfortunately for the moment" (*Los Angeles Times*, November 19, 1972).

175 "A superior biographic movie" (*Boston Globe*, October 14, 1972).

175 "the action film in which the action" (*Saturday Review*, November 25, 1972).

175 "A rousing adventure story" (*New York*, October 16, 1972).

176 "a big, balsa-wood monument" (*New York Times,* October 11, 1972).

176 "While Miss Bancroft looks faintly ludicrous" (*Washington Post,* October 18, 1972).

10. Motherhood and More Roles to Follow

178 "I wonder what her husband" (Sumner Long, *Never Too Late* edition of *Playbill*).

178 "She never thought" (Lunney interview).

178 "She was thrilled to death" (Bobbi Elliott, interview by author, October 17, 2014).

179 "She was very fearful" (ibid.).

179 "We are doting parents" (*New York Post,* December 29, 1973).

179 "I'm sorry, didn't someone explain" (*TV Guide,* November 23, 1974).

179 "I tried very hard" (*New York Daily News,* May 2, 2000   ).

179 "It was quite a thing" (Phyllis Italiano, remarks in October 2010 at the East Hampton Library in East Hampton, N.Y.; https://www.youtube.com/watch?v=C9uy8r1vPAg).

180 "Let's say an order came down" (*Boston Globe,* July 27, 1975).

181 "*The Odd Couple* and *Barefoot*" (Simon, *The Play Goes On,* 20).

182 "The film is more of a drama" (*Variety,* December 25, 1974).

183 "all too rarely on screen" (*New York,* March 17, 1975).

183 "a quietly beautiful portrayal" (*Los Angeles Times,* March 19, 1975).

183 "The concept's just the same" (*TV Guide,* November 23, 1974).

184 "She was very musical" (Nancy Lunney, interview by author, September 8, 2014).

184 "I didn't feel like I was teaching" (ibid.).

185 "Look, the material's hysterical" (*TV Guide,* November 23, 1974).

185 "She was so beautiful" (Gail Parent, interview by Nancy Harrington, July 16, 2013, Archive of American Television).

185 "Mel, as you know" (*Chicago Tribune,* November 25, 1974).

185 "The movement does one bad thing" (*TV Guide,* November 23, 1974).

185 "Her flair for song-and-dance" (*Variety,* December 4, 1974).

185 "sank slowly in a swamp" (*New York Times,* December 1, 1974).

186 "There was no laugh track" (*Chicago Tribune,* December 3, 1974).

187 "I was caught up" (Emery, *The Directors: Take One,* 39–40).

188 "We had no idea" (*American Film,* November 1975).

188 "My experience on that film" (Colby Chester, interview by author, September 11, 2015).

188 "What impressed me about her" (ibid.).

189 "Was he a bank *guard?*" (ibid.).

189   "You could tell" (ibid.).
189   "Nobody got hurt" (Emery, *The Directors: Take One*, 39–40).
189   "One of the problems" (*American Film*, November 1975).
190   "She was Mrs. Robinson" (Chester interview).
190   "thinking man's disaster epic" (*Los Angeles Times*, December 21, 1975).
190   "dull and formula scripting" (*Variety*, December 24, 1975).
190   "I wouldn't have missed" (*New York Times*, December 26, 1975).
191   "People don't want to see" (*Times* [London], March 22, 1977).
191   "But I realized I was asking" (Zeffirelli, *Franco Zeffirelli's Jesus*, 22).
191   "There's little money" (ibid.).
192   "It was the most interesting thing" (Paramount press release with *Lipstick* publicity, Anne Bancroft clippings file, NYPL).
192   "That's my first responsibility" (ibid.).
192   "I had all the jet lag" (ibid.).
192   "The world's trickiest role" (*Times* [London], March 22, 1977).
193   "The spell of Jesus" (ibid.).
193   "We had to do it all over" (Zeffirelli, *Franco Zeffirelli's Jesus*, 99).
193   "We decided, however, to carry her there" (ibid.).
194   "Finally, we were able to drag" (ibid., 100).
194   "In most cases I've chosen" (*New York Times*, October 27, 2010).
195   "It had nothing to do with" (Tobey Shaffer, interview by author, October 1, 2015).
195   "Of course everyone was all over her" (ibid.).
196   "We had a whole conversation" (ibid.).
196   "Anne was really tuned into it" (ibid.).
196   show a little cleavage (Mimi Gramatky, interview by author, July 23, 2014).
196   "She was just a fun person" (Shaffer interview).
197   "My father took me" (Hemingway, *Out Came the Sun*, 84).
197   "nice and supportive" (ibid., 82).
197   "an engrossing melodrama" (*Boston Globe*, April 5, 1976).
197   "a nasty little item" (*Chicago Sun-Times*, April 6, 1976).
197   "Under the guise of examining rape" (*Chicago Tribune*, April 5, 1976).

11. Pulled between Home and Work

199   "It wasn't like a mansion" (Nancy Lunney interview).
199   "huge phalanx" (Langella, *Dropped Names*, 260).
200   "When you and Mel" (*Merv Griffin Show*, October 31–November 1, 1979).
200   "She was very volatile" (Nancy Lunney interview).
200   "I always rather felt" (Jan Haag, e-mail to author, October 26, 2015).
200   "weather her storms" (Langella, *Dropped Names*, 253).

200 "Her responses to things were emotional" (Pendleton interview).

200 "Anne had a volatile temper" (Alda, *Things I Overheard While Talking to Myself*, 155).

201 "Her reaction was an immediate" (ibid., 156).

201 "From beginning to end" (*Boston Globe*, April 27, 1969).

201 "There was a dark side" (Gramatky interview).

201 "I heard this huge argument" (ibid.).

202 "loving, warm, and fiercely loyal friend" (Langella, *Dropped Names*, 253).

202 "She was one of the first women" (Gramatky interview).

202 "She was a girlfriend" (Elliott interview).

202 "In some cases, she was actually" (Gramatky interview).

202 "Mel was unbelievable" (Nancy Lunney interview).

202 "First of all, she was smart" (Elliott interview).

202 "Cocaine was a drug" (Biskind, *Easy Riders, Raging Bulls*, 159).

203 "My parents weren't baby boomers" (Max Brooks, interview by Dennis Miller, November 20, 2012; https://www.youtube.com/watch?v=2fRQ-RCWhiY).

203 "Music was always going" (Elliott interview).

203 "Without question she was one" (ibid.).

203 Griffin's son and *The Graduate* (Julann Griffin to author, undated phone conversation).

204 "People asking that are expecting" (Brooks interview by Miller).

204 "She would record" (*Library Journal*, July 1, 2013).

204 "It was hard for her" (*New York Times*, June 23, 2013).

205 "People expect me" (*Daily Record* [Glasgow, Scotland], February 25, 2012).

205 "Well, are you going to ask me?" (*Chicago Tribune*, August 2, 1976).

205 "Well, I think we'll take a chance" (ibid.).

207 "You know who that is?" (Nancy Lunney interview).

208 "We wanted to explore the turning points" (*New York Times*, November 20, 1977).

210 "I can't say that I identify" (*New York Times*, September 3, 1976).

210 "Perhaps we who hold feminist attitudes" (ibid.).

211 "They were two bitches" (*Washington Post*, November 14, 1977).

211 "It was late" (Emery, *The Directors: Take Two*, 223).

212 "You can't organize" (*LA Stage Times*, May 8, 2013).

212 "That wasn't in the script" (*Joy Behar Show*, aired on CNN on April 18, 2011).

212 "Poor Annie had to look like" (*Seattle Times*, June 13, 2010).

212 "Of course, because I was" (MacLaine, *Dance While You Can*, 194).

212 "Annie was a little aloof" (*Hollywood Reporter*, March 30, 2015).

213 "The whole idea" (Haag, e-mail to author).

214 "The actresses, as it turned out" (Haag, "Women Directors in Hollywood," http://janhaag.com/ESTheDWW.html).

214 "He said, 'Well, what would she do?'" (David Lunney interview).

214 "It was a treat" (Gramatky interview).

215 "Sally started to direct Hope" (ibid.).

215 "She was the first person" (ibid.).

215 "She looked at me" (ibid.)

215 "She gave me her Saks" (ibid.).

216 "She looked at it" (ibid.)

216 "The women all received" (ibid.)

216 "one of the most visually beautiful" (*Washington Post,* April 3, 1977).

216 "Rarely have both the humanity" (*Newsweek,* April 4, 1977).

217 "There is an admirable daring" (*New York Times,* April 3, 1977).

217 "the only bit of casting" (*Washington Post,* April 3, 1977).

217 "a reject from *The Godfather*" (*New York Times,* April 3, 1977).

217 "solemn, stately and dull" (*Boston Globe,* April 3, 1977).

217 "One doesn't know quite what" (*Newsweek,* April 4, 1977).

217 "That wasn't difficult" (Philip Langner, interview by author, November 2, 2015).

218 "We went to him first" (ibid.).

218 "the dream aspired to" (Gibson, *Notes on How to Turn a Phoenix into Ashes,* 9).

219 "When I read the parts" (*New York Times,* August 14, 1977).

219 "I could see what was happening" (*New York Times,* August 14, 1977).

219 "The idea was that Annie" (Gibson interview by Segaloff).

219 "When she opened the door" (*New York Times,* August 14, 1977).

219 "Annie and Golda fell in love" (Gibson interview by Segaloff).

219 "wasn't one who didn't love her" (Gibson, *Notes on How to Turn a Phoenix into Ashes,* 32).

220 "Something that would be a clue" (*New York Times,* August 14, 1977).

220 "There is a type of woman" (*New York Times,* December 9, 1978).

220 "The next time I see you" (Gibson, *Notes on How to Turn a Phoenix into Ashes,* 32).

220 "I'm going back to New York" (*New York Times,* August 14, 1977).

221 "It was the noisiest sendoff" (Gibson, *Notes on How to Turn a Phoenix into Ashes,* 15).

221 "Our instinct for realism" (ibid., 16).

221 "It just had too many damn scenes" (Langner interview).

221 "Penn and I were delighted" (Gibson, *Notes on How to Turn a Phoenix into Ashes,* 17).

222 "When I asked an actor" (ibid., 30).

222 "I wish I could" (Gibson interview by Wood).

222 "terrific" (*New York Times,* November 7, 1977).

223 "She had to say frankly" (Gibson, *Notes on How to Turn a Phoenix into Ashes,* 31).

223 "Golda made quite a speech" (Langner interview).

223 "Now you have to be specific" (Gibson, *Notes on How to Turn a Phoenix into Ashes,* 32).

223 "Anne was well able to take it" (Langner interview).

223 "Grit personified" (Gibson, *Notes on How to Turn a Phoenix into Ashes,* 33).

223 "I don't know how" (ibid.).

224 "one of the best films of this era" (*Variety,* October 9, 1977).

224 "powerhouse performances" (*New York Times,* November 15, 1977).

224 "enormously appealing" (*Washington Post,* November 13, 1977).

224 "vivid moviemaking" (*Los Angeles Times,* November 13, 1977).

224 "A brave, bravura performance" (*Time,* November 21, 1977).

224 "She is dazzling to see" (*Los Angeles Times,* November 13, 1977).

224 "Bancroft has lately shown a tendency" (*Newsweek,* November 28, 1977).

224 "Bancroft is as usual unbearable" (*New Republic,* November 19, 1977).

225 "When the rear-screen projections" (*New York Daily News,* November 15, 1977).

225 "A conscientious, reverential, monumental bore" (*Time,* November 28, 1977).

225 "*Golda* isn't a play" (*New York Post,* November 15, 1977).

225 "extraordinary portrait of a leader" (*New York Times,* November 15, 1977).

226 "Golda wanted a dignified portrait" (*New York Times,* March 1, 1978).

226 "Not for quite some time" (ibid.).

226 "an artistic and financial failure" (ibid.).

12. A First-Time Director's True Calling

229 "I don't think a studio" (Jonathan Sanger, interview by author, October 30, 2015).

229 "Normally they might" (ibid.).

229 "That was an important thing for her" (ibid.).

230 "There was so much" (Italiano remarks at East Hampton Library).

230 "I know a part of him" (*Merv Griffin Show,* October 31–November 1, 1979).

230 "Dom was all over the place" (Sanger interview).

230 "She wanted the humor" (ibid.).

231   "I just knew what she wanted" (Candice Azzara, interview by author, July 14, 2014).

231   "Anne's a genius" (*Los Angeles Times,* May 27, 1979).

231   "She relied on her instincts" (Sanger interview).

232   "It was very different" (Azzara interview).

232   "She hasn't asked me" (*Chicago Tribune,* March 15, 1979).

232   "Her humor is much more subtle" (*Los Angeles Times,* May 27, 1979).

232   "It has a few nice moments" (*New York Times,* February 1, 1980).

232   "What in the world persuaded" (*New Republic,* February 23, 1980).

232   "One trembles to imagine" (*Washington Post,* February 9, 1980).

232   "It wasn't her thing" (Italiano remarks at East Hampton Library).

233   "She hated the actors" (Mel Brooks to Robert Osborne, TCM airing of *Fatso* in 2015).

233   "If she didn't like the actors" (Lombard interview).

233   "She said, 'Yeah, but actors are too difficult'" (Sanger interview).

233   "Italians love this movie" (Azzara interview).

233   "It's the only one" (Italiano remarks at East Hampton Library).

233   Bancroft's breast cancer: mentioned by her younger sister, Phyllis, at East Hampton Library; her older sister, JoAnne, confirmed the illness in an undated interview with the author.

235   "There was a real separation" (Sanger interview).

235   "She was really a big fan of his work" (ibid.).

236   "She treated David" (ibid.).

236   "She wasn't interested in David" (ibid.).

237   "Neither meant a thing" (Palin, *Halfway to Hollywood,* 135).

237   "He could see me do it" (*New York Daily News,* October 24, 1984).

239   "Under Friedkin's direction" (*Newsweek,* December 28, 1981).

239   "She said when we went backstage" (Coletti interview).

241   "A subject far from the realm" (*New York Times,* March 7, 1942).

241   "The American audiences don't laugh" (*New York Times,* March 29, 1942).

241   "By using the medium" ("With Comedy, We Can Rob Hitler of His Posthumous Power," interview with Mel Brooks, *Spiegel Online International,* March 16, 2006, www.spiegel.de/international/spiegel/spiegel-interview-with-mel-brooks-with-comedy-we-can-rob-hitler-of-his-posthumous-power-a-406268.html).

241   "I think he realized it was a load" (Alan Johnson, interview by author, November 2, 2015).

242   "It was still Mel's movie" (ibid.).

242   "She was on the set" (ibid.).

242   "She loved just being there" (Sanger interview).

242   "I was sitting next to her" (Johnson interview).

242 "It was a stupid idea" (ibid.).

243 "Do not expect the usual" (*Newsweek*, December 19, 1983).

244 "Do you still love each other?" (Mink, *This Is Today*, 104).

244 "I'm more than content" (ibid.).

244 "The real reason" (*Town & Country*, August 5, 2014).

245 "She always insisted that gardening" (Grant and Harper, *The Cassoulet Saved Our Marriage*, 80).

245 "Italian peasant heritage" (ibid.).

245 "No one was more tireless" (Jackie Eliopoulos, interview by author, October 15, 2015).

246 "It was hard to prevent Mel" (ibid.).

246 "The thing that was extraordinary" (ibid.).

246 "I was amazed at their generosity" (ibid.).

246 "I've never encountered someone so generous" (ibid.).

246 "Max had a wicked sense of humor" (Sanger interview).

13. Old Ladies and Liberation

248 "Do I need a light here" (Johnson interview).

248 "People don't write wonderful parts" (*New York Times*, October 15, 1984).

248 "The truth is, there aren't all that many roles" (*New York Daily News*, October 24, 1984).

249 "I didn't like that feeling" (*Globe and Mail*, March 13, 1987).

250 "Sidney, believe me" (*New York Times*, October 15, 1984).

250 "If Sidney saw a take" (ibid.).

250 "My mother doesn't even need" (ibid.).

250 "Maybe that's why I like this lady" (*New York Daily News*, October 24, 1984).

250 "Crawford fascinated me" (*Los Angeles Times*, September 15, 1985).

251 "With age your memory starts" (*Los Angeles Times*, October 14, 1984).

251 "That's one of the best scenes" (Wagner interview).

251 "so thoroughly and entirely satisfying" (*Los Angeles Times*, October 12, 1984).

251 "A well-acted and well-meant but empty" (*Washington Post*, November 16, 1984).

251 "fuzzy, emotionally tawdry melodrama" (*Washington Post*, November 20, 1984).

252 "timeless human conflict" (Jewison, *This Terrible Business Has Been Good to Me*, 243).

253 "I'm married to a director" (ibid., 245).

253 "I realized she would be" (ibid.).

253 "They were both, of course" (John Pielmeier, interview by author, December 1, 2015).

254 "He rehearsed the movie script" (ibid.).

254 "She is supposed to be sacrificed" (Jewison, *This Terrible Business Has Been Good to Me*, 246).

255 "That was a choice I made" (Pielmeier interview).

255 "There are people" (*Los Angeles Times*, September 22, 1985).

255 "It was great locking horns" (United Press International, August 22, 1985).

255 "She found it fascinating" (*Los Angeles Times*, September 22, 1985).

255 "The material itself" (*New York Times*, September 13, 1985).

257 "I don't remember anybody" (Tom Moore, interview by author, January 25, 2016).

257 "When Anne came in to meet" (ibid.).

258 "Anne was not easy" (ibid.).

258 "Mama exists in me" (Universal publicity profile, production files, AMPAS).

258 "I write characters who make mistakes" (*New York Times*, August 10, 1986).

259 "That's just the way she was" (Moore interview).

259 "I think he does know what he's doing" (ibid.).

259 "You had to stay" (ibid.).

259 "She felt she had given" (ibid.).

260 "You know, Tom" (ibid.).

260 "There will be nothing stronger" (*Newsweek*, September 22, 1986).

260 "Anne Bancroft gives the performance" (CBS, quoted in *Los Angeles Times*, September 19, 1986).

261 "an irresistible momentum" (*New York Times*, September 12, 1986).

261 "I think she was very disappointed" (Moore interview).

261 "I've just read something" (Hanff, *84, Charing Cross Road*, vii).

262 "I was very moved" (*New York Times*, March 15, 1987).

263 "The writer Hugh Whitemore and I" (*Sunday Times* [London], March 29, 1987).

263 "It was all there in the writing" (*Globe and Mail*, March 13, 1987).

263 "Without signaling to the audience" (*New York Times*, March 15, 1987).

264 "Why didn't that silly woman" (*Chicago Sun-Times*, March 27, 1987).

264 "She hurls apostrophes to the walls" (*Time*, March 2, 1987).

264 "A joyous celebration of the life" (*Los Angeles Times*, March 20, 1987).

266 "You don't have the luxury" (*Los Angeles Times*, July 17, 1988).

266 "I realized every mother in the world" (ibid.)

266 "We really liked each other" (Harvey Fierstein, commentary track for DVD of *Torch Song Trilogy*).

267 "Is homosexuality any less funny now?" (*Los Angeles Times,* July 17, 1988)

267 "It's hard to believe" (*Los Angeles Times,* December 14, 1988).

267 "emphasizes the lovable at every turn" (*New York Times,* December 14, 1988).

268 "extremely odd" (*New York Times,* February 24, 1989).

268 "simply appalling" (*Los Angeles Times,* February 24, 1989).

268 "very nice" (*Los Angeles Times,* February 22, 1989).

14. All in the Doing

269 "She was torn" (Ackerman interview).

269 "She'd always refer to it" (ibid.).

270 "She signed my *Playbill*" (ibid.).

270 "She was so bright" (ibid.).

270 "I think Anne was going through" (ibid.).

271 "graceful and life-affirming play" (*Los Angeles Times,* November 17, 1989).

271 ideal casting (*Los Angeles Times,* November 16, 1989).

271 *monstres sacrés* (Levine, *Manuel Puig and the Spider Woman,* 352).

271 "It was almost as if they both" (Ackerman interview).

272 "Good-bye, good luck to all of you" (ibid.).

272 "She loved the rehearsal process" (ibid.).

273 "magnificently forgettable" (*Sunday Times* [London], December 30, 1990).

273 "a rich, ribald, classy exercise" (*Toronto Star,* February 15, 1994).

274 "It looked just like a house" (Corey Parker, interview by author, February 8, 2016).

274 "It was very relaxed" (ibid.).

274 "He kept coming down the stairs" (ibid.).

275 "She looked up through the mirror" (ibid.).

275 "She was a very hard worker" (ibid.).

275 "Anne Bancroft is all we could ask for" (*Newsday,* March 22, 1992).

275 "Looking old and tired" (*Chicago Sun-Times,* March 23, 1992).

276 "Bancroft is, as usual, wonderful" (*Chicago Tribune,* March 23, 1992).

276 "That's how I got into making films" (Ackerman interview).

277 "She loved complex characters" (ibid.).

277 "It was so disappointing" (Associated Press, May 17, 1992).

277 "What makes you say that?" (*New York Times,* May 19, 1992).

278 "She said that would not be fair" (Dale Launer, interview by author, January 25, 2016).

278 "I like restrained, dry comedy" (ibid.).

278 "She nailed it, every single line" (ibid.).

279 "I said, 'Well, what did you think?'" (ibid.).

279 "She said that she did not like" (Badham and Modderno, *I'll Be in My Trailer,* 199).

279 "It's very difficult in every field" (*New York Times,* May 19, 1992).

280 "The pleasure and the thrill" (*Los Angeles Times,* October 20, 1988).

280 "After *The Graduate*" (Gibson interview by Segaloff).

283 "It was interesting giving direction" (Mark Jean, interview by author, February 22, 2016).

283 "She was demanding in the best way" (ibid.).

283 "She was nervous about the whole thing" (ibid.).

283 "Like any great actress" (ibid.).

284 "a first-rate family film" (*USA Today,* April 12, 1996).

284 "Anne Bancroft was always my first" (Knapp and Kulas, *Ridley Scott,* 140).

284 *Living with Cancer* production (Fred Silverman, interview by author, March 9, 2015).

285 "I've been getting good scripts" (*Calgary Herald,* October 22, 1995).

286 "I hated directing" (ibid.).

286 "I won't let you do this" (John Carucci, "Brooks Recalls Anne Bancroft as Wife, Collaborator," *San Diego Union-Tribune,* February 3, 2010).

287 "Being happy is a very complex thing" (*Charlie Rose Show,* April 25, 2000).

287 "We can never let Mel see this" (*Charlie Rose Show,* June 8, 2005; introducing a rebroadcast of the interview, Rose recounted her off-camera remarks).

287 "It was the loveliest thing I ever saw" (Pendleton interview).

288 "A kind of cosmic talk show" (*New York Times,* February 17, 2002).

289 "It's about a woman fighting the traditions" (*New York Times,* December 7, 2001).

289 "My problem in rehearsal" (Neal Huff, interview by author, February 18, 2016).

289 "It was hard for Anne" (ibid.).

290 "She seemed weak, really frail" (ibid.).

290 "I really never thought that" (ibid.).

290 "I promise you I will be back" (ibid.).

290 "I have never, ever worked" (ibid.)

292 "In Rome, it was a feast" (Ackerman interview).

292 "She was like a schoolgirl" (ibid.).

Conclusion: Inch by Inch, Yard by Yard

293 "She told me she had gone to the doctor" (Ackerman interview).

294 "They thought it was successfully dealt with" (ibid.).

294 "She was a woman" (Kelley, *I Oprahed,* 61).

294 "What's wrong?" (ibid., 63).

295 "She said, 'You know, you better talk to Mel'" (Ackerman interview).

295 "marvelous inventions of texture and color" (Alda, *Things I Overheard While Talking to Myself,* 158).

295 "It was kept pretty quiet" (Sanger interview).

295 "We set up a room and she came there" (ibid.).

295 During her illness Max was working (his routine is described in Steve Julian, "The Brooks Family of Writers: Michelle, Max, and Mel," *LA Stage Times,* November 9, 2010).

296 "one of the most versatile and resourceful actors" (CNN, June 7, 2005).

296 "fiery, funny, larger than life" (*Boston Globe,* June 8, 2005).

296 "both tough and vulnerable" (*New York Times,* June 8, 2005).

297 "We have a motto in our family" (*Globe and Mail,* March 13, 1987).

Bibliography

Archives

Academy of Motion Picture Arts and Sciences, Margaret Herrick Library.
———. Core Collections Files: production files, biography files, subject files.
———. Special Collections: Leonard Goldstein Papers, William "Billy" Gordon Papers, John Huston Papers, MGM Wardrobe Department Records, Gregory Peck Papers.
British Film Institute: Jack Clayton Papers.
Library of Congress, Manuscript Division: Howard Teichmann Papers.
New York Public Library for the Performing Arts, Billy Rose Theatre Division: Anne Bancroft clipping collection, Cheryl Crawford Papers, Jerome Robbins Papers, Patricia Zipprodt Papers.
Stanford University, Manuscript Division, Department of Special Collections: Delmer Daves Papers.
University of California, Berkeley: Pacific Film Archive.
Wisconsin Historical Society, Wisconsin Center for Film and Theater Research: Fred Coe Papers.
Zipprodt, Patricia, with William Woodman. "If the Song Doesn't Work, Change the Dress: A Life in Costume Design." Unpublished manuscript. In Patricia Zipprodt Papers, New York Public Library.

Books

Alda, Alan. *Things I Overheard While Talking to Myself.* New York: Random House, 2007.
Badham, John, and Craig Modderno. *I'll Be in My Trailer: The Creative Wars between Directors and Actors.* Studio City, Calif.: Michael Wiese Productions, 2006.
Baker, Roy Ward. *The Director's Cut: A Memoir of 60 Years in Film and Television.* London: Reynolds & Hearn, 2000.
Balio, Tino, ed. *Hollywood in the Age of Television.* Boston: Unwin Hyman, 1990.
Barney, Richard A., ed. *David Lynch: Interviews.* Jackson: University Press of Mississippi, 2009.

Basinger, Jeanine. *Anthony Mann.* Middletown, Conn.: Wesleyan University Press, 2007.

Battaglio, Stephen. *David Susskind: A Televised Life.* New York: St. Martin's, 2010.

Becker, Christine. *It's the Pictures That Got Small: Hollywood Film Stars on 1950s Television.* Middletown, Conn.: Wesleyan University Press, 2008.

Behlmer, Rudy, ed. *Memo from Darryl F. Zanuck: The Golden Years at Twentieth Century-Fox.* New York: Grove, 1993.

Bennett, Charles. *Hitchcock's Partner in Suspense: The Life of Screenwriter Charles Bennett.* Lexington: University Press of Kentucky, 2014.

Biskind, Peter. *Easy Riders, Raging Bulls: How the Sex-Drugs-and-Rock-'n'-Roll Generation Saved Hollywood.* New York: Simon and Schuster, 1998.

Brecht, Bertolt. *Brecht Collected Plays: Five.* John Willett and Ralph Manheim, eds. London: Bloomsbury Methuen Drama, 2006.

Bryer, Jackson R., ed., *Conversations with Lillian Hellman.* Jackson: University Press of Mississippi, 1986.

Burkett, Elinor. *Golda.* New York: Harper, 2008.

Burstyn, Ellen. *Lessons in Becoming Myself.* New York: Riverhead, 2006.

Carnes, Mark C., ed. *Past Imperfect: History According to the Movies.* New York: Macmillan, 1996.

Carney, Ray, ed.. *Cassavetes on Cassavetes.* New York: Faber and Faber, 2001.

Carter, Graydon, ed. *Vanity Fair's Tales of Hollywood: Rebels, Reds, and Graduates and the Wild Stories behind the Making of Thirteen Iconic Films.* New York: Penguin, 2008.

Chio, Michael. *David Lynch.* London: BFI Publishing, 1995.

Churchwell, Sarah. *The Many Lives of Marilyn Monroe.* New York: Metropolitan, 2005.

Dixon, Wheeler W. *Collected Interviews: Voices from Twentieth-century Cinema.* Carbondale: Southern Illinois University Press, 2001.

Duke, Patty, and Kenneth Turan. *Call Me Anna: The Autobiography of Patty Duke.* New York: Bantam, 1987.

Emery, Robert J. *The Directors: Take One.* New York: Allworth, 2002.

———. *The Directors: Take Two.* New York: Allworth, 2002.

Erskine, Thomas L., and James M. Welsh, eds. *Video Versions: Film Adaptations of Plays on Video.* Westport, Conn.: Greenwood, 2000.

Eyman, Scott. *Print the Legend: The Life and Times of John Ford.* New York: Simon & Schuster, 1999.

Fleischer, Leonore. *Agnes of God.* New York: Signet, 1985.

Fonda, Henry, and Howard Teichmann. *Fonda: My Life.* New York: New American Library, 1981.

French, John. *Robert Shaw: The Price of Success.* London: Nick Hern, 1993.

Friedkin, William. *The Friedkin Connection: A Memoir.* New York: Harper, 2013.

Fujiwara, Chris. *Jacques Tourneur: The Cinema of Nightfall.* Jefferson, N.C.: McFarland, 1998.

Funke, Lewis, and John E. Booth. *Actors Talk about Acting II.* New York: Avon, 1961.

Garfield, David. *A Player's Place: The Story of the Actors Studio.* New York: Macmillan, 1980.

Gibson, William. *A Cry of Players: A Play.* New York: Atheneum, 1968.

———. *Notes on How to Turn a Phoenix into Ashes: The Story of the Stage Production, with the Text, of "Golda."* New York: Atheneum, 1978.

———. *The Seesaw Log: A Chronicle of the Stage Production.* New York: Knopf, 1959.

Goudsouzian, Aram. *Sidney Poitier: Man, Actor, Icon.* Chapel Hill: University of North Carolina Press, 2004.

Granger, Farley, and Robert Calhoun. *Include Me Out: My Life from Goldwyn to Broadway.* New York: St. Martin's, 2007.

Granger, Stewart. *Sparks Fly Upward.* London: Granada, 1981.

Grant, Caroline M., and Lisa Catherine Harper, eds. *The Cassoulet Saved Our Marriage: True Tales of Food, Family, and How We Learn to Eat.* Boston: Roost, 2013.

Gussow, Mel. *Edward Albee: A Singular Journey.* New York: Simon and Schuster, 1999.

Gussow, Mel, and Harold Pinter. *Conversations with Pinter.* New York: Limelight, 2004.

Hanff, Helen. *84, Charing Cross Road* (1970). Introduction by Anne Bancroft. Mt. Kisko, N.Y.: M. Bell, 1991.

Harris, Mark. *Pictures at a Revolution: Five Movies and the Birth of the New Hollywood.* New York: Penguin, 2008.

Hemingway, Mariel. *Out Came the Sun: Overcoming the Legacy of Mental Illness, Addiction, and Suicide in My Family.* New York: Regan Arts, 2015.

Herrmann, Dorothy. *Helen Keller: A Life.* New York: Knopf, 1998.

Holtzman, William. *Seesaw: A Dual Biography of Anne Bancroft and Mel Brooks.* Garden City, N.Y.: Doubleday, 1979.

Hughes, David. *The Complete Lynch.* London: Virgin, 2001.

Jewison, Norman. *This Terrible Business Has Been Good to Me: An Autobiography.* New York: Thomas Dunne, 2005.

Jones, Jenny M. *The Annotated Godfather: The Complete Screenplay with Commentary on Every Scene, Interviews, and Little-Known Facts.* New York: Black Dog & Leventhal, 2009.

Jowitt, Deborah. *Jerome Robbins: His Life, His Theater, His Dance.* New York: Simon & Schuster, 2004.

Kelley, Susan. *I Oprahed: And Other Adventures of a Woman of a Certain Age.* New York: CreateSpace, 2011.

Kellow, Brian. *Can I Go Now? The Life of Sue Mengers, Hollywood's First Superagent.* New York: Viking, 2015.

Kisseloff, Jeff. *The Box: An Oral History of Television, 1920–1961.* New York: Viking, 1995.

Knapp, Lawrence F., and Andrea F. Kulas, eds. *Ridley Scott: Interviews.* Jackson: University Press of Mississippi, 2005.

Koprince, Susan. *Understanding Neil Simon.* Columbia: University of South Carolina Press, 2002.

Kramer, Joan, and David Heeley. *In the Company of Legends.* New York: Beaufort, 2015.

Lahr, John. *Tennessee Williams: Mad Pilgrimage of the Flesh.* New York: W. W. Norton, 2014.

Langella: Frank. *Dropped Names: Famous Men and Women as I Knew Them.* New York: HarperCollins, 2012.

Lash, Joseph P. *Helen and Teacher: The Story of Helen Keller and Anne Sullivan Macy.* New York: Delacorte, 1980.

Leaming, Barbara. *Marilyn Monroe.* New York: Crown, 1998.

Lear, Norman. *Even This I Get to Experience.* New York: Penguin, 2014.

Lennon, J. Michael. *Norman Mailer: A Double Life.* New York: Simon and Schuster, 2013.

Levine, Suzanne Jill. *Manuel Puig and the Spider Woman: His Life and Fictions.* Madison: University of Wisconsin Press, 2001.

Levy, Emanuel. *Vincente Minnelli: Hollywood's Dark Dreamer.* New York: Macmillan, 2009.

Lumet, Sidney. *Making Movies.* New York: Knopf, 1995.

MacLaine, Shirley. *Dance While You Can: On Relationships, Feelings, and Family.* New York: Random House, 1991.

———. *What If . . . : A Lifetime of Questions, Speculations, Reasonable Guesses, and a Few Things I Know for Sure.* New York: Atria, 2013.

Mailer, Adele. *The Last Party: Scenes from My Life with Norman Mailer.* New York: Barricade, 1997.

Mann, William J. *Hello, Gorgeous: Becoming Barbra Streisand.* Boston: Houghton Mifflin Harcourt, 2012.

Manso, Peter. *Mailer: His Life and Times.* 1985. Reprint, New York: Washington Square, 2008.

Martin, Lois. *A Brief History of Witchcraft.* Philadelphia: Running Press, 2010.

Mayer, Geoff. *Roy Ward Baker.* Manchester, U.K.: Manchester University Press, 2011.

McBride, Joseph. *Searching for John Ford: A Life.* New York: St. Martin's, 2001.

Medavoy, Mike. *You're Only as Good as Your Next One: 100 Great Films, 100 Good Films, and 100 for Which I Should Be Shot.* New York: Simon and Schuster, 2013.

Meisner, Sanford, and Dennis Longwell. *Sanford Meisner on Acting*. New York: Vintage, 1987.

Miner, Worthington. *Worthington Miner*. Metuchen, N.J.: Scarecrow Press, 1985.

Mink, Eric. *This Is Today: A Window on Our Times*. Kansas City: Andrews McMeel, 2003.

Mirisch, Walter. *I Thought We Were Making Movies, Not History*. Madison: University of Wisconsin Press, 2008.

Moonjean, Hank. *Bring in the Peacocks: Memoirs of a Hollywood Producer*. Bloomington, Ind.: AuthorHouse, 2004.

Murray, Nicholas. *Aldous Huxley: A Biography*. New York: Thomas Dunne, 2003.

Orrison, Katherine. *Written in Stone: Making Cecil B. DeMille's Epic, The Ten Commandments*. Lanham, Md.: Vestal Press, 1999.

Palin, Michael. *Halfway to Hollywood: Diaries, 1980–1988*. New York: Thomas Dunne, 2009.

Parish, James Robert. *It's Good to Be the King: The Seriously Funny Life of Mel Brooks*. Hoboken, N.J.: Wiley, 2007.

Parker, Stephen. *Bertolt Brecht: A Literary Life*. London: Bloomsbury, 2014.

Peary, Gerald, ed. *John Ford Interviews*. Jackson: University Press of Mississippi, 2001.

Poitier, Sidney. *This Life*. New York: Knopf, 1980.

Ramsden, John. *Man of the Century: Winston Churchill and His Legend since 1945*. New York: Columbia University Press, 2002.

Rapf, Joanna E., ed. *Sidney Lumet Interviews*. Jackson: University Press of Mississippi, 2006.

Reiner, Carl. *I Remember Me*. Bloomington, Ind.: AuthorHouse, 2013.

Robinson, Gabrielle. *A Private Mythology: The Manuscripts and Plays of John Whiting*. Lewisburg, Pa.: Bucknell University Press, 1988.

Robinson, Harlow. *The Last Impresario: The Life, Times, and Legacy of Sol Hurok*. New York: Viking, 1994.

Rodley, Chris, ed. *Lynch on Lynch*. New York: Faber and Faber, 2005.

Rollyson, Carl. *Hollywood Enigma: Dana Andrews*. Jackson: University Press of Mississippi, 2012.

Segaloff, Nat. *Arthur Penn: American Director*. Lexington: University Press of Kentucky, 2011.

———. *Stirling Silliphant: The Fingers of God*. Duncan, Okla.: BearManor, 2014.

Simon, Neil. *The Play Goes On: A Memoir*. New York: Simon and Schuster, 1999.

———. *Rewrites: A Memoir*. New York: Simon and Schuster, 1996.

Sinyard, Neil. *Jack Clayton*. Manchester, U.K.: Manchester University Press, 2000.

Slide, Anthony. *The Silent Feminists: America's First Women Directors*. Lanham, Md.: Scarecrow, 1996.

Smith, Glenn D. *Something of My Own: Gertrude Berg and American Broadcasting, 1929–1956*. Syracuse, N.Y.: Syracuse University Press, 2007.

Bibliography

Spoto, Donald. *The Dark Side of Genius: The Life of Alfred Hitchcock.* Boston: Little, Brown, 1983.

———. *Marilyn Monroe: The Biography.* New York: Cooper Square, 2001.

Suskin, Steven. *Second Act Trouble: Behind the Scenes at Broadway's Big Musical Bombs.* New York: Applause, 2006.

Taylor, William R. *Sydney Pollack.* Boston: Twayne, 1981.

Turman, Lawrence. *So You Want to Be a Producer.* New York: Three Rivers, 2005.

Unwin, Stephen. *A Guide to the Plays of Bertolt Brecht.* London: Methuen, 2005.

Zeffirelli, Franco. *Franco Zeffirelli's Jesus: A Spiritual Diary.* New York: Harper & Row, 1984.

———. *Zeffirelli: An Autobiography.* New York: Weidenfeld & Nicolson, 1986.

Zinnemann, Fred. *A Life in the Movies: An Autobiography.* New York: Charles Scribner's Sons, 1992.

Major Articles

Ardmore, Jane. "Anne Bancroft: Rediscovering the Joy of Acting." *Northeast Woman Sunday Times,* December 25, 1983.

Attenborough, Richard. "The Birth of 'Young Winston.'" *Times* (London), July 8, 1972.

Brodesser-Akner, Taffy. "The Entertainers: Mel and Max Brooks." *Town & Country,* August 5, 2014.

———. "Max Brooks Is Not Kidding about the Zombie Apocalypse." *New York Times Magazine,* June 21, 2013.

Burke, Tom. "Annie: Even in Hollywood She's Never Far from the South Bronx." *TV Guide,* November 23, 1974.

Clark, John. "Escaping Mrs. Robinson." *Los Angeles Times,* August 17, 1997.

Croyden, Margaret. "When the Telephone Rang, Did You Know It Meant War?" *New York Times,* August 14, 1977.

Darrach, Brad. "Playboy Interview: Mel Brooks." *Playboy,* February 1975.

Drury, Michael. "She May Be the Most Exciting Actress of the Century." *McCall's,* May 1962.

Goodman, Joan. "Inch by Inch, Anne Bancroft Finds Fulfillment." *Globe and Mail,* March 13, 1987.

Gratz, Roberta Brandes. "Anne Bancroft's Long Voyage Home." *New York Post,* March 11, 1967.

Gussow, Mel. "How and Why 'Golda' Sank." *New York Times,* March 1, 1978.

Hammel, Faye. "The Second Miracle." *Cue,* October 17, 1959.

Hopper, Hedda. "The Craft of Bancroft." *Chicago Tribune,* October 31, 1965.

"It Isn't Easy to Play the Role of a Sex-Starved Matron." *Los Angeles Herald-Examiner,* June 7, 1968.

Bibliography

Julian, Steve. "The Brooks Family of Writers: Michelle, Max, and Mel." *LA Stage Times*, November 9, 2010.

Kelly, Kevin. "Anne Bancroft Places Herself in History at Stockbridge." *Boston Globe*, July 7, 1969.

King, Doreen. "An Incandescent Actress." *Baltimore Sun*, May 26, 1966.

Lear, Frances. "Interview: Anne Bancroft." *Lear's*, November 1990.

Marks, Peter. "Hollywood Maverick, Broadway Baby." *New York Times*, February 24, 2002.

McManus, Margaret. "Pursues Another Goal." *Boston Globe*, November 27, 1960.

Millstein, Gilbert. "Seesaw Saga of an Actress." *New York Times*, February 9, 1958.

Mitchell, John G. "Anne Bancroft: She's Only the Greatest." *New York Journal-American*, September 2, 1962. First in a five-part series.

Morris, Joe Alex. "Second-Chance Actress." *Saturday Evening Post*, December 9, 1961.

Murray, William. "Viva Interview: Anne Bancroft." *Viva*, December 1973.

Rosenfield, Paul. "Bancroft Talks of Fame, Acclaim and Pain." *Los Angeles Times*, October 14, 1984.

Ryan, Jack. "Anne Bancroft: Happiness Is More Than Oscars." *Family Weekly*, March 31, 1968.

———. "Anne Bancroft: She Won the Biggest Prize." *Hollywood Citizen-News*, March 30, 1963.

Seamon, Richard. "Who Is Stanislavsky?" *Time*, December 21, 1959.

Wall, Michael. "Miss Italiano Thriving on Challenges." *Washington Post*, September 15, 1963.

Wagner, Ruth. "Seesaw's Star in Step." *Washington Post*, December 17, 1957.

Weinraub, Bernard. "Director Arthur Penn Takes on General Custer." *New York Times*, December 21, 1969.

———. "Even a Star Can Identify with Rage." *New York Times*, May 19, 1992.

Weir, June. "The Real Bancroft." *Washington Post*, June 2, 1968.

Wilson, Earl. "Star Analyzes Own 'Miracle.'" *Los Angeles Times*, May 19, 1962

Index

BOOKS IN THE SERIES

Mae Murray: The Girl with the Bee-Stung Lips
  Michael G. Ankerich
Hedy Lamarr: The Most Beautiful Woman in Film
  Ruth Barton
Rex Ingram: Visionary Director of the Silent Screen
  Ruth Barton
Conversations with Classic Film Stars: Interviews from Hollywood's Golden Era
  James Bawden and Ron Miller
You Ain't Heard Nothin' Yet: Interviews with Stars from Hollywood's Golden Era
  James Bawden and Ron Miller
Von Sternberg
  John Baxter
Hitchcock's Partner in Suspense: The Life of Screenwriter Charles Bennett
  Charles Bennett, edited by John Charles Bennett
My Life in Focus: A Photographer's Journey with Elizabeth Taylor and the Hollywood Jet Set
  Gianni Bozzacchi with Joey Tayler
Hollywood Divided: The 1950 Screen Directors Guild Meeting and the Impact of the Blacklist
  Kevin Brianton
He's Got Rhythm: The Life and Career of Gene Kelly
  Cynthia Brideson and Sara Brideson
Ziegfeld and His Follies: A Biography of Broadway's Greatest Producer
  Cynthia Brideson and Sara Brideson
The Marxist and the Movies: A Biography of Paul Jarrico
  Larry Ceplair
Dalton Trumbo: Blacklisted Hollywood Radical
  Larry Ceplair and Christopher Trumbo
Warren Oates: A Wild Life
  Susan Compo
Improvising Out Loud: My Life Teaching Hollywood How to Act
  Jeff Corey and Emily Corey
Crane: Sex, Celebrity, and My Father's Unsolved Murder
  Robert Crane and Christopher Fryer
Jack Nicholson: The Early Years
  Robert Crane and Christopher Fryer
Anne Bancroft: A Life
  Douglass K. Daniel
Being Hal Ashby: Life of a Hollywood Rebel
  Nick Dawson
Bruce Dern: A Memoir
  Bruce Dern with Christopher Fryer and Robert Crane
Intrepid Laughter: Preston Sturges and the Movies
  Andrew Dickos
Miriam Hopkins: Life and Films of a Hollywood Rebel
  Allan R. Ellenberger